Annual World Bank Conference on Development Economics 1997

Edited by **Boris Pleskovic and Joseph E. Stiglitz**

The World Bank   Washington, D.C.

© 1998 The International Bank for Reconstruction and Development / THE WORLD BANK
1818 H Street NW, Washington, DC 20433, U.S.A.
All rights reserved. Manufactured in the United States of America.

First printing April 1998

The Annual World Bank Conference on Development Economics is a forum for discussion and debate of important policy issues facing developing countries. The conferences emphasize the contribution that empirical and basic economic research can make to understanding development processes and to formulating sound development policies. Conference papers are written by researchers in and outside the World Bank. The conference series was started in 1989.

Conference papers are reviewed by the editors and are also subject to internal and external peer review. Summaries are included of floor discussions, which attempt to convey the sense and substance of what was discussed, interventions by participants from the floor, and responses by panelists. These summaries have not been reviewed by the presenters, the discussants, or other participants. Participants' affiliations identified in this volume are as of the time of the conference, April 30–May 1, 1997.

The findings, interpretations, and conclusions expressed in this volume are entirely those of the authors and should not be attributed in any manner to the World Bank, to its affiliated organizations, or to members of its Board of Executive Directors or the countries they represent.

The material in this publication is copyrighted. Requests for permission to reproduce portions of it should be sent to the Office of the Publisher at the address in the copyright notice above. The World Bank encourages dissemination of its work and will normally give permission promptly and, when the reproduction is for noncommercial purposes, without asking a fee. Permission to copy portions for classroom use is granted through the Copyright Clearance Center, Suite 910, 222 Rosewood Drive, Danvers, MA 01923, U.S.A.

Meta de Coquereaumont, Paul Holtz, Barbara Karni, and Ilyse Zable edited this volume. Garrett Cruce and Wendy Guyette were responsible for composition and layout, and Daphne Levitas helped with proofreading and coordination. All are with Communications Development Incorporated.

Annual World Bank Conference on Development Economics is indexed in *Human Resources Abstracts,* the *Index of Economic Articles,* the *Index of Social Science and Humanities Proceedings,* the *Index to International Statistics,* the *Public Affairs Information Service, Sage Public Administration Abstracts,* the *Standard Periodical Directory,* and *Ulrich's International Periodicals Directory* and online by ABI/INFORM and DIALOG.

ISSN 1020-4407
ISBN 0-8213-4115-4

Contents

Introduction   1
Boris Pleskovic and Joseph E. Stiglitz

OPENING REMARKS
Using Research to Reach the Poor   9
James D. Wolfensohn

IN MEMORIAM
A Tribute to Michael Bruno
Stanley Fischer   11
William Easterly   14

KEYNOTE ADDRESS
An Agenda for Development in the Twenty-First Century   17
Joseph E. Stiglitz

Corruption: Catalysts and Constraints   33

Corruption and Development   35
Susan Rose-Ackerman

    COMMENTS
    Diego Gambetta   58
    Edgardo Buscaglia   62
    FLOOR DISCUSSION   66

What Can Be Done about Entrenched Corruption?   69
Michael Johnston

    COMMENTS
    Jeremy Pope   91
    Augustine Ruzindana   95
    FLOOR DISCUSSION   99

Incentives and Performance in Public Organizations — **101**

Incentive Reforms in Developing Country Bureaucracies:
Lessons from Tax Administration — 103
Dilip Mookherjee

> COMMENTS
> *Barry Nalebuff* 126
> *Mary M. Shirley* 132
> FLOOR DISCUSSION 137

Incentives, Efficiency, and Government Provision of Public Services — 139
Sherwin Rosen and Bruce A. Weinberg

> COMMENTS
> *Richard Zeckhauser* 167
> *Robert P. Inman* 173
> FLOOR DISCUSSION 178

Leaders in Growth: Can Others Follow? — **181**

What Can Developing Countries Learn from East Asian Economic Growth? — 183
Takatoshi Ito

> COMMENTS
> *Deborah Bräutigam* 201
> *Andrés Rodríguez-Clare* 207
> FLOOR DISCUSSION 213

The Political Economy of High and Low Growth — 217
Alberto Alesina

> COMMENTS
> *T. Ademola Oyejide* 238
> *Ravi Kanbur* 242
> FLOOR DISCUSSION 245

Poverty and Environment — **249**

Environment, Poverty, and Economic Growth — 251
Karl-Göran Mäler

> COMMENTS
> *Edward B. Barbier* 271
> *John A. Dixon* 277
> FLOOR DISCUSSION 282

Where Development Can or Cannot Go:
The Role of Poverty-Environment Linkages   285
Ramón E. López

    COMMENTS
    Cielito F. Habito   307
    Jeffrey R. Vincent   312
    FLOOR DISCUSSION   316

Introduction

Boris Pleskovic and Joseph E. Stiglitz

The Annual World Bank Conference on Development Economics is designed to expand the flow of ideas among development policy researchers and practitioners from all parts of the world. The conference provides a forum for presenting and disseminating cutting-edge thinking on some of the most important issues in development and for revisiting issues of long-standing interest. It thus contributes to the global debate on development and offers an opportunity to examine lessons of experience for policy. Finally, this conference series is intended to challenge and improve our understanding of development policy in practice. To advance these goals, conference participants are drawn from a broad range of research, academic, and policymaking institutions in both developing and industrial countries.

The ninth conference, held at the World Bank on April 30 and May 1, 1997, addressed four themes: corruption, incentives and performance in public organizations, the transferability of high-growth experience, and poverty and the environment. Though the articles in this volume focus on a broad agenda for development—examining the role of national and international institutions in eliminating corruption and strengthening the rule of law and in promoting sustainable development and raising living standards—several common themes unite them: What is the appropriate role of the government? How should incentives in the public sector be structured? And what are the relationships among economic growth, poverty, and environmental sustainability?

The keynote address by Joseph E. Stiglitz provides a general framework for the discussions that follow. He sets out an agenda for development for the twenty-first century that tempers optimism about the possibilities for economic success with the sober reality of the need to adhere steadfastly to appropriate policies. The articles expand on some of the themes Stiglitz outlines. Susan Rose-Ackerman and Michael Johnston discuss the role of government and international institutions in preventing corruption. Dilip Mookherjee and Sherwin Rosen and Bruce Weinberg explore incentives and performance in public organizations. Expanding on Stiglitz's keynote

---

Boris Pleskovic is deputy administrator, Research Advisory Staff, at the World Bank. Joseph E. Stiglitz is senior vice president, Development Economics, and chief economist at the World Bank.

Annual World Bank Conference on Development Economics 1997
©1998 The International Bank for Reconstruction and Development / THE WORLD BANK

address, these articles examine the role of government as an institution and the need to reexamine how regulations and incentive structures can improve the effectiveness of government and the productivity of the economy.

Takatoshi Ito and Alberto Alesina look at the experiences of high-growth economies to determine how transferable those experiences are to other developing countries. They note that successful development is enhanced by appropriate government policies. Karl-Göran Mäler and Ramón López emphasize the importance of strengthening institutional structures such as property rights and land tenure and of establishing new markets, all of which may positively affect the environment and improve the living conditions of the rural poor.

An Agenda for Development

In his opening remarks James D. Wolfensohn, president of the World Bank, comments on the relevance of the Annual World Bank Conference on Development to some of the new approaches of the World Bank by supporting cutting-edge research, building partnerships with outside institutions, providing background research for project work in client countries, and challenging conventional wisdom. Wolfensohn stresses the importance of research for strengthening development effectiveness, highlighting several research projects that have improved the Bank's lending policies and its understanding of development. The agenda of this year's conference, notes Wolfensohn, reflects the core mission of the Bank. He emphasizes the vital importance of combating corruption and stresses the need for ensuring that anticorruption measures are properly integrated into economic reform.

In the keynote address Joseph E. Stiglitz presents an agenda for economic development for the coming century. Always, he contends, we need to keep in view a broad set of objectives that embrace democratic development, sustainable development, and improvements in living standards as well as rising gross domestic product. His address expands on traditional prescriptions that focus on macroeconomic stability, trade liberalization, and privatization to incorporate broader goals (democratic, egalitarian, and sustainable development) and new instruments (such as competition and regulatory policy and macroeconomic policies) that stabilize the economy and promote economic growth. He emphasizes not only the need to redefine the appropriate scope of government activity and the role of government as a complement to the private sector, but also the potential strategies for improving the efficacy of government, including using more market-oriented policies. Thus the new agenda does not simply consider whether a particular activity should be in the public or in the private sector. Rather, its sees the government and the private sector as working together as partners, each with its own responsibilities. In some circumstances it sees government as helping to create markets, and in others as providing the essential regulation without which markets cannot function. Stiglitz argues that for developing and industrial countries alike, the new agenda requires an openness that both groups have often resisted. He emphasizes the need to extract the appropriate lessons from theory and history, from best practices, and from what has worked. Development, he argues, involves closing the knowledge gap between rich and poor economies and achieving the right balance between the roles of the state and the roles of the private sector.

What Can Be Done about Corruption?

Corruption occurs throughout the world, Susan Rose-Ackerman observes, but it is of special concern in poor countries, where bribes can expropriate a nation's limited wealth, leaving little for its poorest citizens. Recent cross-country studies indicate that strong legal and government institutions and low levels of corruption help foster both domestic and foreign investment and economic growth. The data support the claim that corruption is a function of the amount of red tape, which is itself partly a function of corruption. International lending organizations such as the World Bank can help to reduce corruption by supporting the establishment of transparent institutional structures that are favorable to equitable growth. Rose-Ackerman argues that reducing the incentives for payoffs, establishing credible law enforcement, reforming the civil service, and increasing accountability to citizens are critical to this effort. Her article examines the costs and causes of corruption, the differences between corruption that is concentrated at the top and corruption that is decentralized, and the policy options available to developing countries whose leaders are committed to reform. Basic institutional reforms, she argues, such as increasing the transparency and accountability of government, may be a precondition for reform in some areas. This may include reforms in tax and customs collection, regulation of private businesses, and development of state-sponsored infrastructure projects. The private sector can be an important check on the arbitrary exercise of power by government, but only if citizens can find out what government is doing. Thus there may be scope for organizations such as the World Bank to provide institutional support to reduce corruption and to help create an environment conducive to equitable growth and poverty alleviation. The Bank, she concludes, needs to make clear that corruption will not be tolerated in its grants and loans, and it must be ready to cancel projects in which corruption is uncovered or where cost overruns suggest that venality or incompetence is pervasive.

Michael Johnston notes that corruption is not a problem that just "happens" to otherwise healthy societies. The most serious cases of corruption, he claims, are entrenched political and bureaucratic corruption. Such systems are tightly organized and internally stable and do not automatically result in collapse. Rather, they create and are sustained by conditions of weak political competition, slow and uneven economic growth, and a weak civil society. Johnston shows that in the medium to long term it is possible to move from a high-corruption equilibrium to a low-corruption equilibrium by guaranteeing civil liberties and basic economic rights, enhancing economic and political competition, and encouraging the growth of a stronger civil society. The transition to a low-corruption equilibrium takes time and requires sustained support. During the initial stages, reform will likely produce an apparent surge in corruption, as formerly concealed practices come to light, and organized corruption gives way to more fragmented and disruptive practices. But these are indicators of a breakdown of the old entrenched system. Sustained political leadership and international support are crucial during this phase. Aid partners can help, according to Johnston, by using program design, delivery, and evaluation as positive incentives to encourage and reward necessary changes. To ensure that aid agencies have continuing anticorruption leverage, they should impose standards gradually, rather than as criteria for initial support. The World Bank's recent emphasis on corruption is welcome, says Johnston, and the debate to which it leads offers an important opportunity to reexamine policies for their impact on corruption, to use anticorruption policies more aggressively, and to establish a comprehensive anticorruption policy.

Public Sector Incentives

Throughout much of the world tax collectors are poorly paid and face vast opportunities for enhancing their income by accepting bribes from tax evaders. How can internal incentive mechanisms be designed to curtail opportunistic behavior and ensure that the goals of the state and the goals of civil servants are congruent? Dilip Mookherjee presents a theoretical model of pay-for-performance schemes, which tie civil servants' remuneration directly to their job performance. He draws on evidence from several countries, including Brazil, India, Mexico, and Peru, that have implemented such reforms in tax collection. Whether such schemes increase or reduce welfare, Mookherjee argues, depends both on their effect on corruption by tax collectors and on their impact on taxpayer compliance and government revenue. Piecemeal approaches only exacerbate incentive problems, but governments truly committed to reform can succeed if they enlarge their scope to accommodate a broad range of instruments. Mookherjee finds that pay-for-performance schemes work best when they are accompanied by other organizational changes, including improvements in task design, information and monitoring systems, personnel policy, and budgeting, accounting, and procurement systems. Peru, for example, instituted tax administration reforms beginning in 1991 aimed at inducing incompetent and dishonest officials to leave, reducing the size of tax administration, and increasing the scope of performance-based promotions. In less than a year, staff numbers were down, salaries were up, and tax revenues rose from 5.4 percent of GDP to 9.0 percent. Similarly, in India improved incentive schemes for tax collectors significantly reduced corruption and increased efficiency. While these and other experiences are still too limited to draw robust inferences about the practical success of incentives reform, says Mookherjee, such examples do indicate that bold initiatives are possible and that they appear to have had the effects on taxes that reformers had hoped for.

Economic development is associated with greater division of labor and specialization in production and increased sophistication of markets and trade. These changes invariably raise the value of market time for women and shift economic activity away from the nonmarket and household sectors toward the market sector.

Because market activities are more easily taxed than nonmarket activities, this shift both enables greater government activity and increases demand for government provision of services such as education and health care. Sherwin Rosen and Bruce Weinberg consider the main efficiency and productivity considerations in government provision of services. One is the effect of distortions associated with tax policies and government finances. Data from several countries show that these are likely to be more important for women than for men, because women's labor supply is more responsive to prices and wages. Specifically, tax and other policies associated with subsidized government social services can cause excessive substitution of market-provided services through the formal government sector for self-produced services in the household sector. Rosen and Weinberg also consider some general issues in the provision of government services. They examine empirically for a set of seventeen countries the importance of government as provider of goods and services (looking at the share of government spending on direct provision) and the tax burden imposed by government provision. They examine government's role as provider of education and medical care in detail. In making a case for indirect rather than direct provision of services, they argue that while it is difficult to see from a theoretical perspective why regulation would dominate government ownership (since government is the principal in both cases), empirically regulation seems to clearly win out. Regulated firms, they argue, tend to be run much more efficiently than comparable government enterprises. The gains from indirect provision are greatest when oversight of nongovernment agencies is possible and monitoring costs are low.

Lessons from High-Growth Countries

Takatoshi Ito argues that much can be learned about development by paying more attention to the initial stage of growth acceleration. When conditions are right, an economy starts to take off from a stagnant state and growth accelerates, often to double-digit rates. This acceleration is generally accompanied by structural changes, as resources shift from agriculture to simple manufacturing and then to more sophisticated manufacturing. In the second stage, the economic growth rate slows, as the share of manufacturing hits a plateau and the technological gap is narrowed. Many models of economic convergence capture only this second stage. Ito applies the metaphor of geese flying in V-formation to explain a pattern of takeoff and industrial development in which later-developing economies grow faster than early developers and in which the order of the formation follows that of the stages of industrialization and per capita income. In this natural order of steps in economic development, Ito argues, there is a critical moment for high-growth takeoff. Getting the fundamentals right and achieving social and political stability seem to be important at this first stage. More controversial is the role of industrial policy. What is apparent, however, is that government intervention in the economy has lessened over time in most cases.

Looking at growth from another perspective, Alberto Alesina argues that providing aid to countries with weak institutions—as measured by bureaucratic efficiency, corruption, property rights protection, and respect for the rule of law—may actually impede development. Because of mistargeting, corruption, inefficiencies, and policy distortions, foreign aid intended to benefit the poor often ends up benefiting special interests, vocal groups, and the middle class. Boosting government consumption in countries with weak institutions retards rather than spurs growth. Further, Alesina demonstrates, the prospect of foreign aid has no effect on policy in countries with poor records of reducing poverty and achieving social goals. Thus international institutions, including the World Bank, should not provide financial assistance to countries with corrupt bureaucracies, weak protection of property rights, and poor records of directing spending toward the poor. Alesina concludes that the World Bank may be able to boost growth and improve social indicators in such countries by withholding aid while providing technical assistance for building the stronger institutions that are critical to accelerated growth and improved social conditions.

Environment and the Poor

Karl-Göran Mäler describes two kinds of demand for environmental resources. The first, common in developing countries, is as an input in household production or in small-scale production units. Such inputs are of considerable value to the people using them since these production activities are often essential to survival. The second kind of demand for environmental resources is as an amenity—that is, as something that directly affects people's well being. The role of environmental resources is less clear when they are viewed as amenities. A few empirical studies, however, including one that analyzed data sets for the United States and Africa, have found that even when environmental quality is an amenity, poor people's access to environmental resources is a necessity, not a luxury. Thus environmental protection is progressive, with low-income groups benefiting relatively more than high-income groups. Demand, however, is only one side of the coin. Mäler argues that supply issues must also be taken into account to fully understand the relationship between economic and ecological systems. The supply of environmental resources is determined by how the resource base is managed and exploited. By strengthening the institutional structures responsible for making such management decisions—for example, by improving property rights, implementing land tenure schemes, and establishing new markets—developing countries may reap substantial gains for the rural poor. Moreover, changes in the resource base may have consequences for fertility rates, and so may affect the future of the resource base. In the long run, Mäler concludes, these general reforms are much more important than technical fixes that solve specific problems but fail to change overall incentive structures.

Ramón López, in analyzing the relationship between environment and poverty, notes that as population density increases, two outcomes are possible: a virtuous cycle of increased income and environmental sustainability, or a mutually reinforcing process of ecological disaster and massive poverty. Why do some societies follow the first path while others follow the second? Evidence suggests that different interactions between environmental, institutional, and population dynamics explain the different outcomes. The three key factors are the resilience of the natural resource base, initial institutional conditions, and the rate of population growth. If the environment is fragile, institutions do not evolve quickly, and population growth is rapid, ecological disaster and large-scale poverty are likely. The process by which institutions adapt to increasing population is crucial. Also crucial are the environmental dynamics—in particular the high costs of rebuilding environmental stocks and, in some cases, the irreversibility of environmental losses once a threshold level of degradation has been passed—and the lack of investment incentives associated with extreme poverty. Thus while rising population density has often been associated with higher incomes and better environments in industrial countries, it has caused massive poverty and ecological disasters in many developing countries. To avoid these undesirable outcomes, says López, government should implement measures that restrain population growth, slow the environmental dynamics, and accelerate the institutional dynamics. Also important are measures that minimize the environmental and conventional efficiency losses associated with rural-urban migration and the transition toward private property rights.

* * *

As in previous years, the planning and organization of the 1997 conference was a joint effort. Our special thanks go to the late Michael Bruno, former senior vice president, Development Economics and chief economist of the World Bank, who was responsible for selecting this year's topics. Particular thanks are due to Gregory Ingram, administrator of the Research Advisory Staff, for his continued support of the conference. We would also like to thank other staff members, in particular several anonymous reviewers for their assistance, and the conference coordinators, Mantejwinder Jandu and Jean Gray Ponchamni, whose excellent organizational skills kept the conference on track. Finally, we thank the editorial staff, especially Meta de Coquereaumont, Paul Holtz, Barbara Karni, and Ilyse Zable, and desktoppers Garrett Cruce and Wendy Guyette.

OPENING REMARKS
Using Research to Reach the Poor

James D. Wolfensohn

It is with great pleasure that I welcome you to the ninth Annual World Bank Conference on Development Economics. This conference series epitomizes everything that we are trying to do at the Bank: partnering with outside institutions and experts, feeding research into operations, and using research to reach the poor.

In recent months we have been carefully analyzing our activities in the Bank in an effort to assess and improve our effectiveness. We know from the past how central research is to this endeavor. Bank research—almost two decades of it—on primary education demonstrated clearly the higher returns to public investment in primary relative to secondary and tertiary education. Bank research based on a series of studies of women's employment and welfare in Africa, Latin America and the Caribbean, the Middle East, and South Asia led to a recognition of the importance of educating girls. Bank research revealing the severe disincentives to agriculture and other rural activities created by policies with an urban bias prompted a move away from Bank support of industrial and urban expansion at the expense of the rural sector. And it was Bank research—the living standards measurement studies and incidence analysis—that showed that the system of social transfers in Russia was not reaching the poor. And there are numerous other examples.

Research is no less important to the future. The agenda of this year's conference is especially relevant to development effectiveness. We know that corruption is a disincentive to investors, that it exacerbates inequities and undermines social stability. But we do not as yet know nearly enough about the exact economic impact of different levels of corruption or about what kinds of policy interventions can make a difference. On incentives and performance in public organizations we know that matching a state's activities to its capacity is central to effective economic management. But we need to know a lot more about how pay-for-performance mechanisms can actually work. On countries learning from the growth experience of others, we need to know much more about why countries grow at different rates.

James D. Wolfensohn is president of the World Bank.
Annual World Bank Conference on Development Economics 1997
©1998 The International Bank for Reconstruction and Development / THE WORLD BANK

What is the role of history and culture, political economy, trade and investment? How important are initial conditions? How do we transfer the best practices of fast-growing countries to the slow growers? On poverty and the environment, we know that over the next thirty years—with world population rising by 800 million people each decade, with agricultural output doubling, and with energy and transport infrastructure needs reaching $500 billion a year in developing countries alone—the pressure on the environment will reach unprecedented levels. We also know that poverty is becoming increasingly urbanized: within twenty-five years the number of urban poor will increase from an estimated 400 million to over 1 billion. What we do not yet know enough about is the exact relationship between poverty and the environment: do the poor cause more environmental damage than the nonpoor? What are the relationships among population growth, poverty, and environmental sustainability, and how do we ensure that antipoverty strategies maximize desirable environmental outcomes?

But as those of you engaged in research well know, it is one thing to identify the issues and quite another to act on them. For the Bank's research to have meaning, we must do more than publish the findings. We must absorb and act on those findings. Research in the Bank cannot be a theoretical exercise. It needs to be a decisive determinant of our policies and programs. And that means relentlessly focusing the spotlight on ways to measure effectiveness. How we can assess our activities? How can our clients assess their activities? How can we best measure development impact? This is a key area for the research agenda of the future.

Finally I would like to take a moment to remember Michael Bruno. As many of you know, Michael came to the Bank after a very distinguished career as professor of economics at Hebrew University and governor of the Bank of Israel; honorary member of the American Academy of Arts and Sciences and the American Economic Association; president of the Econometric Society and the International Economic Association; visiting professor at Harvard, MIT, and the London School of Economics; and author of numerous books and articles. Michael was committed to driving the Bank's research agenda forward, never cutting the intellectual corner or shirking the difficult question. More than an economist, though, Michael was also a friend. With his intellect and his candor he taught me a lot. He left a permanent mark on the Bank and the work we do. We will all miss him.

In Memoriam
A Tribute to Michael Bruno

Stanley Fischer

Michael Bruno died in Jerusalem on December 26, 1996, less than two months after retiring as senior vice president, Development Economics, and chief economist of the World Bank.

Michael was born in Germany and moved to Israel one year later, in 1933. After serving in the Israeli army as a member of a kibbutz settlement group, he enrolled briefly at Hebrew University to study mathematics before transferring to King's College in Cambridge. There he started in mathematics and ended in economics, graduating in 1956. On his return to Israel he worked for a few years in the Research Department at the Bank of Israel, where he met Hollis Chenery—former chief economist of the World Bank, about whom Michael spoke at this conference in 1995.

Michael began his graduate studies at Hebrew University, then transferred to Stanford University, where he completed his Ph.D. in two years, having arrived, it is said, with his thesis written. He went to Stanford to work with Hollis Chenery, who nevertheless left soon after Michael's arrival to work at the U.S. Agency for International Development, starting his long and distinguished career of public service.

After graduating from Stanford Michael returned to the Bank of Israel, where he became director of research. In 1963, while still at the bank, he joined the faculty of the Department of Economics at Hebrew University. He was a member of the department until his death, serving as chairman from 1968 to 1970.

Michael was an outstanding economist whose achievements were recognized inside and outside Israel with numerous awards and honors. We think of him as an economist for his role in the Israeli stabilization program of 1985, for his achievements as governor of the Bank of Israel and chief economist of the World Bank, and for his research on inflation, stabilization, income distribution, and policy design over the past decade.

But Michael was an outstanding economist well before 1985. His early contributions to development theory and capital theory and his study of the Israeli economy earned him the honor—rare for an economist—of membership in the Israel Academy

---

Stanley Fischer is first deputy managing director of the International Monetary Fund. This tribute is based on remarks delivered at the memorial service for Michael Bruno held at the World Bank on February 6, 1997.

Annual World Bank Conference on Development Economics 1997
©1998 The International Bank for Reconstruction and Development / THE WORLD BANK

of Sciences in 1975. His work over the next decade on Israeli tax reform and on the dynamics of Israeli inflation, and more broadly on macroeconomics and—jointly with Jeffrey Sachs—on worldwide stagflation and Eurosclerosis, will not be forgotten, in Israel or the world over.

Israel's inflation and economic performance began worsening in the late 1970s. By the early 1980s Michael was thinking about the challenge of stabilization. Through his writing and in discussions with others he honed his ideas concerning the problem. When in June 1985 he was appointed to the small group charged with developing a stabilization program, the moment met the man. He became the intellectual leader of the group, and within less than a month—of extraordinary, intense, creative effort—Prime Minister Shimon Peres's coalition cabinet had accepted the group's plan.

The theory was simple: stabilization would require cutting the budget deficit and tightening monetary policy. But to reduce the risk of unemployment, inflation had to be addressed using a fixed exchange rate and direct measures to contain wage and price increases. This was one of the earliest explicit applications of the heterodox approach to stabilization—and it worked. While the theory was simple, its implementation was not, and Michael contributed as much to the success of the stabilization through his hands-on involvement in the program's implementation as he had in helping formulate it.

In mid-1986 Michael was appointed governor of the Bank of Israel. Prime Minister Peres later said that he had known Michael was a tough nut who would not give the government an easy time—and Michael did not disappoint him. It was during his five years as governor that Michael secured the success of the stabilization plan that he had helped formulate. During that time he restored much of the luster that the bank had lost since he had served there in the 1960s.

At the start of his term Michael was preoccupied with stabilization. By the end of his term he was dealing with something far more to his taste—the absorption of Soviet immigrants and the growth opportunities it presented. The remarkably successful plan for absorbing the massive Soviet immigration that began at the end of the 1980s was his second crucial contribution as governor. The principle guiding the program was to rely on the market as much as possible—for instance, giving immigrants housing allowances rather than assigning them apartments, and creating wage flexibility by adopting a two-tier wage structure. At the same time the program increased government investment in physical and educational infrastructure. This balanced approach, recognizing both the powers of markets and the need for well-focused government intervention, was a hallmark of Michael's approach to economics.

From the Bank of Israel Michael returned to his longtime academic home, the Department of Economics at Hebrew University, of which he had been chairman many years before. His devotion to the department was reflected in his desire, when he left the World Bank in November 1996, to help build a new school of economics, named after our friend and mentor, Don Patinkin, at Hebrew University.

Soon after Michael left the Bank of Israel, other job offers began arriving. Michael chose to come to the World Bank as chief economist, a position he described in his farewell to the Bank as having chased him all his life. He was right to come, and right for the Bank.

Michael set out his approach to development economics in the keynote address to this conference in 1994, "Development Issues in a Changing World: New Lessons, Old Debates, Open Questions." His eclectic approach recognized that we know many of the necessary conditions for sustaining growth and reducing poverty, including macroeconomic stability, sufficient human capital, good policies, and appropriate microeconomic incentives embodied in institutions. Assessing the progress made in his more than thirty years of thinking about these issues and dealing with them as a policymaker, he ended on a typical note: "A sober assessment of past predictions should instill humility. But a hard core of knowledge—small but increasing—has been sustained and buttressed through the turbulence." By his own active involvement in research to the end of his life, Michael left no doubt of the importance he attached to adding to that hard core of knowledge.

Michael's achievements and his reputation as an economist are not based solely on the quality of his technical work. He was a man with a strong social conscience and a clear and practical mind. The many ministers of finance and governors of central banks who mourned his passing respected him for his professionalism, but they valued him even more for his humanity, the clarity of his thought, and the honesty of his advice. Michael never pulled any punches, but no one ever doubted the spirit in which his advice was offered—from a desire to help policymakers do what was right for their countries and their people.

Michael was greatly admired both in Israel and elsewhere. He was intensely patriotic—all the more so for being critical of his country's shortcomings and seeking to correct them. He was an active member of Peace Now before he became governor of the Bank of Israel, but there was never a hint of partisanship while he was in office. At the same time he was a citizen of the world whose easy charm, open mind, broad interests, and impressive accomplishments made him the most pleasant of company, welcome as a friend everywhere.

Michael Bruno was a complex man, tough, charming, and brilliant, a compelling speaker whose powerful and mellifluous voice added to the persuasiveness of his logic, an outstanding policymaker and adviser—no less so for being an intellectual to the core who always wanted to understand how things worked and why they were the way they were, a man of culture, a patriot, a proud father and grandfather. We loved and admired him, and we shall remember him forever, as the prayer "*El male rachamim*—Lord full of mercy," which was sung at his memorial service at the World Bank in February 1996, asks:

Zachrah lo latova—remember him for good
Ve-yanuach beshalom—and may he rest in peace.

In Memoriam
A Tribute to Michael Bruno

William Easterly

Just over a year ago I was in San Francisco, California, at the American Economic Association annual meetings. As I was about to leave to fly back to Washington, D.C., all flights were canceled because of a blizzard on the East Coast. Worried about my family and about the work deadlines I was going to miss, I desperately tried to rebook a flight home—to no avail.

After more than a day of this I was feeling very sorry for myself. I was trying to do some work in my hotel room, without much success. Suddenly the telephone rang. I picked it up, thinking it was the airline with another excuse as to why I could not get a flight any time in the next week. Instead, I heard a cheerful voice on the other end. I knew that this was not the airline.

It was the deep, familiar voice of Michael Bruno, who was also in San Francisco. He told me that he and a few colleagues had rented a car and were going to explore Napa Valley and asked if I wanted to come along. Of course I jumped at the offer.

That was the memory that came to my mind when I heard the news of Michael's passing: "Bill, we've rented a car, and we're going to explore Napa Valley." It was a small example of his kindness to his colleagues, of his ability to make the best of a bad situation. Never have I exited so quickly from despondency. That day in Napa Valley was like a dream.

It is ironic that it was then, during our exploration of Napa Valley, that I saw more clearly than I had before Michael's gift for research. His gift, complemented by his formidable intelligence, was his intense curiosity about how the world works.

We toured one vineyard after another, Michael bombarding the tour guides with questions about how winemaking works. His curiosity extended to U.S. history, as he asked me (as the representative American) how, when, and why California had been settled. I answered as best I could from my slim knowledge of California history; I doubt that my answers would have withstood expert scrutiny.

William Easterly is lead economist in the Macroeconomics and Growth Division of the Policy Research Department at the World Bank.

Annual World Bank Conference on Development Economics 1997
©1998 The International Bank for Reconstruction and Development / THE WORLD BANK

We explored the valley from one end to the other. We went to the Napa Valley Wine Museum, with its amazing Smell-o-Rama display of the aromas that make up the bouquet of wine. Then we had a wine tasting, with Michael asking the guide why one swishes the wine around in the glass before tasting.

The day ended back in San Francisco. Over dinner, Michael questioned me about the many kinds of beer on the menu. That, at least, was a subject that I knew better than California history.

Although I had already had the pleasure of performing joint research with Michael, I started to realize on that day in Napa Valley that his intense curiosity had a lot to do with his originality as a researcher. A research project never sated his curiosity, because he always thought of new valleys to explore. There was always one more valley.

Other, more complacent explorers climbed out of the valley to stand forever triumphantly on the mountaintop. Michael knew that there was always another valley on the other side of the mountaintop.

I learned a lot watching Michael's curiosity in action. Combined with his tremendous courtesy, his curiosity gave him a great gift for listening to and learning from other people. He listened carefully to what previous researchers had learned about a topic, often inviting them to his office for conversations.

As chief economist of the World Bank, Michael took the same delight when visiting new countries. There was always one more valley. There was always one more country to visit. On such visits Michael was the exact opposite of the stereotypical international bureaucrat. That bureaucrat spends time in meetings with government officials telling them what they should do, takes notes on what he tells them, then goes home and writes a report about what he told them.

That was not Michael's approach. He listened with curiosity and compassion as local residents and officials told him of their hopes and disappointments. He was flexible and creative in proposing solutions to their difficulties. It was this quality that made governments from Moscow to Bogotá seek out his advice.

In his research Michael delighted in the process of exploration. There was always one more valley. He was always curious about what the valley mapped out by the data was going to look like. While working on a research paper with Michael, it was wonderful to watch his almost childlike curiosity about how the results were going to come out. This infectious curiosity about statistical data was one of his greatest gifts to me as a researcher. When we met to discuss a joint paper, he would always express pleasure that he could take a break from his administrative responsibilities to examine data.

Michael got especially excited when we were about to test a new hypothesis. We were exploring a new valley, and he was intensely curious about what it looked like. His eyes shone like those of an explorer who suspects that he might be the first ever to see a particular valley. His eyes shone even brighter when the valley turned out to be far different from what we had expected.

Let me give a small example from our research on inflation and growth. We thought that we would learn that countries take a long time to recover from high-inflation crises, even after they had finally reduced inflation.

But the data said something different. The data said that countries did better after recovering from high inflation than they had done before they had high inflation. They even did better than other, similar countries that had never experienced high inflation. We had stumbled into a new valley that we did not fully understand. Perhaps the findings will be explained by the fact that countries that stabilized high inflation had implemented other reforms. Perhaps severe inflation crises help countries mobilize more sweeping reforms. Characteristically, Michael was open to an unorthodox map of the valley, if that was what the data indicated.

Michael appreciated how each research finding expands knowledge a little bit, then leads to more research. There was always one more valley. We were planning further joint research on how, when, and why high-inflation crises lead to reform. Michael's curiosity to see this valley was as intense as usual.

Michael did not live to see this valley, or any of the other new valleys that he wanted to explore. In memoriam, we grieve that a great explorer and a good man is no longer with us.

We take inspiration from the example that Michael left us, of relentless intellectual exploration, of open-minded intellectual curiosity. There is always one more valley. We need Michael's inspiration more than ever as we address research questions that are deep valleys indeed: understanding growth tragedies as well as growth miracles. For my part I will be inspired by the memory of Michael's voice on the phone in a hotel room in San Francisco, saying, "Bill, we've rented a car, and we're going to explore Napa Valley."

KEYNOTE ADDRESS
An Agenda for Development in the Twenty-First Century

Joseph E. Stiglitz

My appointment as chief economist of the World Bank—the largest international organization devoted to promoting development—provides an occasion for reflection on where we have been, where we are, and, most important, where we are going. I want to take this opportunity to set forth my vision of an agenda for development.

This is an exciting time for those of us committed to advancing economic growth, reducing poverty, and sustaining policy reform in developing countries and countries that are making the transition to a market economy. The success not just of one but of several countries in breaking out of the poverty in which they had been mired for centuries shows that development is possible. In Latin America the debt crisis and the growth stagnation to which it gave rise seem to be behind us, and the latest data show that developing countries are growing faster than industrial countries.[1] Although the financial crises in East Asia have attracted much attention lately, we should not allow that to obscure the amazing achievements of the East Asian countries. Per capita income in the Republic of Korea has increased tenfold in just over three decades. There is almost no one in Korea, Malaysia, or Thailand living on less than $1 a day, and Indonesia is within reach of that goal. Even Africa, where many countries experienced negative growth in the 1970s and 1980s, has at last started to experience growth, and countries such as Uganda that have sustained reforms over several years are showing consistent growth averaging 6 percent—still not in the league of China, but far better than was the case a few years ago.

It is now clear that countries that pursue appropriate policies have a better chance of economic success than those that do not (World Bank 1994). And there is mounting evidence that economic assistance, when combined with good policies, promotes economic growth, especially among the poorest countries (Burnside and Dollar 1997). That is, of course, good news not only for the countries involved, but also for those of us who offer advice and dispense aid. We can make a difference. The challenge is to understand which policies are appropriate and how to target our assis-

Joseph E. Stiglitz is senior vice president, Development Economics, and chief economist at the World Bank.

Annual World Bank Conference on Development Economics 1997
©1998 The International Bank for Reconstruction and Development / THE WORLD BANK

tance to promote growth and reduce poverty most effectively. There is clearly no magic formula: if there were, the number of successes would be far higher than it is. And the fact that the messages that we have emphasized have changed over time—and that many of the countries that were successful did not take the particular medicine that was then being dispensed by the development community—should, at the very least, induce a modicum of humility as we consider future directions.

Changed Perspective

It is an exciting time too because of the fast pace of change in the world around us and the concomitant changes in the world of ideas—changes that inevitably would have necessitated modifying our development strategy, even if we had had one that had worked unfailingly in the past. Over the past decade three changes in particular have influenced thinking about effective development strategies.

The first is the collapse of the socialist economies. There was an immediate lesson. For almost a hundred years two theories had competed for the hearts and minds of people struggling to break free of poverty—one focusing on markets, and the other on government. The failure of the socialist economies appeared to demonstrate that the second model was not viable. But another conclusion sometimes drawn, that markets by themselves would provide the answer, also has not been justified by economic theory or by historical experience. As I argue in my book *Whither Socialism* (Stiglitz 1994), had the assumptions under which markets have been shown to yield (Pareto) efficient outcomes been satisfied, market socialism would have been a success—or at least not the great failure that it proved to be. Neither has the historical experience been kind to the view that by themselves markets would have generated development: almost all the major successes—the economies of East Asia, the United States, many countries in Europe—involved heavy doses of government involvement. There is a remarkable similarity between the government activities undertaken by the East Asian tigers and those undertaken by the United States in a comparable period of its development. There are few examples on the other side, of success without government involvement.

One of the striking lessons that emerged from the post–Cold War era is how difficult it is for markets to get established. Most of us in the more advanced industrial economies take for granted a rich institutional infrastructure, much of which requires government action to establish and maintain. This is a theme to which I will return later.

The second major change is the success of the East Asian economies. I have already referred to the intellectual impact that this has had, teaching us that development is possible and that successful development requires (or at least is enhanced by) governments undertaking appropriate policies that go well beyond simply getting out of the way of the market. While there remains an active debate about the precise lessons to be learned and the extent to which the experiences of East Asia are replicable elsewhere, there remains little doubt that government played a critical, catalytic role (Stiglitz 1996; Stiglitz and Uy 1996).

But East Asia's success has had another consequence: these economies have been an engine of growth for much of the rest of the world. U.S. merchandise exports to East Asia, for instance, more than doubled between 1990 and 1996, and exports to developing countries were responsible for roughly one-sixth of U.S. GDP growth in this period. China, while still a developing country in terms of GDP per capita, could soon become the second largest economy in the world. Developing countries have become an economic force to be reckoned with.

The third major change is the globalization of the world economy. This is partly attributable to the tremendous drop in transport and communication costs in recent decades. Globalization has increased trade and capital flows, and developing countries that have opened their economies have especially benefited. Since 1990 private capital flows to developing countries have increased more than sixfold (World Bank 1997a). And East Asia's success was driven by exports: production was not limited by the size of domestic economies, competition in exporting raised standards and increased efficiency, and exports helped transfer advanced technology and management practices. Increasing integration of the world economy has meant that a factory in Indonesia can be closely linked with markets in the United States and Europe, with changes in preferences and demands there being quickly translated into changes in what is produced. Computer programmers in India can be linked with programmers in California's Silicon Valley. Distances have been shrunk, and geographical isolation has been reduced. These trends are just beginning, and they open up a host of new opportunities and challenges for all countries—and for developing countries, the hope of narrowing the knowledge and resource gap that has separated them from more developed countries, but also the challenge that the target they are chasing may be moving that much faster as well.

These changes in the global economy must guide development strategies in the coming decades.

Changed Objectives

But another set of changes was equally important in affecting thinking about development strategies: a change in objectives. It used to be that development was seen as simply increasing GDP. Today we have a broader set of objectives, including democratic development, egalitarian development, sustainable development, and higher living standards.

We recognize that there is more to living standards than is typically captured in GDP accounting. Improvements in education or health are not just means to an end of increased output, but are ends in themselves. Growth by itself does not ensure that the fruits will be equitably shared. We recognize the costs, both to individuals and to society, of economic insecurity. We no longer take for granted our environment—and we recognize that in the struggle to increase GDP, the air in many developing country cities became so polluted as to make them almost unlivable. We know that cutting down an irreplaceable hardwood forest provides an increase in measured GDP that is probably not sustainable.

Fifty years ago the common wisdom was that there was a tradeoff between rapid growth and democracy—Russia could grow faster, but at the cost of basic liberties. In retrospect we realize that people living under totalitarian regimes gave up their freedoms and sacrificed economic growth. We know that in a regime without a free press, millions of people can starve, even starve to death, without public outrage mobilizing efforts to save them. And within developing countries there is a growing recognition of the virtues of democratic development as an end in itself (Drèze, Sen, and Hassain 1995; Sen 1996).

This broadened set of objectives leads to quite different development strategies: for instance, democratic development leads to increased emphasis on participation and the development of political institutions and education.

As always, we have to maintain some perspective: while increasing GDP is not an end in itself, or not the only end, increasing GDP is essential to achieving the other objectives. Raising education levels and improving the health status in a country require resources, and resources are scarce. We should not confuse the fact that some countries have not used their increased resources in ways that comport with these broader development objectives with the fact that increased resources increase the opportunity set of a country.

Similarly, while greater participation is essential to democratic development, we must constantly scrutinize what we are doing: how representative, for instance, are those whose voices are being expressed?[2] In some cases participation can improve other outcomes (for instance, the amount of learning that occurs). But in other cases the effect on outcomes may be less certain. Some studies have found no correlation between rankings of perceived health impacts of various environmental hazards by scientists and rankings by nonscientists (USEPA 1987; Slovic, Layman, and Flynn 1993). Those who want to ensure that funds are spent on improving the environment to reduce overall health risks would surely want to rely more on the informed judgments of scientists than on a broader set of participatory views—while at the same time recognizing the importance of educating people more broadly about the scientific evidence on actual health risks associated with various hazards.

Reflections on the Past

Given the changes in the world around us, in our ideas, and in our views of development objectives, it is not surprising that development strategies have changed markedly over the past half century. When I was a graduate student, development planning was all the rage, and development economics was a mechanistic exercise. A country had a certain amount of resources that had to be allocated efficiently. Development strategies consisted of increasing those resources—in particular, the amount of physical capital—and ensuring, through development planning, that those resources were optimally used and that the various investments were coordinated. Government was required because markets were not sufficiently developed to provide the signals for resource allocation or to perform the coordination role that they were supposed to perform.[3]

Even when behavior was introduced into these models, it was done in a mechanistic manner. Savings rates were fixed, and they were lower among workers than among capitalists. Increasing the savings rate thus required shifting the distribution of income toward capitalists and away from workers.

Throughout this period, however, another strand of thought argued that government was part of the problem, not the solution; that more private initiative and entrepreneurship was required; and that government was inhibiting that private initiative. In the academic literature this perspective was reinforced by data showing the responsiveness of peasants to price signals: peasants in developing countries were just as rational as their urban cousins in the developed world. From here it was an easy step to suggest that the government should simply get out of the way, liberalize trade, and get the prices right. Development would follow.

This simplistic advice ignored the background from which the development planning literature had emerged: many developing countries lacked markets for many commodities, and there was little reason to believe that markets would develop on their own. Market imperfections—imperfections that imply that the resource allocation that the market would provide on its own will not be (Pareto) efficient—while common in industrial countries, are rife in developing countries. Not only were more markets absent, but competition was often more limited and information more imperfect.

There was a curious incongruity: economic practitioners were preaching the free market gospel just as economic theorists began to realize its lack of robustness. One of the central theoretical results of the 1950s was to establish rigorously the conditions under which Adam Smith's insight about the invisible hand guiding the efficiency of markets is valid (Arrow and Debreu 1954; Debreu 1959). Yet one of the central theoretical results of the 1980s was to show that whenever information is imperfect and markets are incomplete—which is essentially always—markets are not even *constrained* Pareto optimal. In other words, taking into account the costs of acquiring information and establishing markets, there are interventions that *in principle* could make some individuals better off without making anyone else worse off (Greenwald and Stiglitz 1986, 1988; Arnott, Greenwald, and Stiglitz 1994).

To be sure, another strand of thought emphasized not the perfections of markets but the imperfections of government. These were taken to be inevitable—or at least a judgment was made that it was better to ignore market imperfections than either to attempt to improve the performance of government or to use imperfect governments to correct the market imperfections.

The debt crisis of the 1980s shifted the focus to macroeconomics: countries could not grow if governments did not provide a stable macroeconomic environment. Governments needed to hold their expenditures to their revenues and to limit the expansion of the money supply.

Many governments began following what came to be called the Washington consensus: they liberalized trade, achieved macroeconomic stability, and got the prices right—yet growth did not follow as quickly or as strongly as envisaged. By contrast, the governments of East Asia took a less dogmatic approach: while they achieved macroeconomic stability, they intervened extensively in the market. They helped create markets, they helped regulate markets, and they used markets to achieve their development objectives. They also experienced the most rapid growth. Since I delivered this paper at the conference in April–May 1997, many East Asian countries have experienced serious financial turmoil. In my view, far from a refutation of the East Asian miracle, this turmoil may, in part, be the result of departing from the strategies that have served these countries so well, including well-regulated financial markets. In part, too, it may be the result of the failure to adapt quickly enough to changing circumstances, especially in the international financial system.

The New Perspective

The new agenda is informed by these experiences and is responsive to the changes in the economic environment and the broadened set of objectives noted earlier.

It sees government and markets as complements rather than substitutes. It takes as dogma neither that markets by themselves will ensure desirable outcomes nor that the absence of a market, or some related market failure, requires government to assume responsibility for the activity. It often does not even ask whether a particular activity should be in the public or the private sector. Rather, in some circumstances the new agenda sees government as helping to create markets—as many of the East Asian governments did in key aspects of the financial market. In other circumstances (such as education) it sees the government and private sector working together as partners, each with its own responsibilities. And in still others (such as banking) it sees government as providing the essential regulation without which markets cannot function.

And behind all of this lies a special responsibility for government: to create the institutional infrastructure that markets require in order to work effectively. At a minimum this institutional infrastructure includes effective laws and the legal institutions to implement them. If markets are to work effectively, there must be well-established and clearly defined property rights; there must be effective competition, which requires antitrust enforcement; and there must be confidence in the markets, which means that contracts must be enforced and that antifraud laws must be effective, reflecting widely accepted codes of behavior. Laws that ensure a level playing field (for example, that restrict insider trading in securities markets) are not just matters of consumer protection: without such laws investors will be reluctant to invest their funds in securities markets lest they be cheated.

The partnership between the government and the private sector has other dimensions:

- Financial regulations that ensure the safety and soundness of banking institutions not only help mobilize capital (by giving depositors more confidence in the banking system), they also help ensure the efficient allocation of investment.[4]
- Government support for education helps ensure a supply of well-trained workers.
- Government either helps provide infrastructure or provides a regulatory structure that ensures the private provision of infrastructure at reasonable prices.
- Government often plays a vital role in developing and transmitting technology, such as through agricultural extension services.
- Government can help promote equality and alleviate poverty, policies that in East Asia contributed to overall growth.

In each of these areas the rationale for government action can be found in the theory of market failure. For instance, knowledge (especially its production) is a public good, and like other public goods it will be undersupplied. But the rationale for government action in these areas can also be found in the historical record: economies in which government performed these roles well also performed better.

The exact role of government will change over time. We used to think of telecommunications and electricity as natural monopolies in which competition was not viable. Government would either have to regulate these industries closely or take charge of production. Today, partly because of changes in technology and partly because of changes in thinking, we know that competition is viable in large parts of these sectors if an appropriate regulatory structure is put in place. What is required is not deregulation, the naive stripping away of regulations, but regulatory redesign, the changing of the regulatory structure in ways that promote competition where it is viable and that ensure that monopoly power is not too badly exploited where it is not.

Improving Government Performance

Once we recognize the vital role that government plays in a development strategy, we must consider how we can improve the performance of government. We know a great deal about markets and market failures, but we know far less about governments and government failures. Still, we have learned a few things:

- Governments can become more effective if they use market and market-like mechanisms. Auctions (both for procurement and for the disposition of government assets) can increase transparency (and thus confidence in government), improve the allocation of resources, and bolster the government's budgetary position. Rather than addressing specific actions or transactions, government regulations may be designed to establish incentives for private firms to act appropriately—for example, by ensuring that banks have adequate net worth.[5]
- Governments that are less frequently subjected to temptation are less likely to give in to it. Discretionary actions, such as the allocation of quota rights, provide opportunities for corruption; corruption has adverse effects on eco-

nomic growth (partly by raising the costs of doing business and thereby discouraging investment) and undermines confidence in government (World Bank 1997c). Thus using transparent, market-like mechanisms has a double set of advantages.
- Governments should constantly reexamine the rationale for the regulations they have imposed. Historical processes often lead to regulations that are not appropriate to today's circumstances: the objectives of the regulations could be achieved at far less cost. For instance, before there were devices that could measure the pollution being emitted by a smokestack, it might have been appropriate to require technologies that met environmental standards. But once reliable monitoring devices are available, regulations should focus on outputs (here, the level of emissions) rather than inputs (technology standards.)
- The quality of a government's bureaucracy depends on the composition and quality of its workforce. Those in turn depend in part on its internal systems for hiring, training, and promotion and, as with any enterprise, in part on wages. Low wages and a mismatch between rewards and results discourage output and result in low performance.
- Government can help stimulate and can use competition: it can create competing public agencies, and it can allow private agents to compete with public agencies. The success of market economies is based on deep institutions that support incentives built around private property and competition. While there is ongoing debate about the relative importance of private property and competition, a plausible case can be made in a variety of settings that competition is what is essential.[6] One of the central themes of the World Bank's report (1993) on the East Asian miracle is that competition played a crucial role (especially competition for exports; see Stiglitz 1996).

Sequencing of Reforms

The simple lesson that emerges from this discussion is that incentives matter: that they matter in both the public and the private sector, that government should make more extensive use of incentives to guide its behavior, and that government should take actions to improve incentives in the private sector.[7]

Government, by the way it sequences reforms, can affect not only the performance of the economy in the short run but also the momentum for the continuation of reforms. Consider, for instance, the consequences of privatization in a large, closed economy before trade is liberalized and before an effective competition law is in place. Under these conditions privatization would convert a government monopoly into a private monopoly. Consumers (or firms who use the privatized firm's output as input) probably would not see any benefits (real prices might actually increase), overall economic performance probably would fail to improve (increased efficiency within the privatized firm is offset by loss of systemic efficiency from higher prices), and a vested interest might be created that would have the incentive and the resources to work against efforts to implement an effective competition law. A regulatory structure might evolve, but it would arrive already compromised, captured by those whom it should regulate.

Or consider the consequences of the privatization of a utility before an effective regulatory law is put in place. Uncertainty about the future regulatory structure could cause the government to receive less from the sale of the assets than it should. There is also the possibility that users, both consumers and firms, will face higher prices and that a vested interest will be created that has the incentive and the resources to resist effective regulatory reform. Moreover, in the absence of an effective regulatory structure, other public objectives that had been pursued by the industry before privatization—such as universal service—may be abandoned. High profits, low sales price, and decreased service will all undermine public support for the continuation of reform.

A regulatory structure can be created to ensure that some of the efficiency gains from privatization are shared by consumers and other users and that other social objectives, such as universal service, are enhanced. But we should never confuse the proposition that privatization can, in principle, increase the efficiency of the economy and achieve other social objectives with the proposition that, in the absence of effective regulatory structures, privatization may do neither in practice.

Neither economic theory nor historical experience gives us clear guidance in these complicated matters. (Even in the case of privatization the principal theoretical proposition, the fundamental privatization theorem, shows how restrictive the conditions are under which privatization can guarantee a welfare improvement.[8]) Theory may tell us that under certain idealized circumstances market economies are efficient. But theory provides us with less clear prescriptions for the second-best situations in which we inevitably find ourselves, in which many of the idealized circumstances underlying the pure theory are not satisfied. And theory gives us even less clear guidance on sequencing: how do we get from here to there? For these decisions we must rely on experience and judgment, perhaps on the guidance that comes from a careful consideration of cross-country experiences.

The Role of High-Income Countries

Most of this discussion has focused on what developing countries must do to succeed in enhancing their economic growth. But there is much that high-income countries can do as well.

The enormous increase in private capital flows to low- and middle-income countries has been a boon to countries that have created a welcoming investment environment. But the magnitude of these flows should not blind us to the fact that they have been very concentrated: ten countries, representing half of the developing world's GDP, have received 75 percent of the funds, and only a handful of low-income countries have received any significant amounts relative to the size of their economies (World Bank 1997a). Moreover, these private flows have not gone to all sectors of the economy: health and education, for instance, remain largely within the public sector.

That is one reason that the decline in official development assistance is so disturbing. In 1996 such aid reached an almost fifty-year low as a percentage of GDP of high-income countries. It is ironic that such cutbacks are occurring just as evidence of the effectiveness of aid is mounting. Development assistance promotes economic growth, especially among low-income countries, if they have put in place good economic policies (Burnside and Dollar 1997). True, aid cannot buy reform, and it works best for countries that can help themselves. But as a complement to local initiatives aid can enlarge and precipitate the positive effects of reforms, and by helping to build political momentum it can make the reforms sustainable. More important, aid may be an effective instrument for transferring knowledge—and as I argue below, the diffusion of appropriate and well-deployed knowledge can greatly enhance development prospects even in the poorest countries.

Some of the high-income countries that have been least forthcoming with aid have emphasized the importance of trade. But here too there is a gap between rhetoric and reality. While preaching the virtues of a market economy, Western producers accused Russian firms that were selling their excess aluminum at international prices of engaging in dumping and encouraged their governments to impose trade restrictions. As an alternative, they proposed establishing what in effect would be an international cartel to restrict worldwide production and raise prices—which is what was done.

How can the advanced economies preach the gospel of competition and free markets, yet turn to managed trade and restricted markets when their own interests are in jeopardy? There are many, many more examples, but the point is clear: the advanced economies should be the role models. They are far more able to absorb the shocks that inevitably occur as a result of changing trade patterns. Why is it that they seemingly find it so acceptable to refer to "political pressures" forcing their deviations from policies of openness while finding such excuses so hard to take from developing countries?

The World Bank's Role in the Development Agenda

Some analysts claim that the huge flows of private capital to developing countries have made the World Bank unnecessary. I obviously disagree. Elsewhere I have set forth at greater length the rationale for the World Bank and for development banks more generally. Here I summarize the main arguments:

- Private capital flows are targeted. Most low-income countries receive very little of this capital, and little of the money goes to vital sectors, such as health and education, that are complementary to the private flows.
- The World Bank and the other international financial institutions have an important role in helping developing countries establish the institutional infrastructure (regulations and laws) that is required to attract capital. This infrastructure is a public good; thus the private sector cannot be expected to provide adequate assistance in its establishment. Moreover, in a world where compet-

- ing private interests are always looking for the establishment of rules and regulations that favor themselves, the World Bank can serve as an honest broker.
- While private capital flows are much more varied in form than they were in the past—there are now substantial equity flows—there are still important gaps.
- The World Bank has a distinct advantage in gathering information and producing knowledge about successful development practices and policies. Knowledge is an international public good that will be undersupplied if left to the market.
- In some cases the World Bank and other multilateral development banks may signal that a developing country has a embraced sound policies and hence boost its credibility, providing an additional incentive for maintaining these policies in the future.

World Bank staff have a special responsibility not only to produce knowledge that will enable developing countries to grow more effectively, but also to ensure that that knowledge gets implemented—including in our lending practices. Earlier I referred to research showing the effectiveness of aid when good economic policies are in place. The flip side of that research suggests that when good economic policies are not in place, aid may have no effect on economic growth. This finding poses a moral dilemma: if a loan does not increase an economy's resources, unless it is explicitly aimed at achieving other social objectives it leaves future generations more impoverished, since they inherit the indebtedness. And even if it does achieve some other social objective, the tradeoffs need to be considered. The issue of the fungibility of funds adds further complications: to the extent that funds are fungible, the issue is not the quality of the project being funded, but what happens as a result of the additional flow of funds. Evidence on the extent of fungibility (or the circumstances under which funds are more fungible) remains somewhat ambiguous. Yet recent studies indicate that, with the exception of sectors such as transport and communications, aid funds are largely fungible and foreign finance does significantly substitute for (rather than complement) domestic spending (Feyzioglu, Swaroop, and Zhu 1997; Pack and Pack 1990, 1993). But we cannot simply ignore the people living in the poorest countries that also do not have good economic policies. We need to help put in place good policies by providing advice and technical assistance. In addition, we should make investments in areas such as human capital that will be ready to support growth once good policies are adopted. And we must seek to find effective delivery mechanisms when governments have demonstrated their lack of capability.

Conclusion

I have sketched in broad outline an agenda for economic development for the next century. It includes a wider set of objectives than have development agendas of the past. It includes a changing role for the state—with a partnership between government and the private sector—that involves a catalytic function for government in helping to create markets. In some areas it includes a more enduring role for government in regulating markets. And it requires governments to improve their own performance, partly by making more extensive use of market-like mechanisms, by using and helping to create competition wherever it can.

For both developing and industrial countries the new agenda requires an openness that both groups have often resisted. The mutual benefits are clear: developing countries will continue to be an engine of growth for industrial countries, providing a broader variety of products at lower prices to their consumers and offering higher returns to their investors. For developing countries the transfer of resources and knowledge will enable a continuation of the growth that I heralded at the beginning of this article.

As I mentioned, there is an important role in this agenda for the World Bank and other international financial institutions. But what that role is and how it can best be performed must undergo a continuing process of reexamination.

There is no room in this agenda for dogma or for doctrinaire approaches. The Washington consensus on basic economic reforms—keep inflation to a moderate level, limit the size of the fiscal deficit, avoid introducing large distortions in the economy, open the economy to foreign competition—addresses issues of fundamental importance and has made important contributions to stabilization in several countries. There is a danger that the Washington consensus has become dogma and, as dogma, may sometimes be applied inappropriately.

One of the principal advantages of the Washington consensus is its simplicity. But the policy agenda of the coming decade will not be as amenable to such a cookie-cutter approach. Regulatory regimes and legal and other institutional structures should be better adapted to country circumstances. And in many cases reforms are far more technically complex than the Washington consensus suggests. For instance, designing regulations that promote competition in telecommunications and electricity is extremely difficult, as we are learning from the experience of the United States and others.

We need to learn from theory and history, from best practices, and from what has worked. But we need to be careful in extracting the appropriate lessons.

- The world today is different from the world thirty, twenty, or even ten years ago. Private capital flows are more important today than they were then; this opens up new opportunities—and new challenges. Thus the fact that some East Asian economies made relatively little use of foreign capital may have little bearing on whether a developing country today should make more extensive use of these flows.
- Some of the most successful economies did not follow all the key prescriptions that are commonly given today. Much of the growth in GDP among low-income countries can be accounted for by the growth in China. China focused on creating new enterprises and engendering competition rather than on privatizing state enterprises. Would these successful enterprises have grown even faster had it followed the alternative strategy? Most observers are doubtful.

The Republic of Korea has been widely criticized during its 1997 financial crisis for its failed economic system—yet that system somehow increased per capita incomes tenfold in three decades, a record unmatched by any large country following the prescriptions now commonly proffered.

- What works in one set of circumstances may not work in others. Analysis is required to identify the factors that determine success and to establish the counterfactuals (what would have happened in the absence of a particular project or policy). Examples of best practices may provide useful and persuasive anecdotes, but they are no substitute for analysis.
- We need to be careful not to confuse means with ends. Macroeconomic stability, deficit reduction, and even enterprise reform are not ends in themselves but means to the broader development objectives described earlier. If a government reduces its fiscal deficit by cutting back vital investments in infrastructure or in human capital, growth may actually suffer. If a government reduces its fiscal deficit by cutting back on food subsidies and that leads to rioting that undermines the country's political stability, is that likely to make the country more or less attractive to foreign investors?
- We also must not confuse ends with means: improved education and health are essential means of increasing GDP, but they are also ends in themselves.
- The broadened set of objectives is an essential aspect of the new development agenda. But while we recognize a richer set of objectives, the constraints provided by limited resources are no less binding. In the words of one of my colleagues, we must approach these issues with soft hearts and hard heads. We face a difficult tradeoff: we might be able to reduce poverty more today, but only at the expense of fewer resources—and therefore more poverty—in the future.
- One of the lessons of East Asia's experience is that there are important instances of policies that increase economic growth, promote equality, and ameliorate poverty. The search for such policies, and their implementation, must be at the center of the development agenda of the future.
- If we truly believe in democratic development, we must recognize the limited role of technical advisers. We can describe our judgments about the consequences of alternative policies. But an essential part of the new development strategies involves the creation of institutions and the changing of cultures—the movement to a culture of change and science, where existing practices are questioned and alternatives are constantly explored. (These cultural changes were, of course, the subject of considerable discussion in the development literature a half century ago.) Deciding how best to effect such changes requires a great deal of local knowledge, and it is not obvious that we have either that local knowledge or the corresponding technical expertise. Moreover, democratically elected governments must, in the end, make the judgments about both the tradeoffs and the political conse-

quences. These are principles that apply to advisers in advanced as well as in developing economies. Having said that, I want to emphasize that there are vast areas in which technical expertise is highly relevant. For example, certain fundamentals in establishing effective banking regulations apply to all countries.

Today we recognize that development is more than the accretion of physical capital and even more than the accretion of human capital. It includes closing the knowledge gap between rich and poor economies. And it includes other transformations, such as those that result in lower population growth rates and changes in economic organization.

I am confident that the coming decade will see enormous growth in the developing world and a reduction of poverty. It will be a struggle. The challenges are great, but the opportunities are many.

The challenge for those of us who advise governments will be to strike those hard-to-find balances: between the roles of the state and the roles of the private sector, and between the doctrinaire positions that have often characterized the policy advice of the past and the agnosticism that gives little guidance to those struggling to make the hard that will affect millions of lives.

Notes

1. Between 1991 and 1995 the growth rate of high-income countries was 2.5 percent, while that of low- and middle-income countries was 4.5 percent (World Bank 1997b).

2. This is a concern even with respect to democratically elected leadership when voter turnout is small: extreme groups may be more likely to express their views. And in some countries the structure of electoral processes in primaries has resulted in centrifugal forces that appear to have more than offset the centripetal forces that Hotelling emphasized. There is concern, too, about the influence of money in electoral processes. But electoral processes in which there is a simple rule of "one person, one vote" still provide the most systematic way of ensuring representativeness.

3. Much of this analysis was conducted in the context of closed economy models, in which material balance equations were critical. The programming problem would have been far simpler if gaps in, say, steel could have been filled by importing the needed good. But there was a companion literature that focused on open economies, in which foreign exchange and capital were the two critical resources that had to be efficiently allocated. For an early and insightful application of the two-gap planning approach, see Chenery and Bruno (1962). For a more general discussion, see Taylor (1979).

4. The dangers from excessive risk taking or looting that occur when banks are undercapitalized have been widely discussed in the aftermath of the banking crises of the 1980s and 1990s.

5. Similarly, government may require commercial firms to have fire insurance, leaving it to the insurance company to ensure that appropriate precautions are taken (such as installing sprinklers), knowing that the insurance company has appropriate incentives.

6. Some view the success of China as bearing witness to this proposition. More narrowly, studies of government-run enterprises that are subjected to competition suggest that they can perform as effectively as private firms (Daves and Christensen 1980). In large organizations, whether public or private, principal-agent problems arise; the scope for putting in place *individual* incentives may differ little between public and private organizations (Stiglitz 1990).

7. The variety of restrictions within the banking sector are examples of actions taken to improve the incentives of banks (Hellman, Murdock, and Stiglitz 1997).

8. Indeed, the conditions parallel many of the conditions underlying the fundamental theorems of welfare economics (Sappington and Stiglitz 1987).

References

Arnott, Richard, Bruce Greenwald, and Joseph E. Stiglitz. 1994. "Information and Economic Efficiency." *Information Economics and Policy* 6(1): 77–88.

Arrow, Kenneth, and Gerard Debreu. 1954. "Existence of Equilibrium for a Competitive Economy." *Econometrica* 22 (3): 265–90.

Burnside, Craig, and David Dollar. 1997. "Aid, Policies, and Growth." Policy Research Working Paper 1777. World Bank, Policy Research Department, Washington, D.C.

Chenery, Hollis, and Michael Bruno. 1962. "Development Alternatives in an Open Economy: The Case of Israel." *Economic Journal* 72 (1): 79–103.

Daves, D.W., and L.R. Christensen. 1980. "The Relative Efficiency of Public and Private Firms in a Competitive Environment: The Case of Canadian Railroads." *Journal of Political Economy* 88 (4): 958–76.

Debreu, Gerard. 1959. *The Theory of Value*. New York: Wiley.

Drèze, Jean, Amartya Sen, and Athar Hussain, eds. 1995. *The Political Economy of Hunger: Selected Essays*. New York: Oxford University Press.

Feyzioglu, Tarhan, Vinaya Swaroop, and Min Zhu. 1997. "Foreign Aid's Impact on Public Spending." Policy Research Working Paper 1610. World Bank, Policy Research Department, Public Economics Division, Washington, D.C.

Greenwald, Bruce, and Joseph E. Stiglitz. 1986. "Externalities in Economies with Imperfect Information and Incomplete Markets." *Quarterly Journal of Economics* 101 (3): 229–64.

———. 1988. "Pareto Inefficiency of Market Economies: Search and Efficiency Wage Models." *American Economic Association Papers and Proceedings* 78: 351–55.

Hellman, Thomas, Kevin Murdock, and Joseph Stiglitz. 1997. "Financial Restraint: Towards a New Paradigm." Stanford Graduate School of Business Research Paper, Stanford, California.

Pack, H., and J.R. Pack. 1990. "Is Foreign Aid Fungible? The Case of Indonesia." *Economic Journal* 100 (March): 188–94.

———. 1993. "Foreign Aid and the Question of Fungibility." *Review of Economics and Statistics* 75 (May): 258–65.

Sappington, David, and Joseph E. Stiglitz. 1987. "Privatization, Information, and Incentives." *Journal of Policy Analysis and Management* 6: 567–82.

Sen, Amartya. 1996. "Social Justice and Public Policy: The Informational Basis of Evaluation." 5 videocassettes. Presidential fellow program, World Bank, Washington, D.C.

Slovic, Paul, Mark Layman, and James H. Flynn. 1993. *Perceived Risk, Trust, and Nuclear Waste: Lessons from Yucca Mountain*. Durham, N.C.: Duke University Press.

Stiglitz, Joseph E. 1990. "The Economic Role of the State: Efficiency and Effectiveness." In Thomas P. Hardiman and Michael Mulreany, eds., *Efficiency and Effectiveness*. Dublin: Institute of Public Administration.

———. 1994. *Whither Socialism*. Cambridge, Mass.: MIT Press.

———. 1996. "Some Lessons from the East Asian Miracle." *The World Bank Research Observer* 11 (2): 151–78.

Stiglitz, Joseph E., and Marilou Uy. 1996. "Financial Markets, Public Policy, and the East Asian Miracle." *The World Bank Research Observer* 11 (2): 249–76.

Taylor, Lance. 1979. *Macro Models for Developing Countries*. New York: McGraw-Hill.

USEPA (U.S. Environmental Protection Agency). 1987. *Unfinished Business: A Comparative Assessment of Environmental Problems*. Washington, D.C.

World Bank. 1993. *The East Asian Miracle: Economic Growth and Public Policy*. A Policy Research Report. New York: Oxford University Press.

———. 1994. *Adjustment in Africa: Reforms, Results, and the Road Ahead*. A Policy Research Report. New York: Oxford University Press.

———. 1997a. *Global Development Finance 1997*. Washington, D.C.

———. 1997b. *Global Economic Prospects and the Developing Countries*. Washington, D.C.

———. 1997c. *World Development Report 1997: The State in a Changing World*. New York: Oxford University Press.

Corruption: Catalysts and Constraints

Corruption and Development

Susan Rose-Ackerman

Corruption occurs throughout the world but is of special concern in developing countries. Widespread corruption is a symptom of a poorly functioning state, and a poorly functioning state can undermine economic growth. What are the policy options for developing country leaders who are committed to combating corruption? Structural reform is often necessary in areas such as tax and customs collection, regulation of private business, and development of state-sponsored infrastructure projects. In addition, institutional reform is often required to increase the transparency and accountability of the public sector and to facilitate the organization of independent oversight groups. Most developing countries also must reform their civil service and improve enforcement. The World Bank can assist such anticorruption efforts as part of its growing interest in creating institutional structures favorable to equitable growth.

Widespread corruption is a symptom of a poorly functioning state. Because such states can undermine economic growth, international development organizations have started to focus on corruption as part of a general rethinking of their role in the post–cold war world. Increasing emphasis is being placed on creating institutional structures favorable to economic development.

Corruption occurs throughout the world but is of special concern in developing countries. Those who pay and receive bribes can expropriate a nation's wealth, leaving little for its poorest citizens. Where corruption is systemic, even countries with extensive natural resources may fail to develop in a way that benefits ordinary citizens. Highly corrupt developing countries face particular challenges, even when controlled by reform-minded rulers. Reforming public institutions and government policies is essential, but poverty limits available options.

Since corruption is usually considered evil, its mere existence is often a cause for concern. Economists, however, can arrive at that conclusion only after understanding corruption's effect on the efficiency and equity of an economic system. If the

---

Susan Rose-Ackerman is Henry R. Luce Professor of Law and Political Science at Yale University.
Annual World Bank Conference on Development Economics 1997
©1998 The International Bank for Reconstruction and Development / THE WORLD BANK

effect is benign, economists will argue for legal reform rather than for the potentially costly step of labeling as illegal practices that are actually functional. Thus it is useful to first consider the costs and causes of corruption.

Costs and Causes of Corruption

All states, benevolent or repressive, control the distribution of benefits and the imposition of costs, usually through agents who possess discretionary power. Private individuals and firms that want favorable treatment may be willing to pay these agents. What is wrong with paying for what you want? That is, after all, the basis of the market system. The problem is that the person receiving the payment is an agent. The agent is responsible to a principal, whose goals seldom align with those of the person making the payment. Low-level bureaucrats are agents of their superior officials, ministers are responsible to the governing coalition, elected officials are responsible to the voting public, judges are responsible to legal norms.

Payments are corrupt when they are illegally made to public agents with the goal of obtaining a benefit or avoiding a cost. Such payments are not merely transfers. They affect the behavior of both payers and recipients. Different societies draw the line between legal gifts and illegal payoffs at different points; in thinking about where to draw that line, one must ask whether payments to agents advance or undermine public goals. An economic analysis of corruption seeks to determine the consequences, for efficiency of purchasing benefits from public agents through bribery.

Recent cross-country studies indicate that strong legal and government institutions and low levels of corruption help foster investment and economic growth.[1] Because the prevalence of corruption is highly correlated with other measures of bureaucratic efficiency—such as the amount of red tape and the quality of the judiciary—these studies cannot determine the effect of any one measure by holding the others constant. The data support the claim that corruption is a function of the amount of red tape, but the amount of red tape is itself partly a function of the prevalence of corruption. Corruption is a symptom of other underlying problems rather than an independent variable.[2]

No region has escaped the negative impact of corruption. For example, one recent study found that foreign direct investment was negatively associated with corruption. Even East Asia's "miracle" economies were not immune (Wei 1997). Another study found that corruption can undermine industrial policy. Again, East Asia was no exception (Ades and di Tella 1995).

To go beyond these macroeconomic findings it is necessary to isolate the structural features that create incentives for corrupt behavior. Six are important:

- The government may allocate a scarce benefit to individuals and firms using legal criteria other than willingness to pay. *Bribes clear the market.*
- Public officials may have little incentive to do their jobs well because of low pay and inadequate monitoring. *Bribes act as incentive payments.*

- Private individuals and firms may seek to lower the costs of taxes, duties, and regulations imposed on them by government. *Bribes lower costs for those who pay them.*
- The government may confer large financial benefits on private firms through contracts, privatizations, and concessions. *Bribes affect the level of monopoly rents and their allocation between private investors and public officials.*
- Bribes may substitute for legal forms of political influence. *Bribery of politicians buys influence, and bribery by politicians buys votes.*
- The judiciary may have the power to impose costs and transfer resources between litigants. *Bribes can override legal norms.*

Bribes That Equate Supply and Demand

Governments often provide goods and services for free or sell them below market prices. In many cases dual prices exist. In China, for example, some producer goods are sold both at state-subsidized prices and on the free market. In 1989 the market price of coal was nearly eight times the subsidized price. Not surprisingly, payoffs to obtain supplies at state prices were reportedly common (China Academy of Social Sciences 1990). Multiple exchange rates and import quotas are frequent sources of payoffs. When the supply of credit and the rate of interest are controlled by the state, bribes may be paid for access to credit.[3]

The incentives to make payoffs are clear enough in these cases, but what are the consequences in terms of economic efficiency? Suppose that the briber is qualified to receive a scarce benefit but is required to pay for it. If the corrupt market operates efficiently, the service will be provided to the applicants willing to pay the most for it. Consider, however, the potential for inefficient or unfair results. First, the goals of programs designed to benefit the needy or the deserving will be undermined if services are provided only to the highest payers. Second, corrupt markets are less open than competitive ones (Cartier-Bresson 1995; Gambetta 1993; Rose-Ackerman 1978). The illegality of bribery induces participants to spend resources to keep the transaction secret. Information about bribe prices will not be well publicized, and prices may be sticky. Some potential participants may refuse to enter the market because of moral scruples or fear of punishment, and public officials may limit their dealing to insiders and trusted friends.

In practice, corrupt officials can exercise monopoly power by determining the quantity of services provided. Like a private monopolist, officials may set the supply of services below the officially sanctioned level to increase economic rents. Conversely, corrupt officials may increase the supply of services if the government has set the supply below the monopoly level. In other situations the service is not scarce but is, like a passport, driver's license, or pension, available to everyone who qualifies for it. However, corrupt officials may have sufficient monopoly power to create scarcity either by delaying approvals or by withholding them unless bribes are paid (Paul 1995).

Finally, bribes are frequently paid to permit the unqualified to obtain a benefit. Shleifer and Vishny (1993, p. 601) call this "corruption with theft." Students pay to alter the results of university admissions tests, patients pay doctors to declare them eligible for disability payments, firms that are not creditworthy pay to obtain loans. People who are the least qualified for the service are often willing to pay the most, since they have no legal way to obtain it.

Bribes As Incentive Payments for Bureaucrats

Bribes can be paid to receive good service or to avoid delays. In some economic models such bribes are effective incentives. For example, payoffs to queue managers can be efficient because they create incentives for the managers to work quickly and to favor those who value their time highly (Lui 1985). Corrupt tax collectors can be efficient as long as the government can impose a binding overall revenue constraint.[4] But tolerating such "routine" corruption is extremely problematic. First, the models assume that officials have only limited discretion—for example, they assume that tax collectors "discover" the tax liabilities of citizens and firms (Flatters and MacLeod 1995). In reality, corrupt tax collectors might create tax liabilities to extract bribes, producing an arbitrary and unfair pattern of payments. Second, there are ways to avoid the costs of illegal payment systems. Queues can be managed through differential fees, and revenue collection offices can be permitted to retain a portion of the taxes they collect. Third, although individual firms may pay bribes to obtain certainty, the ultimate result can be very different operating conditions across firms.[5] Overall uncertainty is increased, not decreased.

Bribes often act as incentive payments to public officials, but tolerance of these payments, especially by outside lenders and donors such as the World Bank, is likely to dim the prospects for long-term reform. Incentive payments that are widely viewed as acceptable should be legalized, but not all incentive pay schemes improve bureaucratic efficiency. Instead, they can encourage inefficient efforts to maximize financial rewards.

Bribes to Lower Costs

Governments impose regulations, levy taxes, and enforce criminal laws. Individuals and firms may pay for relief from these costs—for example, by colluding with tax collectors and customs officials to lower the sums collected. The economic impact of bribes paid to avoid regulations, lower taxes, and supersede laws depends on the efficiency of the underlying systems. In an inefficient legal framework, payoffs to avoid onerous regulations and taxes may increase efficiency.[6] This argument is commonly espoused by investors in the developing world. It is a pragmatic justification that grows out of frustration with the existing legal order.

But are individuals and firms obligated to obey only those laws they judge to be efficient and just? In industrial countries firms generally do not respond to rules they find burdensome by bribing officials or enlisting the help of criminals to evade the law. Instead, firms work to change the laws by making legal campaign contributions, lobbying public agencies, and bringing lawsuits that challenge laws and regulations. Although many observers believe that money and corporate interests have too much influence on modern politics, well-documented lobbying activities and campaign contributions are superior to secret bribes in maintaining democratic institutions. Yet some of the same firms that engage in legal political activity at home feel less constrained about violating laws in developing and transition economies. Because the United States does not allow its companies to pay bribes to obtain business abroad, U.S. multinational corporations face a domestic legal constraint. The importance of this constraint, however, suggests that multinationals generally do not feel obliged to obey the law in the developing countries in which they operate.

Investors do not just pay bribes to avoid inefficient rules and taxes; they pay bribes to reduce the impact of *all* state-imposed burdens, justified or not. Tolerating such corruption can cause serious damage in nations struggling to build viable states. Such nations need to develop public institutions that translate popular demands into law, that establish a credible commitment to the enforcement of those laws, and that provide legal recourse to people or firms that think they have been wronged. If, instead, investors and ordinary citizens are left to decide which laws are legitimate, efforts to create viable institutions will founder. Legal reform can help legitimize the state if the resulting laws reinforce general public goals such as economic efficiency and fairness. International efforts to reduce the acceptability and increase the cost of bribery also can help change behavior.

Bribes to Obtain Contracts and Concessions and to Privatize Firms

Bribes paid to win major contracts and concessions and to privatize companies are generally the preserve of large businesses and high-level officials. Such bribes appear analogous to cases in which government disburses a scarce benefit. Is there anything distinctive about such corruption other than the size of the deals?

One difference is the likelihood that these officials are effectively insulated from prosecution and thus can be less restrained in their corrupt demands than lower-level officials. A second difference is that bribery of top officials can have more far-reaching economic consequences. Consider a logging concession that a company obtains illegally over the higher bids of its competitors. If corruption does not restrict who bids and if the official granting the concession cannot affect its size, then the firm that pays the largest bribe values the concession the most. The lost revenue from the higher bids, however, will be felt in the form of higher taxes and canceled public programs. The payoff may be "just" a transfer, but it is harmful to the well-being of ordinary citizens.

Now consider the firm that has obtained a secure long-term timber concession at a bargain price even with the bribe. If the firm operates in the international market, its subsequent actions should depend on the market for timber. That is, it should seek to maximize profits, and the bribe should be considered a sunk cost. But a corruptly obtained contract may be neither secure nor long term. Corruption introduces uncertainties into the economic environment that may give the firm an inefficient short-run orientation.[7] There are two reasons for this. First, the concessionaire may fear that those in power are vulnerable to overthrow because of their corruption. A new regime may not honor the old one's commitments. Second, even if the current regime remains in power, the concessionaire may fear the imposition of arbitrary demands once investments are sunk. Competitors may be permitted to enter the market, or the contract may be voided. Thus the corrupt firm may cut down trees more quickly than it would in less corrupt countries. It also may be reluctant to invest in immovable capital that would be difficult to take out of the country if the corrupt deal went awry.

In some countries systemic high-level corruption coexists with strong growth. These are states, mainly in Asia, that have managed to create secure economic environments so that state-supported deals represent credible long-term commitments (Campos and Root 1996). Even in such countries, however, corruption is not beneficial (Wei 1997). In addition to its distributive costs, corruption distorts allocative choices. Consider, for example, the ability of Hanbo Steel in the Republic of Korea to obtain bank loans despite its lack of creditworthiness (*Far Eastern Economic Review*, 20 February 1997). Similarly, the aging of an authoritarian ruler may intensify rent seeking by his family and close associates that distorts investment choices. In Indonesia those close to President Suharto appear to be trying to lock in gains for the future (Campos and Root 1996, pp. 136–37). The costs to the nation include lost tax revenue and inefficient investment projects.

Bribes to Buy Political Influence and Votes

Democracy gives citizens a role in choosing their political leaders. Thus corrupt elected officials can be voted out of office. But democracy is not necessarily a cure for corruption. Some democracies harbor corrupt politicians even though citizens are aware of their malfeasance. Moreover, bribes are often used to fund political parties and election campaigns.

Modern political campaigns require enormous amounts of money. In the absence of public funding, businesses that have a stake in politicians' decisions are the most convenient source of funds. Even if certain contributions from business are legal, firms and politicians may prefer to keep them secret if a quid pro quo is involved. An entrenched system of illegal payoffs can undermine efforts to reform campaign financing. In France and Italy, for example, some observers claim that political parties are now dominated by "business-politicians" (Mény 1996).

The testimony of Italian political operatives in the recent "Clean Hands" investigations reveals how corrupt practices can become entrenched in nominally democratic systems. According to the testimony, political "bosses" were in charge of mobilizing voters. This could be done with campaign funds, state resources, patronage jobs, and other government favors designed to create webs of obligation (Della Porta 1996). In Japan Prime Minister Tanaka Kakuei developed a system under which businesses were assigned candidates to fund and elect (Reed 1996). There and in the Republic of Korea politicians accused of amassing illegal campaign war chests justified their actions by noting the high cost of campaigning in countries where voters expect favors from candidates (Park 1995; Reed 1996).

In some countries the purchase of votes is quite open. Such payments have a long history, going back to the nineteenth century in England and the United States. Although reforms have limited such payoffs in most industrial countries, they remain a feature of electoral politics elsewhere. For example, the recent election in Thailand carried on a long-standing practice of small payoffs to voters (*Far Eastern Economic Review,* 28 November 1996; for background on Thailand see Phongpaicht and Piriyarangsan 1994).

In some countries officials in the executive branch buy the votes of legislators. Discretionary budgetary funds fuel this practice in a number of countries, especially in Latin America. For example, when Brazilian President Fernando Collor's impeachment was before Congress, observers worried that his allies were trying to bribe members into delivering a favorable verdict (Geddes and Ribeiro Neto 1992).

Conflicts of interest faced by politicians and bureaucrats are an underappreciated problem in many developing and transition economies. Many countries have few laws regulating the private business activities of public officials, leaving them open to accusations of favoritism. Campaign finance laws are often similarly permissive, although in some cases the rules are so restrictive that off-the-books transfers are almost required to finance campaigns. Recent scandals in France, Italy, Japan, Korea, and the United States point to the importance of clear rules governing the solicitation of private money and the provision of sufficient legal sources of campaign financing.

Bribes to Buy Judicial Decisions

Through their decisions judges have the power to affect the distribution of wealth. Thus, like any public official with similar powers, they may be tempted to accept bribes. This temptation is stronger when judges are underpaid and overburdened and have poorly equipped and understaffed offices. Even if judges are not themselves corrupt, clerks in charge of assigning cases and advising judges may demand or accept bribes. In some Latin American countries, for example, the lack of formal court fees creates incentives for court employees and judges to charge unauthorized fees (Buscaglia 1995).

Bribes can expedite decisions. Buscaglia (1995) found that between 1973 and 1993 judicial delays and backlogs in Latin America increased dramatically, creating incentives to pay bribes. Bribes can also influence decisions. In some cases bidding wars have erupted in which opposing parties have competed—using bribes—for legal judgments in their favor.[8]

When the judiciary is considered corrupt, it introduces uncertainties into the business climate. Laws may not mean much, and those with disputes may avoid bringing them before the courts unless they are certain to be the higher briber. Courts can be circumvented by, for example, hiring private arbitrators or resorting to the protection provided by organized crime. One study of the judiciary in Latin America found that most businesspeople try to avoid using the courts to resolve disputes (Buscaglia 1995). In Eastern Europe and Russia murders of businesspeople and bankers are common. Many appear to be execution-style killings that are part of a brutal private system of dispute resolution.[9]

Corruption and the Organization of Government

A country's level of corruption depends not just on the potential for economic rents but also on the political structure. An outside organization such as the World Bank can help fight corruption only under certain political-economic conditions. Kleptocracies, in which corruption is entrenched at the highest levels of government, must be distinguished from states in which corruption is the province of a large number of officials. The other side of the bribery "market" must be specified as well. Is there a small number of major corrupt private actors, or is the payment of bribes decentralized? Combining these two dimensions produces four stylized types of corrupt states: kleptocracies, bilateral monopoly states, mafia-dominated states, and competitive-bribery states (table 1).

In a pure kleptocracy the head of government organizes the political system to maximize the possibilities for extracting rents and reallocates these rents for personal use. Because such a ruler faces a large number of potential bribers, he or she might be expected to act like a private monopolist—what Mancur Olson (1993) calls a "stationary bandit," striving for productive efficiency but restricting economic output to maximize profits (Findlay 1991). In economic models of monopolies, however, property rights are stable and markets exist. Because kleptocrats may not face such constraints, they can expropriate property and extract wealth from private citizens through the threat of violence. Kleptocrats who have secure tenure may avoid such exploitive behavior. Still, over time, rent extraction can increase the uncertainty of a ruler's tenure.

Furthermore, most kleptocrats are not all-powerful. Their goal is to maximize their personal wealth, but the tools at their disposal are imperfect. They may have a disloyal civil service, a poor resource base, and a weak legal framework. Such rulers are likely to favor an excessively large state to maximize rent-seeking opportunities. Thus, even though they prefer to avoid waste by subordinates, they may be unable to prevent them from shirking and taking bribes (Coolidge and Rose-

Table 1. Types of Corrupt States

	Multiple bribers	Few bribers
Few recipients concentrated at upper levels of government	Kleptocracy (either a pure extortionary state or a weak state)	Bilateral monopoly state
Multiple recipients at lower levels of government	Competitive-bribery state with a possibility of spirals	Mafia-dominated state

Ackerman 1997). Strong kleptocrats run brutal but efficient states; weak ones run intrusive and inefficient states in which some of the inefficiencies are part of the effort to extract bribes from the public and the business community.

In the second type of corrupt state, a bilateral monopoly, a corrupt ruler faces a single major briber. The possibilities for rent extraction are shared by the briber and ruler. Their relative strength will determine how gains are shared as well as the overall size of the pie. If some rents can be generated only with the help of the ruler but the ruler fears losing all the gains to the briber, the ruler will not act. Similarly, the ruler may threaten to expropriate property, or the briber may threaten to engage in violence.

In some bilateral monopoly states rulers form an alliance with a mafia—an organized crime group that provides protective services that in ordinary societies are provided by the state (Gambetta 1993). In some cases the state and the mafia share the protection business, even sharing the same "customers." In this context corrupt rulers extort a share of the mafia's gains. Alternatively, some states depend on a few firms that extract minerals or produce agricultural products. Such firms may form an alliance with a country's rulers to share the wealth. If the firm has invested in fixed capital or if its product is a valuable raw material available only a few places on earth, the country's rulers are in a strong position. By contrast, if the firm produces an agricultural product and can easily relocate, or if the raw material is available elsewhere, the firm has a bargaining advantage and can demand that the state provide infrastructure, guard against labor unrest, and impose low taxes.

While corruption may not be overt in such regimes, the harm to ordinary citizens may nevertheless be severe. The state becomes an appendage of the large investor, incurring distributive and efficiency losses and forfeiting the ability to tap the profits of economic activity. Some rapidly growing states, especially in Asia, may fit into this category, but their economic success appears to undermine this claim. Instead, the mutual interests of rulers and large investors have produced a peaceful business-state alliance that has avoided the worst pathologies of the bilateral monopoly state (Campos and Root 1996). Still, if the state proves unable or unwilling to branch out beyond a few favored investors, the long-run costs may be high, because the economy will lose its ability to respond efficiently to changing conditions.

The third variant, the mafia-dominated state, is weak and disorganized, with many officials engaged in freelance bribery. As in the bilateral monopoly state, these officials face a monopolist briber in the private sector. The briber could be a domestic mafia or a large corporation. In either case the private group dominates the state, buying the cooperation of low-level officials but unable to organize the state into a unified body. The state's disorganization and weakness limit the private group's ability to buy the benefits it wants, since making an agreement with one official will not discourage another from coming forward.

Finally, a competitive-bribery state is one in which many corrupt officials deal with large numbers of ordinary citizens and firms. A fundamental problem in such situations is the potential for an upward spiral of corruption. The corruption of some officials can encourage others to accept bribes until all but the unreconstructed moralists are corrupt.

The challenge for reformers in such states is moving from a high level to a low level of corruption (see Andvig and Moene 1990; Besley and McLaren 1993; and Cadot 1987). One way out of the corruption trap is to tie the expected penalty to the level of bribery. High-corruption equilibria develop when the rewards for corrupt behavior increase with the incidence of corruption. By contrast, corruption remains limited if the probability of being caught increases with the size and incidence of bribery. In the latter case fewer people pay bribes, and those who do must pay very large ones.

Some states experience corruption at all levels of government. Where should reform efforts be concentrated in such cases? Some analysts are more concerned about decentralized corruption, where lower-level officials "overfish" a common pool in their search for rents, than about kleptocracy (Shleifer and Vishny 1993; Olson 1993; Rodrik 1996). In this view corruption at the top is designed to maximize monopoly rents and will lead to inefficient restrictions on supply but will have no effect on productive efficiency.

From this view it follows that anticorruption efforts should focus on low-level corruption. This is a problematic conclusion. The model assumes a fixed level of private rents (the common pool) that public officials try to extract. In reality, officials may have the power to expand the pool, and higher-level officials are generally better able to increase the reach of the state than lower-level ones. Moreover, since corruption can be a source of insecurity, rulers often take a short-term perspective that encourages additional stealing, making them even more insecure—a vicious circle. And, as noted, few kleptocrats are all-powerful. Their tools are inefficient and confiscatory. Thus there are few cases in which one can be confident that the kleptocrat will behave like a private monopolist, and many in which the kleptocrat will cause more damage than low-level corrupt officials.

Determining how international organizations should confront and cope with the various types of corrupt states is no easy task. Still, some response is crucial. The World Bank needs to make some hard choices about where to make loans and when to support policy reform. It should concentrate on countries whose rulers are committed to clean government at the top as well as at the bottom. States dominated by kleptocratic rulers or by corrupt outsiders are poor candidates for support. Of course, most developing countries fall somewhere between these two extremes. Corruption may be entrenched, yet some officials are committed to reform. In such cases the Bank must take a comprehensive view—bearing in mind that economic development is not well served if the proceeds from, say, tax and customs reforms accrue to a corrupt ruler.

Reform Programs

What steps can a reform-minded government take to reduce corruption? The possibilities depend on the state's capacity and the country's level of development. In addition to changing social attitudes and expectations, anticorruption efforts should limit public officials' opportunities for corruption and increase the benefits of being honest and the costs of being corrupt. Many such reforms can be assisted by World Bank projects and loans—but only if a country's political leaders are willing to bear the costs of change. The incentives for corruption are influenced by:

- The benefits and costs under the discretionary control of officials.
- The formal laws on corruption, bribery, conflicts of interest, and campaign finance, and the credibility of law enforcement.
- The conditions of civil service employment and the incentive systems within the civil service.
- The extent of auditing and monitoring within government.
- The ability of citizens to scrutinize government activities and file complaints.
- The level of press freedom and the freedom of individuals to form nongovernmental organizations.
- The level of active political opposition.

Here I focus on four broad categories of reform: reducing the discretionary power of government officials, enforcing anticorruption laws, reforming the civil service, and increasing the accountability of government to citizens.

Reducing the Incentives for Payoffs

The most basic anticorruption reforms are those that reduce the level of benefits under the control of public officials. A reform strategy must do this, however, without eliminating programs that have strong public justifications and without simply shifting the benefits to the private sector, where they will show up as monopoly profits. Since such reforms are in line with World Bank development priorities, Bank staff can be especially helpful in providing technical assistance in this area.

The most obvious approach is simply to eliminate laws and programs that breed corruption. If the state does not have the authority to restrict exports or license businesses, no one will pay bribes in those areas. If a subsidy is eliminated, the bribes that accompanied it will disappear as well. If price controls are lifted, market prices will reflect scarcity values, not bribes. If a parastatal is a locus of corrupt payoffs, privatizing it will eliminate the corruption.

For example, although firms involved in foreign trade often engage in corrupt activities, reform of Pakistan's export processing rules appears to have made exporting firms less corrupt than nonexporting ones (Rose-Ackerman and Stone 1996). After a brief experiment with Prohibition, the United States repealed the Eighteenth Amendment to the Constitution, which outlawed the manufacture and sale of "intoxicating liquors." Its time in force, between 1919 and 1933, was a period of widespread illegal production and sale of alcohol and corruption of law enforcement officers. The debate over legalizing drugs in the industrial world turns on the feasibility of controlling the industry through criminal law. Gambling, once outlawed in many jurisdictions, has recently been legalized in many U.S. counties and states, albeit under heavy state supervision and even state ownership.

In general, any reform that increases the competitiveness of the economy will reduce incentives for corrupt behavior. Thus policies that loosen controls on foreign trade, remove entry barriers for private industry, and privatize state firms in a way that ensures competition will help control corruption. Such reforms will also encourage firms to move from the informal into the formal economy, where they can obtain access to capital at market rates and be effectively regulated and taxed. In general, going "underground" is a substitute for bribery, although in some cases firms bribe officials in order to avoid official status.[10]

But any move toward deregulation and privatization must be carried out with care. Deregulating one area may increase corruption elsewhere. For example, a project sponsored by the U.S. Agency for International Development successfully reduced corruption (in the form of bribe extraction checkpoints) in the transport of onions in Niger—only to increase corruption along the same transport route in neighboring Côte d'Ivoire (Rogers and Iddal 1996). Privatization and the new regulatory institutions it demands also can be corrupted. Instead of bribing a parastatal to obtain contracts and favorable treatment, bidders bribe privatization officials. Moreover, company insiders often receive special treatment (Manzetti and Blake 1996; Celarier 1996).

The integrity of privatization is especially important in transition economies. The risk is not simply corruption and insider deals but domination by organized crime groups, which drive competitors, especially Western firms, away. Thus the privatization process should also establish a transparent and reliable legal environment. Many countries that have privatized ignored this step—with predictable results (Rose-Ackerman 1994; Shelley 1994). Privatization and deregulation are desirable in a wide range of cases, but reformers must carefully examine the incentives for rent seeking created by such reforms (Rose-Ackerman 1996).

Many corrupt regulatory and spending programs have strong justifications and should be reformed, not eliminated. The solution to corrupt tax collections obviously does not lie in abolishing taxes. Rather, laws should be clarified and streamlined in ways that reduce official discretion. Mexico's customs service, for example, cut from sixteen to three the number of steps in the customs process at the Mexico City airport (*El Economista,* 13 February 1992; Reuters News Service, 24 February 1993). Reformers have often suggested that procurement officers favor standard goods sold in private markets and that taxes and subsidies be simplified (Rose-Ackerman 1978).

Making rules more transparent also helps limit opportunities for corruption—as with simple, nondiscretionary tax spending and regulatory laws. Governments can also use market prices as benchmarks against which to judge public contracts (Ruzindana 1995). With clear rules, violations will surface even if bribery remains hidden.

The value of such reforms depends on the costs of limiting the flexibility of public officials. In developing countries that lack trained personnel, simplifying public policies has a strong appeal. Sometimes, however, a risk of corruption must be tolerated because of the benefits of a discretionary approach to program administration.

Transparency and publicity can help overcome incentives for corruption in such cases, but only if the systems of accountability discussed below are in place. If they are not, clear rules can simply permit a top ruler to extract payoffs more effectively.

Economists have long recommended reforming regulations in areas such as environmental protection by introducing market-based schemes that limit the discretion of regulators. Analysts also recommend user fees for scarce government services. These reforms have the advantage of removing incentives for corruption by replacing bribes with legal payments. For example, the sale of water and grazing rights and of import and export licenses can improve the efficiency of government operations while limiting corruption. However, developing countries whose regulations are poorly enforced may have trouble implementing such reforms since violators are not currently bearing any of the costs of existing rules.

Finally, administrative reform may reduce incentives for corruption. Corruption is often embedded in the hierarchical structure of bureaucracies. Low-level officials collect bribes and pass a share on to higher-level officials, perhaps in the form of an upfront payment for the job itself (Wade 1982). Conversely, higher-ups may organize the corrupt system to avoid wasteful competition among low-level officials—and to collect the spoils themselves. Breaking such patterns may require fundamental reorganization.

One way to lower officials' bargaining power is to introduce competitive pressures within government. When bribes are paid for benefits that are not constrained by budgetary limits, such as licenses and permits, overlapping and competitive bureaucratic jurisdictions can reduce corruption. Since clients can apply to any of a number of officials and go to a second one if turned down by the first, no one official has monopoly power. Thus no official can demand a large bribe. For qualified clients bribes will be no larger than the cost of reapplication. Unqualified clients will still pay bribes, but even they will not pay much as long as they too can try another official. And if some officials establish honest reputations, qualified applicants will prefer those officials, reducing the gains to the corrupt. This reduction in benefits may induce some marginal officials to become honest, further reducing the benefits to the remaining corrupt officials. A small number of honest officials can reform a corrupt system unless long queues develop in front of the honest officials (Rose-Ackerman 1978, pp. 137–59). If those who pay bribes are unqualified, however, the honesty of some officials increases the gains to those who are corrupt, inducing more officials to become corrupt.

In situations where officials, such as police officers, can impose costs, another type of overlapping jurisdiction is possible. Police officers seeking bribes from illegal businesses can be given overlapping enforcement areas. People engaged in criminal activity will not pay much to an individual policeman if a second one may later demand an additional payoff. As a result some officials may shift from the corrupt to the honest category. Bribery is no longer worthwhile, given the risks of exposure (Rose-Ackerman 1978, pp. 159–63). This system may work better if the officers belong to different police forces—local, state, or federal, for example—thereby reducing the likelihood of collusion among officers. In the United States the Federal

Bureau of Investigation investigates corruption at the municipal level. In Great Britain the Audit Commission is a national agency that monitors local governments (Great Britain Audit Commission 1993). Sometimes jurisdictional overlap has an international dimension. The involvement of U.S. drug enforcement authorities in investigating the drug business in Colombia led a defector to choose the U.S. justice system over the Colombian and to provide information on drug cartel payoffs to Colombian politicians (*The Washington Post*, 28 January 1996).

Establishing Credible Law Enforcement

A basic condition for corruption control is a viable legal framework that enforces the law without political favoritism or arbitrariness. Such a system deters those tempted to engage in corrupt acts and encourages the public to resist criminal conduct by officials. Tough laws are not sufficient, however. Many highly corrupt countries have exemplary formal statutes that are essentially meaningless because they are seldom enforced. A country that is serious about reform must also have effective agencies to investigate and prosecute corruption and an independent judiciary that is not itself corrupt.

An independent judiciary can be particularly effective in checking official malfeasance. In India the Supreme Court pushed forward a corruption investigation that the government had wanted to quash (*Times of India*, 2 March 1996). In Brazil the Supreme Court's insistence that the congressional vote on President Collor's impeachment be public helped keep the process honest (Geddes and Ribeiro Neto 1992). Judicial reform requires more than just changing personnel, however. Without changes in underlying conditions, fundamental change is unlikely. The first step in reform is improving pay and working conditions for judges and supporting personnel, but this must be accompanied by better monitoring of the system's performance, by both insiders and outsiders. For example, information on delays by court and type of case could be collected and made public.

Judges may require additional training if they are to deal responsibly with the disputes that come before their courts. Increasing the professionalism of judges should reduce the incidence of corruption. But all these reforms will be of little use if the judiciary is not granted independence from the executive and legislative branches. Independence can be achieved in a number of ways. Whatever the mechanism, the goal is a judiciary that has constitutional constraints on its power but that is insulated from day-to-day political pressures. The judiciary can play a role not just in hearing corruption cases brought by state authorities but also in helping citizens review state actions. In countries where the judiciary provides an independent voice for the rule of law, citizen suits requiring the executive to obey the law may be a useful supplementary tool. The World Bank is beginning work on judicial reform, especially in Latin America, but the projects are at an early stage (Rowat, Malik, and Dakolias 1995) and may not focus strongly enough on the judiciary's overall contribution to government reform.

One way to make the judiciary more effective is to have well-written laws. Courts cannot avoid exercising discretion, but a clear body of laws helps resolve disputes and make judicial decisions less arbitrary. Some developing countries' laws are written in the language of the former colonial power and are difficult for citizens to understand. Others continue to rely on outdated statutes borrowed from industrial countries. Thus, while reforming and upgrading the judiciary can help control incentives for corrupt behavior, comprehensive reform also requires a review of the legal system in which judges operate.

Judicial reform will have little impact in the absence of an effective prosecutorial system. When ordinary law enforcement offices are ineffective or corrupt, an alternative is an independent anticorruption commission or an inspector general reporting only to the chief executive or the parliament. The best-known commission is Hong Kong's Independent Commission Against Corruption (ICAC), which reported only to the governor general and had extensive powers (Klitgaard 1988; Quah 1993; Manion 1996). The commission was charged with investigating allegations of corruption and with educating the public. Surveys carried out during 1977–94 indicate that public perceptions of corruption fell in the early years of the ICAC, and indirect evidence suggests that corruption declined as well. Yet the ICAC is not without its weaknesses. In systems less committed to the rule of law its widespread powers could be abused. A tough, independent anticorruption agency can be a potent tool—as long as it represents a credible long-term commitment and includes checks on its ability to be misused for political ends. Botswana, Malawi, Malaysia, Singapore, and the Australian state of New South Wales have similar institutions (Skidmore 1996). It will be valuable to study their experiences as well as that of the ICAC under Hong Kong's new status as part of China.

Legal and judicial reform may, however, be beyond the reach of developing countries in which corruption is endemic. In such cases reform should focus on reducing the incentives for payoffs and on increasing the state's accountability to ordinary citizens.

Reforming the Civil Service

In many developing countries civil servants are poorly paid, and officials often supplement their pay with second jobs or payoffs. A recent cross-country study found that high civil service wages (relative to private sector wages) are associated with low corruption levels (Van Rijckeghem and Weder 1997). Civil service reform projects supported by the World Bank should make an explicit effort to reduce corruption (Nunberg and Nellis 1995), but the effort will not be easy. Civil service reform is generally a long-term undertaking, especially if the system is caught in a trap in which high corruption begets even higher corruption.

If officials are paid much less than people with similar training elsewhere in the economy, only those willing to accept bribes will be attracted to the public sector. In order to recruit based on merit and to permit those selected to serve without resorting to corruption, civil service pay should be set at least equal to that for equivalent positions in the private sector. If officials have control over extremely valuable benefits, however, parity may not be sufficient. Instead, civil service wages may need to be set higher than the going private sector wage, with generous benefits, such as pensions, that will be received only if the worker retires in good standing (Becker and Stigler 1974).

It is seldom possible, however, to raise civil service salaries to levels that reflect the discretionary benefits under officials' control. Moreover, recent evidence from industrial countries suggests that such a costly solution may be unnecessary—parity may be sufficient (Van Rijckeghem and Weder 1997). This strategy, however, must be combined with effective monitoring and a transparent, merit-based system of selecting civil servants. In addition, penalties for corruption must be tied to its marginal benefits. Conversely, if the only efficiency cost of corruption stems from its illegality, bribes could be converted to legal payments. In designing such systems, however, it is important to avoid giving bureaucrats monopoly power that they can use to extract ever higher rents.

In some developing countries the problem is not so much low pay as excess employment. Wage disparities between the civil service and the formal private sector overstate the effective pay differential. For most officials the true opportunity wage is found in the informal small business sector or in farming. High-wage jobs in the formal sector are rationed so that not all of those who are nominally qualified can expect to be hired. In such cases reform of the public sector requires an improvement in private sector job opportunities. The best way to improve the quality of the civil service may be to encourage strong private sector growth, so that it becomes politically possible to cut civil service jobs. To avoid adverse selection and continued corruption, wages will probably need to be raised as well, but a reform that focuses only on pay levels will not succeed. Across-the-board pay increases with no link to productivity are exactly the wrong strategy. Yet they may be difficult for politicians to avoid. For example, Ghana increased all civil servants' wages by 80 percent before an election, thus undermining its attempts to achieve fiscal balance (World Bank 1995).

Increasing Accountability to Citizens

The private sector can be an important check on the arbitrary exercise of power by government—but only if citizens can find out what the state is doing and use this information to hold public officials accountable. As a first step governments must publish budgets, revenue collection data, statutes and rules, and proceedings of legislative bodies. Financial data should be independently audited. Chief executives and top ministers should not have access to secret funds. Several World Bank and United Nations Development Programme projects have helped developing and transition economies publish timely and accurate documents on the basic operations of government. Others have helped countries, especially in Latin America and Africa, make their budgetary processes more transparent (World Bank 1994). These reforms provide an important background for anticorruption efforts.

Public procurement regulations must ensure that the process is open and fair (Pope 1996). Many procurement scandals have occurred because top officials overruled the tender board or because subordinate officials operated without formal controls. But procurement rules must not be perceived as silly or overly intrusive. For example, requiring that the lowest bidder always win a contract can lead to low-quality work or facilitate bid rigging (Klitgaard 1988, pp. 134–55). Transparency International, a nonprofit organization committed to fighting corruption worldwide, recommends that potential bidders sign an "integrity pact" under which they pledge to refrain from corruption. Such pledges appear redundant, since corruption is illegal, but they draw attention to the issue in countries where there is little respect for the rule of law. Nevertheless, any serious attempt to implement an integrity pact requires more than just a pledge—it also requires an institutionalized mechanism for lodging complaints about corruption.

Disappointed contractors are an important source of information in any integrity system (Alam 1995). However, losers have an incentive to accuse the winner of corruption even if none occurred. Countries need to make constructive use of the information contractors provide without having to investigate the claims of every disappointed bidder. The international community could help by developing some kind of forum for hearing such claims.

Those who lose from corruption can be involved in anticorruption efforts in other ways. Sometimes bribers are themselves losers who would be better off in an honest world. But if such bribers are to help fight corruption, they need mechanisms though which to voice their complaints. Along these lines, the World Bank could help countries experiment with low-level tribunals and ombudsmen that help ordinary citizens faced with routine bribery demands. An alternative is the creation of corruption "hotlines" that citizens can call to complain directly to the government. Mexico has established such a system for businesses harassed by inspectors (Federal Executive Power of Mexico 1996), and the Mexican state of Chihuahua has experimented with a similar program to combat police corruption.

Information is a precondition for anticorruption efforts. Freedom of information acts in the United States and a number of European countries contribute to effective public oversight. These laws allow citizens to request information without having to show how that information affects them. But information is of little value unless people can use it to influence government. In countries without democratic elections or independent courts, other forms of citizen voice need to be encouraged. For example, executive agencies could hold hearings at the national and local levels so that people affected by a government policy can voice their opinion on it. The World Bank's operating procedures tend to focus on high-level rather than low-level consultation; this approach may need to be revised. Publicity is another option—even an undemocratic ruler is likely to be sensitive to public opinion. The World Bank's Economic Development Institute has made a start in this area with investigative reporting courses for African journalists.[11]

Individuals face a free rider problem in seeking to control political and bureaucratic processes and limit malfeasance. Information may be available in principle, but no one has an incentive to look at it. Laws that make it easy to establish watchdog associations and nonprofit organizations can help. Some corrupt rulers, worried that nongovernmental organizations will be used to monitor their performance, limit such groups, make it costly for them to organize, or subject their members to surveillance and harassment. The World Bank should help countries promulgate statutes facilitating the incorporation of nonprofit organizations.

Such organizations can play a constructive role. For example, with the help of the World Bank and bilateral donors, local branches of Transparency International have organized integrity workshops in some countries. These workshops bring together concerned people from the public and private sectors to discuss corruption. Nonprofits can also carry out and publish surveys that reveal public attitudes toward government services. Pioneering work has been carried out by the Public Affairs Centre in Bangalore, India, which produces "report cards" on services to the urban poor in five cities. The assessment revealed that up to one-third of slum dwellers had had to bribe officials to obtain services (Paul 1995).

Conclusion

Where should reform efforts begin? Countries serious about fighting corruption will require a detailed, country-specific assessment along the lines of those recently completed by the World Bank for Bangladesh and Nigeria. Still, some guidelines apply to all countries where corruption is common. The first step is to determine where corruption is imposing the most costs. Several government activities tend to harbor corruption:

- Tax and customs revenues may be far below the level needed to provide basic government services, and the pattern of payments may be highly inequitable because of payoffs. Reform options include simplifying the tax laws to reduce bureaucratic discretion and reorganizing the bureaucracy to improve monitoring and create incentives for good performance.
- Another potential fiscal drain is state sponsorship of infrastructure projects that are too large and complex. Here the cost of corruption derives not from bribes but from the cost of inefficient projects. Even if direct evidence of corruption is not available, the inappropriate scale and design of such projects should justify canceling them. Such cancellations must, however, be accompanied by better procedures for future project approvals.
- Regulation of business may be so complex, time consuming, and intrusive that it impedes the development of a healthy private sector. Here the answer is a hard look at the laws, to see which can be eliminated or simplified and which require better enforcement.

Basic institutional reforms—for example, increasing the transparency and accountability of government and facilitating the organization of independent watchdog groups and grassroots citizens groups—may be a precondition for reform in some sectors. Some of these reforms may be politically difficult, but they are not particularly expensive. The challenge is to institutionalize such reforms so that they will outlive changes in personnel and political leadership.

Once institutional and policy problems have been tackled, most developing countries still face the difficult task of civil service reform. Such reform is often financially costly and politically painful, but it is essential to any serious anticorruption effort. Reform policies must reduce the size of the civil service, raise base salaries for workers who remain, establish merit-based recruitment, and give officials an incentive to be honest and to perform efficiently. Of course, this is much easier said than done, especially in developing countries. The World Bank's experience in this area, even in projects that were ultimately unsuccessful, should be made broadly available.

Many developing and transition economies lack credible institutions capable of hearing complaints and enforcing the law. Thus another important reform should be to improve existing institutions, such as the courts, or to create new bodies, such as independent inspectors general or anticorruption commissions. The experience of other countries—both successful experiments and those that backfired when corruption fighters became corrupt themselves—needs to be understood. And the problem of anticorruption campaigns being used to undermine political opponents and discipline troublesome constituents must be addressed when new institutions are proposed.

Even if the basic constitutional framework remains unchanged, serious reform can be carried out within any structure of government—so long as there is a long-term commitment from the top. By contrast, governments that silence critical voices will have a hard time making a credible commitment to honest and transparent government. Such governments might make progress in the short run but always risk policy reversal in the future.

How can the World Bank help reduce corruption in developing countries? Priorities are difficult to establish in the abstract, but a few areas stand out:

- The Bank needs to make it clear that corruption will not be tolerated in its grants and loans, and it must cancel projects in which corruption is uncovered or cost overruns suggest that venality or incompetence is pervasive. It should be skeptical of supporting projects that make it easy for public officials to hide private gains, and it may need to discontinue lending to countries in which corruption at the top appears endemic.
- Recent international efforts are focusing on reducing bribery in international business and checking the flow of illicit funds. The Organization for Economic Cooperation and Development is seeking to end the tax deductibility of overseas bribery and to draft a convention on the criminalization of such behavior. Members of the Organization of American States have signed a treaty pledging to fight corruption, and codes of conduct have been developed for international business. The Bank should support such initiatives and encourage efforts to establish international standards for budgeting, accounting, and procurement.
- Bank projects should increasingly focus on creating an environment conducive to equitable growth and poverty alleviation. The Bank's experience with government reform should be evaluated for the lessons it can provide.

Projects should be designed so that country officials and Bank staff work to isolate the most serious problems and design solutions. The Bank might select a few countries to serve as examples for such efforts. Piecemeal reforms that benefit corrupt autocrats should not receive support.

The World Bank is concerned that its projects are not sufficiently "owned" by borrowing countries. A focus on corruption puts an ironic spin on that concern. Ownership at the top is not desirable if patronage and corruption are rife or if projects help keep corrupt regimes in power. In such cases projects with the greatest ownership potential are unlikely to be targeted toward the poor or to help achieve overall development objectives. Since the Bank is a development institution, it should work to counteract the distortions introduced by corrupt rulers seeking to amass personal wealth and by private firms with monopoly power. Helping countries fight corruption can improve the legitimacy and effectiveness of both governments and international development efforts by making it easier to target projects that alleviate poverty and facilitate equitable growth.

Notes

1. Mauro (1995, 1997) demonstrates that high levels of corruption are associated with lower levels of investment (as a share of GDP) in a cross-section of countries. A standard deviation improvement (2.4) in the corruption index is associated with an increase of more than 4 percent in the investment rate and of more than 0.5 percentage point in annual per capita GDP growth (Mauro 1997).

2. Mauro (1995) presents an investment risk index (based on eleven factors from the *Business International* index, including the corruption index) that shows that higher-risk countries record both lower investment rates and lower growth rates. Keefer and Knack (1995) find that an index of the quality of government institutions is a significant determinant of investment and growth.

3. Surveys of businesspeople in Eastern Europe and Russia have found that payoffs are often required to obtain credit (De Melo, Ofer, and Sandler 1995; Webster 1993; Webster and Charap 1993). A similar survey in Lebanon found that loans are not available without the payment of bribes (Yabrak and Webster 1995).

4. In this case tax officials should set a revenue target, a nominal tax liability schedule, and the wage rate of the tax collector. Corruption gives tax collectors an incentive to seek tax revenue and is tolerated as long as the collector turns in a sum equal to the revenue target (Flatters and MacLeod 1995).

5. World Bank–sponsored surveys of businesspeople in Pakistan and Ukraine indicate that different firms operate under very different conditions (Rose-Ackerman and Stone 1996). Businesspeople in developing countries often cite legal and regulatory uncertainty as a problem (Economisti Associati 1994; Webster 1993; Webster and Charap 1993). Pritchett and Sethi (1994) show how higher tariffs are associated with lower proportional collections and greater variance in rates paid.

6. If state bureaucracies are inefficient and the regulation or taxation they impose is excessive, bribes can have three possible benefits: they can push profitable projects to the head of the queue, limit excessive regulation, and reduce tax payments (*Oxford Analytica*, 5 June 1996).

7. See Coolidge and Rose-Ackerman (1997). On the short-run orientation of corrupt timber concessionaires in Malaysia, see Vincent and Binkley (1992). Deacon (1994) reports that insecurity of tenure and weak property rights are negatively associated with deforestation.

8. According to an Englishman living in Egypt in the 1820s, judicial decisions were influenced by the rank of the parties or a bribe from either: "On some occasions, particularly in long litigations, bribes are given by each party, and a decision is awarded in favour of him who pays the highest" (Johnson 1991, p. 686).

9. According to the Russian government, 269 businessmen and financiers were murdered in 1995 in execution-style slayings (*The Economist*, 9 November 1996).

10. The link between intrusive state regulation, corruption, and the informal economy in Ukraine is documented by Kaufmann (1994) and Kaufmann and Kaliberda (1996).

11. To see how an accountable process might work in a developing country, see Oldenburg's (1987) description of a successful effort to control corruption in the land consolidation process in Uttar Pradesh, India, in the 1980s. Key elements included time pressures, speedy and fair appeals, and open processes that encouraged participation by affected parties. Government officials managed the process, and no one could proceed with planting until the new land distribution system was complete. Disappointed households could appeal and obtain quick decisions that the participants generally viewed as fair.

References

Ades, Alberto, and Rafael di Tella. 1995. "National Champions and Corruption: Some Unpleasant Competitiveness Arithmetic." Oxford University, Keble College.

Alam, M.S. 1995. "A Theory of Limits on Corruption and Some Applications." *Kyklos* 48 (3): 419–35.

Andvig, Jens Christopher, and Karl Ove Moene. 1990. "How Corruption May Corrupt." *Journal of Economic Behavior and Organization* 13 (1): 63–76.

Becker, Gary, and George Stigler. 1974. "Law Enforcement, Malfeasance, and Compensation of Enforcers." *Journal of Legal Studies* 3 (1): 1–19.

Besley, Timothy, and John McLaren. 1993. "Taxes and Bribery: The Role of Wage Incentives." *Economic Journal* 103 (416): 119–41.

Buscaglia, Edgardo, Jr. 1995. "Judicial Reform in Latin America: The Obstacles Ahead." *Journal of Latin American Affairs* (fall/winter): 8–13.

Cadot, Olivier. 1987. "Corruption as a Gamble." *Journal of Public Economics* 33(2): 223–44.

Campos, Edward, and Hilton Root. 1996. *East Asia's Road to High Growth: An Institutional Perspective.* Washington D.C.: Brookings Institution.

Cartier-Bresson, Jean. 1995. "L'economie de la corruption." In Donatella Della Porta and Yves Mény, eds., *Démocratie et Corruption en Europe.* Paris: La Découverte.

Celarier, Michelle. 1996. "Stealing the Family Silver." *Euromoney* 332 (February): 62–66.

China Academy of Social Sciences. 1990. *Zhongguo Wujia* (China Price). Finance and Trade Institute, Price Reform Group, Beijing.

Coolidge, Jacqueline, and Susan Rose-Ackerman. 1997. "High-Level Rent-Seeking and Corruption in African Regimes: Theory and Cases." Policy Research Working Paper 1780. World Bank, Washington, D.C.

Deacon, Robert T. 1994. "Deforestation and the Rule of Law in a Cross-Section of Countries." *Land Economics* 70 (4): 414–30.

Della Porta, Donatella. 1996. "Actors in Corruption: Business Politicians in Italy." *International Social Science Journal* 48 (149): 349–64.

De Melo, Martha, Gur Ofer, and Olga Sandler. 1995. "Pioneers for Profit: St. Petersburg Entrepreneurs in Services." *The World Bank Economic Review* 9 (3): 425–50.

Economisti Associati. 1994. "Eastern Africa—Survey of Foreign Investors." Vols. 2 and 3. Report prepared for the World Bank, Africa Department, Washington, D.C.

Federal Executive Power of Mexico. 1996. *Program for the Modernization of Public Administration 1995–2000.* Mexico City.

Findlay, Ronald. 1991. "Is the New Political Economy Relevant to Developing Countries?" In Gerald M. Meier, ed., *Politics and Policymaking in Development: Perspectives on the New Political Economy.* Washington, D.C.: World Bank.

Flatters, Frank, and W. Bentley MacLeod. 1995. "Administrative Corruption and Taxation." *International Tax and Public Finance* 2 (3): 397–417.

Gambetta, Diego. 1993. *The Sicilian Mafia: The Business of Private Protection.* Cambridge, Mass.: Harvard University Press.

Geddes, Barbara, and Artur Ribeiro Neto. 1992. "Institutional Sources of Corruption in Brazil." *Third World Quarterly* 13 (4): 641–61.

Giglioli, Pier Paolo. 1996. "Political Corruption and the Media: The Tangentopoli Affair." *International Social Science Journal* 48 (149): 381–94.

Great Britain Audit Commission. 1993. *Protecting the Public Purse: Probity in the Public Sector—Combating Fraud and Corruption in Local Government.* London: HMSO.

Johnson, Paul. 1991. *The Birth of the Modern: World Society 1815–1830.* New York: Harper Collins.

Kaufmann, Daniel. 1994. "Diminishing Returns to Administrative Controls and the Emergence of the Unofficial Economy: A Framework of Analysis and Applications to Ukraine." *Economic Policy* 9 (December): 51–69.

Kaufmann, Daniel, and Aleksander Kaliberda. 1996. "Integrating the Unofficial Economy into the Dynamics of Post-Socialist Economies: A Framework of Analysis and Evidence." In Bartlomiej Kaminski, ed., *Economic Transition in Russia and the New States of Eurasia.* Armonk, N.Y.: M.E. Sharpe.

Keefer, Philip, and Stephen Knack. 1995. "Institutions and Economic Performance: Cross-Country Tests Using Alternative Institutional Measures." *Economics and Politics* 7 (3): 207–27.

Kilby, Christopher. 1994. "Risk Management: An Econometric Investigation of Project-Level Factors." Background paper for the *Annual Review of Evaluation Results 1994.* World Bank, Operations Evaluation Department, Washington, D.C.

Klitgaard, Robert. 1988. *Controlling Corruption.* Berkeley: University of California Press.

Lui, Francis T. 1985. "An Equilibrium Queuing Model of Bribery." *Journal of Political Economy* 93 (4): 760–81.

Manion, Melanie. 1996. "Policy Instruments and Political Context: Transforming a Culture of Corruption in Hong Kong." Paper prepared for the annual meeting of the Association for Asian Studies, Honolulu, Hawaii, 11–14 April.

Manzetti, Luigi, and Charles Blake. 1996. "Market Reforms and Corruption in Latin America: New Means for Old Ways." *Review of International Political Economy* 3 (4): 662–97.

Mauro, Paolo. 1995. "Corruption and Growth." *Quarterly Journal of Economics* 110 (3): 681–712.

———. 1997. "The Effects of Corruption on Growth, Investment, and Government Expenditure: A Cross-Country Analysis." In Kimberly Ann Elliott, ed., *Corruption and the Global Economy.* Washington, D.C.: Institute for International Economics.

Mény, Yves. 1996. "Fin de Siécle Corruption: Change, Crisis and Shifting Values." *International Social Science Journal* 48 (149): 309–20.

Nunberg, Barbara, and John Nellis. 1995. *Civil Service Reform and the World Bank.* World Bank Discussion Paper 161. Washington, D.C.

Oldenburg, Philip. 1987. "Middlemen in Third World Corruption: Implications for an Indian Case." *World Politics* 39 (4): 508–35.

Olson, Mancur. 1993. "Dictatorship, Democracy, and Development." *American Political Science Review* 87 (3): 567–75.

Park, B.S. 1995. *Political Corruption in Non-Western Democracies: The Case of South Korea Party Politics.* Seoul: Kim Dae-Jung Peace Foundation.

Paul, Sam. 1995. "Evaluating Public Services: A Case Study on Bangalore, India." *New Directions for Evaluation* 67 (fall).

Pendergast, William F. 1995. "Foreign Corrupt Practice Act: An Overview of Almost Twenty Years of Foreign Bribery Prosecutions." *International Quarterly* 7 (2): 187–217.

Phongpaicht, Pasuk, and Sungsidh Piriyarangsan. 1994. *Corruption and Democracy in Thailand.* Bangkok: Chulalongkorn University, Faculty of Economics Political Economy Centre.

Pope, Jeremy, ed. 1996. *National Integrity Systems: The TI Source Book.* Berlin: Transparency International.

Pritchett, Lant, and Geeta Sethi. 1994. "Tariff Revenue and Tariff Reform: Some New Facts." *The World Bank Economic Review* 8 (1): 1–16.

Quah, Jon S.T. 1993. "Controlling Corruption in City-States: A Comparative Study of Hong Kong and Singapore." Paper presented at a conference on World Bank, *The East Asian Miracle: Economic Growth and Public Policy* (New York: Oxford University Press, 1993), 25–26 October, Stanford University, Palo Alto, Calif.

Reed, Steven R. 1996. "Political Corruption in Japan." *International Social Science Journal* 48 (149): 395–405.

Rodrik, Dani. 1996. "King Kong Meets Godzilla: The World Bank and *The East Asian Miracle.*" In Albert Fishlow, Catherine Gwin, Stephen Haggard, Dani Rodrik, and Robert Wade, eds., *Miracle or Design? Lessons from the East Asian Experience.* Washington, D.C.: Overseas Development Council.

Rogers, Glenn, and Sidi Mohammed Iddal. 1996. "Niger: Reduction of Illegal Road Payments." In Center for Institutional Reform and the Informal. Sector *Governance and the Economy in Africa: Tools for Analysis and Reform of Corruption.* College Park, Md.

Roodman, David Malin. 1996. *Paying the Piper: Subsidies, Politics, and the Environment.* Worldwatch Paper 133. Washington, D.C.

Rose-Ackerman, Susan. 1978. *Corruption: A Study in Political Economy.* New York: Academic Press.

———. 1994. "Reducing Bribery in the Public Sector." In Duc V. Trang, ed., *Corruption and Democracy.* Budapest: Institute for Constitutional and Legislative Policy.

———. 1996. "Una administración reducida significa una administración más limpia?" (Is Leaner Government Cleaner Government?) *Nueva Sociedad* 145 (September–October): 66–79.

Rose-Ackerman, Susan, and Andrew Stone. 1996. "The Costs of Corruption for Private Business: Evidence from World Bank Surveys." World Bank, Private Sector Development Department, Washington, D.C.

Rowat, Malcolm, Waleed H. Malik, and Maria Dakolias, eds. 1995. *Judicial Reform in Latin America and the Caribbean: Proceedings of a World Bank Conference.* World Bank Technical Paper 280. Washington, D.C.

Ruzindana, A. 1995. "Combating Corruption in Uganda." In Petter Langseth, James Katorobo, E.A. Brett, and J.C. Munene, eds., *Uganda: Landmarks in Rebuilding a Nation.* Kampala: Fountain Publishers.

Shelley, Louise. 1994. "Post-Soviet Organized Crime." *Demokratizatsiya* 2 (3): 341–58.

Shleifer, Andrei, and Robert Vishny. 1993. "Corruption." *Quarterly Journal of Economics* 108 (3): 599–617.

Skidmore, Max J. 1996. "Promise and Peril in Combating Corruption: Hong Kong's ICAC." *Annuals of the American Academy of Political Science and Sociology* 547 (September): 118–30.

Stella, Peter. 1992. "Tax Farming—A Radical Solution for Developing Country Tax Problems?" IMF Working Paper 92/70. International Monetary Fund, Washington, D.C.

Van Rijckeghem, Caroline, and Beatrice Weder. 1997. "Corruption and the Rate of Temptation: Do Low Wages in the Civil Service Cause Corruption?" IMF Working Paper 97/73. International Monetary Fund, Washington, D.C.

Vincent, Jeffrey R., and Clark S. Binkley. 1992. "Forest-Based Industrialization: A Dynamic Perspective." In Narendra P. Sharma, ed., *Managing the World's Forests.* Dubuque, Iowa: Kendall/Hunt Publishing.

Wade, Robert. 1982. "The System of Administrative and Political Corruption: Canal Irrigation in South India." *Journal of Development Studies* 18 (3): 287–328.

Webster, Leila M. 1993. *The Emergence of Private Sector Manufacturing in Hungary.* World Bank Technical Paper 229. Washington, D.C.

Webster, Leila M., and Joshua Charap. 1993. *The Emergence of Private Sector Manufacturing in St. Petersburg.* World Bank Technical Paper 228. Washington, D.C.

Wei, Shang-Jin. 1997. "How Taxing Is Corruption on International Investors?" Harvard University, Kennedy School of Government, Cambridge, Mass.

World Bank. 1994. *Adjustment in Africa: Reform, Results, and the Road Ahead.* A Policy Research Report. New York: Oxford University Press.

———. 1995. "Ghana Country Assistance Review." Report 14547-GHA. Washington, D.C.

Yabrak, Isil, and Leila Webster. 1995. "Small and Medium Enterprises in Lebanon: A Survey." World Bank, Private Sector Development Department and Middle East and North Africa Country Department II, Industry and Energy Division, Washington, D.C.

Comment on "Corruption and Development," by Susan Rose-Ackerman

Diego Gambetta

Susan Rose-Ackerman's article effectively summarizes much of what we understand about corruption and how to fight it—not least because she has greatly contributed to that knowledge throughout her career. I claim no similar knowledge about corruption. Several years ago, however, I did some research on the Sicilian mafia. As a result I am now regularly invited to conferences on "unlawful topics" ranging from the white-slave trade to glue sniffing. This situation is rather tricky: the more I protest that I know nothing the less they believe me.

There are, however, a number of ways in which organized crime and corruption feed on each other. Rose-Ackerman discusses mafias at a macro level, analyzing corruption and the organization of governments. Here I focus on the relations between organized crime groups and corruption at a micro level. Most of what I say is supported by empirical evidence, though space prevents me from presenting it here.

Organized Crime and Corruption

Contrary to a common view, corruption is not the defining feature of mafia-like groups. Such groups are more accurately seen as agencies that supply protection to illegal markets. (For our purposes *illegal markets* refers not only to the trade of outlawed commodities but also to the adoption of illegal practices in the trade of otherwise legal commodities.) The protection supplied by organized crime groups may be of poor quality or impose extortionate prices, or both, but it differs from mere extortion.

Mafia protection is supplied in many different markets and does not necessarily play a part in the market for corrupt services. Conversely, corrupt services are exchanged in many parts of the world in the absence of mafia protection. When available, however, mafia protection fosters corruption in at least three ways: it provides enforcement to corrupt exchanges, it promotes illicit cartel agreements

---

Diego Gambetta is reader in sociology at the University of Oxford and fellow of All Souls College. He wrote this comment while he was visiting fellow at the Italian Academy of Advanced Studies at Columbia University.

Annual World Bank Conference on Development Economics 1997
©1998 The International Bank for Reconstruction and Development / THE WORLD BANK

Enforcing Corrupt Exchanges

Corruption requires trust. Yet trust is harder to come by among partners engaged in illicit practices than among law-abiding dealers. Consider the reasons why trust is in short supply among villains: by breaching the law, agents cannot avoid giving a strong sign that they are more likely to breach other pacts as well. So villains are the first to be wary of other villains' trustworthiness—and corrupt exchanges offer numerous opportunities for defection. Suppliers of corrupt services can fail to deliver after they have been bribed. They can sell the same secret twice. And they can raise the agreed price later on. Corrupters, for their part, can forget to pay up or pay less than agreed. There are no courts to turn to in case of cheating. And both parties work under the constant threat of being turned in by the other. Even if we charitably assume that there is some honor among thieves, agents involved in corruption operate in secrecy and are more likely to vanish or be caught by police.

Although often disregarded, these disincentives to corrupt behavior are some of the most important ways honest dealings are sustained. Even if people face large incentives for corruption, they will refrain from it if they cannot trust their partners in crime. The generic policy implication is that anything that lowers trust among corrupt agents lowers corruption, while anything that increases their mutual trust makes corruption grow. The mafia valiantly contributes to increasing mutual trust by providing enforcement services. If the mafia is stable, it can supply stability to a corrupt market that, left to its own devices, would be uncertain and unstable. If the mafia provides good-enough enforcement, corrupt agents behave and corruption works smoothly.

Stabilizing Corrupt Cartels

Some forms of corruption are a consequence of cartels. Even though firms can make cartel agreements work without help from the public agencies that allocate the contracts or oversee the industry, they typically need to include the agencies in the conspiracy to make their agreements stick. Unless they are corrupt, public agents could spot the collusion, refuse to pay higher prices, and inform the antitrust authorities.

Luckily, however, oligopolies often prove unstable. For cartel agreements to be effective, dealers need to coordinate their activities and abstain from free riding. For example, when a cartel relies on public contracts, its member firms must agree on ways to share the cake—say, by arranging queues for bidding or by dividing the territory or type of work among themselves. Member firms also require mutual trust. When trust is absent, cartels founder or fail to emerge. Successful cartels involve only a small number of firms. But cartels can work only if all firms in the industry are involved. If some contractors are left out, they become, as Rose-Ackerman points out, a danger in that they have a personal interest in informing the authorities.

The mafia supplies the muscle needed to make cartels emerge where they otherwise would not. By increasing the number of viable cartels, the mafia indirectly increases the related corruption. Furthermore, the mafia also increases the number of participants that can join the queue without destabilizing the cartel. Economic textbooks state that no more than twelve firms can participate in a cartel. Beyond that number market competition—which cartel members view as cheating—creeps in. But if the mafia intervenes, the number of firms can reach into the hundreds (Gambetta and Reuter 1995). Thus, by enabling more firms to benefit from collusion, the mafia removes one of the mechanisms that can undermine corruption, namely disappointed contractors. Every firm expects to get its share of the corrupt spoils at some point, and consumers and taxpayers will foot the bill.

Lowering the Cost of Corrupt Services

Mafia members are themselves consumers of corrupt services. They try to corrupt judges, juries, police officers, civil servants, and politicians. To use Rose-Ackerman's distinctions, mafiosi use corruption to lower the cost that the judicial system imposes on them and to secure benefits for themselves and their customers. In this respect mafiosi are superficially no different from other corrupting agents. However, mafiosi do differ in that they can resort to an alternative option: if corruption attempts fail, mafiosi can use the threat of violence to achieve their aims. The prospect of violence lurking in the background has a peculiar effect: it increases the number of people ready to be corrupted—the alternative now having been made worse—and it makes them accept lower prices for supplying corrupt services. If mafia services are widely available, people will pay no more in bribes than they would pay to achieve the same goal by resorting to violence.

The most effective mafioso do not even have to pay for corrupt services. People are so afraid that they provide them free of charge, at most expecting other favors in return. (Here the gift economy cherished by many anthropologists studying precapitalist societies takes on a nasty twist.) An environment thick with mafia activity gives people access to corrupt services more cheaply than elsewhere. In such an environment even corrupters reluctant to use the mafia to obtain favors will find that corruptees may yield faster and charge less (other things being equal). This happens if corruptees find it difficult, as they often do in that world, to discriminate between ordinary corrupters and mafia-backed corrupters, for they cannot risk imposing different prices. As a consequence, the demand for corruption grows and corruption becomes endemic. Ultimately, it results in a through-the-looking-glass world where everything is reversed. People will come to believe that something is wrong with you if you are not corruptible. Norms, as Hume said, emerge following interests.

Conclusion

The most pervasive threat that the mafia poses to economic development is not its ability to boost markets of illegal commodities such as narcotics. Such markets may even end up supporting growth because they generate considerable revenue and make cheap capital available for investment. Rather, the mafia's greatest threat lies in its ability to make illegal practices more attractive to ordinary citizens and legal firms, enabling them to rely on collusion and corruption rather than on proper practices and market competition.

Although the mafia can become entrenched in industrial countries (as in Italy and the United States), developing countries are especially at risk because illicit enforcers can play a more pervasive role. States with weak and confused property rights legislation and enforcement are at risk because people seek alternative sources of protection. Countries with disbanded soldiers, former terrorists or guerrillas, poorly paid police, unemployed secret agents, and other groups skilled at violence are at risk because these swell the crowd of thugs clamoring to supply protection. Developing countries that suffer from pressures on both the demand and the supply side of the protection market, such as Russia, are the most exposed of all.

References

Gambetta, Diego. 1993. *The Sicilian Mafia: The Business of Private Protection.* Cambridge, Mass.: Harvard University Press.

Gambetta, Diego, and Peter Reuter. 1995. "Conspiracy among the Many: The Mafia in Legitimate Industries." In Gianluca Fiorentini and Sam Peltzman, eds., *The Economics of Organized Crime.* Cambridge: Cambridge University Press.

Comment on "Corruption and Development," by Susan Rose-Ackerman

Edgardo Buscaglia

Susan Rose-Ackerman's article provides an outstanding overview of the microsocial and macrosocial conditions related to entrenched corruption. But an economic theory of corruption must do more than describe the general situations that foster corruption and its immediate effect on efficiency. Three additional considerations are important. First, the effect official corruption has on the average citizen's perception of social equity helps determine whether efficiency-enhancing economic activities or rent seeking activities will prevail (Buscaglia 1997). Second, a scientific approach to the study of corruption must be empirically verifiable if we are to develop reliable public policy prescriptions in the fight against official corruption. Finally, Rose-Ackerman's economic theory of corruption should recognize that official corruption is a significant source of institutional inertia in developing countries attempting public sector reforms. Thus the private costs and benefits of such reforms, as perceived by public officials, must also be considered.

Corruption, Efficiency, and Social Equity

Rose-Ackerman's article describes many of the negative effects corruption has on the efficient allocation of resources. It does not, however, consider the effects corruption has on social equity. For example, Rose-Ackerman believes that payoffs to queue managers can be efficient because they create incentives to work quickly and to favor those who value their time highly. She also states that some widely accepted illegal payoffs should be legalized. This analysis, however, disregards the effects entrenched corruption has on people's perception of social equity and on long-term efficiency. Official corruption affects future efficiency through its effect on the average citizen's perception of social equity (Buscaglia 1997, p. 283). Homans (1974) shows that in any group the relative status of any member is determined by the group's perception of the member's contribution to the group. An increase in a member's wealth without a perceived increase in that member's contribution to the group will generate

---

Edgardo Buscaglia is research fellow at the Hoover Institution at Stanford University, vice president of the Inter-American Law and Economics Association, and professor of law and economics at Washington College.

hostility among the other group members. In cases of corruption an unjustified increase in wealth violates the average citizen's notion of what constitutes an equitable hierarchy within society. Envy also contributes to the average citizen's condemnation of the perceived inequity.

Homans's theory of ethics can help us understand the effect official systemic corruption has on human behavior within a dynamic efficiency framework. Members of society who are not able or willing to pay bribes are excluded from the provision of any public good (for example, court services) that corruption transforms into a private good subject to an uncertain price. Corruption may remove red tape for those who pay the bribe, but the provision of public services is inequitable for those who do not. This inequity has a long-term effect on social interaction and economic efficiency: a perceived inequitable allocation of resources discourages noncorrupt people from generating wealth (Buscaglia 1997).

Some people might argue that by eliminating red tape, bribes can enhance economic efficiency. This is a fallacy. Corruption may benefit the individual who is willing and able to pay the bribe. But the macrosocial environment is adversely affected by diminishing economic productivity over time—caused by the general perception that the allocation of resources is determined by corrupt practices and so is inherently inequitable. In such an environment productive activities take a back seat to rent seeking.

An Empirical Model of Corruption and Its Causes

A number of studies have described corruption and analyzed its effects on economic development. Low compensation and weak monitoring are generally considered the main causes of corruption. Becker and Stigler (1974) and Klitgaard (1991) show how official corruption (through bribery) reduces expected punishment and thus deterrence. In this context increasing the salaries of public enforcers or paying private enforcement agencies based on their performance will improve the quality of enforcement. Rose-Ackerman (1978), Macrae (1982), Shleifer and Vishny (1993), and Mauro (1995) provide alternative approaches to the economic analysis of corruption. These studies view corruption as a behavioral phenomenon in the interactions between the state and the market.

All these studies rely on economic models that assume that, in responding to incentives for corruption, people and firms take into account the likelihood of apprehension and conviction and the severity of punishment (Becker 1993, pp. 234–37). That is, corruption increases if the marginal returns from crime exceed the marginal returns from legal behavior by more than the expected value of the penalty. In addition, all these studies cite the role of individual ethics in determining the "temptation threshold."

Rose-Ackerman's article tries to address the market-related causes and effects of corruption, yet it identifies only six general situations in which corruption may arise, and they are neither overlapping nor exhaustive. Moreover, her article does not analyze the corruption-enhancing elements arising from the procedural, substantive, market-related, and internal organization of the public sector. If the study of corruption is to enter the mainstream of social science, an empirically testable paradigm that can explain the causes of all types of corruption is required.

Critical institutional gaps and specific organizational patterns make developing countries especially prone to systemic corruption at every level of government. Thus I have developed an organizational–market power model in which to test claims about corruption (Buscaglia 1997, p. 282). First assume a specific level of deterrence, external monitoring, and salary structures within a public agency. The model predicts that the capacity of public officials to extract illicit rents will be enhanced by:

- Uncertainty about prevailing doctrines, laws, and regulations (for example, inconsistencies in judicial rulings).
- Numerous and complex procedural steps, coupled with a lack of procedural transparency, in a public agency supplying a service (for example, closed bids in government procurement).
- A high concentration of internal organizational roles overseen by a few decisionmakers in a public agency (for example, judges concentrating a large number of administrative and jurisdictional roles within their domain).
- The absence of alternative sources for the good or service provided by the public agency (for example, passports or driver's licenses).
- Limited collusion among the parties demanding a service from the public agency (for example, bribes offered by individuals rather than by organized groups).

Corruption, Institutional Inertia, and Public Sector Reform

Finally, future studies must take into account not only the present and future costs and benefits to society of eradicating corruption, but also the reduction in illicit rents to public officials resulting from changes in perceived present and future individual rents. Institutional inertia in enacting reform often stems from the long-term nature of the benefits of reform, such as increased economic growth or investment (Buscaglia, Dakolias, and Ratliff 1995). In the short term these benefits cannot be directly captured by potential reformers within the government. Thus reform sequencing must ensure that short-term benefits compensate for the loss of rents faced by officials responsible for implementing the changes. In turn, proposals generating longer-term benefits for officials should be implemented in later stages of reform (Buscaglia and Dakolias 1996).

Conclusion

Strategies to be incorporated in a corruption prevention plan should address organizational issues such as managerial accountability, employee performance indicators, and internal and external monitoring of the organizational power of each member of a public or private enterprise. These strategies should concentrate on improving systems and procedures, changing the attitudes of staff, and improving the integrity and performance of the organization. As explained above, development of an anticorruption plan should also be linked to an effective incentive-based restructuring of the reorganization, coupled with budget reallocations and changes in leadership. Implementation of this anticorruption plan may need to be frequently adapted to reflect changes in some of the environmental—market-based—factors Rose-Ackerman mentions.

In short, four conditions are needed to overcome institutional inertia during development and implementation of a corruption prevention plan: managerial support of the new organizational power structure brought by the anticorruption measures, staff knowledge and support of the anticorruption plan, adequate human and material resources to implement the plan, and implementation of corruption risk assessment and management procedures. These risk assessment procedures are designed to identify the major functional areas of the organization, assess and rank the risk in each area, and assess the probability of corruption actually occurring (Buscaglia 1995). Involving managers in the risk assessment process is a good way to raise their awareness of the opportunities for corruption in the areas they control and to get them thinking about strategies for preventing corruption. These proposals add an organizational dimension to the environmental factors already analyzed by Rose-Ackerman.

References

Becker, Gary. 1993. "Nobel Lecture: The Economic Way of Thinking about Behavior." *Journal of Political Economy* 108: 234–67.

Becker, Gary, and George Stigler. 1974. "Law Enforcement, Malfeasance, and Compensation of Enforcers." *Journal of Legal Studies* 3 (1): 1–18.

Buscaglia, Edgardo. 1995. "Stark Picture of Justice in Latin America." *The Financial Times*, 21 March, p. A13.

———. 1997. "Corruption and Judicial Reform in Latin America." *Policy Studies Journal* 17 (4): 273–86.

Buscaglia, Edgardo, Maria Dakolias, and William Ratcliff. 1995. *Judicial Reform in Latin America: A Framework for National Development*. Palo Alto, Calif.: Stanford University, Hoover Institution.

———. 1996. *Judicial Reform in Latin American Courts: The Experience of Argentina and Ecuador*. World Bank Technical Paper 353. Washington, D.C.

Cooter, Robert. 1996. "The Rule of State Law and the Rule-of-Law State: Economic Analysis of the Legal Foundations of Development." In Edgardo Buscaglia, William Ratliff, and Robert Cooter, eds., *Law and Economics of Development*. Greenwich, Conn.: JAI Press.

Homans, George C. 1974. *Social Behavior: Its Elementary Forms*. New York: Harcourt Brace Jovanovich.

Klitgaard, Robert. 1991. *Adjusting to Reality: Beyond State versus Market in Economic Development*. San Francisco: ICS Press.

Leiken, Robert S. 1996. "Controlling the Global Corruption Epidemic." *Foreign Policy* 5: 55–73.

Macrae, J. 1982. "Underdevelopment and the Economics of Corruption: A Game Theory Approach." *World Development* 10 (8): 677–87.

Mauro, Paolo. 1995. "Corruption and Growth." *Quarterly Journal of Economics* 110 (3): 681–711.

Rose-Ackerman, Susan. 1978. *Corruption: A Study in Political Economy*. New York: Academic Press.

Shleifer, Andrei, and Robert W. Vishny. 1993. "Corruption." *Quarterly Journal of Economics* 108 (3): 599–617.

Smith, Adam. 1978. *Lectures on Jurisprudence*. Oxford: Oxford University Press.

Floor Discussion of "Corruption and Development," by Susan Rose-Ackerman

A participant from the International Finance Corporation asked Susan Rose-Ackerman (presenter) whether governments suffering from corruption can effectively advise private enterprises on their fiduciary and other responsibilities, given the governments' inability to address the same issues. Rose-Ackerman replied that such anticorruption efforts could be like inflation crises—that is, hard to endure but able to provide valuable lessons and experience, particularly if they force needed action. Moreover, such efforts are usually led by reformers who recognize the need for and benefits of change. The World Bank, she added, faces similar challenges when trying to encourage governments to adopt desirable reforms.

A participant from the Foreign Investment Advisory Service, drawing on Rose-Ackerman's comments about the importance of client ownership of the World Bank's projects and programs, asked whether selectivity is just as important. Should the Bank, with its limited resources, focus on helping governments that are most receptive to reform, where its efforts are most likely to succeed?

Yes, Rose-Ackerman said, for the most part it should. Otherwise, she said, the Bank runs the risk of having dozens of "enclave" success stories. Broader efforts are needed to draw more universal and replicable conclusions. And by concentrating on countries where progress seems possible, the Bank could learn from its mistakes and so provide more effective aid. While working at the Bank, Rose-Ackerman had been struck by its limited reliance on monitoring and analysis—gauging initial conditions, implementing reforms, and measuring their results—particularly in governance reforms and social service projects.

Dilip Mookherjee (presenter in another session) asked how, given the distinction she had made between stationary bandits and roving bandits—with the first, being more secure, taking a long-term view of their corrupt behavior, and the second seeking out rents at every opportunity—Rose-Ackerman explained the entrenched and pervasive corruption of certain dictators and authoritarian governments. For example, given his secure hold on power in the former Zaire, why was Mobutu Sese Seko so corrupt?

This session was chaired by Sven Sandström, managing director at the World Bank.
Annual World Bank Conference on Development Economics 1997
©1998 The International Bank for Reconstruction and Development / THE WORLD BANK

In Mobutu's case, Rose-Ackerman said, it appeared that he had kept himself in power—and amassed enormous personal resources at the country's expense—by allowing lower-level officials to engage in free-lance rent seeking. Despite tremendous inefficiency and corruption at the lower levels, this approach was successful because the country is rich in natural resources. Private monopolists or roving bandits, by contrast, generally do not have as much control over the resources they exploit. Still, she said, the distinction she had made was by no means universal: very secure rulers can also be kleptocrats. Diego Gambetta (discussant) added that rulers' propensity for corruption could not be gauged simply by their opportunities to engage in it. Their natural tendency to be predators also must be taken into account.

Mookherjee then asked Gambetta to clarify his point about the mafia's ability to democratize access to illegal services. Since bureaucrats presumably can act as discriminating monopolists, they can lower their prices when approached by the mafia and raise them when approached by anyone else, resulting in different sets of prices.

His point, Gambetta replied, was slightly ironic. That is, the mafia democratizes access to rents for colluding firms in a cartel. By increasing the number of firms able to participate in a cartel and protecting their access to rents, the mafia ensures widespread participation. Firms are no longer afraid to join cartels because they no longer fear that other firms will jump the queue, submit competing bids, and so on. Problems can arise, however, in an environment thick with mafia, because it becomes impossible to tell who is and who is not a member of the mafia.

Richard Zeckhauser (discussant in another session) noted that corruption means different things in different countries. In some countries corruption is concentrated among low-level officials, such as customs agents. In others corruption is the province of top officials, as with recent campaign finance scandals in the United States. Because the two forms are completely different, should anticorruption theorists be prescribing different treatments, or are they merely two manifestations of the same disease?

Rose-Ackerman agreed that a wide range of situations generate incentives for corruption and said that she had not meant to imply that it was a single phenomenon. If the problem is low-level corruption in routine bureaucratic activities, efforts should initially focus on civil service reform. Are bureaucrats being paid so little that they have few alternatives to moonlighting or taking bribes? Are better monitoring and regulation needed? Do the rules bureaucrats enforce serve any purpose other than generating rents? A number of World Bank studies, for example, have found that simplifying business licensing systems reduces corruption and limits the number of people engaged in informal activities.

If the problem is high-level corruption, Rose-Ackerman continued, it results from the way a political system functions and from the relationship between private wealth and political activity. In terms of campaign financing, it is hard to imagine that a democracy could survive without sources of funds to carry out elections. Still, there is a need for transparency in those dealings.

The challenge, she said, is that many countries have corruption on both levels. Some analysts recommend going after corruption that involves large sums of money—big contracts, big concessions, big privatizations. Others believe that low-level bureaucratic corruption is a more serious problem. Rose-Ackerman, however, did not think that focusing on low-level corruption would be effective in a country like the former Zaire. If a government structure is corrupt at the top, there is no way to restrain corruption at the bottom. Thus she agreed that different policies were needed to address different problems.

Edgardo Buscaglia (discussant) closed the discussion by noting that, despite its various manifestations and symptoms, entrenched corruption has some common denominators. On the macro side these include a lack of political competition and a weak civil society. On the micro side a lack of internal and external monitoring of public institutions and complex and uncertain procedures (for example, in the judiciary) are often to blame. Addressing these weaknesses, Buscaglia continued, will require studying agencies and institutions to determine the causes. There is an urgent need for such studies: without them it will be impossible to develop policy recommendations and anticorruption reforms. To date there have been few such studies; most studies of corruption focus on its effects on growth and investment rather than on its causes.

What Can Be Done about Entrenched Corruption?

Michael Johnston

Corruption is not a problem that "happens to" otherwise healthy societies, nor does it necessarily lead to social, political, or economic collapse. Rather, it is one of a constellation of development problems, endogenous to societies and often a symptom of deeper difficulties. In the most serious cases—entrenched political and bureaucratic corruption—it represents equilibrium, a tightly organized and internally stable system that creates and is sustained by insufficient political competition, slow and uneven economic growth, and a weak civil society. Countries can move from a high- to a low-corruption equilibrium, however, by guaranteeing civil liberties and basic economic rights, enhancing economic and political competition, nourishing a strong civil society, and adopting legal and institutional anticorruption measures. While difficult, such transitions do not require fully democratic systems or advanced economic markets. Aid partners can help fight corruption by judiciously applying conditions to aid and by using program design, delivery, and evaluation to encourage and reward necessary changes.

Corruption is often spoken of as a serious illness—a cancer or, as one official recently put it, "the AIDS of democracy"—spreading relentlessly from official to official and agency to agency, undermining institutions until the political system they represent collapses. In this view corruption must be eradicated so that the system can return to health or—better yet—corruption must be stopped before it starts.

The attraction of such metaphoric language is understandable. Corruption can be a frightening problem: governance and social conditions deteriorate, and venality seems to be everywhere. Moreover, the illness metaphor grabs headlines—no small consideration for a problem that once drew little serious attention. Still, it is misguided to think about corruption in this way. In some countries, such as Singapore and the United Kingdom, eras of entrenched corruption eventually gave way to honest politics

---

Michael Johnston is professor of political science at Colgate University.
Annual World Bank Conference on Development Economics 1997
©1998 The International Bank for Reconstruction and Development / THE WORLD BANK

and administration. Others, such as Germany and the United States, have been able to prosper through long periods of moderate corruption. Major scandals in Italy have led to positive changes in electoral and judicial institutions. In China an outbreak of corruption has accompanied rapid economic growth, while the political regime, though under considerable stress, has changed relatively little. Even more remarkable are countries like Bangladesh and Nigeria, which have experienced prolonged episodes of extreme corruption without ever reaching the point of total collapse. Corruption does not always undermine regimes and institutions: sometimes it does its harm by propping them up past the time when basic changes are needed, as in the former Soviet Union and its member states. Ironically, those countries now face new forms of corruption growing out of political and economic reform.

Illness metaphors likewise do not facilitate reform. Corruption is not something that "happens to" otherwise healthy societies: no country has ever been free of it, and those that reduce it still have other problems. Rather, corruption is one of a constellation of interrelated development problems endogenous to societies and the changes they experience. It is not only worrisome in its own right but also a symptom of deeper difficulties (Rose-Ackerman 1997). This view is supported by empirical analysis: corruption is associated with slow economic growth (Mauro 1997), reduced investment, feeble property and contract rights, ineffective institutions (Knack and Keefer 1995), limited social interaction and weak rule of law (Cooter 1997), poor economic competitiveness (Ades and di Tella 1994), deep ethnic divisions and conflicts (Easterly and Levine 1996), low popular participation in politics and weak protection of civil liberties (Isham, Kaufmann, and Pritchett 1995, 1996), low educational attainment (Mauro 1997), and closed economic and political systems (Elliott 1997). Thus while it will always be important to combat corruption, it is also crucial to understand the broader context in which it occurs and with which it interacts. For aid agencies this means not only combating abuses within programs but also using programs to fight corruption as a development problem.

The Most Difficult Cases

All countries have corruption, but in more developed systems reformers have several advantages. Corruption is usually the exception, not the rule. Anticorruption laws, agencies, and nongovernmental organizations and independent courts, auditors, and news media are generally in place. Anticorruption efforts receive political and popular support, and the basic vocabulary of reform—what is public or private, and which actions are considered abusive—is generally agreed. The government can draw on a fund of political capital—legitimacy, credibility of basic policies and the rule of law, established lines of accountability, and laws consistent with social norms—in its pursuit of reform. If these efforts fail, the government can be changed without destroying the political order (Przeworski and Limongi 1993).

In many of the countries that borrow from the World Bank, however, corruption is entrenched, embedded in a social setting that both shows its consequences and helps sustain it. Entrenched corruption can be political, bureaucratic, or both, though these variants differ and the relationships between them are important. Entrenched corruption is not necessarily more visible—watchdogs may be too weak to make an issue of it—or frequent. Indeed, it is often marked by a shift to fewer but significantly larger cases of self-dealing (Rose-Ackerman 1996). Nor is it necessarily disruptive: entrenched corruption is tenacious because it generates a kind of equilibrium.

Entrenched corruption is of particular concern to the World Bank because it grows out of and helps perpetuate the development problems—feeble and sporadic political competition, slow (or negative) and uneven economic development, and a risky investment climate—found in many of the poorest nations. In such a setting many citizens and investors see corruption as inevitable and reform as futile. There are few alternatives to dealing with corrupt officials on their terms. Those officials preserve that situation as long as they can, and few citizens or businesses are willing or able to confront them directly. Entrenched corruption diverts development resources and saps the political and social vitality societies need to use aid effectively. Moreover, entrenched corruption resists many of the institutional and civil service reforms commonly deployed in more advanced nations. For all these reasons it is a particularly challenging worst-case scenario: if we are serious about corruption as an aid and development issue, we must confront it in countries where the odds of reform seem least favorable. It is in such cases that corruption does the most to keep poor nations poor.

While entrenched corruption is one kind of equilibrium, it is possible to move to other, lower-corruption equilibria. Analyzing corruption in terms of multiple equilibria is not new (Rose-Ackerman 1996, 1997). But my approach differs in scope—I suggest that we can produce, and institutionalize, such a transition "from without," by changing the environment in which corruption is embedded—and emphasizes political as well as economic and legal reforms. While the reform scenario outlined here has never been pursued in its entirety in any one country, it is based on the kinds of changes that helped shift some of today's low-corruption societies out of "corruption traps."

Entrenched Corruption and Its Social Settings

Entrenched corruption, far from being the endgame of a long slide into chaos, is well organized and embedded in a political and economic context that both reveals its effects and helps sustain it. At times these extended aspects of the problem—such as extended clientelism and the dependency it can foster—are as harmful to development as the corrupt actions themselves. Thus entrenched corruption is best thought of as an equilibrium—or, to borrow a less strict term from complexity theory, as a "settling point"—an understanding of which can help explain its origins and tenacity. But it is not the only possible equilibrium: by altering the political and economic environment it is possible to shift toward low-corruption, higher-growth equilibria that benefit from and help sustain accountable politics and administration. Aid agencies are well placed to help with this process, using their resources, staff, and knowledge of the countries in question.

Although political and bureaucratic corruption differ, I consider both entrenched if they are pervasive, organized, and monopolistic. *Pervasive* means that corruption is so common—throughout an entire country or subunit—that there are few practical alternatives to dealing with corrupt officials. This does not necessarily mean that every citizen encounters corruption every day; indeed, as corruption becomes entrenched the most significant abuses often shift upward to elite levels. Moreover, the perception that corruption is pervasive may be as much a matter of expectations as a matter of fact—expectations possibly cultivated by political and bureaucratic middlemen with a stake in maintaining public dependence on their services (Oldenburg 1987; Sacks 1976). Still, corruption that is pervasive is no longer an exception to the political or administrative norm.

Organized corruption involves internal coordination, shared knowledge, and a vertical exchange of benefits. It facilitates (and, in its structure, reflects) an internal economy linking principals and agents. Principals provide protection, make major decisions, control agents' discretion and powers, and confer or withhold shares of the take. Political or bureaucratic agents pay for their spoils through loyal support— by rigging the count at the neighborhood polling station, for example, or by providing services to clients in exchange for payments to be shared with the principals. Organized corruption closes off clients' alternatives, giving the organization more leverage. It creates a network of operatives sharing not only rewards but also risks; thus operatives have a stake in keeping corruption hidden, increasing its proceeds, and freezing out critics and noncorrupt agents and clients. Well-organized corruption is often a sign that political opposition, bureaucratic checks and balances, and private economic alternatives have been weak for some time.

Monopolistic means that corruption faces no meaningful political opposition or economic competition, making it harder to eradicate and allowing corrupt operatives to generate maximum benefits over a long period. Officials enjoying a monopoly on corruption can deliver important benefits in exchange for large payments from major economic interests, who have few alternatives to engaging in corruption on the officials' terms. The monopoly dimension of entrenched corruption is complex, differing between the political and bureaucratic realms and potentially creating instabilities.

These three features of entrenched corruption—pervasiveness, organization, and monopolistic control—are not necessarily related: some corruption is pervasive without being organized, monopolistic without being pervasive, and so on. But when the three characteristics combine—when corrupt officials extend their activities throughout a jurisdiction, organize their practices, and drive out their political or bureaucratic competitors—corruption is especially damaging. Moreover, it creates an equilibrium that is difficult to eradicate, particularly if only administrative and personnel remedies are used.

Entrenched Political Corruption

No example illustrates all these ideas with perfect clarity. Still, when mass politics and policymaking are affected by corruption—including bribery, extortion, election fraud, abusive patronage, and official intimidation of opposition groups—the effects can be classified according to corruption's degree of entrenchment (table 1).

When political corruption is entrenched, political activity is dominated by a monopolistic organization or faction that maintains its power in part through corruption and reaps large rewards from it. Haiti's Tonton Macoute, with its mix of violence and intimidation, is one example. Political machines—found at various times in U.S. cities and elsewhere—are another (Scott 1972; Chubb 1981; Theobald 1992). When the leaders of such organizations have effectively eliminated their competitors, they can extract monopoly rents from their official roles and functions without fear of political reprisal.

Where many factions compete for power, it is difficult to build and maintain a disciplined following: supporters have many political alternatives, and competitors may buy them off. Leaders must bribe their supporters and tolerate disloyalty and suboptimal political support. Meanwhile, their chances of winning lasting power, and therefore their leverage for extracting rents, are small. Discipline can be tighter in a political oligopoly because disgruntled followers have fewer political alternatives. But organizational maintenance will still draw off significant resources, and leaders, facing fewer but better-organized competitors, may still find power difficult to win and to hold.

A political monopoly, however, means that dealing with the organization's leadership, on its terms, is the only political game in town. Leaders can extract monopoly rents, while supporters must work long and hard before seeing any but the most trivial rewards. The focus of corruption shifts from broadly based petty patronage toward fewer but much larger deals at the top: machine leaders demand large payments in exchange for utility franchises and construction contracts, for example, while those seeking such benefits have no reason to believe that the next election will put anyone else in office. Such organizations are not entirely stable, however: leaders face internal conflicts for which patronage or harsh political discipline are awkward remedies, and they may distribute rewards in counterproductive ways or draw off too many resources for personal enrichment (Johnston 1979). Monopoly rents can theoretically rise to infinity, choking off economic activity (Shleifer and Vishny 1993) and turning those who must pay into potential enemies.

Still, the ability of such organizations to close off political alternatives means that their corrupt influence can extend deep into government and society. The leadership not only can politicize the bureaucracy; through arbitrary policies and regulations it can also keep economic growth tightly controlled and uneven. Rent-producing sec-

Table 1. Degrees of Entrenchment of Political Corruption

Is political corruption	1	2	3	4
Pervasive?	No	Yes	Yes	Yes
Vertically organized?	No	No	Yes	Yes
Monopolistic?	No	No	No	Yes

Source: Based on Sherman 1974.

tors may be allowed to grow in order to channel more wealth to corrupt elites, while overall growth is held down to maintain mass dependence on political favors—keeping the costs of political discipline low—and to protect politically favored enterprises from competition. Monopoly political organizations will also fight potential competitors for the loyalties of the public even when the competitors are not seeking official power. Many U.S. political machines, for example, were hostile to the settlement-house movement, which offered the poor aid without a political price tag, and to the early stirrings of labor unions (Rosenbaum 1973). Surveys of African-American community leaders in the late 1960s found that they were much less independent and critical in their political views in Philadelphia, a machine city, than in Detroit, a city without a machine tradition (Webman 1973).

Meanwhile, those harmed by entrenched corruption are more likely to adapt to it than combat it. Alam (1995) identifies three kinds of "countervailing actions" that losers from corruption might take: evasive actions, to reduce dependence on corrupt officials (relocating, finding alternative goods, or forgoing goods altogether); direct actions, to raise the cost or risk of corruption to officials (protest, political action, complaints to oversight bodies, or violence); and illicit actions, to fight corruption with corruption. Where corrupt organizations have eliminated political competition and reduced economic alternatives—and particularly where they protect their monopoly using intimidation or violence—direct action is risky. Evasive and illicit responses are more attractive but will do little to reduce corruption or create effective opposition to it.

Entrenched Bureaucratic Corruption

The situation for corrupt bureaucrats is somewhat different. Most do not face full-blown competition from other governments or agencies performing identical functions (partial exceptions include some over-the-counter services such as passport issuance and a state enterprise that competes with privatized enterprises). Several agencies might deal with one sector of the economy, but in specialized ways: one might regulate working conditions, another inspect products, and yet another collect taxes. These agencies usually cannot abolish one another or drive each other out of the corruption business. But they can collude, creating lasting and lucrative corruption networks that feed on and help sustain economic and political dependence (table 2).

Where bureaucratic corruption is not pervasive, some officials may take bribes as opportunity allows. Most do not, however, nor do they systematically seek them out. Indeed, many deals are initiated by private individuals, such as motorists seeking to avoid fines. Payments, and the discretion they buy, are likely to be modest. By contrast, corruption is pervasive when it occurs (or is perceived as occurring) more often than not. More members of the public may offer payments, and individual functionaries or small groups may seek out bribes and practice extortion on a regular basis. They may share the take and perform specialized roles ("bagman," "enforcer," accountant), but what is taken at the street level or at the front counter stays there. Agents do not share with principals, and rents are likely to be moderate.

Table 2. Degrees of Entrenchment of Bureaucratic Corruption

Is bureaucratic corruption	1	2	3	4
Pervasive within an agency?	No	Yes	Yes	Yes
Vertically organized?	No	No	Yes	Yes
Horizontally coordinated with other agencies?	No	No	No	Yes

Source: Based on Sherman 1974.

Vertically organized bureaucratic corruption, however, is a significant step toward entrenchment. Here a portion of the agents' take is shared with principals. This may begin as protection payments to superiors, but it can evolve into a condition of employment (Rose-Ackerman 1996). Emphasis also shifts from "corruption without theft" to "corruption with theft" (Shleifer and Vishny 1993). In the first case agents keep a side payment but pass the full nominal price of a good (say, a license fee) on to the public treasury. In the second case agents keep some or all of the fee and the treasury receives little or nothing. Low-level agents who do not enjoy protection will find corruption without theft easier to conceal or will at least keep theft within limits to avoid notice. But with vertical organization, corruption with theft grows rapidly, both because of the increasing number of claimants to the take and because of the official protection that corruption enjoys. Indeed, where bureaucrats' salaries are unrelated to the cost of living, organized corruption with theft may be a matter of survival. But barring close integration of bureaucratic and political corruption (see below), theft is still unlikely to be total: for political reasons, tax collectors must generate some revenue and police must make some arrests.

Specialization can be a source of instability in pervasive, vertically organized bureaucratic corruption. If many agencies with specialized functions can extract monopoly rents—theoretically, without upper limits—from the same industry, they can kill off the source of bribes. A business might relocate or close, or shippers might move to another route or port—examples of Alam's (1995) evasive actions. As a result rents would collapse. But if agencies coordinate corruption among bureaucratic functions or levels of government, creating a joint monopoly instead of independent monopolies, the result could be smaller individual payments, but a much larger take over time:

> A helpful analogy is to tollbooths on a road. The joint monopoly situation corresponds to the case of one toll that gives the payer the right to use the entire road. The independent monopolists solution means that different towns through which the road passes independently erect their own tollbooths and charge their own tolls. The volume of traffic and aggregate toll collections fall. In fact, they fall to zero when any party can erect its own tollbooth on this road. The competitive case corresponds to multiple booths competing with each other for the right to collect the toll, or alternatively to the case of multiple roads. In this case, the volume of traffic is obviously the highest, and toll collections the lowest. (Shleifer and Vishny 1993, p. 608)

Independent monopolies can persist if one agency, such as the police, deals with many economic activities, or if a business cannot easily move or is itself a monopoly. But pervasive, organized, and coordinated corruption is stable and difficult to uproot. As with monopoly political corruption, opportunities for large, high-level deals grow, and coordinated bureaucratic harassment and selective law enforcement can be used to pressure those who are reluctant to pay. Unless political leaders send credible signals that critics of corruption will be protected and supported, direct countervailing action will be rare. In this way corrupt bureaucrats extend their influence outward into society, creating an unfavorable economic and investment climate whose shortage of alternative opportunities can further solidify their power.

A Low-Corruption Equilibrium

Entrenched corruption is persistent and difficult to combat not only because of its inner workings but also because it is embedded in a wider political and economic environment that helps sustain it as an equilibrium. Can this environment be altered to create incentives for officials to reduce corruption and for groups in society to combat it and begin to move toward a low-corruption equilibrium? Yes—and international aid, trade, and political organizations can help. Reform need not rely on virtue alone, but can offer real rewards and incentives of its own (which, as George Washington Plunkitt would observe, is essential): in a changed political and economic setting many of the interests now engaged in entrenched corruption can be enlisted to help fight it.

Reformers have more options in countries where corruption is less entrenched. In these countries resistance to corruption is based not just on fear of punishment but also on legitimate norms and traditions that have evolved over time and are shared by contending political and economic interests—interests that help hold the state and private actors in check. Political and economic opportunities are sufficiently plentiful that there is less need to use wealth to buy political power or to use power to extract wealth (Huntington 1968; Johnston 1997). The political officials who oversee bureaucrats know that they can lose power because of corruption or ineffective policies. Supervision from above, scrutiny from without, and structural checks and balances mean that individual officials or small groups do not possess monopoly discretion and find it difficult to organize and coordinate corruption on a large scale. The result is a different sort of equilibrium: corruption may occur, but it is kept within limits and does not become entrenched. This is not the only possible low-corruption scenario: tight political control, as in Singapore and Pinochet's Chile, is the basis of others. But the situation sketched out above is more desirable on political and social grounds and is more feasible in countries larger than city-states.

Moving between Equilibria

Variations on the low-corruption equilibrium can be found in many politically and economically advanced parts of the world—Canada, New Zealand, Scandinavia—

and often reflect long processes of political and economic contention that brought past periods of extensive corruption to a close. There is no quick recipe for this transition, and it will always require supporting legal and institutional reforms. But it is a manageable transition: starting it does not require wholly democratic politics or an advanced market economy, and aid partners can help by adopting policies that change the political and economic setting of entrenched corruption. The goal is to encourage developments that undermine the monopolies and organization of entrenched corruption while strengthening the forces that help sustain low-corruption equilibria. Stronger political and economic competition can increase accountability, open up alternatives to dealing with corrupt networks, and create incentives for political leaders to fight corruption. Reduced corruption can encourage economic growth, further broadening economic alternatives and strengthening interests in civil society while weakening the political and bureaucratic leverage underlying entrenched corruption. Over time this virtuous circle of development fosters a low-corruption equilibrium and entrenches reform, not corruption, in the broader political and economic system (figure 1).

As noted, this process does not require the establishment of a fully institutionalized democracy. Meaningful civil liberties are a good starting point (Isham, Kaufmann, and Pritchett 1995, 1996). An independent press, opposition groups, and an active civil society are more likely to develop if they can express themselves publicly and are free from intimidation. Civil liberties are also essential if the losers from corruption are to confront it in direct, rather than evasive or illicit, ways (Alam 1995).

On the economic side credible property and contract rights, which in the short to medium term help increase investment and weaken incentives to extract short-term profits (Keefer 1996), are a first step analogous to meaningful civil liberties. The economic alternatives that this move would generate would make it easier for firms, investors, and individuals to avoid corrupt officials and harder for officials to keep such groups dependent on their favors. The move to such rights would also, over time, strengthen civil society and social interaction. Here again a full transition

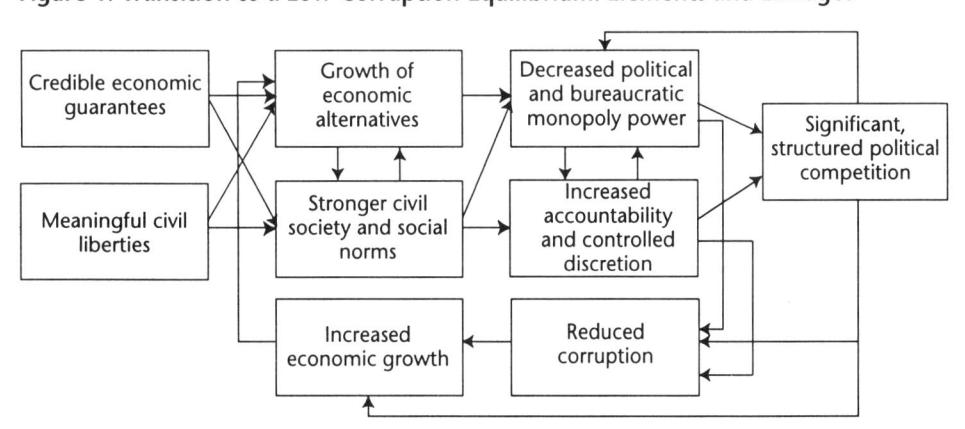

Figure 1. Transition to a Low-Corruption Equilibrium: Elements and Linkages

to prosperity is not essential: aid for emerging sectors of the economy and for growth in a country's most deprived regions (admittedly complicated tasks) can create new economic opportunities outside of established corrupt networks and empower new political constituencies.

Broadened political alternatives also can weaken corrupt monopolies. A first step is to establish independent arenas in which appeals against corruption and other abuses can be filed—mainly the courts but also investigative agencies, inspectors general, and ombudsmen open to public complaints and scrutiny. The goal is to encourage, protect, and follow through on direct countervailing actions, thus strengthening checks and balances. The second, longer-term task is to foster significant and institutionalized political competition, creating opportunities for political forces to win or lose power through open, public processes. Competition is beneficial even if the main political groups do not represent all citizens. England's seventeenth-century parliaments, for example, were strikingly unrepresentative by modern standards, yet they played major roles in resisting the abuses of royal patronage both before and after the civil wars (Peck 1990). Competition must be meaningful but structured: one party offers no choice, but twenty or thirty parties are unlikely to have agendas much broader than the personal interests of their leaders or to win enough power to govern effectively. Indeed, small and numerous parties are more likely to indulge in corruption, both for self-enrichment and to build a political following.

An important distinction between political competition and insecurity applies here. Many scholars have noted that political insecurity leads to voracious corruption, since officials do not know how much longer their power will last (Knack and Keefer 1995; Scott 1972). Why should the threat of losing power through political competition be any different? The answer lies in the way in which power is lost and won, and in what happens next. Insecurity—the threat of a coup, for example—means that the identity and strength of one's opponents, and their timing and tactics, may be difficult to know or predict. Uncertain timing is of particular importance because it creates an incentive to enrich oneself as quickly as possible. The issues and grievances involved are likely to be personal or factional and thus are resistant to negotiation or compromise because they are aimed at overall dominance. When power is lost, it is lost altogether and permanently: rather than remaining as an opposition group or coalition partner, the losers may be killed, imprisoned, or exiled. Thus the contest is not just for spoils, but for survival.

Political competition, on the other hand, involves known opponents, tactics, and timing. The broad outlines of competitors' strengths, appeals, and support are discernible, and competition, if well institutionalized, takes place within agreed rules and social norms. Many of the main issues can be addressed through routine policy, are open to compromise, and can be made matters of public commitment—facts that encourage accountability and careful political oversight of policy formation and implementation. While the winners obtain agreed powers for a limited period, the losers remain to fight another day—an incentive in itself to refrain from last-minute looting of the public purse. Unlike political insecurity, political competition creates incentives to avoid rather than to indulge in corruption. But such competition is a matter of contending forces, not just institutional architecture: where opposition is weak, elected elites engage in entrenched corruption. The point is that orderly competition can undermine political monopolies and create incentives to control corruption.

Interconnections between Bureaucratic Corruption and Political Corruption

Political corruption and bureaucratic corruption can flourish in each other's absence. France, for example, experiences political corruption but retains a highly professional bureaucracy. In Poland, by contrast, former Communist Party figures have created personal bureaucratic fiefdoms, while political activity is open and competitive. But in most cases the two types of corruption coexist and may be interlinked. Political corruption can intrude into the bureaucracy, as when a police department or an inspectorate is staffed with patronage appointees. And bureaucratic corruption can become a factor in politics, as when agencies grant favors to the politically connected to maintain cover for their own corruption. Different connections between political and bureaucratic corruption produce different patterns of extended clientelism in society, as Khan (1997) argues in his comparison of countries in South and Southeast Asia.

The more serious either type of corruption becomes, the less likely it is to exist independently. An interlocked system of entrenched bureaucratic and political corruption is a powerful force: rents can be coordinated and shared across both realms, while monopoly power allows politicians to preempt opposition. Economic policies can maximize corruption while curtailing competition. There will be few opportunities for direct countervailing actions, and illicit responses will require the indulgence of corrupt officials (Alam 1995). Indeed, the functional distinction between political and bureaucratic corruption might all but disappear.

China comes close to this situation: official and market activities, roles, and resources are tightly interlocked—and corruption flourishes—in a large gray area neither wholly public nor wholly private. The same agency or official may deal in consumer goods, access to bureaucratically controlled commodities, and Party preferments, often in collusion with private entrepreneurs (Hao and Johnston 1995; Solinger 1992). Public resentment runs deep, and officially orchestrated anticorruption campaigns are common. But attempts to confront the issue directly are confined to small groups of dissidents willing to criticize the political order (Johnston and Hao 1995).

In other cases political leaders may have the formal duty and power to confront bureaucratic corruption but do so only in response to compelling problems or crises. McCubbins and Schwartz (1984) term this "fire alarm" oversight and compare it with a continuing "police patrol" approach. Despite their argument that the fire alarm model is not altogether ineffective, unsystematic oversight after the fact is an inadequate safeguard. If networks are sufficiently organized and coordinated, corrupt bureaucrats can respond by covering up their dealings more effectively.

Whatever the model of oversight, political initiatives against bureaucratic corruption will depend on the balance of power between the two realms, and in this competition bureaucrats have significant advantages. In the absence of compelling domestic or international pressure, political leaders may tolerate bureaucratic corruption if it:

- Allows them to share in its spoils or if their position is weak or compromised.
- Benefits favored interests or helps buy off potential opponents.
- Provides enough income to bureaucrats to make tax increases (or the systematic collection of the taxes that are on the books) less necessary.
- Helps build support for political leaders' desired policies or cushions their impact.
- Moderates conflicts among bureaucratic factions, particularly if corruption cleanups seem likely to mobilize elite opposition.

Similarly, if reform seems likely to produce major economic disruption, as was arguably the case in the final decades of the Soviet Union, politicians may conclude that its immediate costs outweigh its prospective, long-term benefits.

Indeed, the first result of reforms that break up the organization or coordination of corrupt networks may be corruption that is more visible and disruptive than the entrenched practices had been. Or reforms could yield an independent monopolies situation (Shleifer and Vishny 1993) likely to be damaging to the economy. Would-be corruption fighters must be confident that reform efforts, economic growth, and their careers could survive such a crisis. On the other hand, political leaders who draw broadly legitimate mandates from institutionalized political competition will have reasons to fight bureaucratic corruption, and can do so from a stronger position. Other motives may reinforce this determination: politicians may act if bureaucratic corruption protects a hostile faction or makes the bureaucracy unresponsive and unaccountable. Also, as Rose-Ackerman (1996) points out, secure political leaders may find it advantageous to fight corruption as a way to increase economic growth.

Countering Bureaucratic Corruption

Once political leaders take on bureaucratic corruption, they must do several things. One problem is material: reforms will fail if bureaucrats are paid so little that they must steal in order to survive. But the salary problem is not easily addressed. Besley and McLaren (1993) show that the "reservation wage" for tax inspectors—the wage they would earn working in the private sector—is substantially higher than the "capitulation wage" that drives them to corruption. An "efficiency wage" comparable to what they earn from bribes would be even higher. An interim step might be to create a legal schedule of fees for services, payable by citizens directly to bureaucrats. These would raise pay, reward efficiency, and create accountability to the client. Such payments might be difficult to supervise and regulate, but enabling a number of officials to compete to provide a service, shifting their postings frequently, and monitoring for signs of collusion could help. Direct payments also would be more difficult for higher-level officials to tap into, both for logistical reasons and because agents who do not need high-level protection to collect payments will fight to protect their living wage.

Many of today's low-corruption countries passed through a phase when payment of direct fees to constables, inspectors, and tax and customs officials was not only common but was viewed as a reform (Johnston 1993)—an important step on the road to comprehensive, professional bureaucratic roles. Still, fee-for-service arrangements should be allowed only on a selective basis and only for routine bureaucratic functions. Rose-Ackerman (1996, p. 14) argues that the best candidates are "cases where corruption's only efficiency cost stems from its illegality." Fees for services can also be introduced through careful and honest privatization or by franchising various functions to officials or private bidders. This franchise approach could be modeled on seventeenth-century English "customs farmers," who paid large fees for the right to collect customs duties.

Political leaders will also need to attack the vertical organization and horizontal coordination of corruption. Increasing agencies' independence from one another and encouraging competition among them where possible will be important, though waste, duplication, and contradictory policies may result. Placing new agency managers and powerful inspectors general into each major agency and making them accountable to top political leaders might also be worthwhile, though this can encounter strong bureaucratic resistance. These new principals can reform relationships among agents and clients (Klitgaard 1988; Rose-Ackerman 1978), changing the monopoly-plus-discretion nexus and increasing accountability.

Attacking bureaucratic corruption is a task fraught with costs and dangers (Anechiarico and Jacobs 1996). But there are also many opportunities to use incentives analogous to those created by competition in the political arena. Bureaucrats' motivations are complex and critical to the question of political accountability (Gruber 1987). Most bureaucrats care about the functions they are supposed to perform; once assured of a living wage they will respond positively to changes that increase their effectiveness and provide clear evidence to them, and to the public, that administration is honest and accomplishes worthwhile social goals. Professional status, a sense of personal security, and meaningful autonomy with respect to illegitimate pressures from above and below are important as well. Klitgaard (1988) demonstrates the effectiveness of raising morale and status and (in some cultures) of shaming those engaged in corruption.

Performance-linked incentive schemes also must be carefully considered. Mookherjee (in this volume) argues that these schemes are often ineffective or even counterproductive. Klitgaard (1997), while acknowledging that circumstances in many developing countries are not favorable to performance-linked incentives, suggests that finding new ways to measure performance and making creative institutional adjustments can make such schemes more likely to succeed. This debate can hardly be resolved here, but careful analysis of and judicious experimentation with incentive schemes can teach political leaders and top officials about the origins of corruption and the prospects for reform, convey to bureaucrats (and their private clients) that their superiors are serious about corruption, and alleviate (at least) the worst "incentive traps" that leave many individuals with little alternative to corruption.

Finally, government officials and powers should be subject to checks and balances—separate routine powers or, in parliamentary systems where full separation is not feasible, independent courts, oversight bodies, and client advocates. If these agencies and the government in general are accessible by opposition politicians, journalists, and members of the public, then checks and balances will not only help fight corruption, they will also draw on powerful forces in society. Hong Kong's Independent Commission Against Corruption, for example, used its extensive legal and investigative powers and adopted innovative social strategies to significantly reduce corruption and alter public attitudes toward it (Clark 1985; Manion 1996).

The Role of Civil Society

The political and economic problems that corruption engenders seriously weaken civil society. Civil society has become a buzzword in recent years, and many claims on its behalf will require further research. But the concept dates back to de Tocqueville's ([1835] 1945 ed.) discussion of "intermediate institutions" in the United States in the 1830s and highlights important aspects of political life in low-corruption countries. Here I use it to refer to organizations and public activities between the level of individuals or families and the state. Organized, active groups in civil society can be a check on the state and on one another, as well as a basis for direct countervailing action. They are critical to accountability because "transparent" procedures mean little if there is no external monitoring: corrupt states abound in inspectors, commissions of inquiry, and record-keeping requirements that create and conceal corruption rather than reveal it, because no one outside the state can demand a meaningful accounting. Without a strong civil society to energize them, even a full set of formally democratic institutions will not produce accountable, responsive government.

A strong civil society also encourages and protects free social interaction. Cooter (1997) uses game theory to show that where people freely interact on a repeated basis, they are likely to form strong mutual expectations of conduct and legitimate social norms (see also Keefer 1996 and Milgrom and Roberts 1982). Surveys of popular conceptions of corruption suggest that most citizens judge public officials, as well as one another, by social norms learned in those everyday interactions (see data and bibliography in Johnston 1991). Moreover, where civil society is strong, a range of social groups—trade and professional associations, community groups—function as "law merchants" (Cooter 1997). They promulgate codes of good practice and can impose modest, but socially significant, anticorruption sanctions relatively quickly using a lower burden of proof than that required for criminal penalties. Particularly when it exists within a legitimate state, an active civil society can thus help form a network integrating legal and social norms—a comprehensive value system more likely to be obeyed than laws alone would be.

The transition to a low-corruption equilibrium takes time and requires sustained support. As noted, during its initial stages reform will likely produce an apparent surge in corruption, as formerly concealed practices come to light, elite consensus breaks down, whistleblowers and media investigators begin to speak, and organized corruption gives way to more fragmented and disruptive practices. But these are indicators of a breakdown of the old entrenched system. Sustained political leadership and international support are crucial during this phase. Over time, however, increased political and economic competition and alternatives, a stronger civil society, and improved government and economic performance should develop considerable synergy. There is no guarantee that the system will never revert to its old ways, but once a low-corruption equilibrium is attained, important political and economic interests will have a stake in sustaining the new situation.

Helping Countries Get There: The Role of Aid Partners

The above reform scenario is obviously an idealized account. If there were an easy or obvious way to control corruption, many nations would have done it already—though it is worth remembering that many of today's low-corruption countries overcame serious corruption through similar processes of political and economic development (Johnston 1993). Still, the question remains: What can international aid organizations do to make such transitions more likely and to get them over with in a matter of years, not generations?

Conditionality requirements have an obvious appeal, but they must be carefully conceived. Linking aid directly to reductions in corruption may produce short-term or cosmetic results, perhaps through repression or the manipulation of scandal. But this would be a step away from the enhanced economic and political competition and revival of civil society central to a low-corruption equilibrium. (Similarly, anticorruption coups, even when sincerely aimed at the problem—as they almost never are—rarely reduce corruption on a lasting basis because they preempt political contention and weaken civil society.) Moreover, conditionality of this sort could lead to a situation in which few programs are funded or renewed, or in which conditions must routinely be waived, making them an empty gesture. Where conditionality links aid to processes, however—expansion of civil liberties, reform of institutions, and enhancement of political and economic competition—it may be considerably more beneficial, particularly when supported by technical assistance for implementing and monitoring those processes.

It is also possible to pursue reform through more positive incentives that encourage leaders to reduce corruption, weaken clients' acceptance of it, and strengthen the social forces supporting such changes. While the goal is a broad transition, the measures themselves must be applied selectively because of variations among countries and their corruption problems.

One factor that will differ is the balance between competition and institutionalization in a nation's economic and political system. The transition away from entrenched corruption will weaken political and bureaucratic links, in part because it is intended to do so. Moreover, the transition requires increased political contention and economic competition and entails a strengthening of interests and organizations in civil society. Where corruption has been entrenched, however, institutions and their links to society will likely be weak, as real power will have been held by corrupt networks behind the organizational facade. Even honest leaders may resist anticorruption strategies that risk greater political insecurity or that increase contention without also increasing the state's capacity to deal with it. For this reason my proposals are divided into the very rough categories of competition-enhancing and institution-enhancing measures. Some address both problems. Together they can attack the monopolies and weaken the organization underlying entrenched corruption while strengthening the institutions and social forces that would benefit from and help sustain a low-corruption equilibrium.

Competition-Enhancing Measures

As noted, meaningful civil liberties are the first political step toward the enhanced political and economic contention needed to break through entrenched corruption, and credible property and contract rights are the first economic step. Aid partners can make these changes criteria for program approval and renewal. Later, overall economic and political competition, with an emphasis on a vital civil society, could become additional criteria for aid and be included in project design, evaluation, and delivery.

Progress toward these goals can be measured by the treatment of the press and of dissidents, the openness and honesty of elections, the status of women and minorities, and the viability of trade and professional associations and other private bodies. On the economic side, aid agencies should reward secure property and contract rights, protection for small businesses, honest privatization (where appropriate), and policies encouraging the free movement of capital and resources and fostering transparency in banking, customs, and taxation. Moreover, allowing various segments of society to assess this process will contribute to a stronger civil society and counteract political and bureaucratic monopolies.

To ensure that aid agencies have continuing anticorruption leverage, they should impose such standards gradually, perhaps emphasizing them at the evaluation and renewal stages of programs rather than as criteria for original support. And at least for all but the slowest-reforming countries, trends should be considered more important than absolute levels of attainment, creating incentives to sustain positive change rather than requiring high thresholds that must be reached before aid can be given or renewed. The threshold approach would punish many of the countries suffering the worst ravages of corruption while playing into the hands of corrupt officials currently feeding off the status quo.

Increased political and economic competition and openness should also be major considerations in program design. Aid for emerging sectors of the economy and economic development in regions and for groups previously left behind are not only desirable but can also strengthen emerging political interests, economic alternatives, and social interaction. So too can microcredit initiatives at the community level. Literacy programs, particularly for women and girls and for peripheral regions and groups, can increase the demand for political participation and help individuals recognize, resist, and take action against corruption. Protection and encouragement for labor unions, trade and business associations, and other groups in civil society are also positive steps.

Requiring public consultation and participation in service delivery and securing guaranteed access for journalists and social organizations would also enhance accountability and transparency. In this regard the World Bank's recently revised procurement processes, including a greater emphasis on broad institutional assistance for all public procurement in borrower countries, are a welcome change; an additional, probably controversial, step would be to publish widely the results of project and procurement evaluations, thus making it easier for opposition groups to turn corruption problems into political issues or for governments to benefit politically from anticorruption successes.

Within the bureaucracy a competition-enhancing measure that could help break down organized, coordinated corruption is Transparency International's idea of "islands of integrity." Briefly, bidders on government contracts mutually undertake not to pay bribes—commitments that bidders back up by posting sizable bonds subject to forfeiture should violations occur. If bureaucrats engage in corruption (or keep silent) because they fear reprisals or because they see no point in honesty when everyone else is on the take, and if some firms pay up because they see no alternative, these "islands" might be useful, creating processes beyond the control of corrupt official networks. The potential difficulty, obviously, is one of follow-through. Without it, islands of integrity might become another way to cover up corruption, or at least to divert attention from it. Still, the approach has been implemented in Argentina and Panama. Close scrutiny of such cases will tell us much about creating alternatives to entrenched bureaucratic corruption.

Changes in the overall structure of administration and service delivery also can weaken monopolies. Federalism can have major benefits—opponents to political machines in U.S. cities often found support at the state level—though such a major constitutional change may not be feasible or desirable. Moreover, fragmented federalism can provide nooks and crannies for hiding or coordinating corruption. Decentralizing public agencies might be a better way to inhibit horizontal coordination. Similarly, jurisdictions at the same level could share or merge various bureaucratic functions, but in differing geographical patterns, inhibiting both coordination and vertical organization of corruption.

Institution-Enhancing Measures

Stronger institutions are required if greater openness and competition are to produce maximum benefits and minimal disruption, particularly during the early stages of anticorruption reforms. One essential step is improved and more systematic tax collection—a measure that helps create a predictable investment and economic climate and yields more revenue with which to upgrade official salaries. Much like fee-for-service arrangements, a better tax system can increase social demands for accountability and transparency. In some high-corruption countries real tax burdens are negligible for many. As a result the state is seen as an independent source of benefits to be plundered rather than as an institution using social resources to pursue common goals.

Greater emphasis on the rule of law is also important, because it replaces arbitrary personal power with predictable institutionalized authority and defines the ways state and society can (and cannot) interact. Enforcing the rule of law requires a strong, independent judiciary, investigative and auditing bodies, and legitimate paths of access between state and society. Where the rule of law is weak, even states with great power, such as China, can have serious problems of state capacity and governance.

Fee-for-service arrangements can increase accountability while bringing bureaucrats nearer to a real living wage, perhaps enabling them to resist corruption. Privatization that shifts commercial activities, such as a national airline, into the private sector can reduce the exposure of the public bureaucracy to market pressures. Greater institutionalization of bureaucracies and a stronger rule of law help build more secure, predictable, and autonomous economic markets. Such an environment enables and encourages individuals and firms to plan for the long term and renders corruption an expensive, unreliable, and ultimately unnecessary form of influence. Thus the same private economic motives that encourage corruption in one setting discourage it in another.

Institutionalized political competition is also important. Parliaments and electoral systems merit particular scrutiny. Do they encourage and reward competition, make public the sources and uses of funds, and offer an effective way of expressing political demands and support? Do elections offer real choices, building a broad base of interests into the legislative process while producing decisive results? Do campaign finance laws protect the political process from international manipulation while allowing new interests and groups to enter politics without unduly splintering government and parliamentary bodies? Do parliamentary processes exacerbate ethnic divisions or encourage groups to work together? What works well in one country may be counterproductive in another; still, consider cases such as Italy, where in the wake of the Mani Puliti and Tangentopoli scandals a fragmented proportional representation system was replaced by one awarding half the parliamentary seats on a first-past-the-post basis. The goal was to replace the old elite stalemate (which had tolerated and concealed corruption for years) with increased political competition by offering fewer but more broadly supported parties the chance to gain or lose real power. Campaign financing and representation systems should be made explicit parts of governance criteria but must be backed up by extensive technical assistance and research.

Perhaps, too, it is time to rethink governance itself. The World Bank (1992, p. 3) has defined governance as "the manner in which power is exercised in the management of a country's economic and social resources for development." There is little to quarrel with here, but the concept could also include the strength of civil society, the vitality of political and economic competition, the security of civil liberties and basic economic guarantees, and the capacity of the system to foster and cope with the changes implied by the notion of sustainable development. Bräutigam (1992), for example, identifies three dimensions of governance: accountability, openness and transparency, and predictability and the rule of law. The Organisation for Economic Co-operation and Development (OECD 1995, p. 14) likewise proposes three features of governance: "the form of political regime; the processes by which authority is exercised in the management of a country's economic and social resources; and the capacity of government to formulate and implement policies and discharge government functions."

A broader definition of governance emphasizing the expansion of freely available political and economic alternatives, a balance between the accessibility of government institutions and the autonomy that enables them to govern (Johnston 1997), and well-institutionalized paths of access and demarcations between government and market forces could shift the emphasis in both aid and governance away from projects and toward a broader-gauged assessment of a country's capacity for development. One such definition of governance might be the degree of institutionalization and openness of the political and economic processes through which social development decisions are made; doubtless better ones can be devised. The point is to think of governance in ways that help us increase the precision and internal coordination of aid programs, and to encourage and reward the kinds of changes that historically helped reduce corruption in many countries.

Conclusion

It is worth emphasizing again that corruption is just one of many interrelated problems—one that does not account for all that is wrong or overwhelm all that may be right in a developing country. And again, the transitions envisioned here are medium to long term in nature and will involve many reversals, just as was the case in many of today's low-corruption countries. Short-term increases in corruption, and in more visible and disruptive varieties of it, may be unavoidable. A balance between institutionalization and competition at all points in the process is unlikely. The energies and dedication of anticorruption watchdogs will always be valuable, and the amount of corruption in any society will never be zero—nor would that be an optimal outcome (Klitgaard 1988). Still, an understanding of corruption as a problem endogenous to development, of what sustains it where it is entrenched, and of the forces that inhibit it where it is low may show us how the political and economic interests that sustain corruption can be used to fight it. To that end extensive research on different types of corruption and on their origins and effects in different sorts of societies might be an excellent investment for any agency concerned with development.

These findings offer major challenges and opportunities for the World Bank and other aid agencies—challenges that are political, economic, and administrative in nature. Sustainable reductions in corruption require solidifying political interests and competition, as well as steadfast leadership to see a country through the rocky transition from a high- to a low-corruption equilibrium. Policies encouraging these developments and their practical consequences for the countries concerned will never be politically neutral: some interests, leaders, and followers will gain considerably, while others will lose.

Is the World Bank, by virtue of the restrictions on political involvement laid out in its Articles of Agreement, closed out of this arena? Not if we think in terms of the capacity-oriented definition of governance proposed above. Indeed, the Articles, as well as the broader idea of faithful stewardship of development resources, require the Bank to consider and, where possible, to enhance the political aspects of countries' capacity to use those resources. The case becomes clearer if we think of politics not as the day-to-day contention among elites and their followers but as a fundamental set of competitive processes just as essential to building development capacity as the growth of market economics. Prohibitions against direct partisan involvement and against political favoritism in Bank programs remain eminently sensible and in no way contradict the reform strategy I have proposed. That strategy involves using aid to enable political groups and processes, to provide mutual paths of access between state and society as well as an outlet for social reactions to the stresses of change, and to encourage the institutionalization of political and economic competition in ways that are likely to make Bank programs more effective.

In such efforts the Bank possesses important resources. These include not just its capital and its unique role as a global development agency, but also its continuing presence in developing countries, its regulations, and its personnel. Most of the reforms discussed here—in political and economic processes, civil society, and the quality of leadership, institutions, and administration—have long been Bank concerns. Similarly, a number of administrative strategies, such as procurement controls and the threat of canceling projects, have always been at hand. The Bank's recent emphasis on corruption is welcome, and the debate it is certain to encourage offers an important opportunity to reexamine familiar elements of policy in terms of their impact on corruption, to use anticorruption sanctions more aggressively, and to combine old and new ideas into a comprehensive policy on corruption. The Bank can pursue such a policy on an international and regional basis—avoiding singling out specific nations for disgrace while encouraging intraregional cooperation—and can facilitate greater integration between countries pursuing genuine reform and their international trade partners.

Looked at this way, corruption is not just a development problem but a central issue in development policy; not a discrete problem with self-contained solutions but an endogenous process that must be attacked using comprehensive strategies. Many countries have overcome serious corruption in the past; those experiencing entrenched corruption today can do much to alleviate it. The task begins by understanding not only corruption but also how it shapes and can be sustained by the broader social and economic environment.

References

Ades, Alberto, and Rafael di Tella. 1994. "Competition and Corruption." Working paper. Oxford University, Institute of Economics and Statistics.

Alam, M.S. 1995. "A Theory of Limits on Corruption and Some Applications." *Kyklos* 48 (3): 419–35.

Anechiarico, Frank, and James B. Jacobs. 1996. *The Pursuit of Absolute Integrity*. Chicago: University of Chicago Press.

Besley, Timothy, and John McLaren. 1993. "Taxes and Bribery: The Role of Wage Incentives." *The Economic Journal* 103 (January): 119–41.

Bräutigam, Deborah. 1992. "Governance, Economy, and Foreign Aid." *Studies in Comparative International Development* 27 (3): 3–25.

Chubb, Judith. 1981. "The Social Bases of an Urban Political Machine: The Christian Democrat Party in Palermo." In Shmuel N. Eisenstadt and Rene Lemarchand, eds., *Political Clientelism, Patronage and Development*. London: Sage.

Clark, David. 1985. "Dirigisme in an Asian City-State: Hong Kong's ICAC." Paper presented at the Thirteenth World Congress of the International Political Science Association, 12 July, Paris.

Cooter, Robert D. 1997. "The Rule of State Law and the Rule-of-Law State: Economic Analysis of the Legal Foundations of Development." In Michael Bruno and Boris Pleskovic, eds., *Annual World Bank Conference on Development Economics 1996*. Washington, D.C.: World Bank.

de Tocqueville, Alexis. 1945. *Democracy in America*. New York: Alfred A. Knopf.

Easterly, William, and Ross Levine. 1996. "Africa's Growth Tragedy: Policies and Ethnic Divisions." World Bank, Policy Research Department, Macroeconomics and Growth Division, Washington, D.C.

Elliott, Kimberly A. 1997. "Corruption as a Global Policy Problem: Overview and Recommendations." In Kimberly A. Elliott, ed., *Corruption and the Global Economy*. Washington, D.C.: Institute for International Economics.

Gruber, Judith E. 1987. *Controlling Bureaucracies: Dilemmas in Democratic Governance*. Berkeley: University of California Press.

Hao, Yufan, and Michael Johnston. 1995. "Reform at the Crossroads: An Analysis of Chinese Corruption." *Asian Perspective* 19 (1): 117–49.

Huntington, Samuel P. 1968. *Political Order in Changing Societies*. New Haven, Conn.: Yale University Press.

Isham, Jonathan, Daniel Kaufmann, and Lant Pritchett. 1995. "Governance and Returns on Investment: An Empirical Investigation." Policy Research Working Paper 1550. World Bank, Policy Research Department, Poverty and Human Resources Division, Washington, D.C.

———. 1996. "Civil Liberties, Democracy, and the Performance of Government Projects." World Bank, Policy Research Department, Poverty and Human Resources Division, Washington, D.C.

Johnston, Michael. 1979. "Patrons and Clients, Jobs and Machines: A Case Study of the Uses of Patronage." *American Political Science Review* 73 (2): 385–98.

———. 1991. "Right and Wrong in British Politics: 'Fits of Morality' in Comparative Perspective." *Polity* 24 (1): 1–25.

———. 1993. "Political Corruption: Historical Conflict and the Rise of Standards." In Larry Diamond and Marc F. Plattner, eds., *The Global Resurgence of Democracy*. Baltimore, Md.: The Johns Hopkins University Press.

———. 1997. "Public Officials, Private Interests, and Sustainable Democracy: Connections between Politics and Corruption." In Kimberly A. Elliott, ed., *Corruption and the Global Economy*. Washington, D.C.: Institute for International Economics.

Johnston, Michael, and Yufan Hao. 1995. "China's Surge of Corruption." *Journal of Democracy* 6 (4): 80–94.

Keefer, Philip. 1996. "Protection against a Capricious State: French Investment and Spanish Railroads, 1845–1875." *Journal of Economic History* 56 (1): 170–92.

Khan, Mushtaq. 1997. "Corruption in South Asia: Patterns of Development and Change." Paper presented at a workshop on corruption and development sponsored by the University of Sussex's Institute of Development Studies, 6 May, Brighton.

Klitgaard, Robert. 1988. *Controlling Corruption*. Berkeley: University of California Press.

———. 1997. "Information and Incentives in Institutional Reform." In Christopher Clague, ed., *Institutions and Economic Development*. Baltimore, Md.: The Johns Hopkins University Press.

Knack, Stephen, and Philip Keefer. 1995. "Institutions and Economic Performance: Cross-Country Tests Using Alternative Institutional Measures." *Economics and Politics* 7 (3): 207–27.

Manion, Melanie. 1996. "Policy Instruments and Political Context: Transforming a Culture of Corruption in Hong Kong." Paper presented at the annual meeting of the Association for Asian Studies, 11–14 April, Honolulu.

Mauro, Paolo. 1997. "The Effects of Corruption on Growth, Investment, and Government Expenditure: A Cross-Country Analysis." In Kimberly A. Elliott, ed., *Corruption and the Global Economy*. Washington, D.C.: Institute for International Economics.

McCubbins, Matthew D., and T. Schwartz. 1984. "Congressional Oversight Overlooked: Police Patrols vs. Fire Alarms." *American Journal of Political Science* 28 (1): 165–79.

Milgrom, Paul, and John Roberts. 1982. "Predations, Reputation, and Entry Deterrence." *Journal of Economic Theory* 27 (2): 280–312.

OECD (Organisation for Economic Co-operation and Development). 1995. *Participatory Development and Good Governance*. Paris.

Oldenburg, Philip. 1987. "Middlemen in Third-World Corruption: Implications of an Indian Case." *World Politics* 39 (4): 508–35.

Peck, Linda Levy. 1990. *Court Patronage and Corruption in Early Stuart England*. Boston: Unwin Hyman.

Przeworski, Adam, and Fernando Limongi. 1993. "Political Regimes and Economic Growth." *Journal of Economic Literature* 7 (3): 51–69.

Rose-Ackerman, Susan. 1978. *Corruption: A Study in Political Economy*. New York: Academic Press.

———. 1996. "When Is Corruption Harmful?" Background paper to *World Development Report 1996: From Plan to Market*. World Bank, Washington, D.C.

———. 1997. "The Political Economy of Corruption." In Kimberly A. Elliott, ed., *Corruption and the Global Economy*. Washington, D.C.: Institute for International Economics.

Rosenbaum, Alan. 1973. "Machine Politics, Class Interest, and the Urban Poor." Paper delivered at the annual meeting of the American Political Science Association, 4–8 September, New Orleans.

Sacks, Paul Martin. 1976. *The Donegal Mafia: An Irish Political Machine*. New Haven, Conn.: Yale University Press.

Scott, James C. 1972. *Comparative Political Corruption*. Englewood Cliffs, N.J.: Prentice-Hall.

Shefter, Martin. 1976. "The Emergence of the Political Machine: An Alternative View." In Willis D. Hawley, ed., *Theoretical Perspectives on Urban Politics*. Englewood Cliffs, N.J.: Prentice-Hall.

Sherman, Lawrence W. 1974. *Police Corruption: A Sociological Perspective*. New York: Doubleday.

Shleifer, Andrei, and Robert W. Vishny. 1993. "Corruption." *Quarterly Journal of Economics* 108 (3): 599–617.

Solinger, Dorothy J. 1992. "Urban Entrepreneurs and the State: The Merger of State and Society." In Arthur Rosenbaum, ed., *State and Society in China: The Consequences of Reform*. Boulder, Colo.: Westview.

Theobald, Robin. 1992. "On the Survival of Patronage in Developed Societies." *Archives Européenne de Sociologie* 33 (1): 183–91.

Webman, Jerry A. 1973. "Political Institutions and Political Leadership: Black Politics in Philadelphia and Detroit." Yale University, Department of Political Science, New Haven, Conn.

World Bank. 1992. *Governance and Development*. Washington, D.C.

Comment on "What Can Be Done about Entrenched Corruption?" by Michael Johnston

Jeremy Pope

As Michael Johnston's excellent article notes, corruption is endemic everywhere. New Zealand, my homeland, is the "cleanest" country in the world according to Transparency International's Corruption Perceptions Index. Yet our former auditor general was recently jailed for stealing public funds. At first sight this would seem to warrant lowering New Zealand's rank in the index. But perhaps the fact that he was jailed demonstrates the effectiveness of New Zealand's integrity system—that is, the system for delivering the checks and balances and ensuring the accountability that is so crucial to anticorruption efforts.

Classifying Countries

Countries can be categorized into three broad groups based on the extent of their corruption:

- Those with functioning national integrity systems (many but by no means all are in the North).
- Those with dysfunctional national integrity systems.
- Those whose national integrity systems have effectively collapsed.

This approach takes a holistic view of the various "pillars" that collectively sustain and support a nation's integrity. These pillars include the executive branch of the government, civil society, the private sector, the news media, the auditor general, the judiciary, and the parliament. Among societies the strength of these pillars may vary, but collectively they must be capable of maintaining a nation's integrity if sustainable development, security, and the rule of law are to thrive.

Most analysts consider a free and independent media to be an essential ingredient—indeed, an essential prerequisite—of any effective integrity system. In Singapore, however, the press is less than free and the parliament is less than robust. Still, other aspects of the integrity system are strong enough to sustain a high level

---

Jeremy Pope is managing director of Transparency International.
Annual World Bank Conference on Development Economics 1997
©1998 The International Bank for Reconstruction and Development / THE WORLD BANK

of integrity and the security and development that accompany it. Such tradeoffs may not have a universal appeal, however. Similarly, some view with incredulity the fact that the U.S. federal attorney general is a watchdog over the president and yet is appointed by the president. On the surface this setup creates an inherent conflict of interest. However, Congress's role in overseeing both officials helps rectify what might otherwise be considered a significant weakness.

No universal formulas can be applied to ensure a nation's integrity. National integrity systems and their components vary, but when it comes to controlling corruption it is useful to think in terms of strengthening the processes—the national integrity system—intended to curb corruption. Efforts should focus on reforming systems, not engaging in witch-hunts. Some anticorruption theorists believe that the key to reform is "frying the big fish"—but experience has shown that the big fish selected for frying is, more often than not, the leader of the opposition. These same theorists say that the cleanup should start with a leading member of the ruling party—an approach that is theoretically acceptable but that is usually politically impossible.

Choosing the Approach

Can the transition to a low-corruption equilibrium be aided by external sources? Although Johnston describes a number of possible scenarios for such support, key questions remain unanswered: How does such a process begin? And what sustains it?

To start with, the process must be led from the top. If top leaders are corrupt, lower-level reforms will be unfair and ineffective and lack moral authority.

But why would a deeply corrupt administration want to transform itself into an honest one—even if it were able to grant itself immunity? And how can people who have risen to the highest levels of leadership in a corrupt system embark on root and branch reform? Why should they even try? To what degree are they prisoners of the very system that brought them to power? Who funded their campaigns, and why?

There are even more fundamental questions: What makes people seek power? What are they prepared to do to achieve it? And why should they reform the very system of which they are the most conspicuous beneficiary? Answering such questions may require the assistance of behavioral scientists, as it is extremely difficult for economists to model irrational behavior.

Transparency International believes that anticorruption reforms must be driven internally by a local champion—perhaps a newly elected president or a courageous chief justice. Outsiders have only a small, although potentially significant, role to play in anticorruption efforts. For reform to be effective it must be driven by local needs and considerations; the people who really understand a country's corruption are the people who live and work there and who have deep insights into their society and its power structures.

Kenya is an example of a country whose government made concessions to meet the demands of outside interests, only to renege on them in short order. Although some of the reforms produced tangible benefits—for example, the role of the auditor general was strengthened—real change will come only when a substantial change of government occurs. Similarly, Italy's successful Mani Puliti reforms were driven by a magistrate with political power and popular support, not by external factors.

A country's people, not its government, are the true owners of reform. And as Johnston's article notes, even a complete set of formally democratic institutions will not produce accountability without a strong civil society to energize them. People are more likely to form strong and legitimate social norms if they are able to interact freely. This is the goal that Transparency International is working to achieve: mobilizing civil society to fight corruption on a nonpartisan basis and to support government reforms.

In this regard it is important to remember that many governments have been elected in free and fair elections and have started with the best of intentions, only to collapse into deeply corrupt administrations after being undermined, at least in part, by a cynical and unsupportive public.

Considering Conditionality

If reforms begin and end with a locally owned and driven process, is there any room for aid conditionality? The Kenya example is debatable: conditionality achieved some progress, but not nearly as much as most observers would have liked. Conditionality certainly has not resulted in any significant or apparent change in the mindset of the country's leaders.

As an organization Transparency International is opposed to conditionality, although within the movement opinions vary. Some, for example, see debt relief as an area in which conditionality might be imposed—that is, forgiven debt could be revived if a change in administration reversed processes of reform and accountability. This approach, the argument goes, would force political successors to continue the transparency and accountability reforms of their predecessors.

Random in-depth audits, with the prospect of blacklistings for corrupt firms, also offer promise. Such audits could be performed by outside institutions, and if they were to do them openly and assertively the audits would help transform the low-risk, high-profit formula that typifies corruption in many countries today into a high-risk, low-profit formula—resulting in less corruption.

Outsiders could also help with surveys of the consumers of public services. Such surveys tell us that in Tanzania, for example, people who pay bribes tend to get worse—not better—service than those who do not, undermining the argument that some corruption is beneficial. Surveys can also identify services for which consumers are willing to pay a lawful fee but for which they bitterly resent having to pay an illegal bribe.

There is also the concept of "islands of integrity," mentioned in Johnston's article. This approach brings together all the prospective bidders for a major government contact to determine the rules that will govern that contract—including an "integrity pact" under which the competitors agree not to pay bribes and which empowers losing bidders to sue the winners should the winners be found to have engaged in corruption. This approach—which merits World Bank support—attempts to make the integrity system function in a specific case against a general background of distrust and failure.

Outsiders can also help maximize the benefits of internal consultations and use them to support similar exercises in other countries. And based on internal diagnosis, outsiders can help overhaul and strengthen the crucial pillars of national integrity systems. Such efforts, however, require coordination among external aid agencies. In the past these efforts have tended to be uncoordinated and less than comprehensive.

Principles and Progress

Johnston concludes that it is the World Bank's duty to maximize the effectiveness of its projects by enhancing the capacity of its borrowers to make the best use of available resources. This position is not only sensible but irresistible. Ordinary citizens seeking to borrow from a commercial bank are unlikely to get the money if the bank believes that the funds will be squandered or stolen. Although the World Bank's lending to governments is not quite so simple, the rationale for prudence is the same. Those who squander their borrowings are unlikely to be able to repay them.

The larger point, however, is that outside assistance is most likely to be effective if there is already a significant and home-grown movement for reform. Thus aid agencies should focus their anticorruption efforts on countries that want to do better rather than on those that lack the impetus to reform. In this regard World Bank President James Wolfensohn's offer to help governments who seek assistance on corruption is entirely appropriate.

Working with the Bank's Economic Development Institute, Transparency International has developed a set of principles to guide external agencies seeking to combat corruption:

- We should act on invitation only.
- There should be two "clients"—one in government, the other in civil society.
- The process should be a partnership, but one that is led by as many local stakeholders as possible.
- The role of the outsider should be limited to facilitating and informing a process in which the outsider is essentially a learner, and never a proscriber.

References

Langseth, Peter, Frederick Stapenhurst, and Jeremy Pope. 1997. "The Role of a National Integrity System in Fighting Corruption." EDI Working Paper 400/142. World Bank, Economic Development Institute, Washington, D.C.

Pope, Jeremy, ed. 1996. *National Integrity Systems: The TI Source Book*. Berlin: Transparency International.

Comment on "What Can Be Done about Entrenched Corruption?" by Michael Johnston

Augustine Ruzindana

Michael Johnston's article provides a clear analysis of corruption, and on most points I agree with him. Here I would like to highlight three of the points Johnston makes about corruption:

- Corruption occurs everywhere but is more harmful in developing countries.
- There are many forms of corruption at both political and bureaucratic levels.
- Corruption is not intractable—something can be done about it.

Johnston also analyzes the causes and effects of corruption, but his analysis is that of a researcher and an academic, and his sources are of a similar nature. My observations are derived from my experience and that of others in Africa with whom I have interacted in the course of my work in Uganda.

Johnston sees corruption as a development problem, possibly because he is addressing a conference on development economics. Corruption is not, however, simply a development problem. It is also a problem of governance, of trade, of morals and ethics, and of a weak and immature system of public order. Besides the element of personal or group gain, corruption involves a deviation from certain standards and norms that themselves rest on the notion that those who hold power abide by the limits placed on that power. The clear distinction between power and authority and between public and private behavior determines what constitutes corruption. At one time those holding public office were not held to any distinction between public and private behavior. Notions of service and merit also did not exist, and the ends of power were little more than self-enrichment. This continues to be the case in most developing countries, particularly in Africa.

Forms of Corruption

Johnston does not spend much time describing the different types of corruption, so let me draw on my experience to illustrate the magnitude of the problem we face in Africa.

Augustine Ruzindana is a member of Parliament and chairman of the Public Accounts Committee in Uganda.
Annual World Bank Conference on Development Economics 1997
©1998 The International Bank for Reconstruction and Development / THE WORLD BANK

Drawing on the experience of other agencies in Africa involved in anticorruption activities and my own, I have identified the following types: bribery, extortion, illegal use of public assets for private gain, over- and underinvoicing, payment of salaries and various benefits to nonexistent ("ghost") workers and pensioners, payment for goods not supplied or services not rendered ("air supply"), underpayment of taxes and duties on exports and imports through false invoicing or other declarations, purchase of goods at inflated prices, fraud and embezzlement, misappropriation of assets, court decisions awarding monetary damages well in excess of any injury suffered, removal of documents or even whole case files, and nepotism and patronage.

Such incidents do not always involve large sums of money, but they occur frequently and their effects are disastrous for governance and development. Corruption in Africa is mainly a problem of routine deviation from established standards and norms by public officials and the parties (multinational corporations, local businesspeople, and members of the public) with whom they interact. Thus the activities of these other parties—for example, corporations from industrial countries seeking business opportunities in Africa—should also be of interest to researchers and corruption fighters.

Effects of Corruption

Corruption also occurs in industrial countries, as Johnston points out, but it does not obstruct the normal functioning of their social systems. In Africa, however, corruption has severely undermined national, social, and economic development. Indeed, corruption often leads to national collapse—witness the former Zaire and Somalia, where nepotism led to self-immolation. Other examples include the collapse of the Marcos regime in the Philippines, the recent collapse of state structures in Albania, and the frequent collapse of governments in Pakistan.

In Africa almost every change of government, violent or peaceful, is driven by pledges to get rid of corrupt governments. Indeed, corruption, coupled with economic and political mismanagement, has led to Africa's political instability and gross abuses of power. To be more specific, corruption has led to bad roads and decaying infrastructure, inadequate medical services, poor schools and falling education standards, and the disappearance of foreign aid and foreign loans and of entire projects without a trace (or their delayed completion, leading to higher costs). Corruption has meant that fewer imported goods enter the country than were paid for; foreign exchange earned from exports is not repatriated; national assets are run down and ruined; production capacity in industry, agriculture, and services has been reduced; and repairs of buildings, equipment, vehicles, and physical and social infrastructure have been paid for repeatedly but never performed. Corruption distorts the economy through the waste and misallocation of resources. Citizens' fundamental needs—food, shelter, health, education—are neglected. Thus corruption creates an artificial need for external assistance to compensate for corrupt and irresponsible mismanagement of local resources. Having created the need, corruption then impedes foreign assistance and investment.

These accumulated losses in every area of public expenditure have disastrous economic consequences. As a result the terms and conditions of service for all workers deteriorate and the majority of the population suffers. If Africa is to make progress at a faster rate, corruption must be curbed to tolerable proportions—what Johnston calls a low-corruption equilibrium.

What Can Be Done about Corruption?

Johnston suggests a number of ways to curb corruption, including legal and institutional reforms and political and economic adjustments. In Uganda (as well as in some other African countries) we have tried to curb corruption using some of the measures suggested by Johnston. In Uganda the key to successful reforms has been a leadership that has brought political stability and that was determined to fight corruption. Systems of control and accountability had broken down during the chaotic first twenty-five years after independence. Thus, soon after President Yoweri Museveni took office in 1986, he implemented a number of economic, political, and governance measures that curbed corruption and increased accountability and transparency.

These measures included the formation of the inspector general of government, which has extensive powers to deal with government corruption and human rights abuses, and the reactivation of the auditor general and Public Accounts Committee of Parliament and the director of public prosecution. Moreover, a code of conduct was enacted that defines expected and prohibited forms of conduct for government leaders. The code requires annual disclosure of income, assets, and liabilities and prescribes sanctions for breaching the code. In addition, the Constitution empowers Parliament to review the backgrounds and qualifications of individuals seeking or being considered for political office or senior civil service positions.

The government has also adopted economic and administrative policies and programs that have helped control corruption. The entire integrity system—comprising the anticorruption agencies, Parliament, the judiciary, the attorney general, the director of public prosecution, and the executive branch in general—has been sensitized to the importance of curbing corruption. In addition, the freedom of the press is generally respected. As a result the press is one of the most important voices in the fight against corruption.

Indeed, it seems that Uganda is on the road to achieving a low-corruption equilibrium. Still, Uganda illustrates the problems associated with this transition because corruption remains and in some areas has even increased (for example, as part of privatization and decentralization efforts). During the transition anticorruption efforts tend to take two steps forward, then one step back. Thus appropriate policies must be found to guide this process. For example, should the government establish a cutoff date and grant amnesty for corrupt activities occurring before that date? Should corruption be forgiven if corrupt people confess and volunteer to pay back what they looted (or at least some of it)? How should the government deal with people who are no longer in office or who have assumed new roles in which their performance is fairly good? These are some of the issues facing reformers and for which there are no easy answers.

Finally, should the World Bank and other international organizations use conditionality to control corruption in their loans and projects? I do not think so. Instead, the Bank should encourage the institutionalization of accountability and transparency to help create integrity and accountability systems. But anticorruption processes and policies should be homegrown; otherwise they will be resisted or sabotaged. Aid and assistance to internal initiatives will ultimately prove more beneficial and enduring than external conditionalities.

Floor Discussion of "What Can Be Done about Entrenched Corruption?" by Michael Johnston

A participant from the Bangladesh Institute of Development Studies asked how the pervasive corruption in nongovernmental organizations (NGOs) should be addressed. Given donors' increasing emphasis on channeling aid through NGOs and the absence of regulations governing NGO activities, such corruption, if not addressed, will likely become an even bigger problem. What can be done about it?

Jeremy Pope (discussant) acknowledged that corruption in NGO activities is a serious problem. To address it, some of Transparency International's national chapters are developing accountability programs that donors can use when dealing with NGOs. These efforts are guided by the view that, where corruption is entrenched, civil society should start practicing the democracy that it wants from its leaders.

Michael Johnston (presenter) added that such efforts should be broadened to include the full range of private organizations working in developing countries. For example, he said, many so-called privatizations simply allocate state assets among powerful insiders. Privatizations and NGO activities are not inherently beneficial; indeed, one of the challenges in combating corruption is determining the extent and terms of private sector involvement in public decisionmaking and the use of public assets.

A participant from the World Bank asked whether Pope's concept of national integrity-supporting "pillars" could be extended. In Latin America, he said, the appointment of an independent prosecutor general has proved quite successful in ferreting out high-level corruption. Pope agreed that many approaches were possible. To that end, he said, Transparency International has been sharing different anticorruption experiences with countries tackling the problem at the grassroots level. Augustine Ruzindana (discussant) noted that Uganda now has an independent director of public prosecutions.

Sherwin Rosen (presenter from another session) wondered whether there is a connection between corruption and the form of government. Addressing Pope, he asked whether New Zealand would have received the highest rating on Transparency

This session was chaired by Jessica P. Einhorn, managing director, Finance and Resource Mobilization, at the World Bank.

Annual World Bank Conference on Development Economics 1997
©1998 The International Bank for Reconstruction and Development / THE WORLD BANK

International's Corruption Perception Index twenty years ago, before reforms were implemented. Pope said that, in fact, many New Zealanders perceive corruption to be a bigger problem now than it was before the country's extensive privatizations. These privatizations alienated citizens from politics to such an extent that, when given the chance to jettison the entire political process, citizens did just that. In its place, Pope continued, a form of proportional representation has been imposed—which is also beginning to sour.

A participant from Transparency International asked what external agencies should or can do in countries where corruption is entrenched but there is little internal momentum for change. Ruzindana replied that external agencies are essentially hamstrung if there is little internal will for reform. Such efforts, he said, are doomed to fail if leaders are unwilling to fight corruption, and could even be harmful. Anticorruption efforts are part of the move toward democracy; isolated from that process, progress is not possible.

Johnston agreed, emphasizing that there are no short-cut solutions to entrenched corruption. Democratization is a long, difficult process that usually generates political conflict, though in some cases that conflict can help focus attention on corruption. Still, he added, incremental changes are possible. Fee-for-service arrangements, for example, can help foster a well-paid and eventually independent civil service. Over the longer term, though, political competition is essential to the fight against corruption.

Before providing loans, a participant asked, should the World Bank require that its borrowers meet certain conditions—for example, implement changes in the system of governance or the method of administering the loans? Johnston's view was that conditionality was simply a way for the Bank to focus on process. Because of that, he said, the Bank should not use conditionality in its anticorruption efforts—tying the release of loans to progress on corruption would only encourage false reporting. Still, conditionality does have a role to play, particularly in efforts to strengthen civil liberties, foster political competition, and establish basic economic rights. Those areas, Johnston concluded, offer genuine opportunities to jump-start anticorruption efforts and to create incentives for the public to get involved in the process.

Incentives and Performance in Public Organizations

Incentive Reforms in Developing Country Bureaucracies: Lessons from Tax Administration

Dilip Mookherjee

What major problems are likely to be encountered in designing and implementing pay-for-performance schemes for public bureaucrats? This article examines that question in the context of tax administration, drawing on economic theory and recent reforms in developing countries. Such schemes may or may not increase corruption among tax collectors; more important is their effect on taxpayer compliance and government revenues. Whether incentive schemes enhance or reduce welfare depends on institutional parameters, including the range of instruments available for providing incentives, the extent of discretion available to bureaucrats, and the relevant dimensions of bureaucratic performance. Also pertinent are levels of teamwork and equity within the bureaucracy, taxpayer appeal mechanisms, and the external legal and political environment. Thus incentive reforms should be accompanied by wider reforms in the internal organization of bureaucracies, including changes in information systems, organizational structure, budgeting and accounting systems, task assignments, and staffing policies.

The restructuring of public bureaucracies is one of the most underresearched topics in economics. Yet such reforms are long overdue in developing and industrial countries alike. Most of the bureaucratic structures in place today are legacies of the 1930s, when governments were viewed as the panacea for all market failures—benevolent protectors of the people from avaricious capitalists, imperialist masters, and the vagaries of markets. That governments might be staffed by people with the same instincts for self-interest was never considered. Marxists, focused on the contradictions inherent in capitalism, failed to notice the contradictions of the system with which they sought to replace it. In the 1930s debates about socialism did not focus on incentives and the institutional aspects of government

---

Dilip Mookherjee is professor of economics at Boston University. Many ideas in this article were developed in joint research with Arindam Das-Gupta and Ivan Png. The author is grateful to Jonathan Bendor, Hadi Esfahani, Gunnar Eskeland, Karla Hoff, Robert Klitgaard, and John McLaren for useful comments on an earlier draft and to Leroy Jones and Pankaj Tandon for useful discussions.

bureaucracies. Rather, the main question was the ability of central planners to get prices right. Thus the bureaucratic structures that evolved during this period paid scant attention to the possibility of internal incentive problems.

Half a century later the communist bloc has collapsed, one developing country after another faces crises prompting structural adjustment programs, and theories of the government as predator rather than protector abound. The pendulum has swung to the other extreme. Resolutions of government failures are now sought by reverting to the market, with the dismantling of barriers to private enterprise, reform of tax systems, restraints on fiscal deficits, and privatization of state enterprises. Because many government interventions occurred in areas without significant market failure, many of these changes are likely to be welfare enhancing.

The main problem lies in areas where markets cannot be relied on—areas like health, education, infrastructure, tax collection, environmental control, antipoverty programs, and law and order. Under the weight of fiscal imbalances many developing countries are finding it increasingly difficult to invest in infrastructure and to protect real spending on human resources and antipoverty programs. And many are unable to control large-scale corruption, to introduce organizational reforms within the public sector, or to effectively regulate the private sector. The institutions that guide such efforts, often taken for granted in industrial countries, played an important role in market-based development in East Asia (Wade 1990; Stiglitz 1996). It has been argued that it is the quality rather than the quantity of state intervention that differentiates the role of the state in East Asia from that in less successful developing countries (Bardhan 1996; Wade 1990; World Bank 1993). This naturally raises the following question: Is it possible for developing countries to improve the quality of their bureaucracies, to transform a predatory state into a developmental one?

At first glance the biggest incentive problems appear to be that bureaucrats' pay is not tied to job performance and that civil servants have little personal stake in the social implications of their efforts. Consider the relationship between the salaries of most tax collectors and tax collections, pollution inspectors and air quality, irrigation officials and water services, forest officials and deforestation, government bank managers and social returns on government-financed investments, or public schoolteachers and education standards. As Adam Smith noted, most producers of goods and services have a limited direct stake in the benefits imparted to the rest of society. The private sector addresses this problem through the price system or contractual mechanisms. Why does the public sector not attempt a similar solution?

For one, the price system cannot be relied on in areas involving market failure, such as law enforcement, public good provision, and poverty alleviation. Nor is wholesale privatization the answer; ultimate responsibility for many activities must lie with government. Broadly stated, the question becomes whether and how internal incentives can be designed for public bureaucrats, who by the nature of their work have monopoly power and private information regarding their tasks. More specifically, what major problems are likely in designing and implementing such incentive schemes, and how should their effects be evaluated?

Some General Considerations

Performance incentives are often resisted because in most countries they run counter to civil service norms. These norms, founded on the presumption of a spirit of benevolence and a tradition of service to public welfare among bureaucrats, cannot be ignored. Received folk wisdom—that 10 percent of officials do 90 percent of the work—raises the question of what motivates the blessed 10 percent to shoulder such a heavy burden. Cultural traditions no doubt play an important role. Consider, for example, how the Confucian ethic underlies the traditions of the Japanese bureaucracy (Morishima 1982). Resistance to incentive reforms within bureaucracies frequently stems from the hope that such traditions will continue to endure.

But recent experience in most developing countries has revealed that hope to be unfounded. With an overarching state and regulatory controls, bureaucrats have immense scope for corruption; as a result a culture of public service can easily be replaced by one of narrow self-interest.[1] Where there is little allowance for such motives, the scope for government failure is immense. Thus there is a need to narrow the gap between the objectives of government institutions and the self-interest of bureaucrats. From this perspective incentive systems would need to be evaluated in a context that presumes bureaucrats are driven primarily by self-interest.

Another common criticism of attempts to improve performance through incentive mechanisms is that the mechanisms may not eliminate corruption. It can be argued that this is irrelevant, since eliminating corruption is not an end in itself. In fact, in some contexts such a goal may be unattainable unless the state retreats altogether. By its nature a nonmarket mechanism imposes restrictions on private voluntary behavior and tempts economic agents to enter into mutually advantageous trades to circumvent them. In this sense corruption is endemic to government once self-interested behavior predominates. In most contexts the only way to eliminate corruption would be to dismantle governments altogether. Thus attempts to reform incentives must not be discarded on the grounds that they do not eliminate corruption. As Acemoglu and Verdier (1996) argue, optimal government mechanisms may simultaneously involve corruption, large rents to government officials, and the misallocation of talent between private and public sectors. The effects of a reform on achieving the original intent of the government intervention—raising revenues, regulating externalities, delivering public services—must be assessed. Hence certain changes may be welfare enhancing even though they induce greater corruption.

A criticism that deserves more serious attention is that government bureaucracies typically pursue multiple social goals, and reforms that succeed in motivating public officials along certain dimensions may generate problems along others. Motivating tax inspectors to collect revenues more aggressively may increase corruption, harassment of honest citizens, and wage inequality. Thus both the costs and the benefits of incentive reform need to be appraised, taking into account major side effects and the general equilibrium responses of the economy as a whole.

Several authors have argued that, given the side effects of incentive reforms, in certain contexts no reforms may be warranted. In the terminology of Besley and McLaren (1993), the public sector might as well accept the widespread corruption induced by low pay and inadequate incentive mechanisms. Other manifestations of the apparent inefficiency of public bureaucracies can also be justified under certain conditions (Tirole 1986, 1994). These include reliance on rules rather than discretion, overlapping authority, capture by private regulated entities, and inability to make long-term commitments. In other words, in certain institutional settings many commonly perceived ills of public bureaucracies are actually in the public interest; they merely manifest underlying problems of information and dissonance of objectives.

This does not mean that it is always futile to try to introduce incentive reform in public bureaucracies. For instance, some countries have effective tax administrations, and elements of these systems can be replicated elsewhere. Moreover, many countries have recently implemented ambitious reform programs. The lesson to be drawn from the work cited above is that the effects of incentive reform depend on the institutional setting in which a public bureaucracy functions. Thus the appraisal of any reform proposal must address two basic questions:

- First, what institutional attributes will affect the success or failure of an incentive reform? Is a reform likely to be effective in the prevailing institutional setting? What overall effect will reforms have, and how should their design be modified accordingly? In posing these questions, the institutional setting is taken as a given.
- Second, how feasible is institutional reform? Only by implementing institutional reform can the root cause of the problem—the monopoly power and private information of bureaucrats—be addressed. While aspects of the external environment may have to be taken as a given, policymakers usually have the power to alter aspects of the internal organization of the bureaucracy. As Klitgaard (1995) suggests, successful incentive reforms may require an accompanying set of "enabling" organizational changes, including changes in personnel systems, task assignments, information systems, budgeting and procurement procedures, and feedback and evaluation mechanisms. If incentive reform has undesired side effects, the range of policy instruments must be expanded to moderate them. In the classical terminology of Jan Tinbergen, multiple goals necessitate a corresponding multiplicity of policy instruments.

Thus there is less ground for pessimism than might follow from an approach that takes institutional structures as a given. Governments that are committed to reform may succeed if they broaden their scope to accommodate instruments aimed at altering the institutional attributes of public bureaucracies.

This article argues that such a perspective is indeed supported by recent experience in the reform of income tax administration in developing countries. The article—based largely on research conducted jointly with Arindam Das-Gupta, most of which is summarized in Das-Gupta and Mookherjee (forthcoming)—examines the considerations involved in introducing incentive reforms for tax collectors. Whether the lessons of tax administration reforms generalize is an issue that must await detailed research on other areas of public bureaucracy.

Theoretical Framework

To assess the effects of instituting a pay-for-performance scheme for tax collectors, consider the example of a taxpayer with true income y who underreports income by amount e.[2] Suppose that both the taxpayer and the tax collector responsible for the return seek to maximize their expected net incomes (that is, they are risk neutral). The tax rate, t, is constant, so the taxpayer voluntarily pays a tax of $t(y - e)$ instead of ty. The probability, p, that the tax collector will detect the evasion through an audit depends on the amount of effort, $E(p)$, devoted to inspection. This effort is unobservable by the tax administration on a routine basis unless there are audits by internal supervisors or external "watchdogs."[3]

When the evasion is discovered, the tax collector decides whether to report it and impose penalties. If the tax collector reports an evasion of amount d (that is, assesses the taxpayer to have a true income of $y - e + d$), the taxpayer must pay additional taxes of td. Penalties at a constant rate f on the amount of income concealed are eventually imposed on the taxpayer with a probability (or time discount factor) of q, which measures the effectiveness of the penalty and the prosecution system. Hence the taxpayer pays back taxes and penalties totaling the expected present value of $(t + qf)d$.

Suppose that d cannot exceed e, the true level of income concealed by the taxpayer—that is, the tax collector cannot overassess, or use the threat of overassessment, as a source of bribes. (Later this assumption is dropped, and the effects of incentive pay on harassment are explored.)

Incentive Components

The tax collector receives a fixed salary, W, in addition to the following possible incentive components. The first is the "stick": if the tax collector underreports tax evasion in exchange for a bribe, the underreporting becomes known with some probability, l, either through an audit by an internal supervisor or external agency or through disclosure by a disgruntled subordinate. A penalty can be imposed on the tax collector in the form of a fine, a transfer to a less appealing location, a denial of promotion in the future, or dismissal. Assume that the penalty has a pecuniary (present value) equivalent that is imposed at a constant rate c on the amount of unreported income (which will be proportional to the level of the bribe taken).[4] At the same time the taxpayer is required to pay the additional taxes owed plus a bribery penalty at the fixed proportional rate g.

The second incentive component is the "carrot": the tax collector is entitled to retain a certain fraction, r, of additional revenue generated. Thus the expected utility of the tax collector equals $W + r(t + qf)d - lce + B - E(p)$, where B denotes the expected value of the bribe. In equilibrium, tax collectors have to be ensured at least a given reservation level of utility, U, if they are to continue to serve in the bureaucracy.

Note that this framework includes different compensation mechanisms as special cases. One is the case of no incentive pay ($c = r = 0$). Such an extreme form of fixed-salary service is rare; in most countries a disciplinary code penalizes egregiously corrupt behavior or incompetent service. Collection-based bonuses are less common, although performance-based promotions have the same effect indirectly. In the typical case the stick is the incentive component. Collection incentives will be low powered, however, if the likelihood (l) and magnitude (c) of penalties for underassessment are small. At the other extreme is the case of privatized tax collection. In this case the tax collector retains all revenue generated at the margin ($r = 1$), and W typically is negative, representing an up-front payment by the tax collector to the government in exchange for the right to collect taxes.

Conditions for Corruption and Level of Bribery

What determines whether there will be corruption and, if so, what the level of bribery will be? Suppose that the tax collector has discovered e, the income concealed by the taxpayer. In this simple linear setting it is easy to check whether the tax collector will report the entire concealment ($d = e$) or give the taxpayer a clean chit ($d = 0$). The expected benefit to the taxpayer from being cleared equals $(t + qf)e - l(t + g)e$, while the cost to the tax collector of not reporting the concealment equals $lce + r(t + qf)e$, the sum of expected penalties for bribery and forgone commissions. Corruption occurs if the collective gains to the pair are positive: $t + qf > l(c + t + g) + r(t + qf)$. This condition is more likely to be satisfied when there is no incentive pay ($r = c = 0$). It will never be satisfied when tax collection is privatized ($r = 1$).

With attention restricted to contexts not involving complete privatization, the condition for corruption in the form of underreporting by the tax collector is

(1) $$t + qf > l(c + t + g)(1 - r)^{-1}.$$

When this condition is satisfied, the expected gains from corruption are assumed to be shared equally by the two parties, as the Nash bargaining solution would predict, so that the bribe level would be

(2) $$b = (e/2)[(1 + r)(t + qf) + l(c - t - g)].$$

Note that in general the impact on corruption of increasing incentive pay is ambiguous: increases in the values of r, c, or l make inequality (condition 1) less likely to hold and in this sense reduce the likelihood of corruption. But if the reforms are not large enough to reverse this inequality, corruption continues to occur and on a larger scale. The bribe level rises to compensate the tax collector for the added cost imposed by the reform. Thus piecemeal incentive reforms may increase corruption. Only a large, discrete reform can eliminate corruption.

That corruption occurs does not necessarily mean that the tax collector serves no useful role. After all, corruption represents a privatized form of tax enforcement. The fact that the taxpayer must bribe the tax collector to avoid being caught evading taxes induces the taxpayer to comply with tax laws to some extent (to avoid having to pay this bribe). And the prospect of collecting a bribe motivates the tax collector to devote effort to the audit in the first place. Thus there is a need to go beyond the question of what levels of corruption occur and to examine induced effects on tax compliance and audit incentives.

Consider two possible regimes, one associated with corruption and one associated with no corruption. In the corrupt regime the expected payoff of the tax collector will be $W + p(e/2)[(1 + r)(t + qf) - l(c + t + g)] - E(p)$, and the expected payoff of the taxpayer will be $y - t(y - e) - p(e/2)[(1 + r)(t + qf) + l(c + t + g)]$. Based on these expectations the two will simultaneously select their respective strategies: the tax collector will select the effort to be devoted to monitoring (that is, p), while the taxpayer will decide how much to evade (e). It is easy to see that this "game" has a unique Nash equilibrium, the exact nature of which depends on the specific parameter values. Either the amount of evasion is "interior," in which case

$$(3) \quad \begin{aligned} p^* &= 2t[(1 + r)(t + qf) + l(c + t + g)]^{-1}, \\ e^* &= 2E'(p^*)[(1 + r)(t + qf) - l(c + t + g)]^{-1} \end{aligned}$$

(this is indeed the equilibrium outcome if the expression for e^* above is smaller than y), or the taxpayer discloses nothing at all ($e = y$) and the equilibrium monitoring intensity p solves $E'(p) = (y/2)[(1 + r)(t + qf) - l(c + t + g)]$.[5] A parallel calculation yields equilibrium levels of monitoring and tax evasion in the "honest" regime where condition 1 does not hold.[6]

Bonus-Based Incentives

These equations can be used to examine the effect that reforming compensation policy has on corruption and tax compliance. From equation 3 it is evident that a small increase in positive incentives (a higher bonus rate) causes tax evasion to decrease. But it also causes the bribe level to increase (see equation 2), which is instrumental in reducing evasion: the higher bribe increases the private benefit to the tax collector from monitoring more intensively, which increases the private cost to the taxpayer of evading taxes. In this case, then, increased corruption is useful in limiting tax evasion.

But that is not always true: increased use of the stick (in the form of higher penalties for corruption) also increases corruption, but it may increase tax evasion as well. If, for example, $E'(p) = p$, evasion increases with increases in c. The intuitive explanation is that increased values of c reduce the ex ante monitoring incentive of the tax collector, since the higher level of the bribe provides only partial compensation for the higher expected penalty borne by the tax collector for taking a bribe. This suggests that in this context the carrot is more effective than the stick.

This point can be illustrated more precisely by calculating the revenue and welfare effects of these reforms. In the corrupt regime the expected value of the government's net revenues is given by the difference between expected tax revenues and the wage bill for tax collectors:

(4) $$NR = t(y - e^*) - W + p^*l(c + t + g)e^*.$$

A utilitarian measure of social welfare (aggregating the shadow value of net government revenues and the utilities of the tax collector and taxpayer) equals

(5) $$SW = y + (\lambda - 1)(ty - W) - (\lambda - 1)[t - p^*l(c + t + g)]e^* - E(p^*)$$

where $\lambda > 1$ denotes the shadow price of public revenues. The compensation policy that maximizes expected net revenues and social welfare sets the fixed salary W at the smallest possible value that induces the tax collector to agree to work in the bureaucracy (that is, $W = E(p^*) + U - p^*b$). Inserting this expression into equations 4 and 5 yields reduced-form expressions for revenue and welfare,

(6) $$NR = ty - E(p^*) - U,$$
$$SW = y - (\lambda - 1)U + (\lambda - 1)ty - (\lambda - 1)E(p^*)$$

at an interior equilibrium described by equation 3 for the corrupt regime. Somewhat surprisingly, when attention is confined to such interior equilibria, both revenue and welfare are locally independent of the level of evasion and depend solely on the equilibrium monitoring rate, p^*.[7] Local increases in the likelihood and magnitude of penalties for underassessment (incentive components l and c) then generate higher net revenues and welfare by allowing economies in the wage bill as a result of reduced intensities of monitoring. However, while an increase in the bonus rate will cause levels of tax evasion to decline, increases in penalties may cause evasion to increase. If c is raised sufficiently, it can switch the system to a corner equilibrium, with taxpayers disclosing nothing at all. Any such corner equilibrium is welfare dominated by an interior equilibrium in the corrupt regime. In this sense welfare and revenue are decreasing in the level of tax evasion. Thus increasing the bonus rate is a better policy than increasing the penalty rate for corruption. Moreover, in this model, as long as the bonus rate can be freely varied, the optimal compensation policy entails increasing it enough to eliminate corruption entirely.[8]

If the bonus rate is constrained to equal zero, the penalty rate becomes the only instrument of incentive design. In this case, if corruption is eliminated by selecting c high enough to cause condition 1 to be violated, tax evasion will rise to the maximal level y, since the tax collector has no incentive to monitor taxpayers. Eliminating corruption then simultaneously eliminates all revenues. Thus if ty is large enough, the revenue implications will be dominant, ensuring that it will be optimal to tolerate some corruption rather than to eliminate all of it.[9]

This outcome is similar to that of Besley and McLaren (1993), who show that the inability to provide positive incentives implies that the optimal compensation policy induces inspectors to take bribes. In the model presented here the virtues of allowing corruption are twofold. First, corruption provides an incentive for taxpayers to comply with taxes, since the prospect of collecting bribes motivates tax collectors to undertake audits. Second, recognizing that tax collectors are expected to take bribes from taxpayers, the government can pay its collectors lower wages. In other words, bribes represent a form of hidden supplementary taxes.

The more general lesson from this example was alluded to earlier: whether it is desirable to tolerate corruption depends on the range of controls available to policymakers. In a similar vein, if policymakers are subject to the additional constraint that the "institutional" parameter l equals zero, then inequality (condition 1) will always hold and it will be impossible to eliminate corruption. Thus eliminating corruption is not an end in itself; the effects on tax evasion and revenue are more important.

Extortion-Based Bribery

A potential drawback of bonus-based incentives ignored by the preceding analysis is that they may increase taxpayer harassment based on threats by the tax collector to overassess the obligations of taxpayers. To see how this would work, allow the tax collector to cite the taxpayer for a worse level of evasion than the tax collector can prove. In other words, let d be greater than e', the level of evasion discovered by the tax collector. That level is either 0 (no evidence collected) or e (the true level of evasion discovered in the audit), with probabilities of $1 - p$ and p.

Suppose that a taxpayer who is overassessed (that is, for whom $d > e'$) can file an appeal, that the cost of doing so (legal fees, time spent, and other costs incurred) is A, and that the probability of appealing the assessment successfully is a. If the assessment is revised, the taxpayer is refunded the excess taxes and fines paid $(t + qf)(d - e')$ as well as some fraction, k, of the costs incurred in appealing the assessment. The evidence of overassessment also results in the tax collector being asked to pay back any commissions earned on that overassessment. Consider the case in which the system imposes on the tax collector sharp penalties for overassessment at a rate of $x > 1$. This implies that the penalty exceeds the total amount of additional collections at stake. In the event of a successful appeal the total cost imposed on the tax collector therefore equals $(x + r)(t + qf)(d - e')$. If the appeal is unsuccessful, the taxpayer receives no refund, and the tax collector keeps the entire commission earned, $r(t + qf)d$.

Consider the case in which the appeal cost that would be incurred by the taxpayer is known to both parties; the results extend without modification to the case in which these costs are not known a priori. The assumption that $x > 1$ implies that going to appeals court is never in the mutual interest of the two parties.[10] Overassessments are not in the mutual interest of the parties as long as the bonus rate is less than 1, since the taxpayer pays more to the government than is received by the tax collector. Nevertheless, the threat of overassessment and of going to appeals court plays an important role in the allocation of bargaining power between the two parties, as captured by the Nash bargaining solution.

The threat points forming the status quo payoffs in this bargaining game result from noncooperative behavior should the tax collector and taxpayer fail to agree on a collusive outcome. When a pay-for-performance scheme is not used and the bonus rate is zero, multiple noncooperative (Nash) equilibria exist. However, there is a unique equilibrium involving undominated strategies at which the tax collector neither overassesses nor underassesses.[11] The corresponding status quo payoffs are W and $y - t(y - e) - (t + qf)e'$.

Now suppose that a pay-for-performance scheme is introduced, and r is positive. Then the noncooperative equilibrium always involves overassessment. Knowing that the taxpayer will go to appeals court whenever the cost of the appeal is less than the expected private benefit $(a^{-1} - k)^{-1}(t + qf)(d - e')$, the tax collector, following discovery of evasion level e', will issue an assessment of $d = e' + A(a^{-1} - k)(t + qf)^{-1}$, which will deter the taxpayer from appealing. Thus the status quo outcome will involve overassessment and no appeal. The status quo payoff for the tax collector is $W + r(t + qf)e' + rA(a^{-1} - k)$, and for the taxpayer it is $y - t(y - e) - (a^{-1} - k)A - (t + qf)e'$. Thus the introduction of the pay-for-performance scheme, even on a small scale, will discontinuously shift bargaining power toward the tax collector by rendering the threat of overassessment credible. The higher is the bonus rate and the appeal cost and the lower is the rate of success of the appeal and the reimbursement rate, the greater will be the magnitude of this effect.

Applying the Nash bargaining solution to this status quo confirms that introducing a pay-for-performance scheme increases the bribe extracted by the tax collector by a constant amount $(a^{-1} - k)(1 + r)(A/2)$ in every outcome. In other words, in the corrupt regime (described by inequality condition 1), bribes are given by equation 2 plus this constant additional amount whenever the tax collector discovers the true level of evasion. Moreover, even when no evidence of evasion is discovered, the tax collector will extract a bribe of $(a^{-1} - k)(1 + r)(A/2)$. This component can thus be viewed as an extortion-based bribe, in contrast to equation 2, which can be interpreted as a bribe for underassessment. Thus an increase in the bonus rate increases the scale of extortion.

What are the welfare implications of such extortion-based bribery? In this simple model bribes rise by a constant amount in all contingencies, redistributing income from taxpayers to tax collectors; there is no effect on monitoring or tax evasion incentives.[12] Indeed, this form of bribery amounts to a hidden lump-sum tax, which increases net revenues and utilitarian welfare. Given these bribes, government collectors can be paid less in salary and still be induced to work for the bureaucracy.

A utilitarian, welfare-minded government would be unwilling to deal with this problem. Citizens of a democratic society will, however, rail against being forced to make illicit payments to government bureaucrats to avoid being cited for offenses they did not commit. Harassment of citizens will render such incentive systems deeply unpopular. In addition, as Banerjee (1994) and Marjit and Mukherjee (1996) argue, such corruption is inherently regressive, as the poor are more vulnerable to extortion. In more realistic settings (for example, with concave utility functions) such incentive systems will also have adverse incentive implications, since tax evasion would tend to increase as tax collectors become less motivated to monitor taxpayers and as the returns to taxpayers from honest behavior diminish.[13] Thus the design of pay-for-performance incentive systems will have to trade off the benefits of reduced underassessments and heightened monitoring incentives against the costs of increased harassment of citizens based on threats of overassessment.

Practical Considerations in Designing and Implementing Performance-Based Systems

A range of problems typically arise in the design and implementation of pay-for-performance schemes in a given institutional setting.

Design Issues

In the design of pay-for-performance schemes, important issues include how to measure performance and what kind of performance to measure.

MEASURING COLLECTION PERFORMANCE. Evaluation of the performance of tax collectors must consider the revenue they help generate. But which measure should be used: additional revenue yielded by audits, prepaid taxes, or both? Should collection costs be incorporated in the measure? Such issues have been studied extensively in the theoretical literature on the design of tax enforcement mechanisms (Melumad and Mookherjee 1989; Sanchez and Sobel 1993).

A related issue concerns the need to limit the risk imposed on tax collectors as a result of variables beyond their control, such as tax legislation, the quality of information available about taxpayer transactions, the state of the local economy, the nature of support staff, and, above all, the behavior of taxpayers. If this risk is not limited, the welfare of tax collectors will be reduced, which will shrink the supply of competent recruits into the civil service. This is a familiar moral hazard problem. One solution recently adopted by some countries is to supplement fixed-salary schemes with collection-based bonuses, thus ensuring that officials are unambiguously better off. In awarding collectors excessive rents, however, the resulting compensation scheme may not minimize the government's wage costs. This may be a small price to pay if the corresponding benefit in terms of increased revenue is substantial and the informational requirements of additional fine-tuning are excessive.

To the extent that limiting the rents accruing to bureaucrats is an important objective—to hold down budgetary costs or to avoid inducing a misallocation of talent between the private and public sectors—various methods can be used to benchmark tax collectors' performance evaluation. These include measuring performance against that of other tax collectors in comparable jurisdictions and using collection projections based on information about current tax laws and the state of the local economy. In addition, collectors can participate in setting their own budgets and performance targets against which subsequent performance is evaluated. Such schemes allow for flexible targets, have desirable incentive properties (Laffont and Tirole 1986, 1993), and can be designed for practical implementation (Reichelstein 1992; Gonik 1982; Groves and others 1995). An extreme version of such information elicitation schemes is auction-based privatization of tax collection, in which the right to collect taxes is sold to the highest bidder (Banerjee 1994).

Collection-based bonuses create incentives for tax collectors to pad their collection figures. In India overassessment is common, with taxpayers subsequently appealing the assessments, which are frequently overturned. The problem is compounded by a lack of consistent penalties for collectors found guilty of overassessment (Das-Gupta and Mookherjee forthcoming).[14] Recognizing the problem, Indian tax administration officials instituted collection-based bonuses that are paid only if the additions were sustained following taxpayer appeals, a remedy that considerably diluted the incentive mechanism.

The theoretical model presented earlier assumes that the tax collector is not involved in the appeal and prosecution process (that is, a and q are exogenous). But in many developing countries tax administration is not functionally specialized, so tax collectors must follow up on assessments if penalties are to be imposed on evaders. In India, for instance, a successful defense of an assessment appealed by a taxpayer requires the tax collector to appear in court to present the tax administration's case. The process is time consuming, often stretching out over many years. And because of frequent job rotation, most cases reach the court after the original assessing officer has been transferred to a different jurisdiction. The case is then argued by officers who are less familiar with the details and who do not have a corresponding stake in the outcome. As a result only a small fraction of additional collections are sustained against taxpayer appeals within a reasonable period. Nevertheless, the need to prevent reckless overassessment requires that bonuses be paid only when additional collections are sustained. The confounding of these two problems implies that bonuses lose much of their motivational effect.

MEASURING PERFORMANCE ALONG OTHER DIMENSIONS. Tax collectors do much more than simply assess tax returns and collect taxes. They also provide assistance to taxpayers, process refunds, pursue delinquent taxpayers, initiate penal action for evaders, and provide information requested by their superiors. Thus providing incentives along only a few dimensions can affect the performance of tax collectors along others, as agents divert their effort across tasks (a general problem identified by Holmstrom and Milgrom 1991 for agents pursuing multidimensional tasks). Performance evaluations should thus assess performance along these other dimensions as well. Most tax administrations, however, lack the ability to incorporate all these dimensions in evaluations of collecting officers, particularly in the absence of sophisticated accounting systems.[15]

Implementation Problems

In addition to the design problems associated with incentive schemes there are several problems related to implementation.

INABILITY TO COMMIT TO PAYING BONUSES. In some countries the tax administration may find it difficult to commit fully to a system of bonuses or rewards. In India decisions by the tax administration that certain earned rewards were too large to be paid out clearly dampened collection incentives. There is also the ratcheting problem: officers hold back on current effort for fear that successful performance will cause future targets and bonus requirements to be raised. To avoid these problems, the administration must commit to paying bonuses based on a formula that will not be changed between the time a bonus is earned and the time it is paid.

LACK OF EQUITY AND GROUP INCENTIVES. Senior officials often criticize proposals to introduce pay-for-performance systems on the grounds that they would increase inequality of pay within the bureaucracy and undermine teamwork and cooperation among officials. Rewards earned would vary according to many factors beyond the control of the official, including the nature of tax evasion in different jurisdictions, the ease of detection, and sheer luck. Even relatively small reward rates can give rise to enormous variations in pay, especially in areas where tax collectors occasionally succeed in making large catches. As a result tax collectors may sometimes earn more than their supervisors—sometimes even more than the highest-ranking officials in the administration. (Payment of bonuses to tax officials could also stir resentment among officials outside the tax administration.)

One solution is to divide any bonus resulting from a revenue addition into an individual and a group component, with the weight of each component based on the relative contribution to audit yields and the importance of equity concerns within the bureaucracy (Meyer and Mookherjee 1987; Itoh 1991). To avoid too much pay dispersion, ceilings could be imposed on the aggregate bonus that any officer could receive. But as Brazil's experience (described below) suggests, such ceilings can have adverse incentive effects.

FAVORITISM. Performance evaluations should be conducted by supervisors who monitor the activities of tax collectors. For incentive schemes to succeed, these evaluations must be impartial and efficient. If supervisors are not motivated to enhance performance along the same dimensions as tax collectors are being encouraged to, such evaluations could be biased and lackadaisical, destroying motivation and morale.[16] These problems imply that the design of incentive schemes for tax collectors must be viewed as part of the more general problem of designing incentive schemes for their supervisors, an issue discussed further below.

POLITICAL INFLUENCE. Other prerequisites for successful incentive reform have been pointed out by Qizilbash (1994). Attempts by a tax official to bring a case against a tax evader who has recourse to higher-level political influence may result in disciplinary action against the tax collector from higher-ups: the collector could be transferred or dismissed on trumped-up charges of poor performance. In those circumstances attempts to pay efficiency wages (in the form of increased pay scales) will raise tax officials' stake in staying in their current jobs, reducing any interest in "upsetting the applecart." In systems with strongly entrenched political corruption at high levels, efforts to eliminate bureaucratic corruption are quixotic at best.

The preceding considerations undermine the hope that some simple formula for incentive reform might be universally applicable. The desirability of any reform depends on its effects on equilibrium evasion and monitoring incentives. Adverse effects of reforms may include increased harassment of citizens and a decline in teamwork and equity within the administration. Whether the schemes are effectively implemented depends on the institutional environment in which the bureaucracy functions. This includes both the organizational attributes of the tax administration (such as the nature of task assignments and accounting systems) and some features of its external environment (such as legal and political systems).

Recent Experience with Pay-for-Performance Reforms

A number of countries have recently introduced incentive reforms for tax auditors (for details see Das-Gupta and Mookherjee forthcoming). Mexico adopted incentive measures as part of a comprehensive reform of its tax administration during 1988–92. Under the Mexican system each office is awarded, as a bonus fund, about 60 percent of additional collections. The fund is distributed among members of the office in proportion to the "proximity" of the official to the discovery and collection process. Bonuses have been substantial, amounting to about 130 percent of the aggregate wage bill in the early 1990s. The amount received by any employee is capped at 250 percent of annual salary for those directly involved and 120 percent for those indirectly involved. As a result of the bonuses the number and yield of audits increased almost overnight. Audits rose from 3.2 percent of taxpayers in 1988 to 5.5 percent in 1990 and 8.9 percent in 1993. The share of audits generating additional revenue increased from 38 percent in 1988 to 90 percent in 1990. The benefit-cost ratio of these audits increased from 4 in 1988 to 27 in 1990 and 46 in 1993. Tax administration officials believe that the incentive scheme was the most important factor behind these changes.

These figures alone do not prove that the reform was successful: evaluating the effect of the reform would require assessing its effect on tax compliance and overassessment. Moreover, it is difficult to disentangle the role of the reform from other changes in tax legislation and administration that occurred at the same time. Nevertheless, the figures are consistent with the view of administration officials that the scheme had a major qualitative effect on the performance of tax collectors.

Brazil implemented a similar reform at about the same time, introducing a bonus program as part of an overhaul of the tax system in 1989 (Kahn and de Silva 1996). The program created a bonus fund for distribution among tax officials that has amounted to 68 percent of fines collected. The fund is divided between individual and group rewards on a 70:30 basis. Group rewards are divided among agencies based on their performance evaluation. Performance measurement criteria include fines collected, targets achieved for aggregate and overdue collections, measures of audit effort, and a measure of the agency's size. Individual rewards are based on subjective evaluations by superiors and are subject to ceilings (defined initially by the salary of the minister of finance, later by the highest salary of a public servant). Kahn and de Silva argue that these ceilings were typically binding in high-productivity jurisdictions, dampening the incentive impact. The large group component and the subjectivity of individual evaluations had a similar effect. In contrast, the group rewards provided incentives to high-level officials to reallocate audit resources from low-productivity to high-productivity regions, probably the most significant effect of the reform.

Peru instituted reforms of a somewhat different nature beginning in 1991 (Das-Gupta and Mookherjee forthcoming). The reforms were aimed at inducing incompetent and dishonest officials to leave, raising standards for training and professionalism within the administration, reducing the size of the tax administration, increasing the scope of performance-based promotions, and raising salaries substantially. In less than a year (September 1991 to July 1992) staff strength shrank by two-thirds and salaries increased almost tenfold. The reform represented a move toward paying efficiency wages (a stick-based rather than a carrot-based approach). Tax revenues as a whole rose from 5.4 percent of GDP in 1990 to 9.0 percent of GDP in 1991. Whether these changes were caused entirely by the tax reform is difficult to gauge, since other administrative reforms were instituted at the same time.

These experiences have been too brief and too limited in number to draw any inferences about the practical success of incentive reforms. But they do indicate that bold initiatives that confront the challenge of implementation are possible, and they appear to have had the effects on audit results that reformers had hoped for. Few countries have attempted incentive reforms, however. Instead, most tax administrations have focused on reforming information systems and tax legislation, as described in the next section.

Reforming the Institutional Setting

We turn now to the second question posed at the outset: To what extent can the institutional setting be reformed in order to directly confront the root cause of the problem—the excessive discretionary power and lack of accountability of bureaucrats? Bureaucrats have excessive discretionary power because of their monopoly on relevant information; they are insufficiently accountable because of inadequate monitoring and supervision systems. In principle these problems could be solved by enhancing the information available to the tax administration, improving monitoring systems, and reducing the discretionary authority granted to local officials. Incentive reforms are more likely to succeed if the scope of reform initiatives is widened to incorporate organizational restructuring, as described below.

Enhancing Supervision

A system of independent third-party audits is required to evaluate the audits carried out by tax collectors. Such a system increases the probability of detecting underassessments and restricts the scope for overassessment. Performance evaluations should incorporate the results of these third-party audits as well as the outcomes of taxpayer appeals. To minimize the possibility of collusion between supervisors and auditors, supervisors should be appointed by an independent wing of the tax administration, and opportunities for private contact between auditors and supervisors should be minimized. In turn, supervisors should face incentive schemes similar to those used for auditors.[17]

Some aspects of Mexico's reforms are notable in this regard. Several measures complement the new bonus system. If an audit yields no additional discovery of taxes owed, the case can no longer be closed by the auditor but must be referred to an officer from a different department. If fifteen days go by without any result, the original audit team is replaced by a new one. Audit results must be reported to a *syndico,* or representative of the industry or service sector of the economy to which the taxpayer belongs. If the *syndico* disagrees with the assessment, the case is referred to the vigilance department. Any auditor found guilty of harassment is subject to prosecution.

Improving Personnel Quality

Peru's reforms focused on improving the quality of tax administration personnel by raising wage levels substantially, instituting stricter screening and promotion criteria for new recruits, and encouraging the early retirement of staff unable to pass competence tests or whose records included reports of unethical behavior.[18] Such reforms complement the use of new incentive schemes.

Limiting Discretionary Authority

India's tax administration awards tax collectors an effective monopoly over taxpayers in their assigned jurisdictions. Filed returns are stored in the local office, with no duplicates, making it difficult to induce competition between tax collectors. A simple reform might involve assigning taxpayers to a group of tax collectors, who select which taxpayers to audit from the pool. An evader would then have to bribe the entire group of tax collectors rather than a single one. Moreover, by creating a common jurisdiction such a reform would make it easier to evaluate the performance of tax collectors relative to that of others in the same range.

A centralized audit selection system could also reduce the scope for tax collector discretion in selecting taxpayers to audit. Implementing such a system would require developing a centralized information base to be used by an audit selection cell in identifying returns that should be audited. If a centralized information base is not available, a strict procedure for audit selection could be substituted (for example, a scoring rule that must be applied to information contained in filed returns, along with a suitable sampling scheme). Direct contact between taxpayers and tax collectors could be avoided by requiring audits to be conducted ex parte or by requiring third-party auditors from a different jurisdiction to be present at meetings between collectors and taxpayers.

The authority of tax officials in follow-up action needs to be made strong enough to minimize opportunities for external political influence. That can mean ensuring the use of objective performance criteria for deciding promotions and dismissals and, sometimes, adopting measures for the physical safety of auditors.

Mexico's reforms stand out as a good example of such initiatives. Audit selection procedures became less decentralized, more transparent, and based on better information. Computerization of tax administration meant that audit selection could be made by the programming departments of local administrative offices. The use of "laptop audits"—a preprogrammed audit procedure—further reduced the scope for auditor discretion. The scope for external political interference in penalty and prosecution activity was substantially reduced. Since 1988 more than 500 tax evasion prosecution cases have been launched; in the preceding 100 years only 3 cases had been tried.

Introducing Functional Specialization

Lack of functional specialization in tax administration—requiring a taxpayer to deal with the same tax officer for such diverse functions as filing returns, obtaining refunds, responding to audits, lodging appeals, and responding to penalty or delinquency notices—increases the scope for collusion and extortion. Moreover, an assessing officer must conduct all these tasks simultaneously, limiting the time available for in-depth audits. These problems are ameliorated with a functionally specialized organizational structure, a structure that also allows for the realization of economies of scale. Adopting such reforms requires modernizing the information system.

Computerizing Information Systems

Computerization of tax administration facilitates the use of pay-for-performance schemes and the emergence of a functionally specialized structure, and it can help control corruption. Computerization allows centralized, automated processing of filed returns and the matching of returns with third-party information on taxpayer transactions and characteristics. Such information can be retrieved instantaneously, simultaneously, and at low cost by numerous authorized parties.

Computerization also makes it harder to tamper with records. In India a common way for tax evaders to avoid detection is to pay low-level officials to "lose" their returns. With the proper security measures, computerized systems make it substantially more difficult to engage in such activities. And by automating the processing of refunds and the generation of overdue notices, computerized systems eliminate opportunities for low-level officials to earn "speed money."

Centralizing the information base also facilitates automated audit selection, reducing the discretion of local officials and ensuring that selections are based on richer information. Audits can be automated to further reduce the discretion of auditors, as was done in Mexico. Thus computerization permits an optimal combination of centralized information and decentralized behavior (Hammer and Champy 1993). Third-party supervisory audits, which are facilitated by the availability of more information at the central level, must continue to be performed, however. Computerization, which allows cases to be tracked more easily, also facilitates follow-up legal action.

Another advantage of computerizing records is that it makes possible an accounting system that keeps track of a wide range of performance variables that enter into a collector's evaluation. In particular, computerization allows credit to be allocated among different officials, and it allows audit quality measures to be developed based on comparisons with third-party audits, outcomes of taxpayer appeals, and other indicators of overassessment. Tracking this information can significantly reduce the likelihood of dysfunctional responses by collectors in pay-for-performance schemes.

Numerous countries, particularly in Latin America, have embarked on large-scale computerization initiatives in the past decade. These initiatives have typically cost less than 1 percent of annual tax collections and yielded substantial returns within a very short time (Das-Gupta and Mookherjee forthcoming). Only a few countries, however, have attempted to use automation to enhance incentive and control systems for auditors.

Establishing Appropriate Staffing Policies

Economic growth often leads to large increases in the number of taxpayers and concomitant increases in the workload of the tax administration. Workload management becomes critical. Without it, both the administration and individual officers focus almost exclusively on clearing an ever-increasing backlog of pending cases. In India, for example, the number of taxpayers nearly tripled between 1970 and the mid-1990s, while the number of assessing officers remained constant (Das-Gupta and Mookherjee forthcoming). No attempt was made to computerize operations or to divide tasks by specialization. Not surprisingly, performance evaluation was increasingly based on the ability to dispose of pending assessments, to the exclusion of most other relevant criteria. As a result the time available for assessments and follow-up legal action has shrunk. Today a scrutiny audit in India is almost exclusively a desk audit, lasting three days on average. In contrast, in other countries for which data are available, detailed audits involve visits to the premises of the taxpayer and take an average of eight to fifteen days (Das-Gupta and Mookherjee forthcoming). If tax collectors are not allowed enough time to pursue in-depth audits, heightening their collection incentive will have little effect.

Reallocating staff across jurisdictions is one way to manage workload. Moving staff from low-productivity to high-productivity jurisdictions can significantly raise the aggregate level of tax compliance. In Brazil the group component of the incentive reforms provided high-level officials with an incentive to reallocate workloads across jurisdictions to enhance productivity (Kahn and de Silva 1996). In India reallocating auditors and support staff across different kinds of tax collector charges based on induced effects on taxpayer compliance would yield significant returns (Das-Gupta and Mookherjee forthcoming).

Incentive-compatible target setting systems can also improve tax administration. Bureaucracies the world over tend to hand down work targets to officials in a hierarchical and inflexible fashion. In addition to creating the flexibility needed for effective performance, systems that enable officers to help set their own targets provide superior incentives (as discussed in the previous section).

Job rotation can reduce collusion between taxpayers and auditors. It can complicate performance evaluation by increasing the gap between short- and long-term performance, however. Moreover, frequent rotation increases the incentive of collectors to manipulate short-term performance measures, and it limits their interest in investing in information gathering within the local jurisdiction or initiating follow-up penalty and prosecution activity. Job transfers can also serve as channels for the exercise of external political influence.

Motivating High-Level Officials

Reforms for auditors cannot succeed unless the higher levels of the bureaucracy that must implement the systems are motivated to do so. Supervisors, for example, must have an incentive to evaluate the performance of their subordinates and to allocate budgets among audit teams under their supervision in the desired manner.

Also important is providing high-level officials with autonomy over a range of decisions concerning budgetary allocations and procurement and tapping local expertise in effective enforcement policies. Even motivated bureaucrats are often hampered by lack of autonomy or by confining procurement rules. The benefits of autonomy over the scale of enforcement effort in preventing undesired equilibria are highlighted in the theoretical literature on tax compliance.[19]

An ideal system of incentives would percolate through all levels of the bureaucracy. Top-down systems such as responsibility accounting and hierarchical budgeting are common in private bureaucracies. The hierarchy can be viewed as a sequence of nested profit or cost centers, with progressive delegation of authority to lower-level officials by their immediate supervisors. Theoretical models help clarify how such mechanisms can produce optimal outcomes under suitable conditions (Melumad, Mookherjee, and Reichelstein 1992, 1995; Mookherjee and Reichelstein 1997). Each layer of the hierarchy receives a budgetary allocation and a performance evaluation scheme from the layer immediately above it. Within that allocation and evaluation scheme the departmental supervisor selects a performance target for the department as a whole. The evaluation is based on the net profit or collections of the department. Supervisors are awarded complete autonomy over allocations and procurement decisions. In turn they design similar performance evaluation schemes and allocate budgets (resources and staffing) among their direct subordinates.

Autonomy over budgets, administration, personnel, procedures, and control was increased in recent tax administration reforms in Argentina, Colombia, Ghana, Jamaica, and Peru, among others (Das-Gupta and Mookherjee forthcoming). In some cases budgets were linked to revenues collected. Some countries liberalized the rules for contracting out operations to the private sector. Tax administrations throughout Latin America have tended to rely on commercial banks to act as tax collection centers and processors of the information contained in filed returns. In Mexico the design and operation of the computerization program and the auditing of large taxpayers were contracted out to the private sector. In contrast, Spain outsourced only minor functions of its tax administration and offered little in the way of bonuses for auditors but implemented a computerized system to track the performance of departments at various levels.

Improving the Appeal Mechanism

The role of the appeal mechanism in limiting the vulnerability of honest taxpayers to strategic overassessment by tax collectors has already been elaborated in the theoretical model. Since in most countries appeals are initiated within the tax administration, the process can be enhanced by improving procedures for filing complaints, setting time limits on judgments, and establishing an appropriate burden of proof.

Conclusion

This study of incentive reform in tax administration reveals several general points about incentive reforms in public bureaucracies:

- The design of incentive systems must be sensitive to the institutional environment in which the bureaucracy operates, since it affects the selection of performance measures and the implementation of the reforms. Possible side effects on other dimensions of performance, such as the quality of citizen services, should be monitored and appraised.
- The nature of the institutional environment determines the overall welfare effect of the reforms.
- Incentive reforms will be facilitated by concomitant organizational changes within public bureaucracies, including changes in supervision systems, information and control procedures, staffing policy, and degree of autonomy and accountability at all levels.

Because reforms in incentive systems and organizational procedures are complementary, reforms are more likely to succeed if they are comprehensive rather than incremental. Partial reforms may achieve only limited success, suggesting that the political will at the highest levels of government is an essential prerequisite to successful reform. The government must be willing to implement comprehensive restructuring and decisively confront ideological doubts over the wisdom of tampering with hallowed civil service traditions.

Notes

1. The question of how norms evolve and how they are influenced by the institutional environment has received little attention from economists, with the possible exception of some recent literature in evolutionary game theory (see Bowles 1996 for an interesting analysis along these lines).
2. The simple theoretical model presented here is based on Mookherjee and Png (1995).
3. This function is assumed to satisfy the typical boundary (Inada) conditions that guarantee an interior solution for p.
4. Some authors identify this penalty with the extent by which the general level of pay within the civil service exceeds that in the private sector, as this defines the loss suffered in the event of dismissal. It also

depends on the likelihood of corruption being discovered, which may depend on the magnitude of the bribe.

5. The taxpayer is indifferent between evading and not evading and randomizes accordingly, resulting in the level of expected evasion given by this expression. Introducing appropriate sources of heterogeneity among taxpayers will "purify" these mixed strategies in the standard fashion.

6. The tax collector's expected payoff is $W + pr(t + qf)e - E(p)$, while that of the taxpayer is $y - t(y - e) - p(t + qf)e$. The equilibrium then involves $p^* = t/(t + qf)$, and $e^* = E'(p^*)/[r(t + qf)]$ if the latter is less than y; otherwise $e^* = y$ and $E'(p^*) = r(t + qf)y$.

7. This property stems from the assumed risk neutrality of the taxpayer and the fact that in an interior equilibrium the taxpayer's expected net payments to the government must be exactly zero (since the taxpayer must be indifferent regarding the level of evasion). However, revenues and welfare are not globally independent of the level of evasion. For example, both are lower at a corner equilibrium, at which taxpayers conceal all their income. Moreover, if taxpayers have heterogeneous risk attitudes or different likelihoods of incurring penalties, intramarginal evaders will derive positive benefits from evading, and net revenues will be decreasing in evasion levels. Such a model would be more complex and yet generate qualitatively similar results.

8. Specifically, the optimal policy involves selecting r large enough so that condition 1 is violated and the solution for p in the equation $E'(p) = r(t + qf)y$ exceeds $t/(t + qf)$. Then the equilibrium monitoring rate equals $t/(t + qf)$ and the maximized level of social welfare is $y - (l - 1)U + (l - 1)ty - lE[t/(t + qf)]$.

9. Here is a sketch of the argument. The optimal value of c within the corrupt regime is easily seen to be c^*, where c^* solves $4t = y[(t + qf)^2 - l^2(c^* + t + g)^2]$, as this minimizes the equilibrium monitoring rate while preventing maximal evasion. The resulting level of social welfare is $y - (\lambda - 1)U + (\lambda - 1)ty - (\lambda - 1)E\{2t[t + qf + l(c^* + t + g)]^{-1}\}$. To eliminate corruption, c must be raised to at least $C = l^{-1}(t + qf) - (t + g)$, which is greater than c^*. The resulting level of social welfare will be $y - (\lambda - 1)U$, since both tax revenues and the monitoring rate will fall to zero.

10. The expected gain to the taxpayer from appealing is $a(t + qf)(d - e') - (1 - ak)A$, and the expected cost to the tax collector is $a(x + r)(t + qf)(d - e')$. The aggregate gain to the two parties is $a(t + qf)(d - e')(1 - x - r) - (1 - ak)A$, which is negative.

11. Overassessment is a dominated strategy for the tax collector, since he or she gains nothing from it (given that there are no positive bonuses) and may lose (if the taxpayer successfully appeals). Similarly, underassessment is associated with a penalty with some probability, while there is no gain to the tax collector when the two do not cooperate (that is, when a bribe is not paid).

12. The extreme simplicity of the model is highlighted by the fact that overassessments and appeals do not actually occur in equilibrium. A more complicated model with private information on appeal costs and chances of success is required to explain why parties actually go to appeals court, an issue that is dealt with in the literature on pretrial settlement.

13. As tax collectors become wealthier from bribes based on extortion threats, their incentive to earn additional bribes by detecting tax evasion diminishes. Moreover, when taxpayers are honest they are poorer, as a result of higher voluntary tax payments, rendering appeals less affordable. This makes poorer taxpayers more vulnerable to extortion threats and correspondingly reduces compliance incentives.

14. To illustrate this problem, the theoretical model above can be modified to set the overassessment penalty, x, equal to 0. Suppose that the bonus rate is positive and bonuses do not have to be refunded in the event a taxpayer appeal is sustained. The cost to the taxpayer of overassessment (and subsequent appeal) is $(1 - a)[(t + qf)(d - e') + A]$, and the benefit to the tax collector is $r(t + qf)(d - e')$. If the bonus rate is large relative to $(1 - a)$ and A, overassessment is in the mutual interest of taxpayer and tax collector. Indeed, the tax collector may bribe the taxpayer into accepting the following deal: "I will overassess you today, and you can appeal it tomorrow and have it restored to the correct assessment."

15. This problem constitutes a serious barrier to the introduction of incentive systems in many other public bureaucracies as well. "Output" is particularly difficult to measure for police, schoolteachers, and health care workers.

16. Laffont (1990) provides a theoretical discussion of the problems with incentive design that arise in the presence of "hidden games" between supervisors and agents.

17. Gangopadhyay, Goswami, and Sanyal (1992) show that even if the supervisors are corruptible, having a single layer of supervisors can effectively eliminate corruption, provided the supervisors face a suitable reward system.

18. Besley and McLaren (1993) analyze theoretically the influence of wage levels and dismissal criteria on the quality of personnel in the long run. Groves and others (1995) provide evidence of increased managerial turnover among Chinese state-owned enterprises in the 1980s, often as a result of adoption of auction-based selection mechanisms for managers.

19. For instance, budgetary constraints may cause the emergence of multiple equilibria. If many taxpayers evade at the same time while budgetary constraints prevent the tax administration from increas-

ing audit resources correspondingly, the resulting dilution of enforcement effort per evader will lower the likelihood of detection, thus justifying the decision to evade (Graetz, Reinganum, and Wilde 1984). Budgetary autonomy can help prevent these outcomes (Melumad and Mookherjee 1989).

References

Acemoglu, Daron, and Thierry Verdier. 1996. "Property Rights, Corruption and the Allocation of Talent: A General Equilibrium Approach." CEPR Discussion Paper 1494. Centre for Economic Policy Research, London

Banerjee, Abhijit. 1994. "Eliminating Corruption." In M.G. Quibria, ed., *Proceedings of the Third Annual Conference on Development Economics.* Manila: Asian Development Bank.

Bardhan, Pranab. 1996. "The Nature of Institutional Impediments to Economic Development." Paper presented at the Institutional Reforms and Informal Sector (IRIS) Conference on Economic Reforms, January, New Delhi.

Besley, Timothy, and John McLaren. 1993. "Taxes and Bribery: The Role of Wage Incentives." *Economic Journal* 103 (January): 119–41.

Bowles, Samuel. 1996. "Markets as Cultural Institutions: Equilibrium Norms in Competitive Economies." Working Paper 1996-5. University of Massachusetts at Amherst, Department of Economics.

Das-Gupta, Arindam, and Dilip Mookherjee. Forthcoming. *Incentives and Institutional Reform in Tax Enforcement: An Analysis of Developing Country Experience.* New Delhi: Oxford University Press.

Gangopadhyay, Shubhashis, Omkar Goswami, and Amal Sanyal. 1992. "Tax Enforcement with a Hierarchy of Corrupt Auditors." Discussion Paper 93-03. Indian Statistical Institute, Economics Research Unit, New Delhi.

Gonik, Jacob. 1982. "Tie Salesmen's Bonuses to Their Forecasts." In Alfred Rapport, ed., *Information for Decision Making.* Englewood, N.J.: Prentice Hall.

Graetz, Michael, Jennifer Reinganum, and Louis Wilde. 1984. "A Model of Tax Compliance with Budget-Constrained Auditors." Social Science Working Paper 520. California Institute of Technology, Pasadena.

Groves, Theodore, Yongmiao Hong, John McMillan, and Barry Naughton. 1995. "China's Evolving Managerial Labor Market." *Journal of Political Economy* 103 (4): 873–92.

Hammer, Michael, and James Champy. 1993. *Reengineering the Corporation.* New York: Harper Collins.

Holmstrom, Bengt, and Paul Milgrom. 1991. "Multitask Principal-Agent Analyses: Incentive Contracts, Asset Ownership, and Job Design." *Journal of Law, Economics and Organization* 7: 24–52.

Itoh, Hideshi. 1991. "Incentives to Help in Multiagent Situations." *Econometrica* 59 (3): 611–36.

Kahn, Charles, and Emilson de Silva. 1996. "Performance-Based Wages in Tax Collection: The Brazilian Tax Collection Reform and Its Effects." Discussion paper. University of Oregon, Department of Economics, Eugene.

Klitgaard, Robert. 1995. *Institutional Adjustment and Adjusting to Institutions.* World Bank Discussion Paper 303. Washington, D.C.

———. 1997. "Information and Incentives in Institutional Reform." In Christopher Clague, ed., *Institutions and Economic Development.* Baltimore, Md.: The Johns Hopkins University Press.

Laffont, Jean-Jacques. 1990. "Analysis of Hidden Gaming in a Three-Level Hierarchy." *Journal of Law, Economics and Organization* 6 (2): 301–24.

Laffont, Jean-Jacques, and Jean Tirole. 1986. "Using Cost Observation to Regulate Firms." *Journal of Political Economy* 94: 614–41.

———. 1993. *A Theory of Incentives in Procurement and Regulation.* Cambridge, Mass.: MIT Press.

Marjit, Sugata, and Arijit Mukherjee. 1996. "Harassment, Corruption and Polarization." Discussion paper. Indian Statistical Institute, Economics Research Unit, Calcutta.

Melumad, Nahum, and Dilip Mookherjee. 1989. "Delegation as Commitment: The Case of Income Tax Audits." *Rand Journal of Economics* 20 (2): 139–63.

Melumad, Nahum, Dilip Mookherjee, and Stefan Reichelstein. 1992. "A Theory of Responsibility Centers." *Journal of Accounting and Economics* 15: 445–84.

———. 1995. "Hierarchical Decentralization of Incentive Contracts." *Rand Journal of Economics* 26 (4): 654–72.

Meyer, Margaret, and Dilip Mookherjee. 1987. "Incentives, Compensation, and Social Welfare." *Review of Economic Studies* 54 (April): 209–26.

Mookherjee, Dilip, and Ivan Png. 1995. "Corruptible Law Enforcers: How Should They Be Compensated?" *Economic Journal* 105 (January): 145–59.

Mookherjee, Dilip, and Stefan Reichelstein. 1997. "Budgeting and Hierarchical Control." *Journal of Accounting Research 35 (2): 129–55.*

Morishima, Michio. 1982. *Why Has Japan Succeeded?* Cambridge: Cambridge University Press.

Qizilbash, Mozaffar. 1994. "Bribery, Efficiency Wages, and Political Influence." Discussion paper. University of Southampton, Department of Economics, United Kingdom.

Reichelstein, Stefan. 1992. "Constructing Incentive Schemes for Government Contracts." *Accounting Review* 67 (4): 712–31.

Sanchez, Isabel, and Joel Sobel. 1993. "Hierarchical Design and Enforcement of Income Tax Policies." *Journal of Public Economics* 50: 345–69.

Stiglitz, Joseph. 1996. "Some Lessons from the East Asian Miracle." *The World Bank Research Observer* 11 (2): 151–77.

Tirole, Jean. 1986. "Hierarchies and Bureaucracies: On the Role of Collusion in Organizations." *Journal of Law, Economics and Organization* 2 (2): 181–213.

———. 1994. "The Internal Organization of Government." *Oxford Economic Papers* 46 (1): 1–29.

Wade, Robert. 1990. *Governing the Market: Economic Theory and the Role of the Government in East Asian Industrialization*. Princeton, N.J.: Princeton University Press.

World Bank. 1993. *The East Asian Miracle: Economic Growth and Public Policy*. A Policy Research Report. New York: Oxford University Press.

———. 1995. *Bureaucrats in Business: The Economics and Politics of Government Ownership*. A Policy Research Report. New York: Oxford University Press.

Comment on "Incentive Reforms in Developing Country Bureaucracies: Lessons from Tax Administration," by Dilip Mookherjee

Barry Nalebuff

Dilip Mookherjee's article begins with a basic truth: incentives matter. If a government is not careful in designing its tax collection scheme, tax collectors will not work hard. And whatever work they do may be aimed at lining their own pockets. What is to be done?

Mookherjee's article starts by accepting the status quo as the game and then finding the best way to play it. A stylized model is written down and solved. While the resulting comparative statics are all internally consistent (within the model), in a larger sense they are misleading and misguided.[1] For example, the model concludes that corruption is valuable since it encourages effort by tax collectors. This effort, in turn, motivates citizens to be more honest in reporting their income—an honest person has less to fear from a corrupt inspector. Thus corruption promotes honesty.

I could not disagree more. The goal of incentive reform is not to come up with an optimal level of corruption as an incentive device. The goal is to recognize that incentives matter and that we have to find a way to motivate tax collectors—specifically, one that is not based on bribes and corruption. The solution to the problem does not come from optimizing the parameters of the model and finding a new, improved equilibrium to the wrong game. Getting the right answer requires changing the game.[2]

There are at least three fundamental problems with a bribery-based incentive system. First, we care about the means as well as the ends. A system built on bribery is noxious. It is unrealistic to expect that the sphere of bribery will be limited to one sector of the economy. When it metastasizes to the police and the judiciary, the result will be a loss of property rights and a destruction of incentives on a much larger scale. Even on a pragmatic level the most successful income tax reporting schemes are those that promote a culture of honesty, even where such honesty appears not to be in a taxpayer's economic interest. Allowing bribery will destroy much of the goodwill that supports the system.

Barry Nalebuff is Milton Steinbach Professor of Economics and Management at the Yale School of Management.

Annual World Bank Conference on Development Economics 1997
©1998 The International Bank for Reconstruction and Development / THE WORLD BANK

Second, as a practical matter it is impossible to optimize or even manage underground activities such as bribery. Because underground activities are by nature unreported, there are no reliable tools for measuring performance.

Most important, there are better alternatives. Both theory and practice tell us that bribery is not the optimal incentive device. The good news is that many countries have developed innovative and successful incentive schemes, as Mookherjee indeed notes. His discussion of practical considerations in the design of incentive schemes focuses not on adjusting the parameters of a flawed system but on changing the whole system. He uses results from procurement theory and principal-agent theory to build on common sense. There is much to learn from the radical reforms undertaken by Brazil, Mexico, and Peru, as well as from the mistakes of India, especially when examined from an economist's perspective of incentives.

Lessons and Unanswered Questions

What are the important lessons regarding the design of a tax collection scheme, and what are the unanswered questions?

In the absence of any alternative scheme for motivating tax auditors to work and to be honest, a bribery scheme might naturally arise. If tax collectors are not motivated to work, taxpayers will have a strong temptation to underreport income, creating an opportunity for "frontier justice." Tax collectors will find dishonest taxpayers and punish them by forcing them to share some of their gains from underreporting.

How can this be stopped? A pessimist might argue that until corruption is eliminated at all levels, there is no solution. I am more of an optimist. Economic models rarely distinguish between what people know and what they know about what others know. The models typically assume "common knowledge." For example, when I know something, we assume that this fact is common knowledge. If I know something, you know that I know it (even if you do not know just what it is that I know), and I know that you know that I know it, and so on.

At first glance the assumption of common knowledge appears innocuous. It does not rule out private information. I may know my ability, and you may not have that information. The assumption of common knowledge simply means that we both have a common understanding of the information structure. This assumption would break down if I knew my ability and you knew that I knew, but I did not know whether you knew that I knew. If you did not know that I knew my own type, you would not expect me to signal, and hence I might not signal.

What this simple example is meant to illustrate is that a failure of common knowledge is very much like saying that the two parties are not quite sure what game they are playing. For economists, that is an uncomfortable assumption. We like to know what game we are playing. But uncertainty about the nature of the game is a fact of life and can dramatically impair—or enhance—how the game is played.

Offering bribes is a tricky business, since people want to offer a bribe only if it is likely to be accepted. If they are not sure what game they are playing, they might well choose not to play.

We do not need everyone to be honest to discourage bribery. Eliminating common knowledge of dishonesty will go a long way. Consider an interaction between A, a dishonest taxpayer, and B, a dishonest tax inspector. A would be willing to offer a bribe, and B would be willing to accept it. But what if dishonesty were not common knowledge? Neither party knows whether the other is honest or dishonest. If the corrupt taxpayer offers a bribe to an honest inspector, the taxpayer is now guilty of a potentially much more serious crime, trying to bribe an official. Thus each waits for the other to make the first move, and neither one does. Corrupt and corruptible individuals may act a lot less corruptly if they are put in an environment in which there is some uncertainty about who knows what about whom.

In fact, B could know that A is dishonest—A misreported income, for starters—and solicit a bribe. But unless A knows that B is dishonest, A might be worried about entrapment. And even though taxpayer A appears to be dishonest, perhaps there is an alternative explanation. Or A could get religion about honesty when it is expedient. If the bribery solicitation is unwelcome, A could claim that the tax official is on the take and threaten the official with exposure unless the bribe is substantially reduced. Of course, this is a high-stakes poker game, since taking the official to court may expose A's own underreporting. But if the courts are lenient with those who expose corruption, the threat may well be credible. It may also be possible to turn in the corrupt inspector anonymously, in which case the threat becomes even more credible. The inspector could even be exposed years later, since corrupt behavior is likely to persist over time.

In the United States we hear about similar games played between speeding motorists and state troopers. It is usually a bad idea to attempt to bribe a state trooper to avoid a speeding ticket. While it might work on some occasions, the consequences can be much worse than the speeding ticket if you guess wrong. As a result some motorists act in ways that can be interpreted ambiguously, such as including a $20 bill inside the registration papers to see whether the trooper bites. But ambiguity is by definition ambiguous. If everyone understands that including a $20 bill with the registration papers is a bribery attempt, then doing so exposes the motorist to the wrath of an honest trooper. And what does the motorist say if the trooper asks, "Is this $20 for me?" Is the motorist being set up or let off? If the action is not clearly understood, it will sometimes be misread, and the two sides will miss an opportunity to transact.

My larger point is that when a system is based on corruption, it is hard to keep it a secret. When the equilibrium of a game is a corrupt system, everyone—including the World Bank—knows this fact and knows that everyone knows it. While it may not be possible to remove all corrupt individuals from the system, it seems less daunting to start by working to break the atmosphere of common knowledge. The promise of reform (and the infusion of some honesty) means that people are no longer sure of what game they are playing. By working hard to break the perception of corruption, it is possible to influence the reality and thereby reinforce the altered perceptions.

There are relatively simple ways to make accepting a bribe even more costly. Tax auditors could be required to work in teams of two, and personnel could be rotated across teams. Then, not only does the bribe have to be split two ways, but each person also has to be confident that the other is on the take. Even if dishonest ones think that they know who is who, a well-placed offer of amnesty can bring down a corrupt group.

Evidence of corruption could be sought out. Mookherjee uses as an example of corruption the practice in India of paying low-level officials to make one's returns disappear altogether. At one level this works perfectly—there is no evidence of a crime; hence there is no crime. But at a higher level it is a dead giveaway: the physical absence of a return is a tipoff that something is amiss.[3]

Reformers should recognize and take advantage of the fact that some people will act honestly without regard to economic incentives. Feinstein and Erard (1994) show that a tax compliance game that takes account of even a small number of naturally honest taxpayers leads to a fundamentally different equilibrium.[4] That equilibrium makes it harder for dishonest people to hide and provides valuable benchmarks.

There are also some naturally honest bureaucrats. Mookherjee refers to Michel's Iron Law of Bureaucracy—that 10 percent of officials do 90 percent of the work. Those 10 percent can be used to break the chain of common knowledge. They also can be used to create benchmarks by which to judge the performance of the other 90 percent. The existence of even a few honest tax auditors will reveal what can be found through diligent and honest auditing. Those 10 percent can be a powerful lever that helps lift the entire system. Thus before we worry about how to motivate the other 90 percent, we should be sure that we have created an environment in which the easiest people to motivate—those who consider honesty to be its own reward—are not punished for their honesty. And yet, as those who have volunteered for committee work well know, all too often "no good deed goes unpunished."

Honest auditors who know that the most senior people are taking bribes will be discouraged and look for other types of work. They may even be fired for being honest. No incentive scheme will work if the person designing and implementing the scheme has corruption as a goal. One suspects from the tales of woe coming from Mookherjee's description of India's system that corruption is encountered at every level. Drug enforcement officers and tax officials have much to learn from each other.

A Return to Some Practical Considerations

In my final comments, I would like to discuss some of the excellent practical considerations Mookherjee raises. One particularly promising approach is to have tax inspectors set quotas for themselves, with achievement rewarded through bonuses. Higher quotas lead to higher bonuses. A comparison of tax auditors will show what is and what is not possible. Laffont and Tirole (1986) have shown the success of this type of incentive design in procurement and defense contracting. Similarly, rewards to auditors based on relative rather than absolute performance will mitigate the difficulty of measuring the effort of tax collectors (Nalebuff and Stiglitz 1983; Lazear and Rosen 1981).

How should the overall effectiveness of an audit scheme be judged? Mookherjee is right to emphasize that the success of tax auditing cannot be judged by how much money it brings in. Nor can a district attorney be judged by the number of convictions obtained in court.[5] The reasons are similar. If the tax collection scheme is well designed, there will be little cheating and hence slim pickings from auditing. An auditing system that raises a lot of money suggests that there is a much larger problem to be dealt with.

Mookherjee is also right to warn about going too far in attempting to create incentives for auditors to find unreported income. Excess or poorly designed incentives can lead to overzealousness. We have to worry about tax collectors making false accusations of unreported income in order to collect bonuses on assessments. One solution is to provide taxpayers with a separate auditor to whom to appeal any judgment made by the initial tax agent. Any tax agent who falsely overreports a person's income should be punished (or even dismissed). Mookherjee discusses how this type of cross-checking system was instituted by Mexico with great success.[6]

Brokerage houses have a similar problem of overreporting income in order to collect bonuses. They understand the need to separate agent and auditor. Barings Bank's billion dollar losses were caused by allowing one person to make trades and to audit those same trades.

Fortunately, it may not be as easy to make up unreported income as it is to hide actual income. In the United States, for example, a taxpayer could fail to disclose certain income, such as capital gains (since original stock purchase prices are not reported to the government). It is harder for an auditor to falsely inflate a taxpayer's true capital gains, since the fraud could easily be revealed by the taxpayer's records.

In conclusion, the theoretical literature on the principal-agent problem may have some of its most important applications when it comes to the design of a tax system. Along with the problem of designing a tax system that gives people an incentive to work, we need to be concerned about taxpayers' incentives to circumvent the system. And we must be concerned with the incentives of bureaucrats to carry out the game they have put in place. Without well-designed incentives for the employees of a tax collection agency, nothing else is likely to work.

Notes

1. On a technical level, many of the comparative statics are counterintuitive. In the model, for example, increasing the bonus rate for uncovering hidden income increases the tax collector's private benefit from monitoring. One might therefore expect the amount of monitoring to increase. But increasing the bonus rate increases the cost to dishonest taxpayers of getting caught, since they must pay higher bribes to compensate the auditor for the lost bonus. Since (for some parameters) the only equilibrium of the model is in mixed strategies, the taxpayer must be kept indifferent between cheating and reporting honestly. Thus in the new mixed-strategy equilibrium, the tax official must actually audit less often in order to keep the taxpayer indifferent. This counterintuitive comparative static result is a common feature of a mixed-strategy equilibrium. In a more complicated model with a distribution of types, the result would be a pure-strategy equilibrium, and this unfortunate result would likely disappear. The counterintuitive comparative static results are an artifact of trying to keep the model simple. But if an oversimplified model gives misleading results, what is the point of the model?

2. This point reflects a larger critique of much of modern game theory. The focus is often on finding the equilibrium to a particular game as opposed to asking the larger question: is this the right game? Of course, designing a game is simply playing a meta-game, the game of what game to play. Although this

may sound like a semantic argument, the tools of game theory are more powerful when applied to designing games than to merely solving them (see Brandenburger and Nalebuff 1996).

3. The return can still be retrieved if taxpayers are required to keep their own records for the period during which audits may be performed.

4. When the fraction of honest taxpayers rises, the tax authorities can afford to audit a larger percentage of low-income returns while still auditing the same percentage of total returns. If the tax administration audits a larger percentage of low-income returns, greater honesty implies fewer low-income returns and therefore more resources available to audit all other returns. Thus greater audit frequency induces less cheating by dishonest taxpayers. Another nice feature of the model is that the auditing frequency and cheating strategies now depend on the distribution of income (since the distribution of income affects the distribution of honest reports); without honest taxpayers, the equilibrium is independent of the income distribution (see Reinganum and Wilde 1985).

5. Since most guilty defendants will accept a plea bargain, those cases that go to trial will consist of defendants who are innocent or are at least confident in the prosecutor's inability to prove their guilt.

6. The response in the model is to argue that the corrupt auditor will overstate income by a sufficiently small amount that the cost of the appeal is not justified by the money to be gained. Of course, this need not be so if a person who wins such a case is also reimbursed for legal (and other) costs incurred in making the appeal. But even without this complication, finding this indifference amount is likely to be a practical impossibility for the corrupt auditor, since some victims may have a low cost of suing. In particular, a person who honestly reports all income, even without an economic incentive to do so, could as easily report a dishonest auditor, even without an economic incentive to do so.

References

Brandenburger, Adam, and Barry Nalebuff. 1996. *Co-opetition*. New York: Currency/Doubleday.

Feinstein, Jonathan, and Brian Erard. 1994. "Honesty and Evasion in the Tax Compliance Game." *Rand Journal of Economics* 25 (1): 1–20.

Laffont, Jean-Jacques, and Jean Tirole. 1986. *A Theory of Incentives in Procurement and Regulation*. Cambridge, Mass.: MIT Press.

Lazear, Edward, and Sherwin Rosen. 1981. "Rank Order Tournaments as Optimum Labor Contracts." *Journal of Political Economy* 89 (5): 841–64.

Nalebuff, Barry, and Joseph Stiglitz. 1983. "Prizes and Incentives: Towards a General Theory of Compensation and Competition." *Bell Journal of Economics* 14 (1): 21–43.

Reinganum, Jennifer, and Louis Wilde. 1985. "Income Tax Compliance in a Principal-Agent Framework." *Journal of Public Economics* 26 (February): 1–18.

Comment on "Incentive Reforms in Developing Country Bureaucracies: Lessons from Tax Administration," by Dilip Mookherjee

Mary M. Shirley

Dilip Mookherjee's analysis of incentive reforms in tax administration provides an excellent sense of the problems and potential of such schemes for improving the performance of public bureaucracies. These problems are not unique to central governments. Many of the challenges to incentive reforms that Mookherjee mentions are similar to our findings from research on the use of performance contracts to improve the productivity of state-owned enterprises (see Shirley and Xu 1997a, b). Moreover, some of the problems he cites under the heading of "practical considerations" are well established in the theoretical literature on incentive contracts in private hierarchies (for a review see Miller 1993). Mookherjee's model would be enriched if some of these practical considerations were incorporated into his theoretical treatment as well.

I would like to expand on two of the problems he identifies—information and commitment—and explain why I think they may be especially difficult to overcome in designing incentive contracts for public bureaucracies.

Information

The problem of information asymmetry—which exists when agents hold private information that allows them to act opportunistically—is common to most contracts, public or private. But I contend that public policy compounds the information problems in government bureaucracies. In our research on performance contracts we found that government increased the information advantage of state enterprise managers over their monitors by setting many different goals that changed with changes in political fortunes (Shirley and Xu 1997a, b). This enabled the managers to negotiate targets that could be achieved without any increase in their effort or in the enterprise's productivity.

In the case of tax administration, tax collectors' information advantage over their supervisors is increased by policy decisions that make the tax code more complicated or

Mary M. Shirley is chief of the Finance and Private Sector Development Division in the Policy Research Department at the World Bank.

Annual World Bank Conference on Development Economics 1997
©1998 The International Bank for Reconstruction and Development / THE WORLD BANK

change it frequently. Tax reforms that simplify the code, eliminate low-return taxes, and reduce the number of filers can reduce information asymmetry and make it easier for monitors to judge whether collectors have earned their incentives. These reforms, however, are often contrary to the interests of political decisionmakers, as I discuss below.

Technology can help reduce information problems, although technological advances can also be undermined by political decisions. Computerization has tremendous potential to ease the problem of monitoring tax collectors, much as it has improved private contracting by making verification of product delivery and quality cheaper, contributing to such innovations as just-in-time inventories. One way computerization can do that, as Mookherjee points out, is by allowing supervisors to compare tax collection and cost patterns across tax collectors, over time, and against benchmarks.

Computers can also help by simplifying tax collection, which reduces the extent to which collectors have to be monitored (or, for that matter, motivated). For example, when Colombia computerized its tax system in 1986–88, it introduced cross-checks that allowed revenue officials to identify obvious cases of underreporting (Vazquez-Caro, Reid, and Bird 1992). The new system automatically sent letters to encourage taxpayers to correct their statements voluntarily, thereby reducing their penalties and interest, which increase with each round of investigation. These letters reduced the number of audits—and saved the government considerable sums, since the cost of the audits averaged 80 percent of the additional revenues they generated before appeals and only about a third of appeals were decided in favor of the tax agency. While the remaining audits were usually more complicated (since the easily identified cases had been eliminated), the smaller number facilitated monitoring because the number of collectors and supervisors was not reduced.[1] (The Colombian example also shows the importance of Mookherjee's suggestion that incentives be based on total collections, not just audit collections. Otherwise collectors will resist cost-saving measures such as efforts to increase voluntary compliance.)

The benefits of computerization may be reduced or even eliminated, however, if the government makes the tax code more complicated or changes it often. Government would not make such changes if it were interested mainly in enhancing revenue. But politicians are more likely than private owners to have objectives that conflict with maximizing net revenues. By its nature tax policy is intensely political. As different politicians with different constituencies take power, there are likely to be corresponding shifts in the tax code. These changes may inadvertently complicate the tax code, but complications may also be the intentional outcome of political bargains that powerful actors prefer not to reveal.

Furthermore, as tax collectors become more effective through computerization and other innovations, they are likely to face greater political interference, as powerful constituents lobby politicians for special protection against tax enforcement. Thus Hunter and Nelson (1995) found large differences in tax enforcement across U.S. states; for example, the share of a state's returns that were audited ranged from 0.79 percent in West Virginia to 4.0 percent in Alaska. After the U.S. Internal Revenue Service (IRS) greatly improved its efficiency through new computer programs beginning in 1969, the portion of a state's returns that were audited was significantly correlated with state representation on the U.S. Senate Finance Committee, reinforcing a finding of Weingast and Moran (1983) that political forces guide agency behavior in important ways.[2]

Would allowing tax collectors to set their own targets help reduce information asymmetries, as Mookherjee suggests? I doubt it. Our analysis of performance contracts with state enterprises did not find that self-targeting improved the productivity effects of the contracts (Shirley and Xu 1997b). Rather, managers in the sample used their information advantages to set targets that were easily achieved. In contrast, competition may help reveal information. Our research on the effects of performance contracts on a sample of 414 state enterprises in China suggests that auctioning incentive contracts was positively and significantly correlated with productivity growth; correlation for the 90 percent of the sample contracts that were not auctioned was negative (Shirley and Xu 1997a). Whether auctioning tax collection contracts would be politically feasible is another question. Since taxes are "compulsory, unrequited, nonrepayable contributions exacted by a government for policy purposes" (IMF 1986, cited in Stella 1993), the public and its representatives are likely to object to the idea, especially if government monitoring of its agents is perceived to be weak.

Commitment

In my view the problem that governments have in credibly committing to pay a promised incentive is not, as Mookherjee presents it, just one of several practical considerations. Rather, it is a major reason why incentive contracts are much more difficult to effect in public bureaucracies than in private hierarchies. True, private owners and managers have strong motivation to renege on incentive contracts with employees (see Miller 1993). But the problem is complicated in public hierarchies, especially in developing countries that lack a neutral enforcement mechanism not controlled by government and in which incumbents may not be able to credibly commit future administrations (Levy and Spiller 1996). Unlike private employees, public bureaucrats may not be able to threaten to sue employers who renege on a contract, or they may have good reason to doubt that courts would be neutral toward a suit against the government that appointed the judges. Even if the current government's commitment is enforced, many developing countries are highly unstable politically and have weak institutions with which to bind new administrations to honor the commitments of their predecessors.

The credibility of government promises to pay incentives to tax collectors is likely to prove politically sensitive, especially where monitoring is weak. Mookherjee points out that governments may find it politically difficult to make good on promised incentives if they lead to pay inequality or very high wages. I think the public may also find large incentive payments to tax collectors offensive, even where pay equality or high wages are not an issue. Taxes are a product of the state's exercise of its monopoly powers over compulsion, and are bound up in issues of rule of law and fairness (Stella 1993). While we economists can weigh the prospect of tax collectors choosing between large bribes and large incentives against the welfare gains from additional revenues, it would likely be much harder for politicians to support this argument. This may partly explain why relatively few countries use incentive pay for revenue officials and why tax farming disappeared.

A risk-averse tax collector might discount the promised incentive highly under such circumstances, and given the same probability of detection of corruption, opt instead for more certain payment in the form of a bribe. Consistent with Mookherjee's model, the net effect of incentive uncertainty may be to reduce the amount of the bribe needed to dominate the incentive, perhaps even to the level that prevailed before the incentive contract was introduced. Thus a government with low credibility could conceivably collect no additional revenues and see no reduction in corruption following the introduction of incentive contracts. Indeed, if tax collectors are allowed to self-select their targets in situations of high information asymmetry and low commitment, the revenues collected could even fall. Our studies of performance contracts in market economies and in China found that the productivity of state enterprises declined under similar circumstances (Shirley and Xu 1997a, b).

Conclusion

Despite these problems, I agree with Mookherjee: incentive reforms are worth considering as an experiment in public bureaucracies. New Zealand's experience in particular suggests that the scope for incentive contracting is much greater in public bureaucracies than previously thought. Considerably more research is needed to measure the effects of incentive reforms and to understand the political economy that leads governments to introduce and enforce them. Mookherjee's excellent article identifies many of the issues involved.

I also agree with Mookherjee that piecemeal reforms that focus on incentives alone will not work. Recent research on private hierarchies suggests that individual gain-sharing plans have mixed to no effects. In contrast, when combined with measures to induce norms of trust and cooperation among employees, incentive schemes based on team outputs were found to result in more production gains than were possible through incentive schemes alone. More research is needed to understand how such cooperative expectations and conventions arise in public hierarchies and how incentive reforms might reinforce—or perhaps reduce—their beneficial effects.

Notes

1. Computerization can also raise the returns from audits. Benefit-cost analysis of the U.S. tax system has shown that certain types of taxpayers are more likely to evade and allowed tax collectors to focus their efforts on cases with potentially higher returns (Hunter and Nelson 1995).

2. Hunter and Nelson's (1995) model, which is similar to the Weingast and Moran (1983) model of congressional dominance of government agencies, controls for efficiency variables that affect IRS auditing probabilities, such as the proportion of high-income taxpayers, taxpayers who itemize, farmers, and other variables.

References

Hunter, William J., and Michael A. Nelson. 1995. "Tax Enforcement: A Public Choice Perspective." *Public Choice* 82 (1–2): 54–67.

Levy, Brian, and Pablo T. Spiller. 1996. *Regulations, Institutions, and Commitment: Comparative Studies of Telecommunications.* New York: Cambridge University Press.

Miller, Gary J. 1993. *Managerial Dilemmas: The Political Economy of Hierarchy.* Cambridge: Cambridge University Press.

Shirley, Mary M., and Lixin Colin Xu. 1997a. "Determinants and Effects of Performance Contracts: Evidence from China." World Bank, Policy Research Department, Washington, D.C.

———. 1997b. "Information, Incentives, and Commitment: An Empirical Analysis of Contracts between Government and State Enterprises." Policy Research Working Paper 1769. World Bank, Policy Research Department, Washington, D.C.

Stella, Peter. 1993. "Tax Farming: A Radical Solution for Developing Country Tax Problems?" *IMF Staff Papers* 40 (1): 217–25.

Vazquez-Caro, Jaime, Gary Reid, and Richard Bird. 1992. "Tax Administration Assessment in Latin America." Regional Studies Program Report 13. World Bank, Latin America and the Caribbean Technical Department, Washington, D.C.

Weingast, Barry R., and Mark J. Moran. 1983. "Bureaucratic Discretion or Congressional Control? Regulatory Policymaking by the Federal Trade Commission." *Journal of Political Economy* 91 (October): 765–800.

Floor Discussion of "Incentive Reforms in Developing Country Bureaucracies: Lessons from Tax Administration," by Dilip Mookherjee

Sherwin Rosen (presenter from another session) said that an efficient tax administration—one that allows government to readily collect taxes from its citizens—is not enough. Attention also must be paid to what government does with the money it collects, and whether those activities are desirable.

Dilip Mookherjee (presenter) agreed that making tax collections more efficient is not always the answer. Still, he argued, most of the problems developing countries have with tax administration involve enforcement of direct taxes, such as income taxes. And because enforcement of direct taxes is weak, these countries rely on distorting and regressive production and trade taxes. Thus if tax reforms are intended to maintain the level of tax revenue, the structure of taxes needs to be changed to increase the role of direct taxes and decrease the role of production and trade taxes.

A participant agreed with Mookherjee's point about the importance of organizational reforms in tax administration but added that reforms must also take into account a country's institutional and political setting. If, for example, the tax administration is being used not to collect taxes but to harass members of opposition parties, then the incentive structure guiding promotions and pay raises is similarly misaligned. Mookherjee's proposed reforms, he said, would not work in that kind of setting.

A participant from the Carnegie Endowment for International Peace argued that reformers should consider not just the cost but also the desired form of the eventual tax administration. Russia, for example, has a number of independent tax authorities. The most demanding branch, the tax police, essentially comprises 40,000 former KGB agents working on commission. Rich, honest companies—such as foreign companies—pay the most taxes under this setup because they do not hide their wealth. Large, politically connected companies pay much less. Tax officials make hit-and-run attacks on the honest companies, essentially looting them. And because there are few legal safeguards protecting companies against such behavior, it is extremely difficult for companies to recover tax money once it has been taken. As a

---

This session was chaired by Gary L. Perlin, vice president and treasurer at the World Bank.

Annual World Bank Conference on Development Economics 1997
©1998 The International Bank for Reconstruction and Development / THE WORLD BANK

result companies are becoming less honest, tax revenues are falling, and production is suffering, because production is hard to hide.

A participant from the International Monetary Fund noted that discussions about tax reforms and incentive systems have been taking place for forty years. The main conclusion of these discussions has been that, whatever the merits of various incentive schemes, a tax administration's success is ultimately gauged by its ability to achieve an acceptable level of voluntary tax compliance. Achieving that goal requires that services be delivered to taxpayers and that audits be used to detect and prosecute noncompliant taxpayers. To ensure widespread compliance, audits must cover all types of taxpayers and all levels of income. If, as had been suggested, tax officials are allowed to keep a portion of the penalties they collect, they will have no incentive to audit small taxpayers. Thus, she concluded, tax officials require only the simplest of incentives: decent salaries and regulations stating that nonperforming or corrupt workers will be fired.

Mookherjee responded that incentives were important, but that they were talking about different kinds of incentives. For example, for audits to be effective, officials need to know what leads people to evade taxes in order to devise effective targeting mechanisms. And in order to step up prosecutions, one first has to figure out how to motivate tax officials to pursue noncompliant taxpayers and take them to court. Both issues, he said, clearly involve identifying and applying incentives.

Mookherjee said that he and Barry Nalebuff (discussant) had different views on the scale of needed reforms. In his article, Mookherjee said, he had prescribed piecemeal reforms. Nalebuff, by contrast, had proposed reorganizing the entire tax administration. Mookherjee believed that from a practical standpoint, his approach was more likely to succeed. Many of the debates on public finance, he said, contrast optimal theoretical approaches with less perfect but more practical approaches. But given the way governments work, most theory remains just that—theory. Wholesale reform may work if governments have the desire and the power to implement it. Such cases are, however, few and far between.

Nalebuff agreed that he and Mookherjee shared many views. However, Nalebuff said, he refused to accept the idea of fine-tuning a corrupt system. There is no point in trying to strengthen a system based on corruption, and no reason to avoid using disincentives to punish corrupt tax inspectors. Indeed, the focus should be on rewarding honest workers and punishing dishonest ones. If that approach fails or makes the system worse, then a new system is needed.

Responding to Mary Shirley (discussant), Mookherjee said that he believed that there was considerable scope for targeted administrative reform in countries with weak legal systems. Mexico, for example, had implemented changes in its tax administration that did not extend to the overall political or legal structure. Moreover, this is often the only viable approach for reformers. Although transparency, political constraints, and issues of fairness and the rule of law are important, many reformers can affect only their immediate surroundings, not the prevailing legal and political system.

Incentives, Efficiency, and Government Provision of Public Services

Sherwin Rosen and Bruce A. Weinberg

Modern economic development is invariably associated with forces that raise the market value of time for women and shift economic activity from the nonmarket and household sectors to the market sector. Because market activities are more easily taxed than are nonmarket activities, this shift enables and encourages greater government activity. At the same time, substitution of market for self-produced goods increases the demand on government to provide services such as education and medical care. Because women are more responsive to price and wage incentives, distortions associated with tax policies and government finance are more likely to affect women's labor supply than men's. Such efficiency considerations also dictate whether the government should provide services directly or indirectly. Data from several countries show that economic development is associated with women's greater participation in the labor force, that governments play a larger role in the economies of industrial countries, and that tax burdens are much larger in industrial countries.

Economic growth and development are associated with the development of markets, growing volumes of trade, an ever-increasing division of labor, and greater specialization of economic activities. Specialization raises personal productivity, the gains from trade, and living standards. It also widens the potential tax base and increases the potential for governments to redistribute income and directly provide goods. The growth of state activity in the economy is one of the most remarkable empirical facts of economic life in the twentieth century. But the state is also one of the least understood sectors of the economy.

The Family, the State, and the Growth of Social Services

To assess the economic consequences of state involvement in the economy, especially state provision of social services, we must first analyze the determinants of the econ-

Sherwin Rosen is professor of economics at the University of Chicago and senior fellow at the Hoover Institution. Bruce A. Weinberg is professor of economics at Ohio State University.

Annual World Bank Conference on Development Economics 1997
©1998 The International Bank for Reconstruction and Development / THE WORLD BANK

omywide division of labor between the nonmarket and household sectors and the market sector. Then we must establish how tax incentives and welfare policies affect those allocations. Whatever causal mechanisms describe the growth of the state and its slight downward drift in recent years, the fact is that the scope of collective economic activity is greatly constrained by the tax base.

There are, to be sure, exceptions and variations. For example, in ancient times collecting taxes was not absolutely necessary for raising an army. Recruits could be enlisted by the promise of pay by "piece rates"—personal claims against the spoils of war or from tribute. Today conscription is a form of direct taxation that greatly reduces the need to tax other members of the population, whereas financing a voluntary army, and one with expensive modern weapon systems, would be unthinkable without an elaborate system of general taxation. Another example: governments of highly state-directed economies have had to institute collective agriculture and state ownership of business to maintain control. But the negative effects on total production have limited state activities even there. The point is that general taxation is possible only if a significant portion of transactions can be taxed or if the severe negative effects of taxation on output can be controlled in other ways.

Economic activities that take place outside of formal markets and without transaction records usually cannot be taxed much. Thus the scope of government activity is limited in countries where much of economic life is organized informally. Perhaps that is why governments remained relatively small until the twentieth century. More important for our purposes, this simple fact is a major explanation (though not the only one) for the much lower levels of government economic activity in developing countries than in industrial countries.

Role of Nonmarket Activities

What are labeled nonmarket activities vary across time and place. In all societies a large share of economic activity takes place within households. Even in modern industrial economies the mostly unmeasured household sector probably accounts for more than half of economic production. Household services are self-produced by combining household producers' time with purchased inputs.

Household services tend to be labor-intensive. The rearing of children is one of the most important of these activities. Family time devoted to children has great economic value, both to parents and to children, in the skills and character that children acquire while growing up and in the lasting family ties that develop. Similar observations could be made about the care of elderly parents. Though few of us think about these activities in such terms, they contribute as much to standards of living as do material goods, even though they are difficult to measure and are not counted in official estimates of output and income. Of course, the size and extent of the nonmarket sector are themselves affected by taxes and the volume of state activity.

Citizens try to minimize taxation and to shift its burdens by moving transactions to the household, informal, and illegal sectors. For example, it is said that in many industrial countries income tax revenues (as a share of total income) could not get much larger, regardless of what tax rates might be set. Economists generally concur with the idea that the untaxed household sector, broadly considered, is a major component of nonmarket economic activity. For example, in the conventional analysis of the economic effects of income taxation, substitution away from labor (given the tax-induced wage reduction) and toward "leisure" is shorthand for self-production of goods within households. Minimal participation in the household sector by men explains why male labor supply is relatively wage inelastic.

Economists have estimated economic activity in the household sector, but estimation is difficult because market transactions are few and far between. Thus there are significant differences among the various estimates. Still, the estimates agree that the household sector is extremely large (Nordhaus and Tobin 1972; Thomas 1992; Quah 1993). If it rivals the size of the market sector in rich countries, it is much larger in developing countries (Usher 1968, 1980). Thus economic growth and development are associated with an increasing division of labor and greater market transactions in household production. Economic development and growth of the market for household goods generate an ever-greater volume of taxable activity—another reason that there is greater government involvement in the economic affairs of richer, industrial economies. The household increasingly becomes "monetized."

From Self-Production to Market Production

The size and extent of the household sector are largely determined by the role of women in the economy. The increasing market value of women's time is the primary reason for the growth of market elements in private and state-provided household services throughout the world. Rising wages and increasing work opportunities for women have raised the cost of staying at home to produce household services and have lowered the demand for such services. Fertility declines as women's labor force participation grows. Economic growth is increasingly associated with greater human capital requirements for people in the labor force. In each generation parents must invest more in their children—raising the cost per child and leading families to bear fewer children. Thus we observe the substitution of higher-quality children for larger numbers of children and a downward trend in fertility rates.

Development also makes market transactions more important. The increasing value of skilled labor requires that there be fewer children per family and that they be educated much more intensively than in the past. In poor countries, where the value of education is smaller and constrained by parents' personal wealth, there is less need for money for such purposes. Families are larger, and the relative productivity of time in the household is greater. Women participate much less in the labor market. But as these countries become wealthier, the same forces observed in the industrial world will bear on them. The demand for marketed household services provided by both the private and the state sector will increase.

Furthermore, technological improvements have made market production of many household services more efficient than self-production, at least in some parts of the world. Changing medical technology and longer lifespans have increased the productivity of and demand for formal medical and old-age services. The relative productivity of self-produced medical care and old-age services has declined greatly. These services are expensive in their intensive use of highly trained professionals and of increasingly sophisticated and expensive equipment and procedures.

As a final example, consider the relative costs and benefits of such traditional household activities as preparing food and washing clothes. In rich, modern, urban economies these activities have been increasingly marketed through the direct hiring of household services, installation of time-saving household machinery and appliances, and development of intermediate products (for example, in food processing). These changes have greatly reduced the time burden of self-production. But in poor, rural settings in the developing world these household tasks remain extremely onerous and time-consuming. They generate greater demand for women's household production over market production.

The monetization of the family and substitution of market for self- and family-provided household services will become increasingly important in the developing world. Taking industrial countries as the best indicators of what lies ahead reveals many different possibilities for allocations between government and a decentralized private sector on the one hand, and between direct provision and subsidization as alternative government allocation mechanisms on the other.

In poor countries, where women care for their own children today, we will increasingly see men and women taking care of and educating the children of other men and women, who in turn will care for the parents of those who are looking after their children. We are all specialists in our own realm, working for pay to hire other specialists to produce goods that we cannot produce as well by ourselves. We are all better off for it. The real choice is the extent to which these allocations will be centralized through the collective decisions of the state or decentralized through private decisions of families. But if in the process of development families are inevitably monetized, will they inevitably be "nationalized" (Lindbeck 1993), as in Scandinavian countries, where the state is a major player in the household sector and controls more than half of the typical family's expenditures?

Government Participation in the Economy

Providing public goods and stimulating the consumption of merit goods (goods whose consumption is deemed intrinsically desirable) are the classic economic justifications for government participation in the economy. This section addresses empirically three aspects of the government's economic role. First, it examines the importance of the government as a provider of economic goods and services. Because the welfare implications of directly providing services differ from those of financing services, the share of government spending on direct provision is compared with that on subsidies and transfers. Similarly, because government production of services may be less efficient than private production, the extent to which governments produce the services they provide is also examined. Second, to produce goods at a low cost, governments must finance expenditures through taxes.

Thus the tax burden imposed by government expenditures is also quantified. Third, government's role as a provider of two services, education and medical care, is examined more closely.

Throughout this section the government's economic role is measured using government expenditures relative to private expenditures—that is, the share of resources controlled either directly or indirectly by the government. Government involvement often takes the form of regulating the private sector; however, because there are no quantifiable measures of regulatory activity, we cannot study it.

Government Provision and Subsidization of Goods and Services

Because our main interest here is in the importance of government as a provider of economic services, defense expenditures and interest payments are netted out before calculating ratios of government disbursements to private consumption expenditures (see figure 1 at end of article). Military spending is left out because countries differ greatly in their defense expenditures, while interest payments are netted out to put the focus on provision of current services. Government transfers and subsidies are included because they affect the quantity and type of goods consumed.

Two strong patterns emerge. First, the government plays a larger role in the economy in industrial countries, particularly in Europe. The ratio of government disbursements to private consumption expenditures ranges from 0.15 or less in Bangladesh, India, Pakistan, and the Republic of Korea to between 0.4 and 0.7 in France, Germany, and the United Kingdom and 0.9 in Sweden. Government expenditures in Japan and the United States, while high compared with expenditures in developing countries, are lower than those in Europe (they were between 0.35 and 0.40 during the 1980s). Even excluding defense expenditures, government expenditures are half of private consumption expenditures in Israel, placing it at the same level as the European countries.

Second, there is a tendency for the size of government to increase over time. In Europe government growth was concentrated in the 1970s. Between 1970 and 1980 government size rose from 0.5 to 0.7 in Germany, from 0.6 to 1.0 in Sweden, and from 0.40 to 0.55 in the United Kingdom, and then stabilized or declined during the 1980s in Sweden and the United Kingdom. In the United States government expenditures grew rapidly between 1970 and 1975 before declining over the rest of the period. In Japan government expenditures grew from less than 25 percent of private consumption in 1970 to 36 percent in 1980, then stabilized during the 1980s. Among developing countries, governments grew significantly throughout the period in Colombia, Greece, India, the Republic of Korea, and Zimbabwe. In Iran the government grew dramatically during the oil boom of the 1970s, from 0.20 to 0.47, then fell to 0.17 in the 1980s. Venezuela, the other oil exporter in the sample, experienced rapid growth in government spending during the 1970s and a decline in the mid-1980s with the fall in oil prices.[1] Of all the sample countries, only Ecuador experienced a significant decline over the entire period.

The government may provide goods or services directly, or indirectly through transfers and subsidies. In general, direct provision is more costly. In providing goods directly, the government decides what goods and what quantity will be available—and individuals incur costs if they deviate from government-set levels. If the government provides schooling directly, for example, students are assigned to schools that meet for a set number of days a year and that have a set ratio of teachers to students and particular course offerings. Individuals must either accept what they are given or make other arrangements. Allowing individuals to choose providers enables them to obtain the services they value most highly at least cost. (Differences in the external benefits of the particular aspects of services provides a justification for subsidizing those aspects of services or regulating the options available to individuals without requiring government provision.) In addition, goods provided directly by the government may be produced less efficiently than privately provided goods because less competition for business reduces the incentives for efficiency in production and in the procurement of intermediate goods. Subsidizing individual purchases preserves competition among service providers.

Industrial countries tend to devote a greater share of government expenditures to transfers and subsidies (figure 2). But the variation here is noticeably smaller than the variation in the size of government. The share of transfers and subsidies ranges from a low of roughly one-third in Ecuador, Iran, the Republic of Korea, and Venezuela to one-half in France, Germany, Greece, Japan, Sweden, the United Kingdom, and the United States. The share of spending on subsidies and transfers is also relatively stable over time. In most countries that share varies by less than 10 percentage points over 1970–90. An exception is Japan, where the share increased from 45 percent in 1970 to 60 percent in 1990, with most of the growth occurring during the 1970s. Ecuador, Iran, and Venezuela also experienced large increases in the share of transfers. Zimbabwe experienced an increase during the 1970s and a large decline during the 1980s (from 60 percent to 10 percent).

The extent to which governments produce the services they provide can be determined using government value added (primarily a payroll measure) as a share of government direct consumption expenditures (figure 3). While the importance of the government as producer of services varies substantially—the government produces 40 percent of the services it provides in Israel and 90 percent in France—there is little relationship between government production and development. Compared with the other series, government production exhibits a high degree of stability over time.

If governments provide goods and services with little or no direct user costs, they must finance expenditures through taxes, which create economic distortions. (In addition, provision of goods at prices beneath their cost encourages people to overconsume government-provided goods.) The tax rate is determined by the present value of government spending relative to the present value of the economy's output. But the link between current disbursements and taxes is inexact because governments may defer current taxation and instead finance spending through borrowing. Figure 1 is relevant for determining the tax burden imposed by current government nondefense activities (that is, the costs of goods provided directly by the government, as well as transfers and subsidies). But in addition to financing current expenditures, taxes must be raised to cover interest on accumulated debt.

Two patterns are evident in the share of government consumption expenditures on defense (figure 4). First, defense spending tends to be relatively low in high-income countries and in Latin American countries (less than 20 percent of total government spending in both). The United States is an exception, with defense spending accounting for 30 percent or more of government spending. Israel and Pakistan stand out, devoting 55–80 percent of government spending to defense. Second, there has been a large decline in defense spending over time. This is true for the Western European countries, Greece, Israel, the Republic of Korea, Pakistan, and the United States (except during the Vietnam War and the early 1980s). Though low, defense spending has not declined among the Latin American countries. Defense spending rose in Zimbabwe during the 1970s, then declined in the 1980s. In Iran defense spending increased until the late 1970s, dropped until the mid-1980s, then rose again.

Interest payments do not contribute directly to the current provision of economic services but certainly contribute to the current tax burden (figure 5). In most countries debt service represents a small but increasing component of government spending. Interest payments are 20 percent or less of noninterest, nondefense expenditures in all the high-income countries in the sample. Japan, Sweden, and the United States experienced large increases in interest payments from the late 1970s to the mid-1980s. Interest payments also rose significantly in Ecuador, India, Israel, and Venezuela during that period. While low in the Republic of Korea, interest payments doubled between 1974 and 1987 before declining. By 1990 interest payments were 40 percent or more of government noninterest, nondefense disbursements in Greece and India. Interest payments are low and declining in Iran (already less than 10 percent of spending in 1970).

Tax Burdens

We measure the tax burden imposed by government activity using the ratio of government expenditures to GDP (figure 6). Inclusion of defense spending and interest payments raises the tax burden far beyond what is needed to finance current expenditures on economic goods and services. Yet measuring the size of government activity relative to total market activity—which includes government expenditures, capital expenditures, and net exports as well as private consumption expenditures—tends to lower the figures. As could be expected, tax burdens follow a pattern similar to that of noninterest, nondefense expenditures relative to private consumption (see figure 1). Tax burdens are high in Western Europe, averaging between 30 and 50 percent of GDP in France, Germany, and the United Kingdom and exceeding 60 percent in Sweden throughout the 1980s. As with noninterest, nondefense spending, the tax burden rose during the 1970s and stabilized or declined (in the case of Sweden and the United Kingdom) during the 1980s. Government expenditures rose somewhat in the early 1990s. The tax burden in the United States ranges between 30 and 35 percent of GDP throughout the period. Japan's tax burden rose from less than 15 percent of GDP in 1970 to 25 percent in 1990.

The tax burden is lower in most other countries. A notable exception is Israel, where high defense and interest payments raised government expenditures to 60 percent of GDP starting in the mid-1970s. Rapid growth in spending in Greece and Zimbabwe forced the tax burden up to Western European levels by the mid-1980s. While Bangladesh, Colombia, India, and Pakistan all experienced rapid increases in government spending, their tax burdens remained far lower than those in Western Europe. Given Korea's high capital expenditures and exports, government spending there rose only slightly relative to GDP. Venezuela experienced rapid growth in government spending during the 1970s and declines during the 1980s. The tax burden also declined during the 1980s in Iran.

Education Expenditures

In most countries education expenditures account for 20–30 percent of government consumption expenditures (figure 7). The share of spending on education is closer to 40 percent in Israel, Japan, the Republic of Korea, the United States, and Zimbabwe. Education expenditures also tend to be high (30–40 percent of government consumption spending) in Latin America. Bangladesh, Greece, and India devote the smallest portion of government resources to education (10–20 percent). The share of government spending on education declined throughout the 1970s and 1980s in Sweden and the United Kingdom and during the 1980s in Germany and Japan. An increasing share of government resources was devoted to education in India, Iran, Venezuela, and Zimbabwe.

The figures on the government share of total education consumption expenditures are striking in their uniformity (figure 8). In almost all countries government directly provides 75 percent or more of education services. In Greece, India, and Zimbabwe the share of education controlled by the government, initially small, has risen dramatically. France, the United Kingdom, and the United States show a decline in the share of education services provided by the government during the 1980s.

Medical Care Expenditures

The share of government consumption expenditures on medical care is highest in Western Europe, ranging from 20 percent in France (where the government also finances a large portion of medical expenditures through transfers and subsidies) to between 25 and 30 percent in Sweden up to 35 percent in Germany and the United Kingdom (figure 9). The share of government consumption devoted to medical care is much lower in the United States (less than 10 percent during the 1970s and 1980s) and is less than 5 percent in Japan. In Bangladesh, Colombia, Ecuador, India, Iran, and Pakistan less than 10 percent of government nondefense spending is devoted to medical care. (The large decline in the share of medical spending in Pakistan in 1979 was caused by a large drop in military spending after the establishment of an Islamic state.) Venezuela and Zimbabwe devote a large share of government expenditures to medical care by non–Western European standards (15–20 percent and 20–30 percent until the end of the 1980s).

To the extent that governments provide a large portion of medical services indirectly through transfers and subsidies to private providers, the figures on the share of medical consumption that governments provide directly understate their full role in financing medical services. In Germany, Sweden, and the United Kingdom the government provides about 80 percent of all medical care. In France the government directly provides 40 percent of medical expenditures (figure 10). The government plays a smaller role in the United States (directly providing 15 percent until the mid-1970s, with the share declining to 8 percent by 1989) and in Japan (7 percent). While in the 1970s government medical expenditures were a small fraction of total medical care in Greece, India, and Israel, this figure rose rapidly. The government plays a small direct role in medical care in the Republic of Korea (5 percent of the total), Colombia (17 percent), and Ecuador (22 percent), and a larger role in Iran (30 percent) and Venezuela (47 percent).

Labor Force Participation

Male labor force participation rates are close to 80 percent in most countries (table 1). Participation rates are somewhat higher in Bangladesh, India, Iran, and Japan (85–90 percent) and somewhat lower in Israel and the Republic of Korea (72 percent). In contrast to the uniformly high participation rates among men, participation rates for women are significantly lower and vary greatly. High-income countries have the highest participation rates for women, from 46 percent in Germany (in 1970) to 68 percent in Sweden. Participation rates are lowest in Islamic countries—Bangladesh (5 percent), Iran (14 percent in 1976), and Pakistan (3 percent). And participation rates are between these two extremes in Latin America (ranging from 20 percent in Ecuador to 31 percent in Venezuela), Greece (29 percent), and India (35 percent). In Korea, Israel, and Zimbabwe participation rates are closer still to those in the high-income countries (between 42 percent and 50 percent).

Public Finances and Tax Incentives

It is a well-studied and well-known proposition in public finance that the marginal social costs of financing collective choices are increasing (Hansson 1984). If services are financed through government taxes, the link between a person's claims to government-provided services and their direct costs is broken. Because everyone is sharing the production costs through general taxation, the private costs of these services appear to be much smaller than their true social costs. And since collective choices are invariably mediated through politics, the voting mechanisms that determine outcomes tend to conceal voters' true valuations and encourage excessive consumption

Table 1. Labor Force Participation
(percent)

Country, year	Men	Women
Sweden, 1980	81.0	67.5
United States, 1980	83.2	58.5
France, 1982	77.4	53.7
United Kingdom, 1981	83.3	52.1
Japan, 1980	86.1	51.6
Zimbabwe, 1982	81.3	49.8
Germany, 1970	82.8	46.2
Israel, 1983	71.7	45.1
Korea, Rep. of, 1980	71.9	41.5
India, 1981	89.3	35.1
Venezuela, 1981	79.5	31.0
Greece, 1981	80.2	29.0
Colombia, 1973	80.6	24.9
Ecuador, 1982	81.7	20.3
Iran, 1976	85.0	14.0
Bangladesh, 1981	85.3	4.5
Pakistan, 1981	82.5	2.6

Source: ILO various years.

of government-provided goods. In addition, the reduction in after-tax returns discourages participation in the taxable activities needed to finance public expenditures, ultimately limiting the extent to which goods can be publicly provided.

Decentralized private market transactions provide much tighter connections between the social costs of goods and a person's evaluation of their worth. Economic efficiency increases when consumers and producers take full responsibility for decisions that are in their best interests. But there is still a role for collective choice and government involvement. Decentralization results in underproduction of goods and services whose consumption or production confers external benefits on others, of goods for which technological conditions and information limitations make private transactions overly costly, and of goods (such as education) for which financial constraints unduly inhibit private choice. Individuals do not see or cannot exploit the full social costs and benefits of their economic actions, and efficient coordination of individual decisions is not achieved without government intervention. Collective decisions can improve matters in principle—if the collective choice mechanism elicits reasonably accurate value assessments from citizens.

Moreover, general tax financing of government services introduces distortions that can be offset by imposing taxes or subsidies in related markets. Still, the larger is the size of the public sector, the larger are the social costs of financing it. So the central question in thinking about the size and role of government involves weighing the benefits of collective decisions against their costs. Somewhere a balance is struck. The balance in Western Europe has favored a large role for the state in family and welfare services compared with that in other countries. These services come at the cost in much larger tax burdens.

How Taxes Affect Household Decisions

For the state to provide services that would otherwise be produced within households or through private markets, many ordinary, inherently personal activities must be reckoned in monetary terms, tax revenues must be raised to finance them, and complex rules and conditions must be imposed to limit undesirable side effects. The chief distortion arises from behavioral incentives to shift part of the private costs of household production onto others. Some of these adverse incentives can be held in check if they are recognized when policies are designed.

The marginal costs of household-produced goods are the most important economic determinant of household production and consumption decisions. These costs depend in turn on the market prices of purchased inputs and on the opportunity cost of using one's time to produce them rather than working in the market sector and hiring someone else to produce them (Becker 1965). Since the scope for substituting nonmarket production for market production among men is small in most countries, most of the economic action at the relevant margin occurs among women. For instance, a woman with small children might be able to earn a substantial salary at a market job and hire someone to look after her children during the day, she might forgo the job and look after them herself, or she might do some of both. Factors such as how much the job pays and how interesting it is, the costs of child care, and the value parents place on continuous contact with children determine this choice. An increase in wages or a decrease in the costs of child care makes paid market work more attractive and tends to increase the time devoted to market activities. This is what lies behind worldwide observations of higher wages, reduced fertility, and greater labor force participation among women.

In evaluating the economic efficiency of state tax policies, it is conventional practice to take expenditures as a given and trace how tax financing affects behavior (Harberger 1971; Atkinson and Stiglitz 1980). Income and sales taxes inevitably lower below its social value the marginal after-tax return to a person supplying labor to the taxable market economy. This difference—the tax wedge—represents the potential unit distortion. A tax's total distortion and efficiency cost is the unit distortion multiplied by the change in allocations that it generates. Thus the total efficiency loss depends on the extent to which individuals respond to price incentives, as well as on the magnitude of taxes. A small tax or subsidy can cause large efficiency losses if it provokes a substantial change in behavior. A large tax or subsidy will not cause large distortions if it does not change behavior very much.

An important example is the effect of taxes on the labor market decisions of women. When marginal tax rates are high, it may not pay for a woman to take a market job and hire child care, even when it is economically efficient for her to do so, because after-tax pay is not large enough to leave a surplus. In industrial countries reducing marginal tax rates and lowering the progressivity of joint returns (such as in the switch from family to individual returns in Sweden in the 1970s) substantially reduced the marginal taxes on women's earnings and increased their private return to working in the marketplace. Many more women entered the labor force as a result. Substantial empirical evidence suggests that women's labor supply is much more sensitive to economic incentives and conditions than is men's. Hence at that margin the efficiency losses due to taxation may be large.

How Subsidies Undermine Efficiency

Income and expenditure taxes inefficiently reduce market production of household services and encourage excessive self-production, especially by women. Since income taxes and sales taxes on purchased goods lower the private return to work below its social return, there is a clear second-best efficiency case for subsidizing certain marketed household products such as day care. Doing so economizes on family time allocations and leads to the production of household goods with efficient proportions of hired and own time (see, for example, Sandmo 1990 and Bergstrom and Blomquist 1996). But such subsidies enlarge the role of the state because they must be financed by even greater taxes on incomes, payrolls, or expenditures.

There is another, indirect effect of the second-best tax increase needed to achieve production efficiency: it reduces the marginal user costs of state-provided or tax-subsidized market household goods below their true social production costs and encourages excessive market production. Production of other kinds of goods is too small. Too many people are involved in the household production of other families, and too few in producing nonhousehold material goods and services. These distortions must be weighed against each other when assessing the economic consequences of family policies. It is generally in the social interest to scale back subsidies that eliminate production distortions in order to control the consumption distortions they provoke.

Detailed analysis yields a surprising result (see Rosen 1997). Suppose that when household subsidies are increased, income, payroll, and value-added tax rates are simultaneously increased to raise enough public revenue to pay for the subsidies. It can be shown that output and total time allocated to material goods production actually declines, while total time allocated to household production—one's own time and that of others—actually increases. State subsidies or direct provision of household services creates a kind of cross-hauling effect. People work more for one another to earn the taxable pay needed to help finance the subsidies that induce them to work for one another in the first place, rather than remain working for themselves in the tax-sheltered nonmarket household sector. Cross-hauling limits the efficient amount of such subsidies, and is the reason they must be bounded.

This analysis of the basic economics of government-provided social services suggests that in the aggregate such services at least partly replace what would have been purchased in other, more decentralized ways and without the associated tax burdens. These costs manifest themselves as incentives to overconsume subsidized government-provided goods and to engage excessively in personal activities that are beyond the reach of tax collectors. By reducing the links between personal contributions to production and claims on social output, these kinds of "welfare" policies encourage people to produce utility that does not have to be shared with others. The real household sector becomes too large on both counts. This unintended consequence imposes a burden on the welfare state model that so many newly reformed and developing economies appear to long for.

Public Provision, Privatization, and Regulation

Economists have analyzed extensively the distortions and incentive effects of government taxes and policies, but they have been much less willing to analyze how services should be provided. In part this is a result of theoretical limitations: the "theory of the firm" has served better as a metaphor for thinking about forces that affect the supply of goods to the market than as a metaphor for thinking about how firms are organized and operated. For instance, in the 1930s, when government responsibility for natural monopolies became well understood, there was little meaningful analysis of the comparative virtues of regulation or government ownership of public utilities. Many market-oriented economists favored state ownership. Even the old debates on socialism and capitalism were relatively silent about such details. And though economists recognized possible conflicts in separating ownership and control of large, widely held firms, little was made of these issues until recently.

Important political events and theoretical advances in the economics of information have changed our thinking. Perhaps more than ever in the period since World War II, there is now worldwide recognition, based on practical results, that decentralized decisionmaking often serves the public interest better than central government control. The increasing privatization of public utilities, airlines, and the like and the trend toward deregulation are not just momentary swings in ideological fashion and abstract theory. These changes are based on concrete empirical results. Government ownership and provision are almost always less efficient and less productive than more decentralized modes. Is there any doubt that the global decline in government control over business and the movement toward private enterprise and private initiative in economic affairs are part of these same forces?

Applying Agency Theory

The economic analysis of agency investigates how contracts can be written to align the interests of workers (agents) and their employers (principals). Given that altruism is limited, what makes it in an employee's self-interest to work on behalf of an employer's best interest? Some coordination is always needed to align common organizational goals with the selfish interests and incentives of individual members. Economists know a great deal about how decentralized market price systems align social interests with the self-interested actions of individuals, and what preconditions on preferences and technologies are needed for markets to function well. This is the whole point of the "invisible hand" and the essential logic of decentralization. But the very rationale for the existence of firms is to take economic transactions off the market—to substitute other control mechanisms in their place. And of course government involvement is sometimes justified in correcting market failures of one kind or another.

The formal apparatus of modern agency theory is built on the assumption of incomplete markets—the problem does not arise if there are enough prices and instruments (Hart and Holmstrom 1987). Market incompleteness usually comes from information differences between contracting parties. For instance, the person rendering a service (say, a mechanic) might know more about a problem than the person on the other side of the transaction (the car owner). Given the specification of why markets are incomplete and the availability of contractual instruments, it is often possible to describe the general features of incentives and contracts that make both parties as well off as possible. These solutions vary widely by problem and depend on the specification and on general institutional sanctions built into the legal, political, and social structure of society. For example, tolerance of official corruption and the sanctions against it vary widely throughout the world. For this reason it is difficult to make universal statements about the problem. Nevertheless, a couple of general points can be made that are relevant for thinking about government enterprises.

The first is that there is never an ideal solution in the Pareto optimal sense of complete coordination akin to the invisible hand. All solutions are "bad" in some sense. But some are worse than others. The second is that performance incentives must be built into contracts to achieve social efficiency. It is not possible to align the interests of selfish agents and their principals unless agents are rewarded for producing the desired behavior and outcomes or are punished for engaging in self-serving actions that do not work in the best interests of others (Lazear 1995). Some type of oversight is generally needed to achieve this outcome.

These points are not terribly far removed from the central idea in economics that people must see the full costs and benefits of their actions to perfectly align self-interest with social interest. In an important sense Pigouvian taxes and subsidies can solve agency problems. But in agency theory the main complication is that institutional and technological barriers make it impossible to cover every margin, so seeing full costs and benefits is not possible. Nevertheless, the basic logic is the same.

Making a Case for Indirect Provision

Two general phenomena tend to work against productive efficiency in government-owned enterprises: public enterprises serve the interests of many political constituents (including employees and the direct consumers of the services) and are usually insulated from competition. These points undermine the case for direct provision of services, tending to favor subsidies or regulation of private agencies. The monopoly position of government enterprises makes them less likely to face the trials and tribulations of open competition. Nor do they have to cater to the interests of final users as normal businesses do. For that reason oversight is much more difficult.

The first point, that public enterprises serve diverse constituencies, is closely related to the problem of soft budget constraints (Kornai 1986) and insulation from the financial distress that disciplines nonpublic enterprises. From a strictly theoretical perspective it is difficult to see why regulation would dominate government ownership. After all, the government is the principal in both cases. And regulated monopolies are subject to the capture problem—suppliers can sometimes manipulate the regulatory process to serve their own interests rather than the public interest. Yet empirically there appears to be little contest between the two forms. Regulated firms tend to be run much more efficiently than comparable government enterprises. They tend to produce higher-quality services at lower cost. For instance, regulated utilities manage with many fewer employees and smaller payrolls, and innovate more often.

One reason is that a greater division of labor in the oversight function often yields better results. It is more difficult for political interests to police themselves when they are both principal and agent. Elaborate bureaucracies, rules of procedure, and red tape are required to prevent conflicts of interest under such circumstances. But these methods are often more costly than direct, decentralized oversight from capital markets and shareholders, as well as political oversight of the regulators. The greater efficiency in transacting that motivates organizations to internalize activities without recourse to markets also motivates employees bent on serving their own purposes when principal-agent roles are mixed.

No doubt, other reasons could explain the empirical results. And there are important exceptions to these statements—cases where public ownership has achieved excellent results. As noted earlier, throughout the world the bulk of education services are state-provided. Some of these systems work extremely well. Two factors appear to be essential when they do. First, a large share of the returns to education are captured by the individual, increasing the incentives for customers to oversee quality. Education is a mix of a private and a public good, and the private component is important enough for consumers to monitor performance.

Second, decentralization—elementary and secondary education is invariably provided by local governments—often allows consumers to act on their information. The main advantage claimed for privatization and voucher programs in public education is that greater choice by parents will provide better oversight than the current system. It is not surprising that many of the most successful privatizations (for example, airlines and telephone service) have been in industries whose products have strong elements of private goods. In the case of public goods the incentives for individual oversight are weaker, the costs are certainly higher, and the oversight gains from competition among providers are usually much smaller.

These observations about oversight have been curiously overlooked in most analyses of the agency problem (Sah and Stiglitz 1986 and Sah 1991 are exceptions), perhaps because agency theory has been preoccupied with the structure of contracts within organizations, not with interactions between organizations and customers. The beauty of competition is that it is the ultimate form of oversight. This is also the reason privatization and property rights may not achieve dramatic results if they are not accompanied by the easing of constraints on entry and openness. Government enterprises are insulated from competitive pressure. They do not allow customers to "vote with their feet" (Tiebout 1991), except at an exorbitant cost. They tend to be slower to change practices and adopt cost-reducing innovations because sharp competitors and superior alternatives are not around to discipline them. The current trend toward more open, competitive provision through privatization is well grounded in economic logic. The wonder is, why has it been so long in coming? Developing countries are well advised to take a cue from what it has taken industrial countries many years to learn.

Conclusion

Modern economic development is invariably associated with forces that raise the market value of time for women, reduce fertility and family size, and shift economic activity from the nonmarket and household sectors to the market sector. Since market activities are more readily taxed than household activities, this shift to the market sector reduces the tax burdens generated by government activity and tends to encourage more of it. At the same time, the substitution of market for self-produced household goods increases the demand for governments to provide services such as education, medical care, and retirement programs. Data from a variety of countries reveal that economic development is associated with greater female labor force participation, that governments play a larger role in the economies of industrial countries (especially in Europe), and that tax burdens are much larger in industrial countries. The government is the primary provider of education services in almost all countries, but plays a greater role in providing medical care in industrial countries.

We considered the two main efficiency and productivity issues associated with government provision of such services. One is the traditional distortions (deadweight losses) associated with tax policies and government finance. These distortions are likely to be more important for women than for men because women's labor supply is more responsive to price and wage incentives. Specifically, tax and other policies associated with subsidized government social services can cause excessive substitution of market-provided household goods through the formal government sector for self-provided household goods in the traditional household sector. In some cases government policies actually cause production of material goods to fall, with more people and resources engaged in the production of household services than of other goods and services. But policies can be designed to deal with these kinds of substitutions.

We also considered some general issues in the provision of government services. Basic economic logic presumes a bias against direct provision by public enterprises and in favor of subsidies and regulation of the private sector. Though agency problems are present in all organizations, they are especially acute in the government sector because oversight often is much more diffused and activities are more difficult to monitor. For these reasons direct government provision of services tends to be less efficient.

The gains to indirect provision are highest when greater oversight of nongovernment agencies is possible and monitoring costs are small or self-enforcing. Private providers can be effectively monitored by the public when producer liability for unacceptable outcomes is easier to assess (for example, in the case of road construction and some other public works) or when stockholders provide financial monitoring that reduces the tendency to rely on a soft budget constraint, evident with direct government provision. And when government-subsidized goods are largely private in nature, customers can often monitor outcomes. Choice among providers disciplines private suppliers to work in the public interest. In such cases local government control can sometimes compete with subsidies to private producers on efficiency criteria. But legal institutions and tolerance for corruption affect all these issues. Empirically, indirect provision through transfers and subsidies accounts for a larger share of government involvement in industrial countries.

Appendix. Data Description

The data on economic activity are from the United Nations, *National Accounts Statistics: Main Aggregates and Detailed Tables* (for 1981, 1986, and 1992) and *Yearbook of National Accounts Statistics* (for 1967, 1970, and 1975). We use direct data on government final consumption expenditures (on defense, education, medical care, and total) and private final consumption expenditures (on education, medical care, and total). In addition to government final consumption expenditures, total current disbursements by government include payments to property income (interest, rents on land but not improvements, and transfers and subsidies). For most countries total current disbursements are calculated by subtracting net savings from the sum of total current disbursements and net savings. For Bangladesh, India, Pakistan, and Zimbabwe direct data on current disbursements are available and are used instead. Transfers and subsidies are calculated by subtracting consumption expenditures and payments to property income from total disbursements. Interest payments are measured using payments to property income. In a few cases the series exhibit breaks between sources. Rather than adjusting the series, we use the reported figures. Data on labor force participation are from the International Labour Office, *Yearbook of Labour Statistics*, 1945–89. We use the fraction of the population that is economically active.

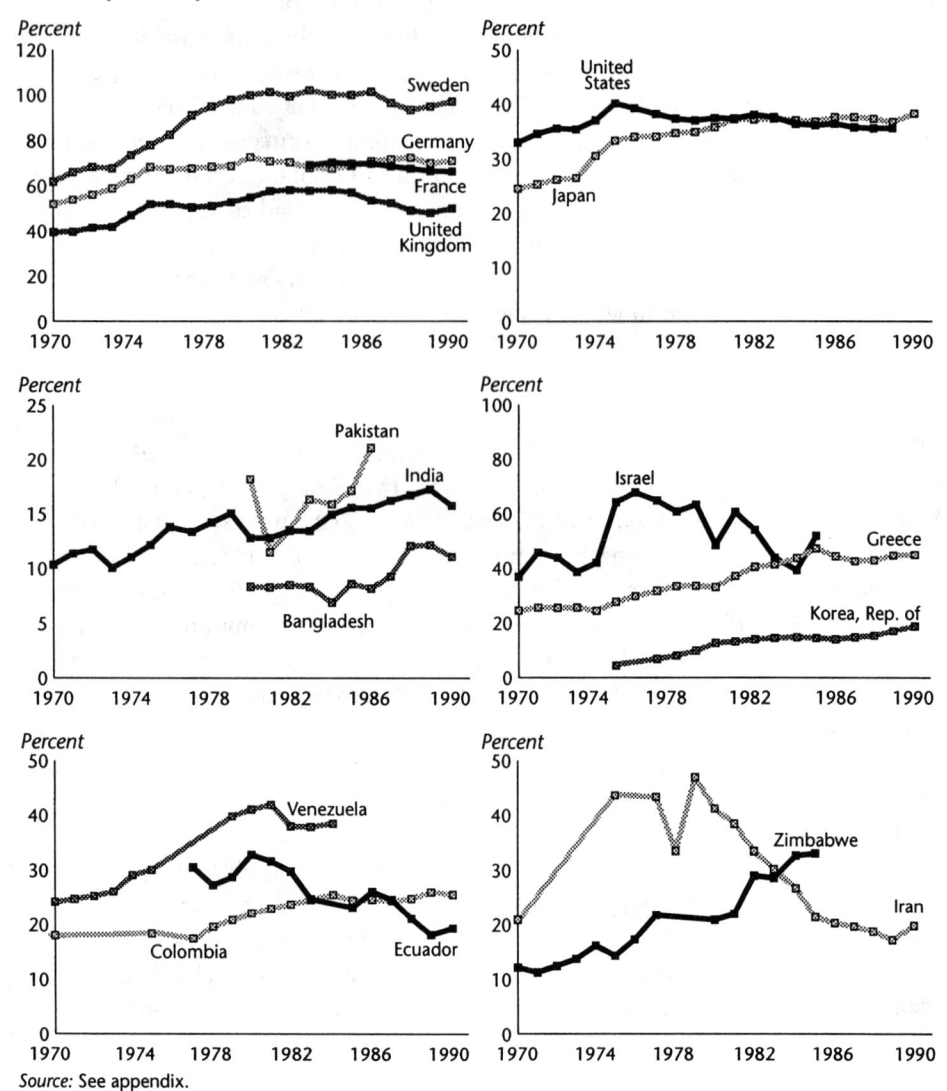

Figure 1. Government Noninterest, Nondefense Disbursements as a Share of Private Consumption Expenditures, 1970–90

Source: See appendix.

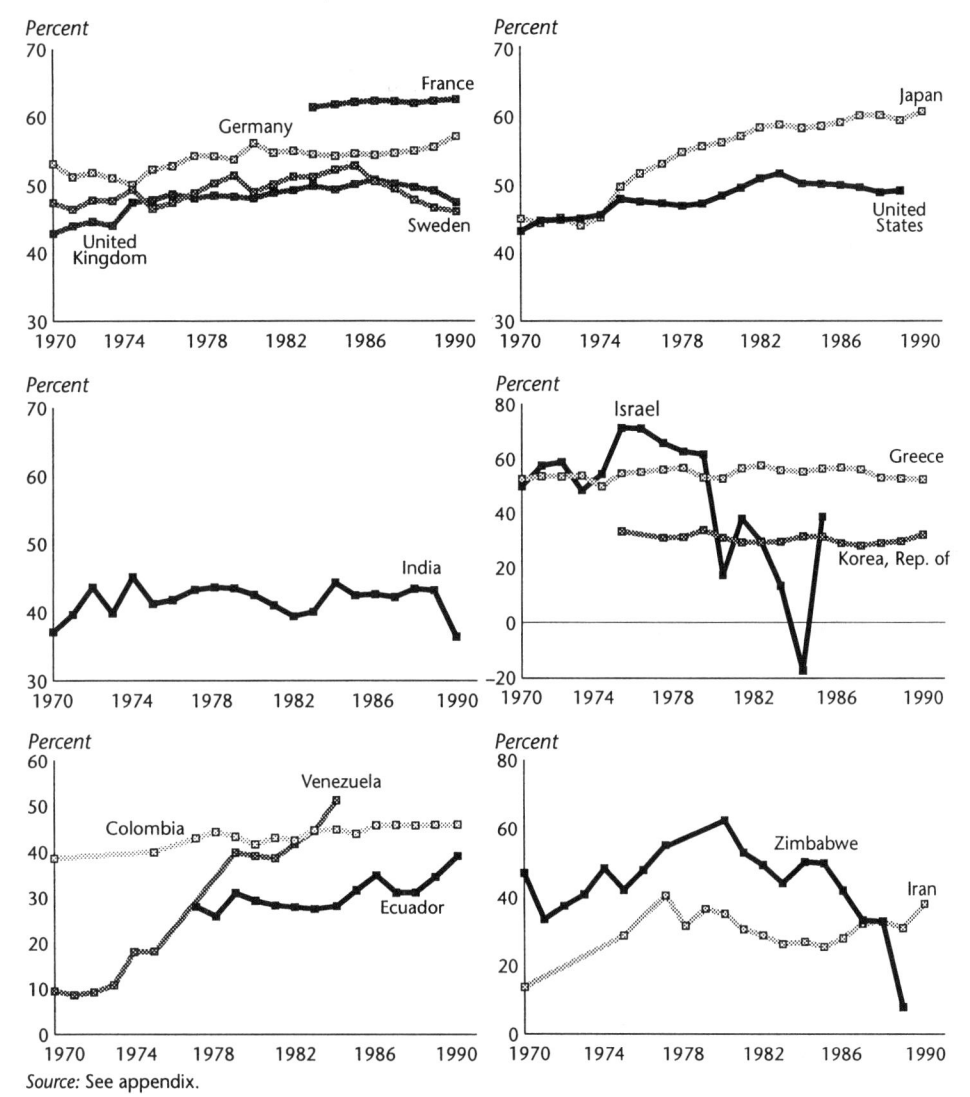

Figure 2. Government Transfers and Subsidies as a Share of Government Noninterest, Nondefense Disbursements, 1970–90

Source: See appendix.

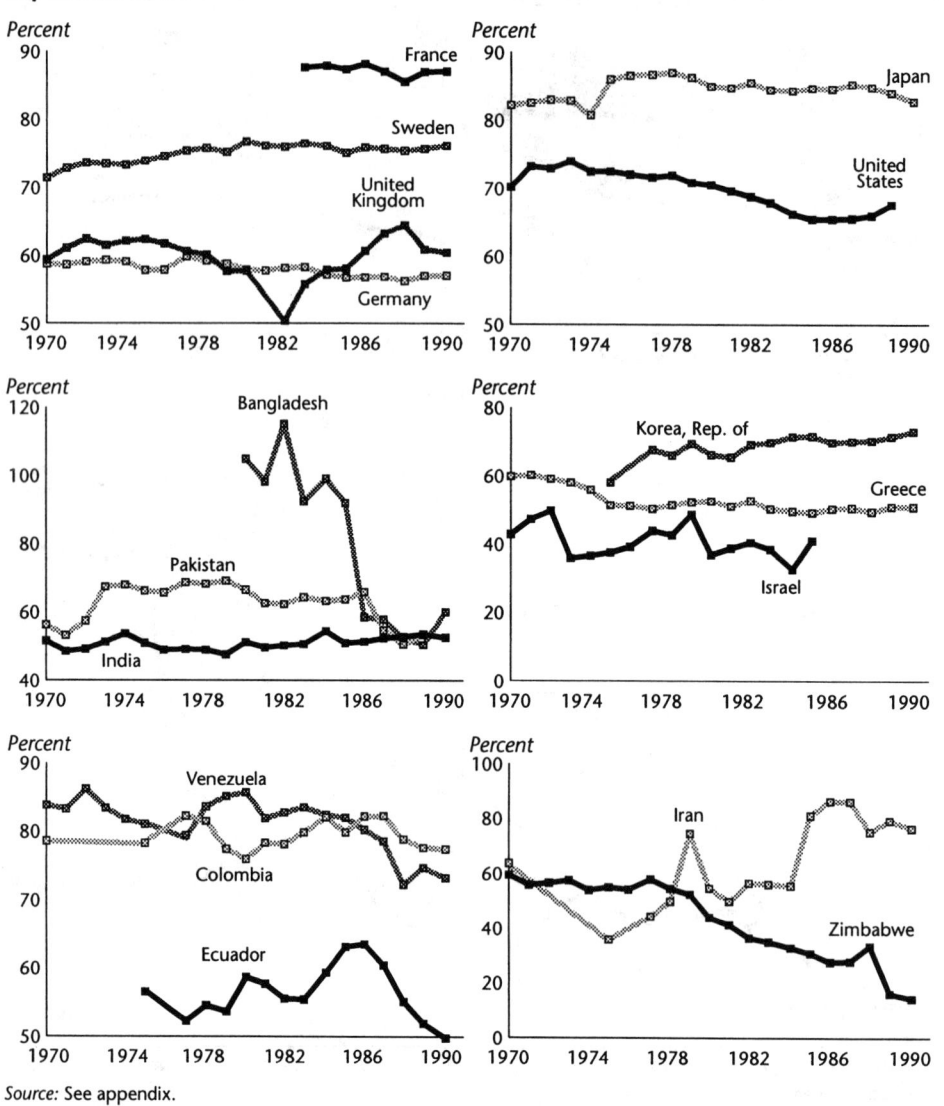

Figure 3. Government Value Added as a Share of Government Consumption Expenditures, 1970–90

Source: See appendix.

Figure 4. Government Defense Consumption Expenditures as a Share of Government Consumption Expenditures, 1953–90

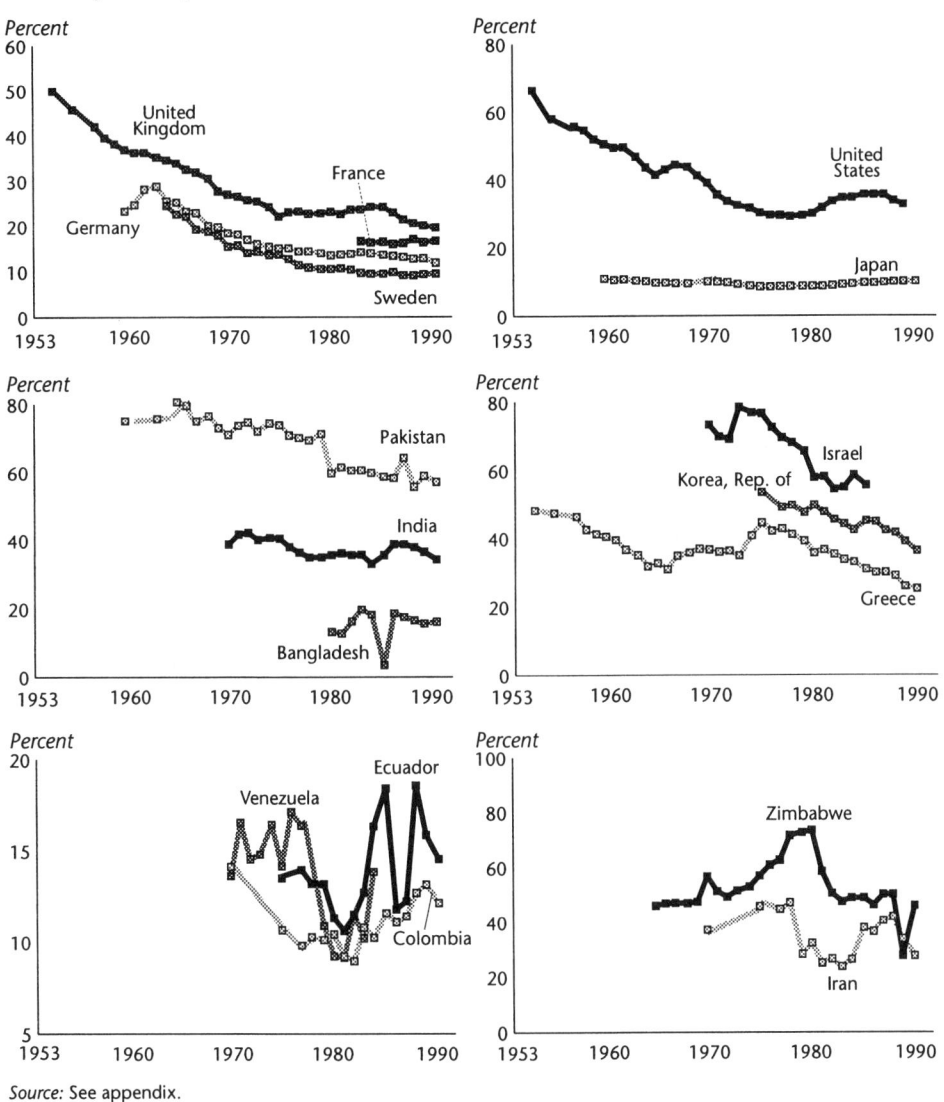

Source: See appendix.

Figure 5. Government Interest Payments as a Share of Government Noninterest, Nondefense Disbursements, 1970–90

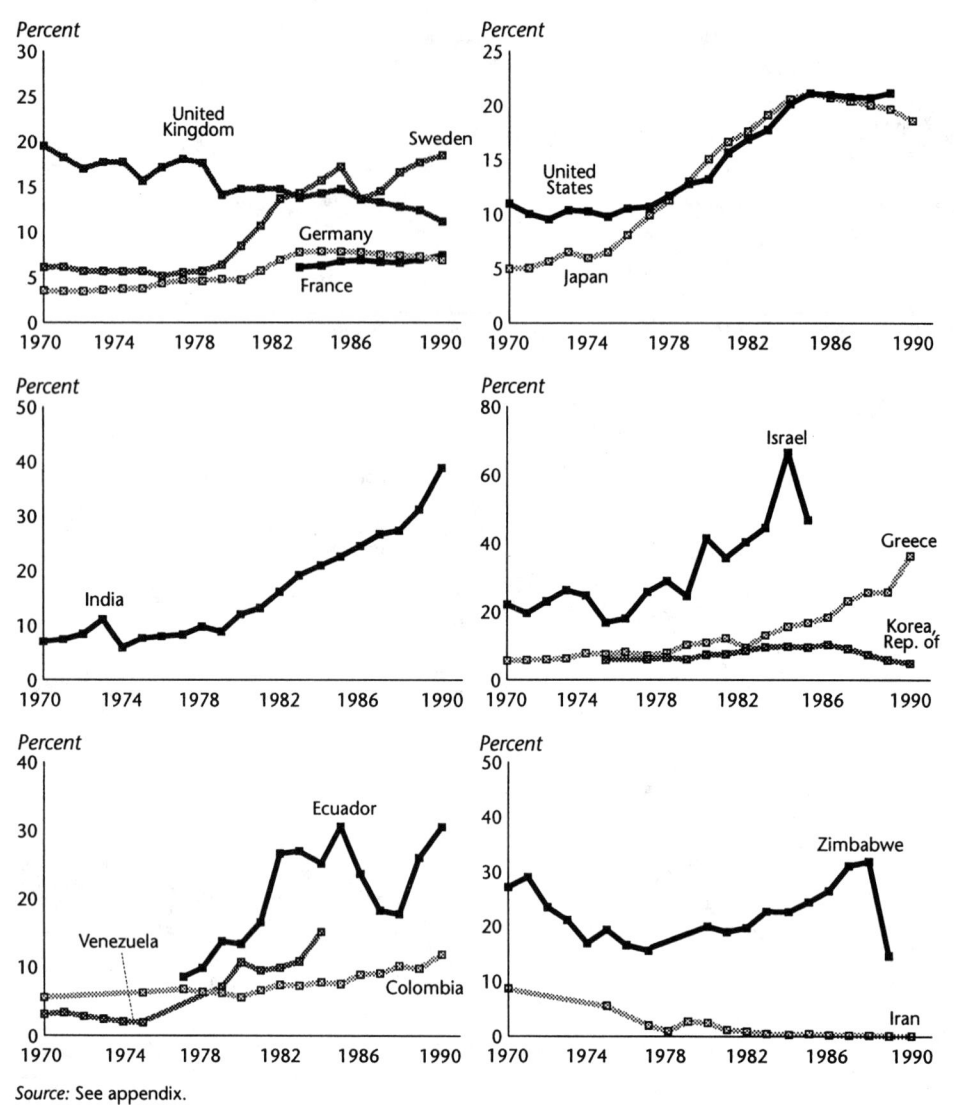

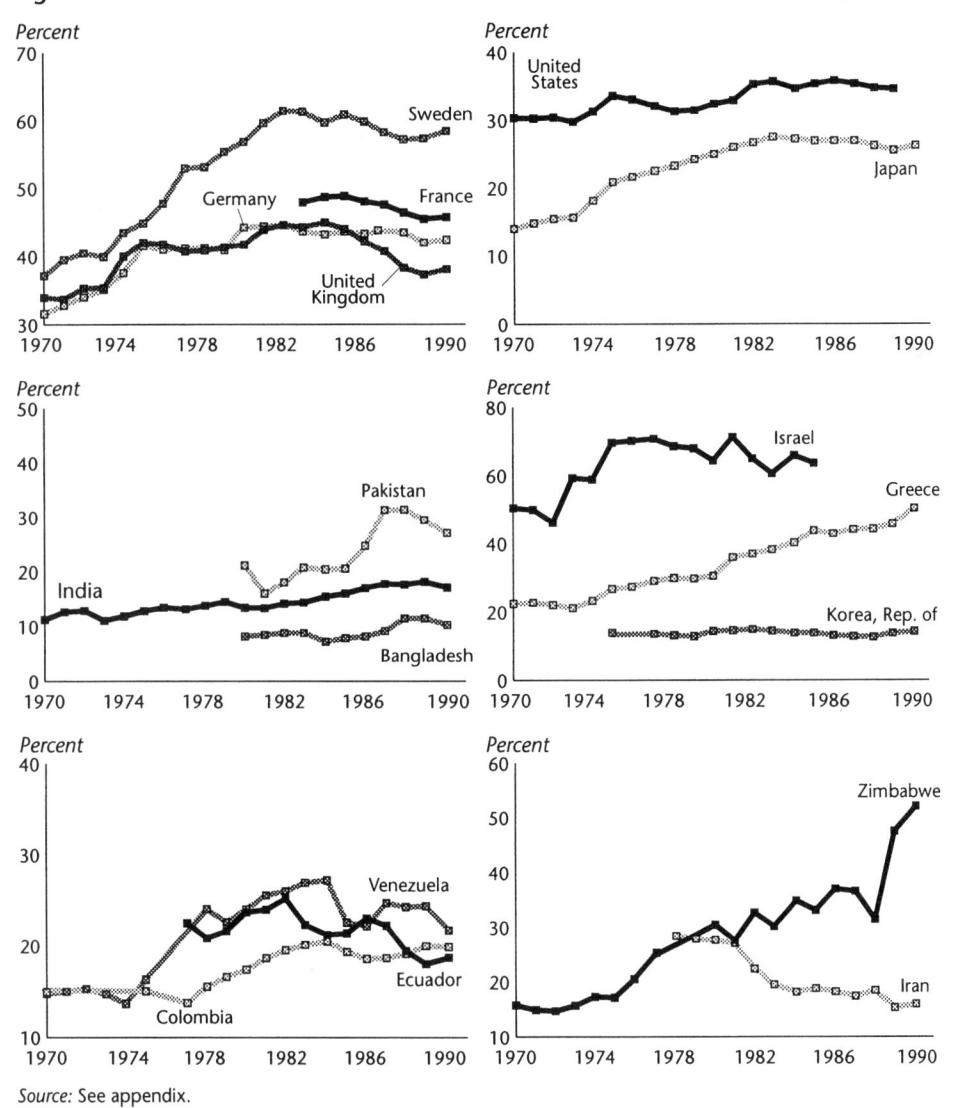

Figure 6. Government Disbursements as a Share of Gross Domestic Product, 1970–90

Source: See appendix.

Figure 7. Government Education Consumption Expenditures as a Share of Government Nondefense Consumption Expenditures, 1953–90

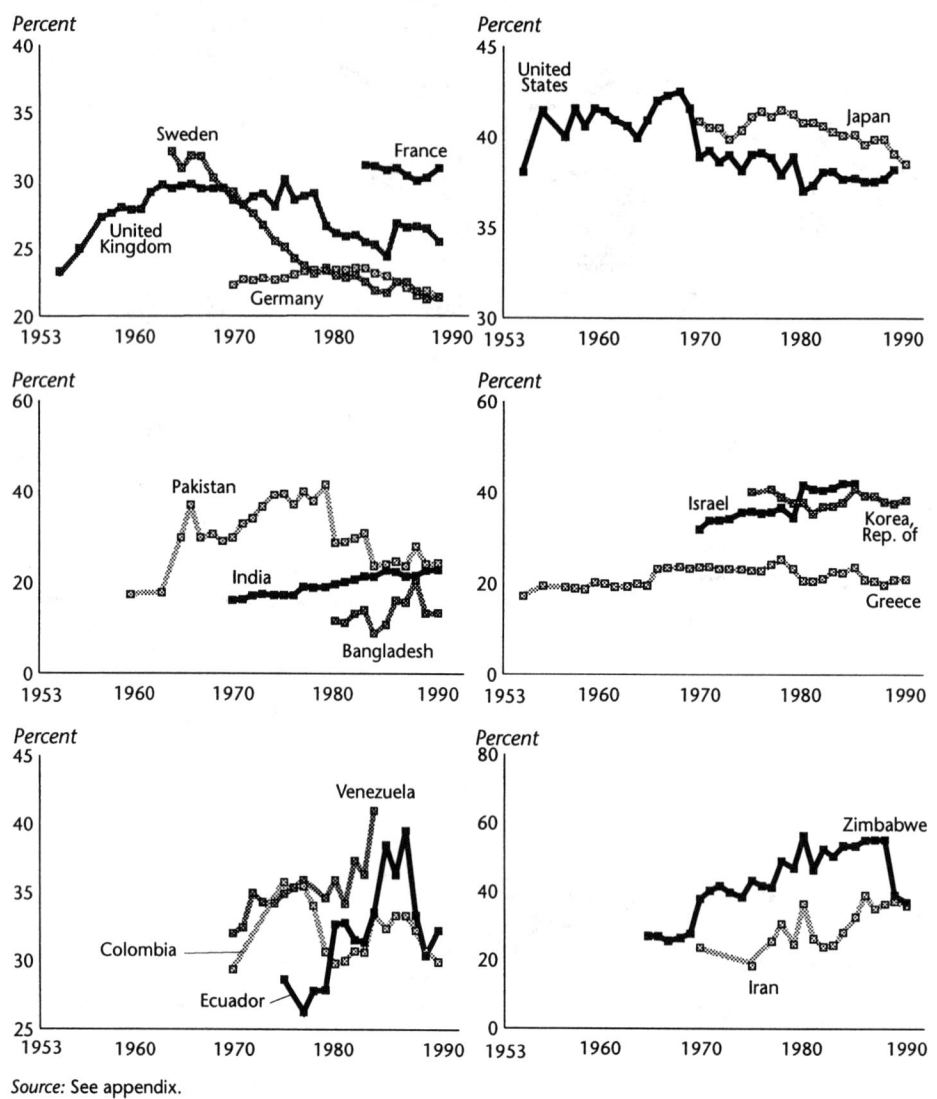

Source: See appendix.

Figure 8. Government Share of Education Consumption Expenditures, 1953–90

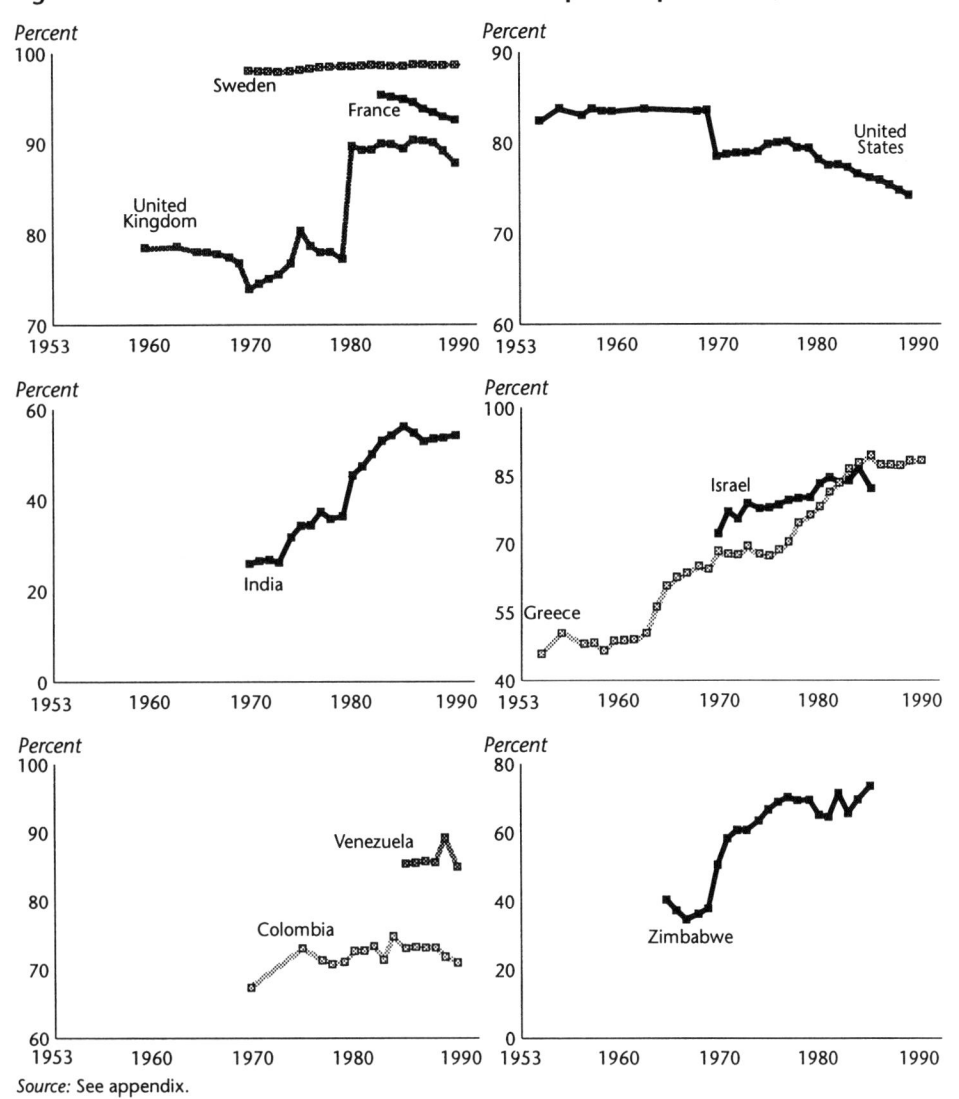

Source: See appendix.

Figure 9. Government Medical Consumption Expenditures as a Share of Government Nondefense Consumption Expenditures, 1953–90

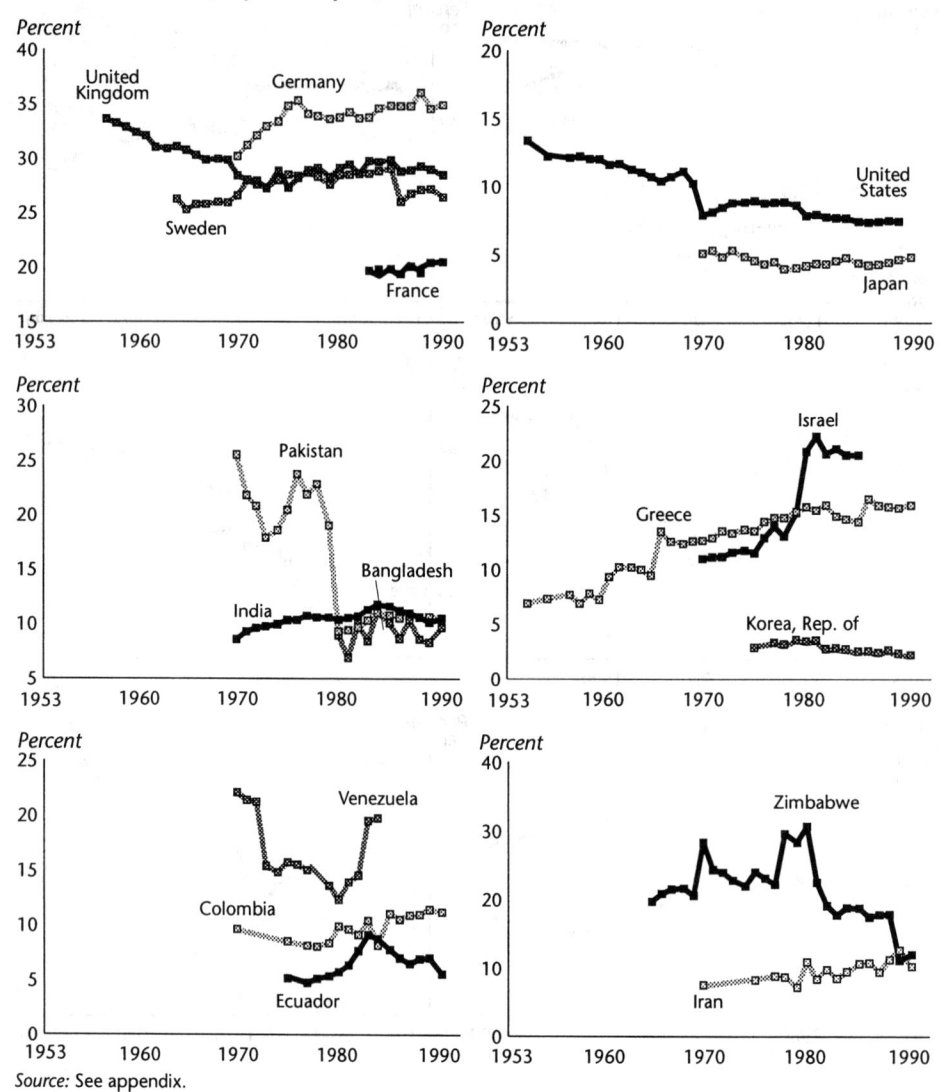

Source: See appendix.

Figure 10. Government Share of Total Medical Consumption Expenditures, 1953–90

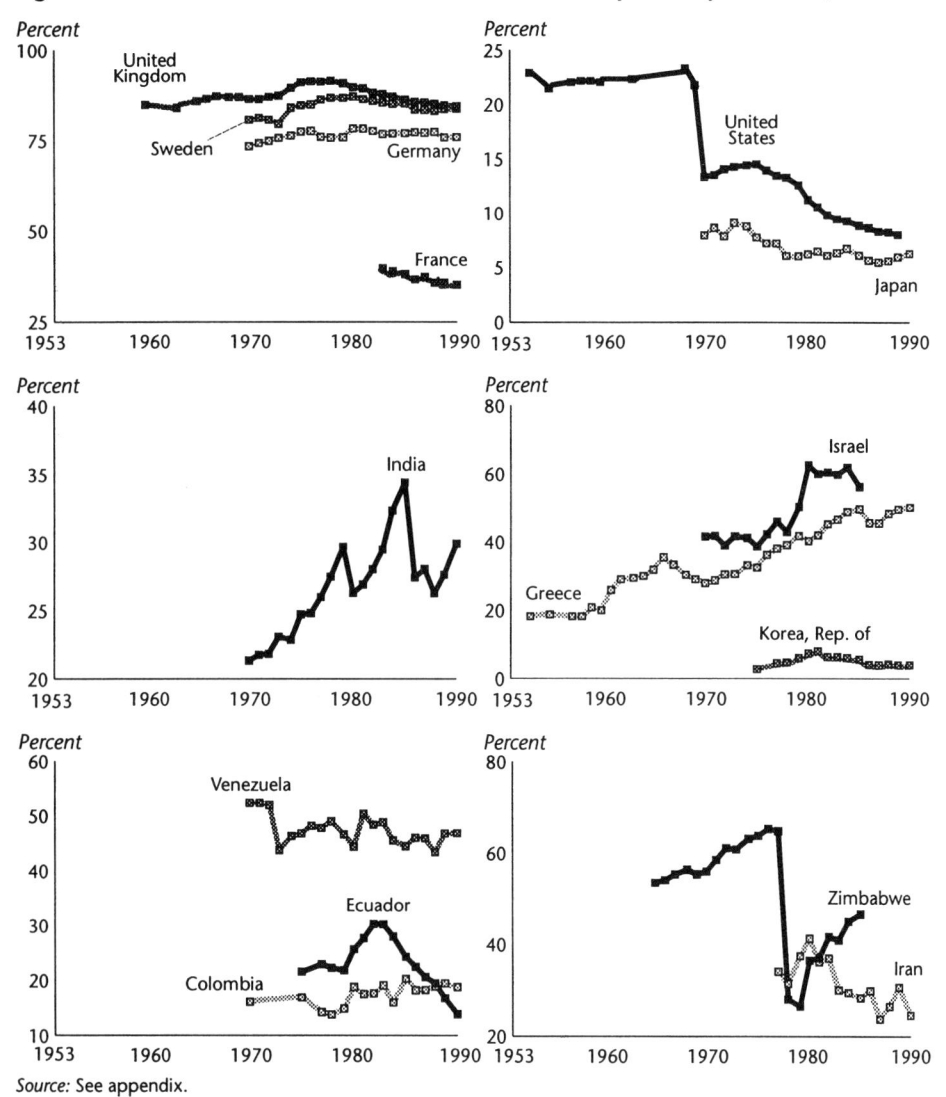

Source: See appendix.

Note

1. Interest payments, which are netted out of this series, are not available for Venezuela after 1983. But other series show a decline in government spending during the 1980s (see figure 5).

References

Atkinson, Anthony B., and Joseph E. Stiglitz. 1980. *Lectures on Public Economics.* New York: McGraw Hill.

Becker, Gary. 1965. "A Theory of the Allocation of Time." *Economic Journal* 85 (299): 493–508.

Bergstrom, Theodore, and Soren Blomquist. 1996. "The Political Economy of Subsidized Day Care and Labor Supply." *European Economic Review* 12 (3): 443–57.

Hansson, Ingemar. 1984. "Marginal Cost of Public Funds for Different Tax Instruments and Government Expenditures." *Scandinavian Journal of Economics* 86 (2): 115–30.

Harberger, Arnold C. 1971. "Three Basic Postulates for Applied Welfare Economics." *Journal of Economic Literature* 9 (3): 485–97.

Hart, Oliver, and Bengt Holmstrom. 1987. "The Theory of Contracts." In Truman F. Bewley, ed., *Advances in Economic Theory.* Cambridge: Cambridge University Press.

ILO (International Labour Office). Various years. *Yearbook of Labour Statistics.* Geneva.

Kornai, Janos. 1986. "The Soft Budget Constraint." *Kyklos* 39 (1): 3–30.

Lazear, Edward P. 1995. *Personnel Economics.* Cambridge and London: MIT Press.

Lindbeck, Assar. 1993. *The Welfare State: Selected Essays.* Vol. 2. London: Edward Elgar.

Nordhaus, William, and James Tobin. 1972. "Is Growth Obsolete?" In Fiftieth Anniversary Colloquium, *Economic Growth.* New York: Columbia University Press (for the National Bureau of Economic Research).

Quah, Euston. 1993. *Economics and Home Production: Theory and Measurement.* Aldershot, United Kingdom: Avebury.

Rosen, Sherwin. 1997. "Public Employment, Taxes and the Welfare State in Sweden." In Richard Freeman, Robert Topel, and Birgitta Swedenborg, eds., *The Welfare State in Transition.* Chicago: University of Chicago Press.

Sah, Raaj K. 1991. "Fallibility in Human Organizations and Political Systems." *Journal of Economic Perspectives* 5 (spring): 67–88.

Sah, Raaj K., and Joseph E. Stiglitz. 1986. "The Architecture of Economic Systems: Hierarchies and Polyarchies." *American Economic Review* 76 (September): 716–27.

Sandmo, Agnar. 1990 "Tax Distortions and Household Production." *Oxford Economic Papers* 42 (January): 78–90.

Thomas, James J. 1992. *Informal Economic Activity.* New York: Harvester Wheatsheaf.

Tiebout, C.M. 1991. "A Pure Theory of Local Expenditures." In A.B. Atkinson, ed., *Modern Public Finance.* Vol. 1. Aldershot, United Kingdom: E. Elgar Publications.

UN (United Nations). Various years. *National Accounts Statistics: Main Aggregates and Detailed Tables.* New York.

———. Various years. *Yearbook of National Accounts Statistics.* New York.

Usher, Dan. 1968. *The Price Mechanism and the Meaning of National Income Statistics.* Oxford: Oxford University Press.

———. 1980. *The Measurement of Economic Growth.* Oxford: Basil Blackwell.

Comment on "Incentives, Efficiency, and Government Provision of Public Services," by Sherwin Rosen and Bruce A. Weinberg

Richard Zeckhauser

In recent years the government's role in developing economies has shrunk dramatically—a development that I argue is a result more of politics than of economics. No powerful underlying forces have worked their magic, nor have governments responded to natural incentives. Rather, citizens and their leaders have responded to the dramatic lessons of the breakup of the Soviet Union and the virtual collapse of socialist ideas. Many countries are following the market-oriented prescriptions—such as selling off state-owned enterprises—espoused by the World Bank, most major international lenders, and most Western economists.

Sherwin Rosen and Bruce A. Weinberg do not applaud this development—not because they do not approve of it, but because they focus on a different phenomenon and on an earlier period. They explain why governments grow, particularly as countries develop. They note that governments play a larger role in industrial countries, suggesting that increases in the level of development and the size of government go together, and that government tends to grow over time. Of the countries they studied, only in Ecuador did the government shrink significantly during the period under examination (1970–90 for most countries).

Their analysis is characteristically Rosen in style. It takes a broad sweep, with wide-ranging implications. It offers intriguing theory, presented in an informal style appropriate for its audience, and provides supportive empirical data from both industrial and developing countries. The Weinberg twist gives somewhat greater credence to welfare economics and to concepts such as public goods and merit goods. Rather than follow the Chicago tradition of attack, I will elaborate on this insightful analysis and address related issues.

Directed Goods

Many government-provided goods and services, such as education, medical care, and child care, benefit primarily the recipient. I label them directed goods, suggesting

Richard Zeckhauser is Frank P. Ramsey Professor of Political Economy at the John F. Kennedy School of Government at Harvard University.

that the benefits are directed to specific individuals. Though such goods may give rise to some externalities and may be justified on a merit-good basis, they are principally an instrument of redistribution to particular parties.

Over the past three decades governments in industrial countries have vastly increased the share of their activities devoted to providing directed goods rather than traditional public goods. In the United States, for example, directed goods went from 32 percent of federal spending on directed and public goods in 1965 to 63 percent in 1995 (Zeckhauser 1996). The relative decline in defense spending contributed to this change but hardly explains the dramatic upsurge. The changing mix of government expenditures is as worthy of economists' attention as their more usual concern, the size and tax burden of government.

Rosen and Weinberg focus on women's work in developing countries and its effects on government activity. With development, the market value of women's labor increases, spurring a shift from the household to the market sector. Because taxation is much more feasible in the market, this shift facilitates the growth of government activity. Thus there is a potential link between the level of development and the size of government. Moreover, working women demand more government services, such as education and medical care. Rosen and Weinberg complement their demand-driven theory with a welfare economics justification for directed goods: they correct distortions in the labor market. If we tax women's wage labor but not their household production, then on a second-best basis we may want to subsidize traditional women's activities, such as child care or medical care, to encourage women to enter the labor force. The authors develop an insightful optimal subsidy argument: governments subsidize the traditional activities of women rather than those of men, since women have far higher elasticities of labor supply.

Whatever the economic justification, what motivates countries to provide for the care of children or elderly parents? Many citizens would say compassion or responsibility. With University of Chicago authors, it might seem more appropriate to invoke Director's Law—that is, governments generally operate to transfer resources from the rich and the poor to the middle class. The emerging field of positive political economy provides a number of additional—and at times conflicting—theories. Despite their vast differences, these theories agree that political forces and considerations trump welfare economics justifications in explaining patterns of redistribution.

For example, the transactions costs theory of politics tells us that identifiable and concentrated interests will be able to organize cheaply and will thus benefit at the expense of diffuse, disorganized interests. One example in the United States is the vast expansion of services to the elderly in recent decades with the Association for the Advancement of Retired People (AARP) serving as the lobbying arm of elderly voters. Similarly, many developing countries concentrate government expenditures in urban areas even though these areas are far richer than rural regions. The celebrated median voter theory would have a hard time explaining such outcomes, since median voters may be neither elderly nor urban.

The political reality is that there are severe cleavages in both developing and industrial societies over government provision of directed goods. The patterns of provision reflect fault lines between generations, ethnic groups, and those who can impose their claims more and less effectively. Many citizens feel that too much government largesse is going to someone else. Such views are reflected in the widespread decline of confidence in government. Consider this question: "Would you say that the government is pretty much run by a few big interests looking out for themselves or that it is run for the benefit of all the people?" In the United States the percentage of respondents who answered "a few big interests" rose from 29 percent in 1964 to 76 percent in 1994 (National Election Studies 1996).[1]

Tax Burdens

Rosen and Weinberg note two trends in government expenditures: an increase with the level of development and over time. The increase with the level of development stems from the challenge of collecting tax revenues in a largely nonmarket economy with poor administrative mechanisms. Rosen and Weinberg note that as the costs of tax collection fall, as they do with development, governments spend more.

The authors' focus on taxes gives us a helpful but incomplete analysis of the sources of government revenue. Developing country governments raise a substantial share of revenue through nontax routes—much more than their industrial country counterparts. Significant potential sources of revenue include natural resources, tariffs, printing of currency, and state-owned enterprises.[2]

When computing the tax burden of government expenditures, we must take into account all aspects of government operations, not just their magnitude. For example, in the regulatory state that characterizes many developing economies, and in the absence of reasonable salaries and opportunities in the private sector, many government officials engage in corruption. The deadweight cost of corruption activities relative to revenue secured can be enormous.

The size of government is far from the determining factor in assessing its net benefits or costs. Anecdotal evidence, and a number of passages in Rosen and Weinberg, suggest the optimistic but reasonable conclusion that the deadweight losses of raising government revenue decline as development proceeds and that the benefits per government dollar increase.

Consider a hypothetical example with one industrial country and one developing country (table 1). The ratio of government to private consumption is much larger in the industrial country. The deadweight loss associated with raising government revenue is far larger in the developing country (perhaps because of corruption), and the benefits per unit of government spending are lower. (Ideally, the benefits per unit of government spending should be much greater than one because government spends to maximize net social benefits.) The total loss to the private sector is the costs of government spending (government revenues plus the deadweight loss of raising them) minus the benefits, namely $0.1(1+1) - 0.1(0.5) = 0.15$ of private production

Table 1. Costs and Benefits of Government Spending in Two Countries

Variable	Industrial country	Developing country
Ratio of government to private consumption	0.3	0.1
Deadweight loss per unit of government spending	0.2	1.0
Benefits per unit of government spending	0.8	0.5
Ratio of loss to private consumption	0.12	0.15

Source: Author's calculations.

in the developing country. In the industrial country that value is 0.3(0.2+1) − 0.3(0.8) = 0.12.

Fads or Learning?

An implicit theme of Rosen and Weinberg's article is that widely observed time series and cross-sectional patterns reflect conscious choices. Their explanations of why government grows with development and over time reflect this theme. A critical question is whether these phenomena instead reflect inevitable responses to underlying forces and, if so, whether the outcomes are desirable. Rosen and Weinberg's cogent arguments relating to deadweight losses from taxation and agency losses when beneficiaries are diffused suggest that a large government is not likely to prove desirable. They do not offer empirical evidence. In future work, I hope that Rosen and Weinberg will provide political economy explanations of why countries, particularly advanced countries, would allow governments to grow undesirably.

A reasonable conjecture would be that the "chosen" outcomes reflect the interests of a few powerful parties but are contrary to the preferences and foreseeable well-being of many citizens. Russia's experience is instructive. Many factions' proposed paths to development are self-serving. What emerges from such a tussle should not be interpreted as desirable, or as a conscious choice of a broad cross-section of the population.

Despite Rosen and Weinberg's disquieting lessons, and despite observations of politically imposed self-serving policies in many countries, I suspect that a fair assessment of economic policies in recent years would suggest that on the whole they have moved in the right direction. Major recent events—a substantial lowering of tax rates in most industrial countries, dramatic privatization across the globe, the dismantling of the Soviet Union, much greater openness to international trade and finance—suggest that the patterns Rosen and Weinberg chronicle may not be inevitable. The pendulum swings back—and its arc covers many places at once. It is not that dramatic changes in world conditions led all countries to seek new approaches at once, but that countries learned from one another, or imitated one another. Ideas matter; so may evidence, which is reassuring.

Transnational learning is a fad when one does not like the lesson; it is learning when one does. Thus the authors and I would label as fads the spread of socialism in the developing world over past decades and the rapid increase in government spending in the 1970s. We would call learning such recent developments as privatizations, tax cuts, and the overthrow of socialism.

Development, Labor Force Participation, and Values

With development comes increased labor force participation, particularly among women. Rosen and Weinberg's explanations for this change emphasize patterns of taxation and government subsidization. Household services are disproportionately subsidized, partly as a way to induce women, who would not be taxed on household production, into the labor force. Nevertheless, high tax rates still encourage home activity, as do supposedly corrective government subsidies. They conclude that for both reasons the real household sector becomes too large.

The authors continually patrol for distortions and tax wedges, but do not cast their discerning eyes on how the activities they study affect values within society. When a developing country adopts policies that boost formal labor force participation, society can be dramatically disrupted. Substantial changes in labor force participation rates or patterns, for both men and women, impinge on marriage and living practices. For example, the HIV/AIDS epidemic in some developing countries may be attributable to the migration of men from rural to urban areas and the accompanying spread of the disease through prostitution.

Economists are comfortable assessing changes in production; effects on values are harder to tally. But when the scorecard for economic development is filled in, many of the effects—both positive and negative—will be due to changes in the structure of society.

Conclusion

Rosen and Weinberg's provocative and broad-ranging article stimulates our interest in the evolving role of government as development and time advance. They present us with profound questions: How much of the growth in government or the rise in directed goods is a response to market imperfections rather than political forces? What metric is appropriate when assessing the dramatic change in women's roles that accompanies development? Are these trends inevitable?

Recent evidence suggests that these trends are not inevitable. Taxes are falling around the world, socialist governments have scrambled toward capitalism, and privatization proceeds apace.[3] Is this the marketplace of ideas working its wonders? Unlikely—since as Rosen and Weinberg chronicle, opposite trends characterized the world in the period they studied.

There appear to be swings in political sentiment that are quite large relative to swings in the business cycle, and probably more significant for the economy. And such swings, alas, only dimly reflect the evidence on the efficacy of alternative government policies. In both industrial and developing countries economic policies would be much improved if we could learn how to control the political cycle.

Notes

1. The percentage increased mononically, except for a drop in 1980–84.
2. State enterprises, which frequently constitute major segments of the industrial sector, rarely yield much government revenue unless they sell natural resources. They often require government subsidies, even when they are protected as monopolies. Many privatized state enterprises are sold at bargain prices—not surprising, given the severe information asymmetries and frequent corruption surrounding such sales. But a positive price plus the potential for future tax revenues may well be preferable to the status quo.
3. While France and the United Kingdom have just replaced conservative governments with socialist or labor governments, these parties are much more moderate than they have been in the past.

References

National Election Studies. 1996. NES 1948–1994 Cumulative Dataset, V605, from http://www.umich.edu/~nes/nesguide/toptables/tab5a_2.htm

Zeckhauser, Richard. 1996. "Directed Goods and Clash Goods." Harvard University, Kennedy School of Government, Visions of Government Project, Cambridge, Mass.

Comment on "Incentives, Efficiency, and Government Provision of Public Services," by Sherwin Rosen and Bruce A. Weinberg

Robert P. Inman

In their overview of economic development and government growth, Sherwin Rosen and Bruce A. Weinberg provide a new answer to an old but still important question: Why does the share of government activities in the national economy grow as economies become more developed? Their article offers both a supply-side and a demand-side explanation.

On the supply side, governments are necessarily constrained by their ability to raise revenue from the population. While head taxes are certainly feasible, large per capita taxes are regressive and often difficult to collect when a significant portion of the population is poor; debtor prisons are the only true enforcement mechanism. As a result most governments tax economic activities to raise money, using value-added and sales taxes, wage taxes, and capital and property taxes. Administering such taxes requires that taxed activities be measured, most plausibly through prices set in the marketplace. Economic development, particularly the adoption of technologies with significant economies of scale, encourages the expansion of market activities. Thus as markets grow, the administratively feasible tax base grows, lowering the cost of collecting each additional unit of government revenue. These lower marginal costs encourage the growth of government.

In addition to lowering the costs of government, Rosen and Weinberg argue, technological adoption and market expansion raise the demand for government services. As market activities expand, the demand for labor in the market rises and with it market wages. As market wages rise, nonwage household activities, performed mainly by women, become economically less attractive. Thus women begin leaving work in the household in search of employment in the market. But as women leave home for the marketplace, new means of providing home services must be found—services such as day care and education for children, nursing and health care for family members, and care for the elderly. Technological advances, particularly in health care and training, provide significant economies of scale in the production of such home services, and

---

Robert P. Inman is professor of finance and economics at the Wharton School at the University of Pennsylvania and research associate at the National Bureau of Economic Research.

Annual World Bank Conference on Development Economics 1997
©1998 The International Bank for Reconstruction and Development / THE WORLD BANK

the resulting cost advantages further favor provision of these services outside the household. But should markets or governments provide these services?

Though Rosen and Weinberg do not stress this point, there are plausible reasons to think that markets might not provide these services efficiently, or at all, in the early stages of economic and market development. Since many home-care services involve a significant insurance component—that is, high demand in times of specific need—private providers must be able to predict demand for each consumer. Problems of asymmetric information arise, and unsophisticated markets might not succeed (see Akerlof 1970). Extended families and small villages often successfully provide home-care services because they can overcome problems of asymmetric information through informal information networks. But impersonal private markets lack such networks, and developing economies may find it difficult to institute formal information systems. If markets cannot provide needed home-care services, government information gathering or direct provision becomes a plausible alternative. Herein lies the demand-side pressure for increased government activity with economic development.

Why Does Development Produce Bigger Government?

The Rosen-Weinberg supply and demand shift hypotheses, diagrammed in figure 1, can help us understand why the government grows as the economy develops. The cost of government activities before economic development can be represented by curve S_0, representing the rising cost of moving an additional unit of tax revenues from the private to the public sector. The curve rises because revenues become more difficult to collect administratively as the amounts increase (the tax evasion effect) and because more revenues mean higher tax rates, which lead to greater allocations away from the taxed activities. The demand for government activities before economic development is shown by the declining demand curve, D_0, in which each additional unit of government spending gives a lower additional benefit. If the government balances the marginal costs of raising revenues against the marginal benefits from spending those revenues, the level of government activity before economic development will be low, say at G_0.

As Rosen and Weinberg argue, industrialization and market expansion are likely to dramatically shift these supply and demand curves in directions that favor the growth of government. The expansion of markets is likely to lower the administrative costs of tax collection and, with a larger tax base, to allow lower marginal tax rates to raise government revenues, thus reducing the misallocations associated with market-based taxation. Both effects shift the marginal costs of raising government revenues downward, say to S_1. Industrialization and market expansion are likely to increase the demand for government activities as well. Industrialization encourages more women to enter the market economy, creating a demand for home-care activities outside the home. But because of asymmetric information, markets may not adequately provide these services. Thus the demand for government services will shift upward to D_1. The new, post-development level of government services will therefore rise to G_1.

Figure 1. The Size of Government

Marginal benefits and costs

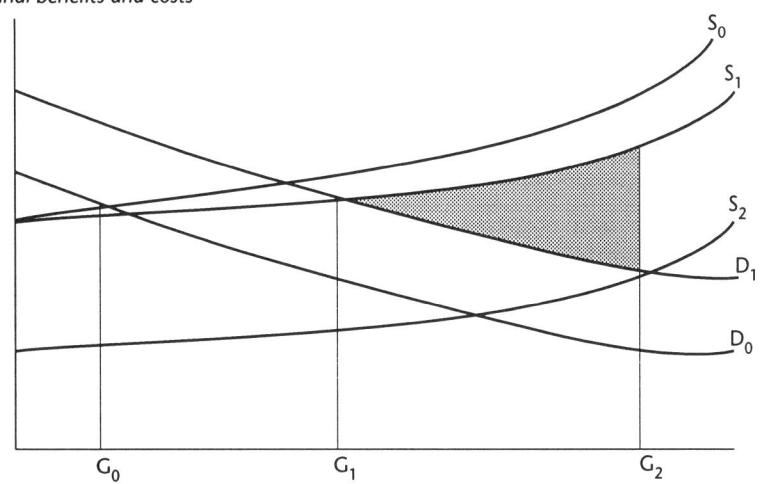

G₀ = Government spending before economic development
G₁ = Government spending after economic development
G₂ = Government spending after economic development and democratic policy choice

What is the evidence for Rosen and Weinberg's explanation of the growth of government? While they do not provide a formal econometric test of their hypothesis—one would presumably want to specify and estimate the supply and demand curves for government spending[1]—they do provide empirical observations in support of their theory. First, they supply considerable evidence that industrial countries have larger public sectors, absolutely and as a share of GDP, than do developing countries. Second, taxation of market activities, not head taxes or extra government borrowing, pays for this growth in government spending. Third, while male labor force participation rates are similar across industrial and developing countries, female labor force participation increases significantly with economic development (though one wants to be careful to control for Islamic countries). Fourth, most of the increased government spending in industrial countries is allocated to services that substitute for household services previously supplied by women who are now in the labor force. Given these supportive facts, it is hard not to take seriously the Rosen-Weinberg industrialization–market expansion hypothesis for the growth of government.

What is not well explained by the hypothesis, however, is the significant variability in the share of government in GDP *within* the industrial and developing country subsamples. The discussions of incentives and government provision hint at one approach to explaining these differences. Rosen and Weinberg rightly note that there is never an ideal solution to the problem of market failure, or what the authors call "market incompleteness," arising from incomplete or asymmetric information. The hope that simply moving an economic activity from the marketplace to the halls of government will solve a market failure is naive. Rosen and Weinberg correctly point out that all solutions are bad in some sense, and some are worse than others. Problems of incomplete contracting that undermine market allocations will make government allocations difficult too. The task is to evaluate the relative performance of markets and governments.

Are Governments or Markets More Efficient?

Whereas markets use prices and legal contracts to allocate resources, governments use votes and informal agreements. In democratic societies any agreement must be approved by at least half the voters or their elected representatives. Since government services are typically financed by a national tax base, the decisive voters—say, the median voters in a referendum or a median coalition in a legislature—will likely bear only a fraction of the economic costs of government spending and, because they are decisive, they may receive a disproportionate share of the economic benefits.[2] If so, a wedge will arise between the marginal costs and the marginal benefits of government spending.

Figure 1 illustrates how this wedge might affect the size of the public sector. If the decisive voters receive the average benefit, then their demand curve remains at D_1. (The decisive voters' demand curve for government services could lie above the average voters' demand curve if the decisive voters receive more than the average share of benefits.) If the decisive voters pay less than the average voters' marginal cost of public services, as is likely, their marginal cost curve will be below S_1, say at S_2.[3] When the decisive voters set government spending, they do so according to their private demand and supply curves. This will be at point G_2, where the decisive voters' demand curve (D_1) intersects the decisive voters' supply curve (S_2). But point G_2 is economically inefficient. At G_2 the average voters' demand curve (D_1, representing social marginal benefits) lies below the average voters' supply curve (S_1, representing social marginal costs). Since social marginal costs exceed social marginal benefits at G_2 ($S_1 > D_1$), government spending is too high. The shaded area in the figure—the wedge measuring the total excess of social marginal costs over social marginal benefits—measures the economic inefficiency that arises with service provision by democratic governments. Note, too, that government spending is larger the greater is the size of the wedge.

Efficient governments seek to limit the size of this wedge. As Rosen and Weinberg note, efficient governments ensure that people recognize the full costs and benefits of their actions so that self-interest can be aligned with social interests. How might this be done? As Nobel Laureate Ronald Coase (1960) pointed out, when there are economic inefficiencies, there are also strong incentives to search for alternative institutions to remove those inefficiencies. Government institutions that might overcome the inefficiencies of crude majority-rule politics include political parties (Wittman 1989) or strong presidents (Fitts and Inman 1992), who negotiate, following Coase, for a cut in excessive government spending in return for sharing the tax savings that those cutbacks offer.

In figure 1 an agreement between the decisive voters and the excluded minority to cut government spending from G_2 to G_1 yields a social surplus equal to the shaded area that can be shared between the majority and minority coalitions (say, through targeted tax cuts). Competition between governments or between governments and private providers might also work to control inefficiencies, as Rosen and Weinberg note. Here is the case for privatization or decentralized federal fiscal systems, both of which allow competition in the provision of government services. It is in this expanded analysis of government spending—one that integrates the fundamental economic forces of development with the capacity of a country's political institutions to manage the public sector—that the most complete explanation for the size and growth of government is likely to be found.

Conclusion

In the end I find two of Rosen and Weinberg's points especially worth emphasizing. First, the economic forces that drive economic development—technological adoption and market expansion—are also likely to drive government growth. Second, government institutions—majority rule, strong executives, strong parties, federalism, political competition—will play a central role in how this growing public sector performs economically. Weak political institutions mean excessive government spending and higher taxes, both of which are likely to adversely affect economic growth. An important lesson follows from these two observations: as economies develop and the public sector commands an increasing share of GDP, the task of practitioners will increasingly be to design and implement political institutions that foster the adoption of efficient tax and spending policies.

Notes

1. See the study of U.S. government spending from 1795 to 1988 by Inman and Fitts (1990). That study finds some tentative evidence consistent with the Rosen and Weinberg model in that urbanization significantly increased government spending. Inman and Fitts assume exogenous shifts in the supply curves of government spending (S_0, S_1, and S_2 in figure 1) to econometrically identify the demand curves (D_0 and D_1) for government spending. A fully specified test of the Rosen-Weinberg model would have to endogenize the supply curves as well, presumably through a fiscal model in which the choice of tax policies was endogenous.

2. There are numerous political economy models with this feature; see, for example, Inman (1987).

3. See Inman and Fitts (1990) for a model with this feature.

References

Akerlof, George. 1970. "The Market for Lemons: Quality Uncertainty and the Market Mechanism." *Quarterly Journal of Economics* 84 (3): 488–500.

Coase, Ronald. 1960. "The Problem of Social Cost." *Journal of Law and Economics* 3 (1): 1–44.

Fitts, Michael, and Robert Inman. 1992. "Controlling Congress: Presidential Influence in Domestic Fiscal Policy." *Georgetown Law Journal* 80 (5): 1737–85.

Inman, Robert. 1987. "Markets, Government, and the 'New' Political Economy." In Alan Auerbach and Martin Feldstein, eds., *Handbook of Public Economics*. Vol 2. New York: Elsevier Science.

Inman, Robert, and Michael Fitts. 1990. "Political Institutions and Fiscal Policies: Evidence from the U.S. Historical Record." *Journal of Law, Economics, and Politics* 6 (special issue): 79–132.

Wittman, Donald. 1989. "Why Democracies Produce Efficient Results." *Journal of Political Economy* 97 (6): 1395–424.

Floor Discussion of "Incentives, Efficiency, and Government Provision of Public Services," by Sherwin Rosen and Bruce A. Weinberg

A participant from the University of Warsaw, agreeing with the points made by Sherwin Rosen and Bruce A. Weinberg (presenters), elaborated on related changes that had occurred in Poland during its transition to a market economy. Almost overnight, she said, there was an enormous increase in the opportunity cost of women's time—particularly among educated women. Women's overall labor force participation rate did not change much, however. Given that women were earning more and paying more taxes, the Polish government should have provided them with more services. Because that did not happen, women had to use their additional income to pay for additional private services.

A participant, drawing on points made by Rosen and by Richard Zeckhauser (discussant), did not agree that there was necessarily a link between increases in female labor force participation and increases in health and education spending. In the United States, for example, it was not the case that many children were being taught at home before women started entering the labor force in large numbers. And, he said, much of the increase in U.S. spending on health care over the past thirty years had resulted from the establishment of Medicare and Medicaid in the mid-1960s. Although there may be a link between increasing numbers of female workers and increasing education and health costs in developing countries, the connection seems unlikely in the United States. Zeckhauser noted that even if health care subsidies were found to increase the number of women in the workforce, the public was unlikely to approve of such subsidies—in the United States or elsewhere.

Another participant agreed with Zeckhauser on the importance of examining the net burden on the public sector in order to get a better perspective on public services. Taking the argument a step further, he argued that the effective burden is even larger when the costs of regulation and corruption are taken into account. And given the enormous spending demands on the public sector—in many countries debt, defense, and civil service costs almost exhaust the government budget—not much is left with which to provide services. As a result many needed services, particularly social services, are provided by the private sector in developing countries.

Rosen agreed that there are different ways to measure the government's role in the economy. In India, for example, government participation in the economy is small when measured as a share of total resources. But when corruption and the enormous regulatory burden are taken into account, the government's role is much larger. Thus, he said, analysts need to carefully define what they mean when discussing government, government growth, and the like.

For services such as military protection, he added, there are alternatives to taxing the general population to pay for them. For example, it used to be that armies were "paid" by their enemies—that is, they were able to pillage and loot the property of the people they attacked. This form of "direct taxation" is much less important in today's world.

For services such as health care, Rosen continued, demand has increased because professional care is much more effective than it used to be. In the United States it used to be that women in traditional families provided a large portion of medical care, because doctors could not provide much better care. Today doctors are much more knowledgeable—and much more expensive. As a result insurance, public or private, is needed to cover costs. U.S. citizens may pay a lot for their health care, he said, but they also receive the best medical services in the world.

Leaders in Growth: Can Others Follow?

What Can Developing Countries Learn from East Asia's Economic Growth?

Takatoshi Ito

The growth experiences of Japan and other Asian countries share some common features. In the first stage the economy starts to grow, often reaching double-digit rates, and the growth is accompanied by structural changes, with resources shifting from agriculture to simple manufacturing and then to more sophisticated manufacturing. In the second stage, as manufacturing hits a plateau and the technological gap is narrowed, the growth rate slows. Convergence regression models capture only the second stage of this dynamic process; more attention should be paid to the initial stage of growth. Getting the fundamentals right and achieving social and political stability seem to be particularly important during the first stage. Other countries, including African countries, can draw lessons from East Asia's experience by identifying their stage of development and the factors that are important at that stage.

In a 1996 article in *The World Bank Research Observer,* Joseph Stiglitz lists his favorite metaphors for economic development. One is the engine metaphor, in which capital accumulation (or a particular sector) is seen as the driving force of growth. Another is the chemical metaphor, in which the government catalyzes growth without necessarily providing significant resources. A third is the biological metaphor, which sees adaptation to changes in the environment as the key to survival. A fourth metaphor, more popular in the literature, views the economy as an equilibrium; Stiglitz mentions it but omits it from his list.

I would like to start with three favorite metaphors of my own. The first is the old idea of economic takeoff, in which a stagnant, agrarian economy beginning to industrialize is seen as an airplane taking off (Rostow 1960).[1] Successful takeoff requires that several conditions be met and that the engine run at full throttle. I like this metaphor because it implies that at the time of takeoff everything has to work for the plane to become airborne. Acceleration (of the growth rate) continues until cruising altitude is achieved (the high-income level). To grow, economies have to face

---

Takatoshi Ito is professor of economics at the Institute of Economic Research at Hitotsubashi University.

demand for their products, often from abroad. Thus export growth often drives takeoff. And just as there may be a limit to how many planes can take off at once, not all developing countries can achieve export-led growth at the same time.

The second metaphor is biological: ontogeny recapitulates phylogeny. That is, the maturation of an individual in a species repeats the steps in the biological evolution of the species. A frog starts as a one-cell egg, transforms into a fish-like tadpole living in the water, and finally becomes a four-legged land-dwelling frog. The process roughly parallels the evolution from primitive organism to amphibian, though at an extremely accelerated pace. Similarly, an economy's metamorphosis from an agrarian state to an economy with a simple industry such as textiles, to an economy with more sophisticated manufacturing, and eventually to a service economy mirrors the history of science and technology. Economies that develop later grow faster. Japan's transformation from an agrarian state in the 1890s to an industrial one in the 1930s was much faster than Britain's earlier transformation. The acceleration of economic development for latecomers was an important topic of investigations in the early literature on development economics (see Kuznets 1959, 1971).

The last metaphor is the "flying geese" hypothesis, which has been popular among academic economists in Asia, particularly in Japan. Originally the metaphor referred to the inverse-V shape of the time series for imports, domestic production, and exports of a given manufactured good (Akamatsu 1961).[2] Today the metaphor is used to describe the Asian economies, likening them to a group of geese flying in V-formation. Japan, flying in front, is flanked by Hong Kong (China) and Singapore, and followed by the Republic of Korea and Taiwan (China). Behind them are Malaysia and Thailand, and the Philippines and Indonesia. The order reflects each economy's stage of industrialization and per capita income. Long ago Japan moved from textiles to steel and chemical industries, leaving to Hong Kong the status of major textile exporter. As Japan progressed from steel and shipbuilding to automobiles and electronics, Korea took over in steel and shipbuilding. Comparative advantage forces the forerunners to vacate the markets for less sophisticated goods, leaving them to latecomers.

These metaphors illustrate the thrust of this article, which is that there is a natural order of development steps, however fast the latecomers are able to climb them, and there is a critical moment in development for economic takeoff—a popular view among East Asian economists and policymakers. The article elaborates this view of development stages and examines East Asia's experience for possible application elsewhere of the lessons of this experience.

The East Asian Miracle

Japan grew by 9–10 percent a year from the mid-1950s to the early 1970s. Growth then slowed to 4–5 percent a year until the end of the 1980s. With these high growth rates and the sharp appreciation of the yen relative to the U.S. dollar, Japan's per capita GDP (converted at the market exchange rate) surpassed that of the United States in the late 1980s.

The four "tigers"—Korea, Taiwan (China), Hong Kong, and Singapore—started to grow rapidly in the late 1970s. In the early 1980s Korea's ratio of external debt to GDP was as high as Mexico's, but Korea rapidly repaid its debt through growth and exports. Taiwan (China) also achieved remarkable growth, though it lacks the large conglomerate-like industrial powers of Japan *(keiretsu)* and Korea *(chaebol)*. Hong Kong and Singapore achieved impressive economic development despite small domestic markets. Both economies benefited from entrepôt trade. Hong Kong emphasized free markets; the other three economies used government guidance to shape export industries. By 1996 Singapore had surpassed small Western European countries in per capita GDP and Korea had joined the Organisation for Economic Co-operation and Development. The International Monetary Fund added the four tigers, along with Israel, to the list of advanced economies in its *World Economic Outlook 1997*.

Thailand, Indonesia, and Malaysia started to grow rapidly in the mid-1980s, and China soon followed. These countries have grown by 9–10 percent a year during the 1990s, and growth of less than 7 percent a year is now considered a recession—a pattern reminiscent of Japan's experience thirty years ago.

The sudden increase in growth rates and the geographical proximity of these economies have caught the attention of economists. Plotting the ratio of East Asian to U.S. per capita GDP (converted to dollars at the purchasing power parity

Figure 1. Per Capita GDP in Selected East Asian Economies as a Share of U.S. GDP, 1950–92

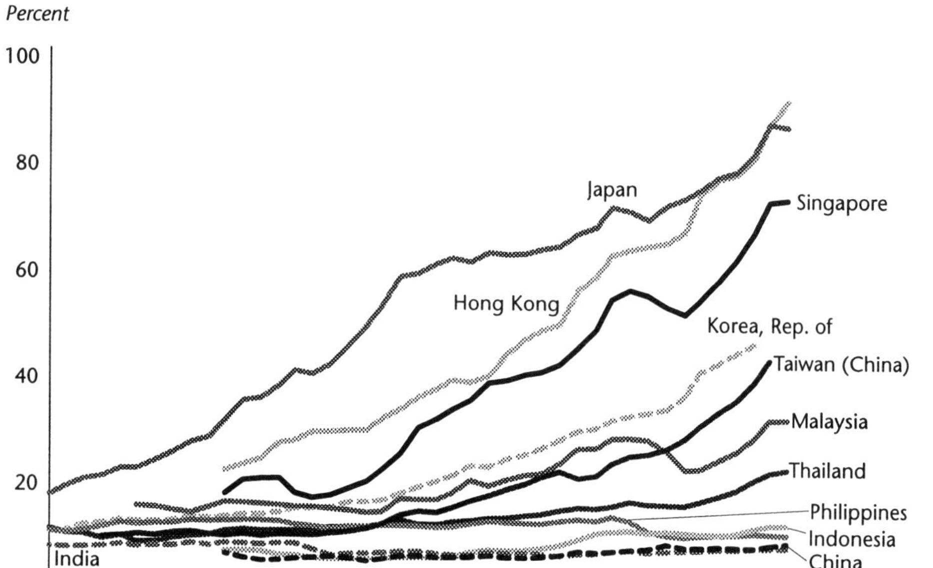

Note: Sample periods may vary. All values were converted to U.S. dollars using purchasing power parity exchange rates (Summers and Heston 1991, Mark 5.6)
Source: For East Asia, IMF 1996; for the United States, Council of Economic Advisers 1996.

exchange rate, using Summers and Heston 1991) shows how Asian economies took off and began to catch up with the United States. It also shows that the per capita incomes of the four tigers are converging to the U.S. level (figure 1).

The East Asian success story raises four important issues. First, why did some economies grow rapidly (by as much as 8 percent a year or more for two decades) and join the group of industrial countries while others (most notably in Africa) failed to grow at all? Second, are there common threads among the economies that did take off? Third, how did productivity growth increase? And fourth, can the lessons of the successful economies be replicated in other economies?

Convergence Models

Neoclassical growth models have been used to explain the rise in East Asia's per capita incomes. Given certain assumptions about the production function, the level of per capita income y is explained by the level of per capita capital k. Given other assumptions, the model has a unique equilibrium at a level of per capita income at which investment is just adequate to make up for the loss of capital through depreciation and the decline in per capita capital through population growth. Given that the economy starts from a low level of income, equilibrium converges. The equilibrium level of per capita income is independent of the savings rate (or the investment rate), although a high savings rate generates faster convergence.

In recent years growth theory has been tested using actual data (see, for example, Easterly 1995 and Barro and Sala-i-Martin 1995). In a typical regression cross-country growth rates for three decades are regressed on initial conditions, including such economic and social variables as openness to trade, political stability, and education levels.

Because the typical model would fail to predict that the East Asian economies would become high achievers, their high-growth experience is often called a "miracle." But these convergence regressions suffer from several weaknesses (Ito 1994, 1995a). First, the production function is assumed to be identical for all economies, and there is assumed to be a unique equilibrium to which all economies converge. The typical neoclassical growth model predicts that economies converge toward that equilibrium linearly. The lower is the initial level of income, the higher is the growth rate. This assumption, however, is contradicted by observations suggesting that there are two distinct types of low-income economies: those that are taking off and those that remain grounded. There is a critical moment at which an economy can grow rapidly. The explanatory variables in the typical convergence regression fail to capture the conditions for takeoff.

Second, reality may be nonlinear, and the apparent miracle of the East Asian outliers may actually be a result of misspecification. According to this argument there are three groups of countries (see Ito 1995a). The first group is the mature economies, with high income levels and low rates of economic growth. The second group is the converging economies—East Asian and other emerging market economies that are on a linear convergence with the first group. They range from low-income (less than $500 per capita), high-growth (10 percent) economies to nearly high-income economies, and there is a negative correlation between income and growth. For this group of economies the convergence regression fits well. The third group is the low-income, low-growth economies. Their income level is similar to that of high-growth countries, but their growth rate remains low. In convergence regressions the second and third groups are distinguished by other exogenous variables, but they often cannot be distinguished completely. Thus the convergence line is biased downward, giving East Asian economies high residuals in the regression.

Third, production functions may differ by country and by sector, and disaggregation of the economy is needed to estimate the development process correctly. The data needed for such sectoral estimates are not available.

Old and New Ideas about Takeoff and the Big Push

What conditions allow an economy to take off? "Old" development theory identified a set of initial conditions for sustained economic growth. Kuznets (1959, 1971), for example, observed that countries that had achieved "modern economic growth," such as Canada, Japan, the United States, and European countries, shared certain characteristics: modern scientific thought and technology were applied to industry; real GDP per capita grew at a rapid and sustained rate, usually accompanied by rapid population growth; the industrial structure was rapidly transformed (changing sectoral output, labor force, and capital stock distribution); and international contacts expanded. With more data from newly industrialized economies, this list of characteristics may require some rethinking.

New growth theory, beginning with the seminal work of Romer (1986, 1990), emphasizes economies of scale (in the sense that production enhances efficiency in the use of capital) and the effect of human capital formation on the increase in labor productivity (Lucas 1988, 1993). (See Barro and Sala-i-Martin 1995 for a survey of this literature.)

Demand spillovers from one industry to another also affect growth, a process that may be captured by input-output tables. When the textile industry grows, for example, it requires machinery and machine parts, and other maintenance-related goods and services have to be developed. The textile industry may stimulate the development of the garment industry and other textile-related industries if there is an advantage to proximity. This idea of the "big push" has been explored theoretically by Murphy, Shleifer, and Vishny (1989a, b). But the question of whether a sequence of industries or a big push of several industries is more important for economic development has not been resolved.

Srinivasan (1995) argues that even an "old" growth model can exhibit some of the characteristics associated with "new" growth models, such as a permanent shift in growth rates in response to a higher savings rate, depending on the shape of the production function. For example, if the marginal product of capital does not fall to zero as capital increases infinitely, a change in the savings rate can cause a permanent rise in the growth rate. Hence what is "new" is not that new results appear to

Table 1. Year in Which Agriculture's Share in GDP Fell to Displayed Levels in Selected East Asian Economies

Share	Japan	Korea, Rep. of	Thailand	Malaysia	Indonesia	China
Less than 30 percent		1967	1967	1964	1976	1984
Less than 20 percent	1956	1978	1982	1983	1991	1992
Less than 10 percent	1963	1989	1988			

Note: In Hong Kong and Singapore agriculture accounted for less than 10 percent of GDP for the entire sample period. In the Philippines agriculture's share in GDP has not fallen below 30 percent. Data for Malaysia are not available after 1984.
Source: For 1960–92, World Bank data. For Japan before 1960, Ohkawa and Shinohara 1979.

have been obtained but that a micro foundation has been established regarding how scale economies may have generated conventional results.

Structural Changes: The Flying Geese Pattern

East Asian economies experienced enormous changes in industrial and export structures over a short period. For economies poorly endowed with natural resources, like Japan, Korea, and most others in East Asia, growth has meant industrialization. Thus the relative shares of agricultural and industrial output provide a benchmark for the level of economic development (table 1). (Notable exceptions are Hong Kong and Singapore, which never had substantial agricultural sectors. Both economies began with commercial entrepôt businesses and developed into manufacturing.) Rapid economic growth is associated with a rise in productivity and a shift of resources toward manufacturing. The rate of growth rises as the share of manufacturing increases, partly explaining why rapid industrialization accelerates growth.

Similarly, the product composition of exports changes rapidly as an economy grows. A traditional primary commodity exporter first exports textiles and simpler (light) industrial products. After these products are well established, production and exports shift to more sophisticated goods, such as machinery, steel, and automobiles (table 2).

Table 2. Year in Which Machinery's Share in Exports Reached Displayed Levels in Selected East Asian Economies

Share	Japan	Singapore	Korea, Rep. of	Taiwan (China)	Malaysia	Hong Kong	Thailand
More than 60 percent	1984						
More than 50 percent	1976	1992					
More than 40 percent	1969	1985	1992	1992			
More than 30 percent		1983	1983	1987	1989		
More than 20 percent		1973	1978	1973	1986	1979	1991

Note: In Indonesia machinery's share in exports has not exceeded 10 percent, and in the Philippines it has not exceeded 20 percent.
Source: World Bank data.

Table 3. Sequencing of Growth of Key Industries in Selected East Asian Economies

Industry	Japan	Korea, Rep. of	Taiwan (China)	Hong Kong	Singapore
Textiles	1900–30; again in 1950		1960s–70s	Early 1950s	Early 1960s again in 1970s
Clothing, apparel	1950s		1960s–70s	1950s–60s	
Toys, watches, footwear	1950s		1960s–70s	1960s–70s	
Refining		Early 1960s			
Steel	1950s–60s	Late 1960s–early 1970s			
Chemicals	1960s–70s	Late 1960s, early 1970s	1970s		
Shipbuilding	1960s–70s	1970s			
Electronics	1970s	Late 1970s, 1980s	1980s		1970s
Automobiles	1970s–80s	1980s			
Computers, semiconductors	1980s	Late 1980s			
Banking and finance				Late 1970s, 1980s	1980s

Source: Ito 1994.

Development of key industries in Japan and other East Asian economies reveals a flying geese pattern (table 3). The pattern of output and exports suggests that these other economies are following a path of economic development similar to that of Japan.

The Young-Krugman Argument on Productivity

Young (1992, 1994, 1995), Kim and Lau (1994), and Krugman (1994) argue that some of East Asia's remarkable success was attributable to factor accumulation rather than a miracle. In estimates of the production function using capital and labor data, the portion of output growth that is not explained by factor accumulation (capital input times its productivity and labor input times its productivity) is called total factor productivity growth.

Young (1992) observes that Singapore invested much more heavily in capital stock than did Hong Kong in the 1970s and 1980s, while output growth was similar and returns to capital were comparable or lower. Detailed estimation with a translog production function, adjusting for changes in labor quality, reveals that output growth in Singapore is explained entirely by factor accumulation.

Young (1994, 1995) extended the study to Korea and Taiwan (China) and calculated total factor productivity in each economy, adjusting for shifts in resources from agriculture to manufacturing and for increases in participation rates and education levels. He concludes that a dramatic rise in factor inputs explains most output growth, leaving little for total factor productivity growth. Kim and Lau (1994) present similar findings. They estimated the production function for the five leading industrial countries (the United States, Japan, Germany, France, and the United Kingdom) and the four East Asian tigers, testing for a null hypothesis of no total factor productivity growth. The null hypothesis was rejected for the five industrial countries but not for the four tigers.

Young (1992) suggests that Singapore's total factor productivity growth was so low because investment proceeded too rapidly. New industries were promoted before old industries had started to enjoy total factor productivity benefits (the returns to scale economies that come from learning by doing). Krugman (1994) argues that if East Asia's growth (particularly Singapore's) was accounted for by increases in capital and labor, the future of these economies is dim, since there is a limit to increases in the mobilization of productive factors, especially labor. Simply put, once all workers attain a secondary education and work the maximum number of days and hours, labor input cannot increase further.

As suggested in earlier work and confirmed in Kim and Lau (1994), total factor productivity growth was key to output growth in the leading industrial countries. During the period of rapid economic growth in Japan, for example, total factor productivity increases accounted for about half of output growth. Denison and Chung (1976) found that more than half (4.9 percent) of Japan's average annual growth of 8.8 percent during 1953–71 could be attributed to technological progress. In the United States annual growth averaged 4 percent during 1948–69, of which 1.9 percent could be attributed to technological progress. (See Ito 1992 for a related discussion.)

These growth results must be interpreted carefully. In simplest terms total factor productivity growth estimates are obtained by the following equation:

$$\text{total factor productivity growth} = Y - K^* - L^*$$

where Y denotes output growth, K^* denotes capital growth times the productivity of capital, and L^* denotes labor growth times the productivity of labor. This is a simple stylized form, since in practice the translog specification (which accounts for the second cross-derivatives as well as the second derivatives) is used.

Total factor productivity growth is hard to determine, for several reasons. First, capital growth is difficult to estimate. The change in capital is estimated by gross investment minus depreciation, which in theory should reflect technological obsolescence as well as physical wear and tear. In practice depreciation is usually calculated mechanically by depreciating existing stock. Second, labor input should be adjusted for changes in the quality of workers; use of education levels provides only an approximate adjustment. Third, the productivity of capital and labor are hard to estimate. These coefficients may change over time, especially when economic structures are changing rapidly. Fourth, it is difficult to estimate value added rather than final consumption. Singapore, for example, has a high ratio of trade to GDP, but much of GDP is value added to exports rather than value added to final consumption in domestic markets. This may bias the estimates downward.

Table 4. Estimates of Total Factor Productivity Growth
(percent)

Economy	Young (1995) 1966–90	Bosworth and Collins (1996) 1960–94	Bosworth and Collins (1996) 1984–94	Sarel (1995) 1975–90	Sarel (1996) 1979–96
Hong Kong	2.3	—	—	3.8	—
Korea, Republic of	1.7	1.5	2.1	3.1	—
Singapore	0.2	1.5	3.1	1.9	2.5
Taiwan (China)	2.6	2.0	2.8	3.5	—
Indonesia	—	0.8	0.9	—	0.9
Malaysia	—	0.9	1.4	—	2.0
Philippines	—	0.4	–0.9	—	–0.9
Thailand	—	1.8	3.3	—	2.0

— Not available.
Source: IMF 1997.

For these reasons estimates of total factor productivity growth vary (table 4). Estimates of total factor productivity growth tend to be higher for the 1980s and 1990s than before. Even for Singapore, the economy at issue in Young's (1992) study, total factor productivity growth seems to have increased in later years, rising from 0.2 percent between 1966 and 1990 to 2.5 percent between 1979 and 1996 (Sarel 1996).

Even if Young's estimates are the most accurate, Young's and Krugman's interpretation may not be correct. First, even growth that comes from the accumulation of factors is better than no growth. Many developing countries invest, but they invest in the wrong kinds of fixed capital and inventory, so productivity does not increase. (This was part of the problem in the Soviet economy, to which Krugman compares Singapore.)

Second, Singapore has received more foreign direct investment in domestic manufacturing sectors than any of the other tigers or Japan. Low returns to capital may not be a real concern for Singapore, at least in the short run. As long as real wages increase with growth, lack of total factor productivity growth may not imply adverse welfare consequences.

Third, technological progress may be realized at the end of sequencing, if not during sequencing, as suggested by the higher estimates of total factor productivity growth in Singapore during the 1980s and 1990s (Sarel 1996) than during the 1960s and 1970s (Young 1992). If growth follows the flying geese pattern, what Young describes as too much investment and too hasty a shift to the next industry may not imply a loss in national welfare. If the time discount factor is sufficiently low, it may be optimal to run up the ladder of industrialization quickly before reaping even larger benefits (in total factor productivity growth) later.

Even if total factor productivity growth is low at earlier stages of development, it may not mean that a development process—that is, a country's combination of policies and market outcomes—is suboptimal. It is more important to sustain a high growth rate, whatever it takes, until the economy approaches the leading industrial countries in terms of per capita income.

Similarities and Differences among East Asian Economies

The geographical proximity and cultural similarities of East Asia's successful economies raise obvious questions about whether a formula for growth can be extracted from their experience. High savings, high investment, and export promotion are often cited as a common denominator among these economies, all of which are poor in natural resources and densely populated with educated and skilled workers. And in many countries, most notably Japan and Korea, the government has intervened in the economy to promote particular industries.

But there are at least as many differences among these economies. Japan's horizontal *keiretsu* and Korea's *chaebol* are dominated by large industrial conglomerates, whereas small-scale businesses propelled growth in Taiwan (China). Japan did not rely on foreign capital for its investment, whereas Korea and Singapore borrowed from abroad before achieving surplus in their current accounts. Financial institutions in Taiwan (China) are owned by the government, whereas Korean financial institutions are private and closely connected to large companies in the chaebol.

Lessons from East Asia and Applicability to Other Regions

Several lessons can be drawn from East Asia's experience and applied to other developing countries. Some common characteristics, such as an excellent education system, were clearly important. The flying geese pattern of industrial development is discernible, although economies that developed later seemed to grow even faster than those that developed earlier.

Neighborhood effects may also be strong (as the flying geese pattern suggests). Peer pressure ("If country A can grow, why not us?"), demand spillovers, and technology transfers may explain some of these effects. Thus it is important that the leader in a region initiate the growth process.

But applying lessons from East Asia's experience requires understanding how incentives have worked within each economic and political environment. For example, if a bureaucracy is fragile and easily influenced by political pressure, relying on government-led industrial policy would be ineffective. A strong meritocracy with an incentive system that is neutral to political force is required for successful government intervention. If financial expertise is limited, allocating resources through the stock market may produce inefficient results, since the stock market requires a broad base of heterogeneous participants to function without excessive volatility. Intermediation through the banking system may be more efficient initially. Financial markets will eventually deepen, but there may be an optimal stage (sequence) for introducing such markets.

Industrial Policy

The effectiveness of policy interventions such as industrial policy remains unclear. While some East Asian economies appear to have succeeded with industrial policy, many countries elsewhere have failed to use it effectively. And even in East Asia industrial policy is in decline. Tariffs and nontariff barriers have been lowered, and restrictions on interest rates and foreign exchange have been lifted. While particular industries have been targeted and promoted, subsidies have been reduced and in most cases phased out as governments move to promote other industries (as the flying geese pattern suggests; Ito 1993). And because protection was afforded to entire industries rather than to specific firms or vested interests, competitive pressure was maintained. Moreover, success in exports, the ultimate test of success, had to be achieved in a reasonable number of years or protection was withdrawn.

Successful industrial policy requires several economic, social, and political prerequisites. Infrastructure, including electricity, highways, airports, schools, and health facilities, must be in place as a precondition for growth. Successful market economies also must have an incentive system to reward economic agents for hard work, a monitoring device that ensures the reward system is not corrupted, a political-economic structure for correcting mistakes based on some balance of power (checks and balances), and a mechanism for competition, although not necessarily in markets.

Industrial policy can be used as an alternative to a market mechanism to achieve these outcomes (Ito 1993, 1995b). It is more likely to be effective in countries where bureaucrats are competent technocrats, hired and promoted on the basis of merit and immune from political influence. Bureaucratic decisions should be checked by others, however, so that the bureaucracy does not turn into an inefficient planning machine driven by inertia. As businesspeople and the general public become better educated and more sophisticated, the role of industrial policy diminishes—and that should be reflected in policy.

Stage-Sensitive Advice

Policies must change as a country develops. For example, although hyperinflation has a negative effect on growth, it is not clear that moderate inflation (of, say, less than 10 percent) should be corrected through monetary tightening. In many cases a high growth rate is associated with a rapid change in industrial structures and the consumption basket. Rapid growth in manufacturing implies a faster rate of change in productivity in tradable sectors than in nontradable sectors. This divergence results in a real appreciation of the currency, an effect known as the Balassa-Samuelson hypothesis. (See Ito, Isard, and Symansky 1997 for a discussion of the relevance of the hypothesis for the Asia-Pacific Economic Cooperation economies.) If the country adheres to a fixed exchange rate, its currency will appreciate if domestic inflation exceeds that of its trading partners. If this is the case, trying to lower inflation may be misguided.

Export promotion is a second policy that should change with development. Industrial policy is more likely to be successful in countries where industrialization has begun but remains at an early stage, because tracks to industrialization are left by other countries that industrialized earlier. If countries are willing to devote resources to promote industries that would be competitive in the world market and would have large spillover effects on other domestic industries, industrial policy should be given a chance—provided the bureaucracy acts in an economically efficient manner, free from politically vested interests.

The timing and method of privatization is a third example. If a developing country has a deep capital market, privatization of a state enterprise can proceed through open bidding for and subscription to stocks sold by the government (as has been done in Japan and the United Kingdom). But if a country lacks active and deep stock and bond markets and there is only a small middle class, privatization through open bidding will be difficult, and privatization through the distribution of vouchers to the public or sale to foreign companies (with proceeds helping the balance of payments) will yield better results. If capital markets are in place, however, privatization through the distribution of vouchers may not result in an efficient allocation of capital and management among industries because the price of the vouchers will not reflect the enterprise's true value on the black market.

Applicability to Africa

There has been keen interest in whether the lessons of East Asia's economic success can be applied to Africa (World Bank 1995; Harrold, Jayawickrama, and Bhattasali 1996). Several issues based on the arguments presented here should be noted.

First, is it reasonable to expect Africa to grow rapidly? According to the growth convergence argument, low-income countries should grow quickly. Without several preconditions, however, economies will not take off. Some of the preconditions, such as social infrastructure, are often made possible by government involvement. Efforts should be made to identify the factors needed for Africa to take off. Relative to Asian economies, many African economies lack basic social infrastructure (tables

Table 5. Social Indicators and Growth in Selected Asian Countries, 1980 and 1994
(percent unless otherwise specified)

Country	GNP per capita 1994 (U.S. dollars)	Share of agriculture in GDP 1980	Share of agriculture in GDP 1994	Infant mortality (per 1,000 live births) 1980	Infant mortality (per 1,000 live births) 1994	Primary school enrollment rate 1980	Primary school enrollment rate 1994	Illiteracy rate 1995	Average growth rate 1980–94
Korea, Rep. of	8,220	14	7	30	12	100	100	2	7.7
Malaysia	3,520	20	15	28	12	93	93	17	3.6
Thailand	2,210	19	10	44	36	99	98	6	6.5
Papua New Guinea	1,160	32	28	65	65	59	74	28	1.1
Philippines	960	23	22	51	40	100	100	5	–0.5
Indonesia	880	24	17	80	53	100	100	16	4.8
China	530	33	21	39	30	100	100	19	8.0
Mongolia	340	11	18	78	53	100	—	—	–1.9
Cambodia	240	—	51	160	100	—	47	—	—
Lao PDR	320	—	51	122	92	100	100	43	2.5
Vietnam	190	—	28	53	42	100	100	6	—

— Not available.
Source: World Bank 1996.

Table 6. Social Indicators and Growth in Selected African Countries, 1980 and 1994
(percent unless otherwise specified)

Country	GNP per capita 1994 (U.S. dollars)	Share of agriculture in GDP 1980	Share of agriculture in GDP 1994	Infant mortality (per 1,000 live births) 1980	Infant mortality (per 1,000 live births) 1994	Primary school enrollment rate 1980	Primary school enrollment rate 1994	Illiteracy rate 1995	Average growth rate 1980–94
Lesotho	700	18	11	60	44	100	98	—	−0.4
Cameroon	680	29	32	88	57	98	87	37	−2.8
Congo, Republic of	640	8	10	124	112	—	—	25	−1.2
Senegal	610	22	17	97	64	46	54	—	−0.4
Côte d'Ivoire	510	24	35	106	90	79	69	60	−4.8
Guinea	510	—	24	157	131	36	44	—	1.3
Zimbabwe	490	13	13	80	54	85	100	15	−0.3
Mauritania	480	30	24	117	98	37	69	—	−0.7
Ghana	430	57	46	98	74	80	76	—	2.0
Benin	370	33	34	118	96	64	64	—	−0.5
Central African Republic	370	39	42	114	100	71	71	40	−1.9
Zambia	350	14	31	88	108	90	100	22	−2.8
Togo	320	27	38	105	81	100	100	48	−2.0
Burkina Faso	300	31	31	149	128	18	38	81	0.8
Nigeria	280	31	42	96	81	100	93	—	−0.3
Kenya	250	29	24	66	59	100	91	—	0.1
Mali	250	57	42	180	125	27	31	—	−0.5

— Not available.
Source: World Bank 1996.

5 and 6), and takeoff has occurred in few, if any, African countries. But even countries with better social conditions—including Kenya, Lesotho, Nigeria, Togo, and Zambia—have failed to take off.

Second, the effectiveness and efficiency of government seem to be important. This does not necessarily mean that government should pursue an interventionist policy. Rather, policies should foster a market-friendly environment. Getting macroeconomic fundamentals right—that is, low inflation, low budget deficits, and few distortionary taxes—is crucial. Transparency in tax and other regulations is also important for businesses.

Third, when the economy reaches the takeoff stage, the orientation of policy may change to promote some industries. Comparative advantage must be carefully considered. From the point of view of donors and international financial institutions it may be too optimistic to hope that all countries can take off at the same time. The countries that get the conditions right should be encouraged to take off. Some export promotion by a country in the initial stage of industrialization may be encouraged.

Fourth, the stages of development are important. Most countries developed by moving from agriculture to textiles, toys, and simple manufacturing (such as stitching bags). First-stage industry is not particularly glamorous to promote. But having experience in light manufacturing is important for human capital formation, and success, however simple the industry, increases confidence among domestic and foreign investors. Skipping a stage in industrial evolution may not be productive. (Exceptions are countries willing to import managerial skills as well as capital.)

Comparing Asia and Africa

The comparison between Asia and Sub-Saharan Africa is relevant because many Asian countries were also low-income countries in the early 1960s. Since then economic development in many Asian economies has been remarkable, while many African economies have stagnated. Between 1961 and 1993 per capita GDP grew at an annual rate of 0.3 percent in Africa, 7.4 percent in East Asia, and 4.3 percent in Southeast Asia (World Bank 1996).

Why has growth been so slow in Africa? To find out, Harrold, Jayawickrama, and Bhattasali (1996) compared Asian and Sub-Saharan African economies. To control for initial conditions, the authors selected three groups of Southeast Asian and Sub-Saharan African countries with similar endowments: Nigeria and Indonesia, Côte d'Ivoire and Malaysia, and Ghana, Tanzania, and Thailand. In each group income levels moved together during the 1960s and 1970s and then deviated in the 1980s and 1990s.

The results showed that sound macroeconomic policy is the most important condition for growth (World Bank 1994, 1995; Harrold, Jayawickrama, and Bhattasali 1996). Keeping the inflation rate low by restraining spending and adopting prudent monetary policy is important. Moreover, the exchange rate policy must allow flexibility (or avoid real appreciation) to keep export industries from being destroyed. In comparing Nigeria and Indonesia, Harrold, Jayawickrama, and Bhattasali (1996) found that Indonesia was able to reduce the adverse effects of Dutch disease by adopting restrictive fiscal policy and prudent monetary policy. Early adjustments of the exchange rate in response to oil price changes (the devaluations of 1983 and 1986) were used to avoid a foreign exchange crisis. In contrast, Nigeria waited until a crisis forced a devaluation when the oil boom was clearly over. As a result Indonesia, which was poorer than Nigeria in 1960, surpassed Nigeria in the early 1980s in real GDP per capita. In 1975 the share of manufactures in export earnings was about 1 percent in both Nigeria and Indonesia. By 1992 the share had risen to 48 percent in Indonesia but remained almost unchanged in Nigeria.

Côte d'Ivoire and Malaysia, the second group of countries, are both endowed with rich agricultural cropland and minerals. Between 1961 and 1970 GDP in Côte d'Ivoire grew by 12.4 percent a year, a higher rate than that of the newly industrialized economies in Asia or the Association of Southeast Asian Nations (ASEAN) economies. Between 1965 and the late 1970s real GDP per capita grew at roughly the same rate in Côte d'Ivoire and Malaysia. Since the late 1970s, however, Malaysia has continued to grow, while GDP per capita has fallen in Côte d'Ivoire. This decline has been caused by fiscal indiscipline and a rigid exchange rate system (Harrold, Jayawickrama, and Bhattasali 1996). Appreciation of the real exchange rate in the early 1980s caused a temporary setback in Malaysia that was corrected within a few years. Malaysia also encouraged investment and exports through taxes and subsidies.

Ghana, Tanzania, and Thailand are the third group of countries compared in the study. Thailand's policies created an economic environment that allowed the private sector to focus on investment; in Ghana and Tanzania private investment was actively discouraged, if not prohibited, by direct controls. The increase in Thai investment was supported by strong banks. Thailand maintained a stable exchange rate policy but gradually depreciated its currency against the dollar by about 15 percent in the late 1980s. Ghana and Tanzania, by contrast, experienced huge swings in their exchange rates. During the first half of the 1980s their currencies appreciated more than 100 percent; by the late 1980s the value of their currencies had fallen to less than 10 percent of their peak levels.

Also seeking answers to questions about Africa's lack of growth, Sachs and Warner (1995, 1996) applied a convergence regression model in which the growth rate is affected by the gap between the equilibrium income level and the current income level. The lower is the income level, the higher is the growth rate. A country's equilibrium income level is affected by policy variables and structural variables. Policy variables include openness to trade, market efficiency, and the national savings rate; structural variables include initial income, physical access to port facilities, and natural resource abundance. The authors' estimates confirm convergence after controlling for policy and structural variables and show that resource endowment has a negative effect on growth. The estimated regression is used to calculate the contribution of each factor to lower growth in Africa by multiplying the difference between the averages for African and other developing countries by the estimated coefficients. The results show that low growth in Africa is explained largely by less openness and a lower savings rate.

This model suffers from faults common to most convergence regressions. First, the convergence path is specified to be linear. The farther away from the equilibrium, the faster the economy is expected to grow. Large positive residuals for East Asian economies and large negative residuals for African countries reflect the obvious fact that some low-income countries grew and others did not. Growth is explained in the model by assuming that the equilibrium (a goal) to which the economy converges is different for different countries. The less open is the economy, the lower is the equilibrium income level. Hence, given initial conditions, the economy with less openness experiences lower growth. Sachs and Warner are optimistic about the future of the African economies, since they believe that introducing economic reforms will raise the growth rate substantially. (According to their estimates, trade liberalization alone should raise average growth rates by 0.7 percent a year in formerly closed economies.)

Second, the Sachs and Warner model does not analyze changes over time for individual countries. Some African countries had high growth rates in the 1960s, but growth slowed considerably in the 1970s and 1980s. These dynamic changes are not addressed by Sachs and Warner (or any other convergence regression model), since their model is basically a cross-country analysis that takes 1970 as the initial condition. Sachs and Warner might explain a slowdown in some of the African countries as a "natural" phenomenon occurring as the economy nears the low-income equilibrium.

Conclusion

The lessons of East Asia's experience should be applied only cautiously to other countries. First, there is no single Asian model. Japan succeeded in import substitution before export promotion. Korea and Taiwan (China) succeeded in industrial policy, promoting investment and exports. Japan and the newly industrialized economies are poor in natural resources, which probably drove them to adopt export-oriented policies. Indonesia, Malaysia, and Thailand grew "despite" their rich endowment of natural resources (which, according to Sachs and Warner, should have retarded growth). Dutch disease can be overcome. These experiences show that having resources, as many African countries do, does not necessarily mean that industrialization, which produces rapid growth, cannot take place.

Second, it is important to determine a country's stage of development, so that appropriate policies can be developed. Different forces of economic development operate during different stages, and policies have to be adjusted to these changing needs. Rigorous modeling and econometric specification for this nonlinear process is left for further work.

Third, although industrial policy may have had a positive effect in Japan, Korea, and Taiwan (China), its applicability to other economies is limited. Without competent bureaucrats and sound governance, government intervention will be counterproductive (Roemer 1996). In fact, less involvement by government may increase growth in Africa. Competent government depends on the quality of human resources, which in turn depends on education. This does not mean, however, that African countries should spend more on education. They already spend a larger percentage of their national output on education than do Asian countries (4.1 percent in Africa compared with 3.7 percent in East Asia), suggesting that the quality of education may not be a function of spending alone (Harrold, Jayawickrama, and Bhattasali 1996).

Fourth, the successful Asian economies serve both as role models and as markets for the goods produced by other developing countries. Rapid growth appears to be contagious, in that neighbors of rapidly growing countries tend to grow faster. This may reflect the spillover of aggregate demand (as asserted in the big-push literature). If a group of countries starts to grow in Africa, it may become much easier for others to follow. Perhaps "flying geese" will migrate to Africa in the near future.

Finally, lessons can be drawn for Africa by focusing on stages of development and the factors that are important at each stage. A common development sequence is for growth to begin from a stagnant state once conditions warrant it. Growth often accelerates to double-digit rates, accompanied by structural changes. Resources shift from agriculture to simple manufacturing and then to more sophisticated manufacturing. As the share of manufacturing hits a plateau and the technological gap is narrowed, growth slows. Convergence regression models capture only the second stage of this dynamic process. More attention should be paid to the initial stage of growth acceleration, when getting the fundamentals right and achieving social and political stability are especially important.

Notes

1. Rostow (1960) defines takeoff as meeting three conditions: the share of productive investment in GNP rising from 5 percent or below to 10 percent or above, at least one strong manufacturing industry growing at a high rate, and having the political, social, and institutional framework to take advantage of economic externalities for expansion in modern sectors.

2. In this early usage, a surge in imports is followed by the start of domestic production. Domestic production increases and replaces imports (import substitution). As domestic production becomes efficient and competitive, imports drop and exports start to rise. This view was also linked to the production cycle theory of foreign direct investment (Vernon 1966).

References

Akamatsu, Kaname. 1961. "A Theory of Unbalanced Growth in the World Economy." *Weltwirtschaftliches Archiv* 86 (2): 196–217.

Barro, Robert, and Xavier Sala-i-Martin. 1995. *Economic Growth*. New York: McGraw-Hill.

Bosworth, Barry, and Susan M. Collins. 1996 "Economic Growth in East Asia: Accumulation versus Assimilation." *Brookings Papers on Economic Activity* 2. Washington, D.C.: Brookings Institution.

Council of Economic Advisors. 1996. *Economic Report of the President*. Washington, D.C.: U.S. Government Printing Office.

Denison, Edward F., and William K. Chung. 1976. "Economic Growth and Its Sources." In H. Patrick and H. Rosovsky, eds., *Asia's New Giant*. Washington D.C.: Brookings Institution.

Easterly, William. 1995. "Explaining Miracles: Growth Regressions Meet the Gang of Four." In Takatoshi Ito and Anne O. Krueger, eds., *Growth Theories in Light of the East Asian Experience*. Chicago: University of Chicago Press.

Harrold, Peter, Malathi Jayawickrama, and Deepak Bhattasali. 1996. *Practical Lessons for Africa from East Asia in Industrial and Trade Policies*. World Bank Discussion Paper 310. Washington, D.C.

Helpman, Elhanan, and Paul R. Krugman. 1985. *Market Structure and Foreign Trade: Increasing Returns, Imperfect Competition, and the International Economy*. Cambridge, Mass.: MIT Press.

IMF (International Monetary Fund). 1996. *International Financial Statistics*. Washington, D.C.

———. 1997. *World Economic Outlook 1997*. Washington, D.C.

Ito, Takatoshi. 1992. *The Japanese Economy*. Cambridge, Mass.: MIT Press.

———. 1993. "Industrial Policy for Development: Japanese Experience and Replicability." Background paper for *The East Asian Miracle*. World Bank, Washington, D.C.

———. 1994. "Comments on 'The East Asian Miracle: Four Lessons for Development Policy,' by John Page." *NBER Macroeconomic Annual 1994*. Cambridge, Mass.: MIT Press.

———. 1995a. "Comments on 'Explaining Miracles: Growth Regressions Meet the Gang of Four,' by William Easterly." In Takatoshi Ito and Anne O. Krueger, eds., *Growth Theories in Light of the East Asian Experience*. Chicago: University of Chicago Press.

———. 1995b. "Japanese Economic Development: Idiosyncratic or Universal?" Paper presented at the International Economic Association World Congress, December, Tunis.

———. 1996. "Japan and the Asian Economies: A 'Miracle' in Transition." *Brookings Papers on Economic Activity* 2. Washington, D.C.: Brookings Institution.

Ito, Takatoshi, Peter Isard, and Steven Symansky. 1997. "Economic Growth and Real Exchange Rate: An Overview of the Balassa-Samuelson Hypothesis in Asia." NBER Working Paper 5979. National Bureau of Economic Research, Cambridge, Mass.

Ito, Takatoshi, and Anne O. Krueger, eds. 1995. *Growth Theories in Light of the East Asian Experience*. Chicago: University of Chicago Press.

Itoh, Motoshige, Kazuharu Kiyono, Masahiro Okuno-Fujiwara, and Kotaro Suzumura, eds. 1991. *Economic Analysis of Industrial Policy*. New York: Academic Press.

Kim, Chung-Yum. 1993. "President Park Chung Hee's Economic Development Policy." Paper presented at the World Bank Colloquium on Lessons from East Asia, 25–26 March, Washington, D.C.

Kim, Jong-Il, and Lawrence J. Lau. 1994. "The Sources of Economic Growth of the East Asian Newly Industrialized Countries." *Journal of the Japanese and International Economies* 8 (3): 235–71.

Krugman, Paul. 1994. "The Myth of Asia's Miracle." *Foreign Affairs* (November–December): 62–78.

Kuznets, Simon. 1959. *Six Lectures on Economic Growth*. New York: Free Press.

———. 1971. *The Economic Growth of Nations*. Cambridge, Mass.: Harvard University Press.

Lucas, Robert E. 1988. "On the Mechanics of Economic Development." *Journal of Monetary Economics* 22 (1): 3–42.

———. 1993. "Making a Miracle." *Econometrica* 61 (2): 251–72.

Murphy, Kevin M., Andrei Shleifer, and Robert W. Vishny. 1989a. "Income Distribution, Market Size, and Industrialization." *Quarterly Journal of Economics* 104 (August): 537–64.

———. 1989b. "Industrialization and the Big Push." *Journal of Political Economy* 97 (5): 1003–26.

Ohkawa, Kazushi, and Miyohei Shinohara, eds. 1979. *Patterns of Japanese Economic Development: A Quantitative Appraisal*. New Haven: Yale University Press.

Roemer, Michael. 1996. "Could Asian Policies Propel African Growth?" HIID Development Discussion Paper. Harvard University, Harvard Institute for International Development, Cambridge, Mass.

Romer, Paul M. 1986. "Increasing Returns and Long-Run Growth." *Journal of Political Economy* 94 (October): 1002–37.

———. 1990. "Endogenous Technological Change." *Journal of Political Economy* 98 (5): S71–102.

Rostow, W.W. 1960. *The Stages of Economic Growth: A Non-Communist Manifesto*. Cambridge: Cambridge University Press.

Sachs, Jeffrey D., and Andrew M. Warner. 1995. "Economic Reform and the Process of Global Integration." *Brookings Papers on Economic Activity* 1. Washington, D.C.: Brookings Institution.

———. 1996. "Sources of Slow Growth in African Economies." HIID Development Discussion Paper. Harvard University, Harvard Institute for International Development, Cambridge, Mass.

Sarel, Michael. 1995. "Growth in East Asia: What We Can and What We Cannot Infer from It." IMF Working Paper 95/98. International Monetary Fund, Washington, D.C.

———. 1996. "Growth and Productivity in ASEAN Economies." Paper presented at the conference sponsored by the International Monetary Fund on macroeconomic issues facing ASEAN countries, 6–8 November, Jakarta.

Shleifer, Andrei, and Robert W. Vishny. 1988. "The Efficiency of Investment in the Presence of Aggregate Demand Spillovers." *Journal of Political Economy* 96 (December): 1221–31.

Srinivasan, T.N. 1995. "Long-Run Growth Theories and Empirics: Anything New?" In Takatoshi Ito and Anne O. Krueger, eds., *Growth Theories in Light of the East Asian Experience*. Chicago: University of Chicago Press.

Stiglitz, Joseph E. 1996. "Some Lessons from the East Asian Miracle." *The World Bank Research Observer* 11 (2): 151–77.

Summers, Robert, and Alan Heston. 1991. "Penn World Tables (Mark 5): An Expanded Set of International Comparisons, 1950–88." *Quarterly Journal of Economics* 106: 327–68.

Vernon, Raymond. 1966. "International Investment and International Trade in Product Cycle." *Quarterly Journal of Economics* 80 (2): 190–207.

Young, Alwyn. 1992. "A Tale of Two Cities: Factor Accumulation and Technical Change in Hong Kong and Singapore." *NBER Macroeconomic Annual 1992*. Cambridge, Mass.: MIT Press.

———. 1994. "Lessons from the East Asian NICs: A Contrarian View." *European Economic Review* 38 (3–4): 964–73.

———. 1995. "The Tyranny of Numbers: Confronting the Statistical Realities of the East Asian Growth Experience." *Quarterly Journal of Economics* 110 (3): 641–80.

World Bank. 1993. *The East Asian Miracle: Economic Growth and Public Policy*. A Policy Research Report. New York: Oxford University Press.

———. 1994. *Adjustment in Africa: Reforms, Results, and the Road Ahead*. A Policy Research Report. New York: Oxford University Press.

———. 1995. "A Continent in Transition: Sub-Saharan Africa in the Mid-1990s." Africa Region, Washington, D.C.

———. 1996. *Social Indicators of Development 1996*. Washington, D.C.

Comment on "What Can Developing Countries Learn from East Asia's Economic Growth?" by Takatoshi Ito

Deborah Bräutigam

Takatoshi Ito's article asks an important question: What can developing countries learn from East Asia's economic growth? Ito makes three points that help frame the debate. First, he argues that economic stages are important, and that economies are likely to need different policies and advice at different stages. Policies such as selective industrial promotion or trade liberalization might be appropriate at one stage of industrialization but could backfire if applied too soon. Second, he reminds us that effective governments played an important role in most East Asian economies, intervening more in the early stages of industrialization than in the later stages. Third, using the "flying geese" metaphor, he emphasizes how later-industrializing East Asian economies benefited from the proximity of early industrializers. I agree with much of what Ito says and so will focus on the areas in which we disagree. I will also attempt to clarify some of the issues Ito discusses and provide some empirical evidence on how parts of Africa are learning from East Asia.

Initial Conditions for East Asian Growth

Revisiting Rostow's (1960) stages-of-growth model, Ito notes that too little attention has been paid to identifying the factors that will enable Africa to accelerate growth. Nevertheless, Ito suggests that infrastructure, incentives, education, and sound macroeconomic policies are basic to any industrial development strategy. These points are not controversial, and they are surely good advice for any government wishing to learn from East Asia. Yet many of the studies that have tried to explain Africa's slow growth have failed to factor in Africa's relatively poor infrastructure and education levels and the structural difficulties these present for effective supply response. For example, as Ito notes, the recent Sachs and Warner (1997) effort to model Africa's experience "explains" low growth rates as a function primarily of highly distorted trade policies. The conclusion of their research is that if African countries liberalize, they too can grow at close to Asian levels. However, their model

Deborah Bräutigam is associate professor in the International Development Program at the School of International Service at American University.
Annual World Bank Conference on Development Economics 1997
©1998 The International Bank for Reconstruction and Development / THE WORLD BANK

fails to include variables for initial levels of education, infrastructure, and other conditions that have been identified by Ito, and others, as critical foundations for East Asian growth.

A comparison of initial levels of manufacturing, transport infrastructure, adult literacy, and electricity output in Taiwan (China) and in three of Africa's largest economies plus Mauritius (included as a successful industrializer) shows that initial levels were much higher in Taiwan (China) and Mauritius, the two successful industrializers, than in the other economies (table 1). Many African countries have not yet reached the levels of literacy and infrastructure development reached by some East Asian economies in the early 1950s. This suggests that factors in addition to economic policy play a crucial role in industrial takeoff, and no doubt make up part of the large, unexplained residual in the Sachs-Warner model.[1]

Two other initial conditions may have been influential in East Asian growth: the high levels of equality in most East Asian societies and the presence of significant security concerns in the neighborhood. Some scholars believe that the relative equality of income and assets explains much of the region's success. Rodrik (1994) found that in the Republic of Korea, Malaysia, Taiwan (China), and Thailand equality of land distribution and unusually high levels of primary school enrollment in 1960 explained a large portion of subsequent economic growth. Studies by Alesina and Perotti (1993) and others suggest that more equitable income distribution, which creates middle-class demand for local goods, eases pressures for destabilizing populist policies, reduces political instability, and may even be a prerequisite for successful industrialization.

Finally, in considering the transferability of the East Asian experience, we need to determine why East Asian governments were motivated to pursue the combination of policies and interventions that produced such spectacular growth with equity. Ito addresses this indirectly in discussing the neighborhood effect and the flying geese pattern. On the one side was Japan, providing technology, capital, and its outgrown industries to some of its neighbors. But we also have to consider the other neighbors: China, the Democratic People's Republic of Korea, Russia, and Vietnam. Security fears and rivalry initially led East Asian governments to invest more in rural

Table 1. Initial Conditions in Taiwan (China) and Selected African Countries

Economy, year	Share of manufacturing in GDP (percent)	Highways (meters per square kilometer)	Railways (meters per square kilometer)	Adult literacy (percent)	Electricity output (kilowatt hours per capita)
Taiwan (China), 1952	13	434	47	69	175
Côte d'Ivoire, 1960	5	107[a]	2	5	20
Kenya, 1960	10	77[a]	12	19	30
Mauritius, 1968	14	897[a]	0	61	246
Nigeria, 1960	5	97[a]	4	25[b]	12

a. Figures are circa 1970.
b. 1970.
Source: Bräutigam 1994.

development because the Communists had strong support from the landless and rural poor. Although only Japan, Korea, and Taiwan (China) implemented significant land reform, Indonesia and Malaysia also poured resources into rural development, thereby mitigating some of the effects of urban bias and establishing agriculture as the initial pillar of economic growth. These actions helped underpin the remarkable equity found in most of the region.

Government Policies and Growth in East Asia

Ito is somewhat ambivalent about the lessons East Asia provides for government intervention. At one point he remarks that although government effectiveness is important, that does not mean that governments should pursue interventionist policies. Shortly thereafter he suggests that governments might consider selective industrial promotion once industrial takeoff has been reached. These seemingly contradictory recommendations reflect the still unresolved debate over the role of government in East Asian industrialization. Until we understand better just what East Asian governments did, and when, this debate is likely to continue.

One of the problems with attempts to model East Asian growth and to look for lessons from East Asia is that, as Ito points out, different forces of economic development work in different ways at different stages. Most analysts of East Asia's experience have focused on more recent policies; few use data from before 1965. But if policies have different effects at different stages, it is crucial to consider what policies East Asian governments used at the start of their successful growth spurts as well as at later stages.

The example of Taiwan (China) is typical for East Asia. Taiwan (China) grew rapidly in the 1960s and 1970s before the economy was liberalized. Although Taiwan (China) began promoting exports as early as 1958, there were few significant changes in import controls and tariff rates until 1970–74. In 1966 tariffs on 60 percent of its imports exceeded 30 percent, and 42 percent of imports faced import controls. Moreover, many industries remained highly protected through the 1970s (Wade 1990). Interest rates were liberalized in 1981, capital market controls were loosened in 1983, and foreign exchange controls were ended in 1987, more than twenty years after the takeoff of export-oriented industrialization. This phased liberalization was also followed in Korea. Both Korea and Taiwan (China) grew rapidly in the 1960s and 1970s while retaining capital market and exchange controls. Chile and China still retain such controls, and their growth rates do not appear to have suffered. This suggests that countries wishing to learn from East Asia need to pay close attention to the optimal sequencing of financial liberalization. In view of the 1997 Asian currency and banking crises, it is clear that financial liberalization requires the oversight of a prudent and capable state, something most African countries presently lack.

Interventionist policies characterized the early stages far more than the later (more often studied) stages of East Asian industrialization. Although Ito recognizes that different policies may be required at different stages of development, he appears to discount the importance of illiberal policies like import substitution, which almost all the East Asian economies adopted early on and retained even after they turned to export promotion (World Bank 1993). A sustained push at developing domestic industry meant that as Taiwan (China) was beginning its export push, manufacturing had already risen to 19 percent of GDP (Council for Economic Planning and Development 1996). Many Sub-Saharan African countries have yet to achieve that level of industrialization: in 1995 manufacturing as a share of GDP averaged 15 percent in the region (World Bank 1997).

The successful mix of interventionist policies was possible in East Asia largely because of the state's high capacity. This suggests that African governments interested in learning from East Asia would do well to study how governments there built state capacity, and whether some of the mechanisms used in the early years by East Asian governments, which achieved stability without liberalization, might also be useful for Africa (Bräutigam 1994, 1996; Stein 1995).

Learning from East Asia: Two African Cases

Case studies of two African efforts to learn from East Asia reveal the importance of one aspect of learning seldom mentioned in studies of East Asia's experience: the way learning is transferred and the likely importance of private sector links and networks in bringing Asian-style industrialization to other developing countries.

Mauritius, a small African country in the Indian Ocean, was a multiethnic, resource-poor, densely populated, commodity-exporting economy at independence, dependent on plantation cultivation of sugar.[2] The first post-independence government set out to learn from East Asia, dispatching a team of experts to visit Taiwan (China) and other East Asian economies that had already begun to attract notice for their efforts in developing export-oriented manufacturing. In 1970 the Mauritian government created the first export processing zone in Africa—one of just ten countries worldwide to establish such a program—and encouraged Asian investors to set up factories. As a result the economy took off: by the mid-1990s Mauritius had been growing by about 6 percent a year for several decades. At more than $3,100, per capita income is far higher than typical African levels and on par with that in Malaysia. Over this period the Gini coefficient of income inequality fell from .50 to .37, and manufactured goods rose from 0 to 67 percent of exports.

When Mauritius began its development push at independence, education and infrastructure basics were already in place (see table 1). The literacy rate was comparable to that of Taiwan (China) in 1952, and primary education was universal by 1965. (At .50, however, the Gini coefficient was relatively high.) In the following years inflation was low, savings rates were high, the exchange rate was not overvalued, and government deficits were relatively low—reflections of the sound macroeconomic policies that most observers agree were crucial in East Asia. Moreover, as in East Asia, trade liberalization was not a big part of this story (at least in the first fifteen or so years after Mauritius began its export push). When exports began growing by 30 percent a year in 1983, the average effective rate of protection on manufactured goods was 89 percent. In 1986 Mauritius was still successfully resisting external pressures to liberalize trade (Bräutigam 1994).

The other case of learning from East Asia does not show up in national economic statistics. The eastern Nigeria towns of Aba, Nnewi, and Onitsha form part of an area known locally as "the Taiwan of Africa," Nigeria's newest industrial axis. Since the early 1980s this area has seen remarkable indigenous industrial development (Bräutigam 1997b). In Nnewi, a town of 100,000 people, some two dozen medium-size factories began operating between 1983 and 1994, creating more than 2,700 new jobs. More than half of these factories were established by Nigerian auto parts traders who had observed manufacturing in East Asia firsthand. Having been exposed to Asian manufacturing practices at about the same time (in the early 1980s) that the Nigerian government was making import licenses for finished goods harder to obtain, these traders decided to manufacture auto parts in Nigeria for local distribution and export. The networks they had formed as traders allowed them to contract for machinery and technical assistance through Asian manufacturers and distributors whom they knew and trusted.

Although Nigeria's difficulties in maintaining macroeconomic stability since 1991 have led to a sharp decline in new investment in Nnewi, both examples show that learning from Asia may be speeded by personal private sector contacts that make industrial dynamism tangible. When these contacts are complemented by government interest and support, as in Mauritius, an entire economy can benefit. When governments are indifferent, or even hostile, to indigenous business, as in Nigeria and much of the rest of Africa, small pockets of Asian-style growth will have only local effects that fail to show up in national data. Growth regressions cannot easily capture the dynamics of the networks and relationships that brought East Asian ideas to Mauritius and Nnewi, suggesting that we need a better understanding of how actual learning can and does occur if we want to understand the relevance of Asia's experience for Africa.

Notes

1. I refer here to the residual that would be left unexplained if Sachs and Warner had not assumed different equilibria for different countries.
2. This section on Mauritius draws on Bräutigam (1994, 1997a).

References

Alesina, Alberto, and Roberto Perotti. 1993. "Income Distribution, Political Stability, and Investment." NBER Working Paper 4486. National Bureau for Economic Research, Cambridge, Mass.

Bräutigam, Deborah. 1994. "What Can Africa Learn from Taiwan? Political Economy, Industrial Policy, and Adjustment." *Journal of Modern African Studies* 32 (1): 111–38.

———. 1996. "State Capacity and Effective Governance." In Benno Ndulu and Nicolas van de Walle, eds., *Agenda for Africa's Economic Renewal*. Washington, D.C.: Overseas Development Council.

———. 1997a. "Institutions, Economic Reform, and Democratic Consolidation in Mauritius." *Comparative Politics* 30 (1): 45–62.

———. 1997b. "Substituting for the State: Institutions and Industrial Development in Eastern Nigeria." *World Development* 25(7): 1063–80.

Council for Economic Planning and Development. 1996. *Taiwan Statistical Data Book 1996*. Taipei.

Rodrik, Dani. 1994. "King Kong Meets Godzilla: The World Bank and the East Asian Miracle." In Albert Fishlow and Catherine Gwin, eds., *Miracle or Design? Lessons from the East Asian Experience*. Washington, D.C.: Overseas Development Council.

Rostow, W.W. 1960. *The Stages of Economic Growth: A Non-Communist Manifesto*. Cambridge: Cambridge University Press.

Sachs, Jeffrey D., and Andrew M. Warner. 1997. "Sources of Slow Growth in African Economies." Harvard Institute for International Development, Cambridge, Mass.

Stein, Howard, ed. 1995. *Asian Industrialization and Africa*. London: Macmillan.

Wade, Robert. 1990. *Governing the Market: Economic Theory and the Role of Government in East Asian Industrialization*. Princeton, N.J.: Princeton University Press.

World Bank. 1993. *The East Asian Miracle: Economic Growth and Public Policy*. A Policy Research Report. New York: Oxford University Press.

———. 1997. *World Development Indicators 1997*. Washington, D.C.

Comment on "What Can Developing Countries Learn from East Asia's Economic Growth?" by Takatoshi Ito

Andrés Rodríguez-Clare

I do not know whether the title of Takatoshi Ito's article was proposed by the organizers of this conference, but for rhetorical purposes I will assume that it was. Confronted with such a title, I think most people would expect the objective to be to extract policy lessons from East Asia's experience. This is not, however, what Ito's article does. And this is a compliment, not a criticism.

Lessons and Pitfalls

The first problem with extracting policy lessons from East Asia's experience is that, even if the newly industrialized economies are included, we are talking about only a few economies—and very different ones at that. There is heavy government involvement in some economies (Japan and the Republic of Korea) but very little in others (Hong Kong). Large conglomerates dominate industry in some economies (Korea) but are absent in others (Taiwan, China). Most of these economies are poor in natural resources and densely populated, but some (Indonesia and Malaysia) are neither. And the list of differences goes on.

The second problem is that extracting policy lessons from a few economies usually leads to a qualitative exploration of the policies they followed, which usually only serves to verify the author's original hypotheses. Proponents of industrial policy, for example, point to policies that seem to have worked, while skeptics point to cases that failed.

The third problem is that even moving beyond qualitative analysis it is difficult to extract policy lessons from the experience of these economies because all those in the sample experienced rapid growth. If one is seeking to determine key elements for growth, looking at these economies may help in discarding a few possibilities. East Asia's experience shows, for example, that large industrial conglomerates are not essential, since they operate in neither Hong Kong nor Taiwan (China). But narrowing the group of possibilities further requires expanding the set of economies being

---

Andrés Rodríguez-Clare is associate professor of business economics in the Graduate School of Business at the University of Chicago.
Annual World Bank Conference on Development Economics 1997
©1998 The International Bank for Reconstruction and Development / THE WORLD BANK

analyzed to find elements common to the successful ones but not to the rest. In doing this it is natural to consider not only the economies of East Asia but all those that achieved high growth rates.

To see why doing this is important consider the ongoing discussion about the role of total factor productivity growth in East Asian economies. According to Young (1995), total factor productivity growth accounts for about a third of per capita income growth for these economies (except for Singapore, which had almost no total factor productivity growth). Some analysts have concluded from this finding that rapid total factor productivity growth is not the key to rapid growth. Before drawing this conclusion, however, it is necessary to compare total factor productivity growth rates across fast- and slow-growth countries. Klenow and Rodríguez-Clare (1997) did this and found a strong positive correlation between total factor productivity growth and growth in output per worker. Furthermore, taking into account the fact that total factor productivity growth naturally leads to some capital accumulation, the study found that almost all the variation in the rate of growth in output per worker is explained by differences in the growth rate of total factor productivity.

In addition to showing the importance of comparing a large number of fast- and slow-growing countries, this result suggests that the key to fast growth is not merely high enrollment and investment rates; high total factor productivity growth is crucial as well. But what policies are most conducive to fast total factor productivity growth? In recent years cross-country growth regressions have been the most common way to answer this question (although not always interpreted this way). As Ito notes, however, there are serious problems with this approach. Even more important than the problems he notes (in particular, that these regressions fail to capture the conditions for takeoff) is the problem of endogeneity of regressors, which makes it hard to conclude anything about causality from cross-country growth regressions. Take, for instance, the role of education in growth. A consistent result in cross-country growth regressions is that, all other things being equal, higher initial enrollment rates lead to faster subsequent growth. In a simple calibration exercise Bils and Klenow (1996) find that the coefficients estimated by Barro and Sala-i-Martin (1995)—that 0.68 more years of male secondary education increase annual growth by 1.1 percentage points, and 0.09 more years of male higher education increase it by 0.5 percentage point—are much too large to reflect the effect of schooling on growth but could easily reflect the effect of expected growth on schooling.

For another interesting example of the problem created by endogeneity of regressors—and one that is important in its own right—consider macroeconomic stability. Ito, and most of the related literature, concludes that macroeconomic stability (particularly low and stable inflation and low volatility in real interest rates and real exchange rates) is essential for fast growth. This is consistent with the finding in cross-country growth regressions that fast growth is associated with low inflation and a low black market premium. This is a reasonable conclusion (macroeconomic stability does appear essential for growth), but I think this piece of common wisdom follows more from intuition and experience than from rigorous empirical analysis.

For one thing, there is the issue of causality: maybe fast growth makes it easier to maintain macroeconomic stability. It is also possible that a third factor, such as income equality, explains both macroeconomic stability and fast growth. Moreover, if we want to go beyond these qualitative statements to a quantitative statement about the effect the degree of macroeconomic stability has on growth (so that we can determine, for instance, whether the government should risk increasing the deficit by reducing tariffs), we need a theory explaining how macroeconomic instability slows growth.

All these problems make me skeptical that we can extract important policy lessons by comparing international experience without first developing proper theories about how different policies affect growth. And naturally, I am even more skeptical that we can learn much about appropriate growth policies by looking at East Asia's experience alone. There is something to be learned from this experience, but it is something more basic: by looking at these cases of accelerated development, we can gain some understanding of development itself.

Models of Development

Here I come to the second part of my comments, the alternative interpretation of the title of Ito's article to which I alluded in my introduction. According to my reading, this alternative interpretation is the thrust of Ito's article. The three metaphors for economic development that he mentions (takeoff, ontogeny recapitulating phylogeny, flying geese) all deal with the nature of development rather than with the policies needed to encourage growth. I think we can learn something useful in this way, especially once we reject the simple neoclassical model that views development as simply the accumulation of physical and human capital. If development is not simply about capital accumulation, what is it about? What explains rapid total factor productivity growth?

It is interesting to think about an economic model of development that would capture the insights of Ito's metaphors (a metaphor for Ito's metaphors!). The first two metaphors, takeoff and ontogeny recapitulating phylogeny, can be captured by a model with multiple steady states: the underdeveloped steady state, in which there is little industrial activity, and the developed steady state, in which the country is competitive in complex industrial processes and machinery is an important part of overall exports. Development entails going from the underdeveloped to the developed steady state, a process during which agriculture diminishes in importance and the economy moves on to ever more complex industrial activities. This process would certainly entail fast total factor productivity growth, as the evidence suggests. But what determines whether the economy embarks on this process?

The "history versus expectations" models of Krugman (1991) and Matsuyama (1991) provide a useful framework for thinking about this question. In these models there are two steady states and multiple equilibria that depend on where the economy starts. If the economy starts close to the underdeveloped steady state, there is a unique equilibrium that entails approaching that steady state, referred to as an underdevelopment trap. If the economy starts sufficiently far away from the underdeveloped steady state, there is an equilibrium that leads to the developed steady state, and there may also be an equilibrium leading back to the underdeveloped steady state.

Interpreted this way, there are two elements for takeoff: the existence of an equilibrium path toward the developed steady state and the "choice" by society of this equilibrium. In other words, development needs both the right fundamentals and optimistic expectations.

This model of development is consistent with Ito's third metaphor, that development spreads in a flying geese–like pattern, with the leader moving on to ever more complex industrial processes (such as automobiles and electronics), leaving more standard and labor-intensive industries (such as textiles) to the countries "flying" behind it. How is this view consistent with the model of development articulated earlier? There are two possibilities, one linked to expectations and the other to fundamentals. The first possibility is that the optimism necessary for development may be contagious; when people see that the country next door is developing, they become optimistic that their own country can do so too. The second possibility is that having neighbors that are developed improves the likelihood that a country's only equilibrium path is the one that leads to the developed steady state.

This view of development, shaped by Ito's three metaphors, is interesting and stimulating. But unfortunately—and this is my main criticism of Ito's article—it does not take us very far in thinking about whether this view is correct. To do this we must first complete the model of development laid out earlier in order to identify the source of the aggregate and external increasing returns to scale that lead to the multiplicity of steady states.

Ito mentions the big-push model of Murphy, Shleifer, and Vishny (1989a, b), but the impressive expansion of exports experienced by East Asian economies makes me think that the aggregate externalities lie more at the production than at the final consumption level and that they arise as firms set up production and demand more inputs, something that generates an expansion in the variety of inputs available in the economy. This, in turn, allows other firms in the economy to use an expanded variety of inputs and increases overall productivity (see Rodríguez-Clare 1996a, b). This is the process that leads to the formation of a "cluster" in Michael Porter's (1990) analysis.

I think it would be interesting to see whether the East Asian miracle can be explained in terms of this kind of model. I am not an expert on East Asia, so instead of doing this I will briefly consider other sources of evidence for and against this view of development. Three pieces of evidence suggest the existence and importance of aggregate increasing returns arising through the variety of intermediate goods available in the local economy. First, industries are very geographically concentrated (Silicon Valley, California, is the best example; see also Ellison and Glaeser 1994). Second, rich countries are usually near one another; the probability of being rich increases when a country is located near a rich country. Just think what would happen if you were to take Honduras and put it between Germany and Italy; things would change drastically even without any change in policies. (As a related exercise, consider southern Italy. It is hard to imagine, given its policies and institutions, that this region would have its relatively high income level if it were located in Africa or South Asia.) The flying geese pattern of development can be seen as a dynamic manifestation of this phenomenon. Third, as Holmes (1995) has shown, plants in areas of industrial concentration rely more on inputs purchased from other firms than do firms in isolated areas.

On the negative side there are two issues that concern me about the practical importance of the heterodox development model outlined above. First, not all economies that go through the structural transformation described by Ito experience the fast growth implied by the model. Second, it is not clear that large economies are richer than small ones. This second issue worries me, but it does not make me lose much sleep because it is not clear how we should define an economy. (Is it a country? A region? A city?) Moreover, even if we could define an economy, it is not clear what variable should define its size (population? density? stock of physical or human capital?).

Implications for Development Policy

I think that we can indeed learn something from the East Asian miracle, but it is more about the nature of development than about which policies promote growth. The fact that these economies developed so rapidly, in sequence, and near one another does not necessarily imply that development is associated with aggregate increasing returns of the kind described above, but it is certainly suggestive evidence.

What does all this imply for development policy? An important if unexciting point is that policies that are bad for growth in orthodox models are also bad for growth in the heterodox model. Development is retarded by macroeconomic instability, high effective rates of protection to politically powerful economic groups, regulation that makes business creation and expansion more expensive, and government policies that impede the normal workings of the market with no clear economic purpose. A second, more adventurous point is that there may indeed be some room for industrial policy that is designed to help an economy embark on the equilibrium path toward the developed steady state. Coming from Latin America, however, I am wary of opening up possibilities for rent seeking and corruption, and I think that such a policy would be desirable only if we had the knowledge needed to implement it systematically rather than leaving it to the discretion of the administration in power. And right now, I think that we lack such knowledge.

References

Barro, Robert, and Xavier Sala-i-Martin. 1995. *Economic Growth*. New York: McGraw-Hill.

Bils, Mark, and Peter Klenow. 1996. "Does Education Cause Growth or the Other Way Around?" Graduate School of Business, University of Chicago.

Ellison, Glenn, and Edward Glaeser. 1994. "Geographic Concentration in U.S. Manufacturing Industries: A Dartboard Approach." NBER Working Paper 4840. National Bureau for Economic Research, Cambridge, Mass.

Holmes, Thomas. 1995. "Localization of Industry and Vertical Disintegration." Staff Report 190. Federal Reserve Bank of Minneapolis.

Klenow, Peter, and Andrés Rodríguez-Clare. 1997. "The Neoclassical Revival in Growth Economics: Has It Gone Too Far?" In Ben Bernanke and Julio Rotemberg, eds., *NBER Macroeconomics Annual 1997*. Cambridge, Mass.: MIT Press.

Krugman, Paul. 1991. "History vs. Expectations." *Quarterly Journal of Economics* 106 (2): 651–67.

Matsuyama, Kiminori. 1991. "Increasing Returns, Industrialization, and Indeterminacy of Equilibrium." *Quarterly Journal of Economics* 106 (2): 617–50.

Murphy, Kevin M., Andrei Shleifer, and Robert W. Vishny. 1989a. "Income Distribution, Market Size, and Industrialization." *Quarterly Journal of Economics* 104 (August): 537–64.

———. 1989b. "Industrialization and the Big Push." *Journal of Political Economy* 97 (5): 1003–26.

Porter, Michael. 1990. *The Competitive Advantage of Nations*. New York: Free Press.

Rodríguez-Clare, Andrés. 1996a. "The Division of Labor and Economic Development." *Journal of Development Economics* 49 (1): 3–32.

———. 1996b. "Multinationals, Linkages and Economic Development." *American Economic Review* 86 (4): 852–73.

Young, Alwyn. 1995. "The Tyranny of Numbers: Confronting the Statistical Realities of the East Asian Growth Experience." *Quarterly Journal of Economics* 110 (3): 641–80.

Floor Discussion of "What Can Developing Countries Learn from East Asia's Economic Growth?" by Takatoshi Ito

A participant from the World Bank, drawing on the comparisons made between Africa and East Asia, asked whether Central Asia could also learn from East Asia's success. Rather than following the Washington consensus on development and growth, he said, should a country like Uzbekistan instead emulate the export promotion, import substitution, and interventionist policies used by, say, the Republic of Korea—even to the point of using directed credit and, possibly, multiple exchange rates? Given the region's tradition of authoritarian leadership and the gradual pace of development it desires, is the Korean model appropriate?

Deborah Bräutigam (discussant) replied that Central Asian countries, because of their landlocked position, would have trouble implementing certain East Asian policies. As a result it is unlikely that trade will become Central Asia's engine of growth. Still, she said, the region could well look to East Asia for lessons on using government intervention in ways that promote growth.

A participant from the Bangladesh Institute of Development Studies noted the importance of initial conditions when comparing economic growth over a long period. Investments during the colonial period were important in determining those conditions, he agreed, but of even greater importance were the different types of colonialism, which had a lasting effect on agrarian transformation and subsequent economic development.

Bräutigam concurred, adding that it is also important to consider the kinds of institutions colonialism left in place. Douglass North's work on institutions, she said, emphasizes the importance of examining the far-reaching effects of these initial institutions and the paths they put countries on.

A participant from the University of Delhi observed that most East Asian economies, despite their considerable heterogeneity, share some common features—notably, high savings rates, high investment in skills formation, and high levels of intraregional cooperation. Given their moderate income levels, he asked, how had some East Asian economies managed to achieve savings rates of 35 percent?

This session was chaired by Lyn Squire, director of the Policy Research Department at the World Bank.
Annual World Bank Conference on Development Economics 1997
©1998 The International Bank for Reconstruction and Development / THE WORLD BANK

Takatoshi Ito (presenter) said that two factors had played an important role in East Asia's high savings rates. First, governments promoted savings through tax policies and through social security and pension plan policies. Malaysia and Singapore, for example, have considerable savings invested in their pension plans as a direct result of government efforts. Such policies are justified if the savings are used for domestic investment. Second, private sector expectations have been important because people are more patient if they have high expectations of future growth and consumption. And patient people are willing to use their money for long-term domestic savings rather than for current consumption. Having both conditions occur, he said, probably requires a virtuous circle between savings and growth.

Grzegorz Kolodko, Poland's former deputy prime minister and minister of finance, agreed with Ito's message that there had been no East Asian "miracle." Rapid growth in East Asia and in Poland in recent years, said Kolodko, was the result of sound economic policy—with an emphasis on building strong institutions and investing in human capital. Rather than hewing to the Washington consensus, which argues that reforming countries must engage in "shock therapy" liberalization, Poland had taken a gradual approach. Slower liberalization made recessions less severe and economic contractions less pronounced, providing therapy without the shocks. Given Poland's experience, Kolodko asked, did Ito have any advice for other transition economies that have not done as well?

Ito agreed that institution building is crucial. Many transition economies have distributed vouchers and securities as part of their mass privatization programs without first establishing a stock market. Such an approach, Ito said, is bound to fail. Institution building efforts should be accompanied by investments in human capital because reformed institutions cannot be effective without properly trained personnel.

A participant from the World Bank asked what could be done about countries that are stuck in the middle. That is, several Latin American and transition economies have made enormous investments in setting up the right initial conditions yet have not experienced rapid growth. What policies, she asked, should these countries use to kick-start development?

Andrés Rodríguez-Clare (discussant) replied that the consistent application of clear policies is an important first step. The public must have an idea of where a country is moving and have faith in the approach being used to get there. Costa Rica, for example, experienced fairly rapid growth until 1994. Since then growth has slowed, leading to a recession, because government policies have stalled. The private sector is no longer receiving clear signals on where economic reform is going.

One of Costa Rica's most effective policies, Rodríguez-Clare continued, involved emphasizing and investing in specific sectors, such as microelectronics. For the past ten years the government has been teaching English and computer skills in primary and secondary schools. As a result Intel has built a plant there, and other high-tech companies are investing or planning to invest in Costa Rica. The government is not subsidizing the microelectronics industry, but it has been active in luring investment from microelectronics companies. Creating such clusters of investment may be one way for countries to get moving again.

A participant from the World Bank questioned Bräutigam's assertion that industrialization was possible in the absence of macroeconomic reform. Bräutigam had cited eastern Nigeria as an example, he said, but in fact industrialization occurred there only after the currency was devalued and trade was liberalized. Both moves made it easier for companies to import raw materials and other inputs, facilitating their development and making them more competitive.

Bräutigam replied that the participant was both right and wrong. True, Nigeria's structural adjustment program and the reforms that accompanied it spurred production, but a third of the companies that Bräutigam had researched were engaged in production before the program began. In the early 1980s there were severe restrictions on imports, so many companies produced goods that otherwise would have been imported. Thus production was occurring in the absence of macroeconomic reform.

But when the restrictions on imports were eased under the structural adjustment program, Bräutigam continued, many companies took the opportunity to import, driving industrialization. During 1986–91 production boomed. Since then, however, it has been fairly stagnant. Many traders are waiting for the situation to stabilize before making investments—that is, waiting for macroeconomic reform.

A participant from the World Bank asked about the emphasis the speakers had placed on manufacturing's role in East Asia's industrialization. Ito, he said, had claimed that in East Asia total factor productivity grew by 3 percent in agriculture and 10 percent in manufactures. Yet, the participant said, most of the data on total factor productivity in developing countries show that it grows faster in agriculture than in manufacturing. Certainly, in high-growth economies agricultural output has declined and capital-intensive sectors have grown. But, he said, that does not mean that total factor productivity growth in agriculture has stagnated, and it should not suggest the need for import substitution policies or for direct taxation of agriculture—approaches that have been spectacularly unsuccessful in Africa.

Ito said that he had not meant to downplay the importance of agriculture or increases in agricultural productivity. Still, he said, productivity growth—both labor productivity and total factor productivity—is limited in agriculture, at least in developing countries. By contrast, continued high growth in manufacturing is possible. Thus agriculture should play only a supporting role in growth.

As for import substitution policies, Ito continued, to some extent they have worked in Japan and the Republic of Korea. In Latin America and the Philippines, however, they failed on a massive scale. The difference in outcomes is determined by whether import substitution is supported by competition in the domestic economy. If just one or two companies has the right to produce import substitutes, rent seeking will emerge and the effort will fail. But import substitution policies can be effective if they foster competition among, say, five or six licensed domestic firms, or even allow free entry. Growth, he said, is often determined by whether industrial policies result in rent seeking.

Lyn Squire (chair) closed the discussion by saying that the main message he had gotten was that both policies and institutions are crucial to development. In the past, he said, the World Bank had probably put too much emphasis on getting policies right and too little on strengthening institutions. Because institutional incentives and institutional capacity generally determine whether policies are implemented, the Bank ought to take a closer look at what its policy recommendations mean in terms of institutional delivery.

The Political Economy of High and Low Growth

Alberto Alesina

Institutional quality—as measured by bureaucratic efficiency, absence of corruption, protection of property rights, and the rule of law—is important for growth. So are political stability and civil and economic liberties. Government consumption is generally not conducive to growth, and is particularly harmful in countries with weak institutions. In addition, government consumption does not seem to improve social indicators or reduce poverty or income inequality—again, especially in countries with weak institutions. Given that foreign aid typically increases government consumption, the World Bank and other international organizations should consider withdrawing financial and technical assistance from countries that do not satisfy minimum standards of institutional quality. Cutting off assistance may increase growth and foster social development in the medium run by creating incentives for institutional development.

Over the past few decades countries' growth rates have been remarkably different, and almost every possible variable has been invoked to explain the phenomenon. In addition to the more standard economic variables (education, savings rates, fertility, and so on), a long list of political-institutional variables has recently been considered. While there is a reasonable amount of agreement on the economic determinants of growth, the picture is much murkier for political-institutional variables.

This article has two objectives. First, it tries to derive robust conclusions about which of the many political-institutional variables suggested in the literature are important for growth, and to explain how these variables influence government performance. Second, it seeks to derive from this analysis policy lessons for an international organization like the World Bank.

The article concludes that institutions are important for growth. Especially important are protection of property rights, a capable and honest bureaucracy, and

---

Alberto Alesina is professor of economics at Harvard University. The author is grateful to Ravi Kanbur and Zanny Minton-Beddoes for comments and to Romain Wacziarg for excellent research assistance.

Annual World Bank Conference on Development Economics 1997
©1998 The International Bank for Reconstruction and Development / THE WORLD BANK

political stability, particularly if initial conditions are favorable for economic take-off. Countries with large public sectors and weak institutions, by contrast, are likely to founder.

It is not easy to create good institutions quickly, and it is not immediately obvious how external forces like the World Bank can help. But one thing is certain: in countries with weak institutions, increasing the level of government intervention, perhaps financed by foreign aid and loans at below-market rates, is not the solution. In fact, it is counterproductive.

The problem is that the poorest countries often have the weakest institutions and unacceptable levels of income inequality. Yet cutting government consumption and foreign aid and concessional lending to these countries may not hurt the poor disproportionately. This implies that the World Bank should make assistance to countries much more dependent on institutional performance. Countries with substandard governance should not receive assistance from the international community. Only countries that show progress in institution building should receive assistance.

Basic Economic Variables on Cross-Country Growth

Differences in country growth rates are very large. When they persist, they result in substantial differences in per capita GDP. In the Republic of Korea, the world's fastest-growing economy between 1960 and 1990, per capita GDP grew an average 6.7 percent a year, rising 700 percent in thirty years (table 1). In Chad, the slowest-growing economy, per capita GDP dropped 50 percent over the same period. The fastest-growing economies are concentrated in East Asia; the slowest in Latin America and Africa. The difference in average per capita growth between Southeast Asia and Sub-Saharan Africa in 1960–90 was a staggering 3.5 percentage points.

Several Asian economies rose many steps on the per capita income ladder between 1960 and 1990 (table 2). Korea rose forty-six steps, Thailand thirty, and Singapore twenty-six. In contrast, many Latin American countries, including Argentina and Venezuela, dropped many steps on the ladder (fourteen for Argentina, twenty for Venezuela). Nicaragua dropped twenty-five steps during its civil war. Most of Sub-Saharan Africa remains relatively poor, as it was in 1960, and several countries in the region—the Central African Republic, Côte d'Ivoire, Gabon, South Africa—have fallen.

Results of a basic regression on cross-country growth rates (based on Barro 1991, 1996a, b) are consistent with the findings of many other researchers: initial income and the share of government consumption in GDP are negatively associated with growth, the investment rate is positively associated, and openness is generally positively associated (appendix tables A.1 and A.2). Male education is positively correlated with growth, but female education is negatively correlated, a result first noted by Barro and Lee (1993). This negative correlation reflects not that female education reduces growth but that large differences in male and female education are strongly correlated with low levels of development.[1]

Table 1. Real GDP per Capita Growth Rates, 1960–90 and 1970–90
(percent)

Region/economy	1960–90	1970–90
World	1.947	1.469
Sub-Saharan Africa	0.759	0.483
Central African Republic	−0.652	−1.274
Chad	−2.130	−2.516
Côte d'Ivoire	0.266	−1.431
Gabon	2.647	0.332
Nigeria	1.875	1.301
South Africa	1.312	−0.009
Middle East and North Africa	2.831	2.351
Algeria	1.591	2.096
Cyprus	4.710	4.009
Egypt	2.867	2.486
Iran	0.470	−1.732
Tunisia	3.240	3.511
South Asia and China	2.012	2.007
Bangladesh	1.262	0.412
China	2.827	3.215
India	1.670	2.275
Pakistan	2.605	1.518
Sri Lanka	1.699	2.613
Southeast Asia	4.225	4.173
Hong Kong	6.295	5.967
Indonesia	3.765	5.078
Korea, Rep. of	6.663	6.896
Singapore	6.516	6.781
Taiwan (China)	6.198	6.522
Thailand	4.447	4.264
Latin America	1.115	0.383
Argentina	0.177	−0.903
Brazil	2.726	2.536
Chile	1.360	0.925
Mexico	2.400	1.897
Nicaragua	−0.720	−3.003
Venezuela	−0.152	−1.236
Industrial countries	2.924	2.363
Germany, Federal Rep. of	2.602	2.099
Italy	3.355	2.504
Japan	5.264	3.368
Portugal	4.622	4.081
United States	2.005	1.656

Note: Regional averages are unweighted.
Source: See table A.1 in the appendix.

The relationship between the share of government consumption in GDP and growth is strong and robust, surviving several permutations of the specification of the basic regression (with and without openness, for example, and with and without fertility). The same result is obtained by Easterly and Rebelo (1993), Barro and Sala-i-Martin (1995), and Commander, Davoodi, and Lee (1997), among others.

Table 2. Real GDP per Capita in International Prices, 1960 and 1990
(purchasing power parity, in constant 1985 dollars)

Region/economy	1960 GDP per capita	Rank	1990 GDP per capita	Rank
World	2,440		5,162	
Sub-Saharan Africa	884		1,266	
Central African Republic	704	83	579	95
Chad	756	82	399	102
Côte d'Ivoire	1,120	67	1,213	76
Gabon	1,789	40	3,958	42
Nigeria	567	91	995	81
South Africa	2,191	32	3,248	49
Middle East and North Africa	1,757		4,217	
Algeria	1,723	43	2,777	53
Cyprus	2,037	36	8,368	25
Egypt	809	79	1,912	64
Iran	2,946	27	3,392	47
Tunisia	1,101	68	2,910	51
South Asia and China	836		1,494	
Bangladesh	952	74	1,390	70
China	567	92	1,324	72
India	766	81	1,264	74
Pakistan	638	87	1,394	69
Sri Lanka	1,259	55	2,096	62
Southeast Asia	1,354		5,917	
Hong Kong	2,247	31	14,849	6
Indonesia	638	88	1,974	63
Korea, Rep. of	904	76	6,673	30
Singapore	1,658	46	11,710	20
Taiwan (China)	1,256	57	8,063	26
Thailand	943	75	3,580	45
Latin America	2,350		3,247	
Argentina	4,462	21	4,706	35
Brazil	1,784	41	4,042	39
Chile	2,885	28	4,338	38
Mexico	2,836	30	5,827	33
Nicaragua	1,606	48	1,294	73
Venezuela	6,338	11	6,055	31
Industrial countries	5,663		12,877	
Germany, Federal Rep. of	6,570	10	14,341	9
Italy	4,564	20	12,488	19
Japan	2,954	26	14,331	10
Portugal	1,869	39	7,478	28
United States	9,895	1	18,054	1

Note: Rankings are based on a sample of 102 countries.
Source: See table A.1 in the appendix.

Estimates of the coefficient of the share of government consumption presented in all these studies are similar and large.

Readers of the recent empirical growth literature often wonder which results are robust and which are not, since changes in specification, sample, measurement, and estimation techniques lead to very different results. (For an early discussion of this point, see Levine and Renelt 1992.) In most specifications and in most samples, however, government consumption has a negative effect on growth.[2]

How well do these regressions explain growth? The purely economic regression run here explains about half the cross-country variance in growth.[3] A different way of assessing the explanatory power of the model is to ask whether these numbers can explain the exceptional achievement of the East Asian economies. Rodrik (1995) suggests that once initial conditions are taken into account there appears to be nothing miraculous about the high-performing Asian economies' growth experience. In a series of papers (1995, 1996, 1997a, b) he notes that among the crucial initial conditions explaining East Asia's performance are a higher level of human capital and a more even income distribution than in Latin America. Rodrik argues that single-minded pursuit of economic growth in East Asia would not have been possible if redistributional conflicts had disrupted the political arena.

When trying to explain growth with a few basic economic variables that capture initial conditions, two puzzles remain: why certain countries with reasonably good initial conditions did not quite make it and why many poor countries did not catch up more quickly. The next section argues that politics and institutions may have something to contribute to the answer.

Politics, Institutions, and Growth

Political-institutional variables have recently been added to cross-country regressions on growth (see Barro 1996a, b and the survey by Alesina and Perotti 1994). Four sets of variables have been used: variables capturing sociopolitical instability, such as riots, coups d'état, and revolutions; variables capturing the quality of government and institutions, such as measures of corruption, protection of property rights, and enforcement of contracts; institutional variables, such as whether the country is a democracy or not; and the socioeconomic characteristics of the country, such as initial income inequality (as measured by the Gini coefficient) and ethnic or religious composition (appendix table A.3).

Two observations about the correlations among these variables and with some economic variables should be noted. First, many of these political-institutional variables appear to be highly correlated (appendix table A.4). One possible interpretation of this observation is that good things go together—that political stability, an efficient bureaucracy, and low levels of corruption are positively associated. A more troublesome interpretation is that this correlation is spurious and derives from measurement problems. Many of these variables (in particular those measuring institutional quality) are obtained from expert surveys, in which local experts are polled by the organization compiling the data. Respondents may be tempted to rank a country high (or low) in every dimension when the feeling about the country's institutions is generally positive (or negative). This is particularly problematic for variables that cannot easily be measured objectively, such as corruption or bureaucratic quality. It is less of a problem for variables that can be quantified more easily, such as coups d'état or ethnolinguistic fractionalization.

Second, many good institutional features are strongly correlated with per capita income. This connection does not establish causation, of course, which probably runs in both directions in a virtuous (or vicious) circle. Good institutions facilitate growth, and at higher income levels it is easier to maintain political stability and efficient institutions.

Political-Institutional Variables and Their Effects

When the values of many political-institutional variables are compared for the ten slowest- and ten fastest-growing economies in the sample for which these variables are available, the results are striking (appendix table A.5). The ten slowest-growing economies tend to be more ethnically fractionalized and more politically unstable (in particular, they have more frequent revolutions and coups d'état). They also tend to have much poorer indicators of the rule of law and institutional quality, much higher black market premiums (an indicator of policy distortions), and greater income inequality.

Among the variables measuring political instability, variables measuring government fragility (frequency of government changes and coups d'état) and variables measuring sociopolitical instability (political assassinations, riots, and revolutions) can be distinguished (appendix table A.6). The results are somewhat murky. Some variables are statistically significant; some are not. Variables measuring frequency of government change tend to be insignificant except for revolutions and coups d'état, which are borderline statistically significant at conventional levels.

Alesina and others (1996) suggest that a much better way to measure the effect of uncertainty about government survival is to study a time series dimension, in which the critical variable is not the actual occurrence of a government change but the uncertainty in expectation caused by the underlying probability of a government collapse. They estimate a two-equation system in a data panel. One equation is a probit regression that estimates the probability of a government change or coup d'état as a function of several political and economic variables, including lagged growth. The other equation estimates growth as a function of several political-economic variables, including the probability of a government collapse. This system allows the effect of the probability of a government change on growth to be evaluated regardless of whether the change actually occurs. Following this procedure Alesina and others find that government fragility has a negative effect on growth.

The variables measuring social conflict, such as assassinations, demonstrations, and strikes, tend to be significant with the expected sign: more instability is harmful for growth. These results are consistent with the findings of Barro (1991). Along the same lines, Alesina and Perotti (1996) and Perotti (1996) construct an index of sociopolitical instability that is a linear combination of several of these variables.

Introducing this measure of political instability into an investment equation, they find a robust negative effect: more instability reduces investment. A plausible interpretation is that political instability creates uncertainty and undermines investor confidence for two reasons. First, frequent government changes may make the policy environment unstable, leading to policy uncertainty. Second, signs of even more extreme instability (coups, civil wars, riots) may threaten property rights, leading to an even more acute loss of investor confidence.

The results of these regressions suggest that political instability, which influences investor confidence and creates an environment not conducive to accumulation and market activities, is a multidimensional phenomenon, difficult to capture with a single variable. In certain countries political instability manifests itself with frequent government change; in others, with frequent riots.

The results on bureaucratic quality, rule of law, and corruption are very clear and strong. Virtually all these variables are strongly significant in all the regressions, with t statistics often greater than 3—much higher than for any other political variable. It is worth emphasizing that many of these variables are highly correlated with one another (see appendix table A.4). Thus while it is difficult to distinguish the effect of, say, corruption relative to bureaucratic efficiency, it is clear that weak institutions have strong and significantly negative effects on growth. This result has been reported by many economic analysts using different cross-country growth regressions.[4] Rodrik (1997b) convincingly shows that bureaucratic quality explains much of the difference between the most successful and least successful East Asian economies. He shows that the residuals of a growth regression in which the control variables are initial income and education have an extremely high correlation with the same indexes of institutional quality used here.

Causes of the Effects

Bureaucratic efficiency and institutional quality influence growth for several reasons. Inefficient and corrupt bureaucracies require lengthy and expensive (because of bribes) procedures for opening businesses, which may reduce foreign investment and channel domestic investment toward the underground economy. An inefficient bureaucracy also provides a low level of productive public goods for given levels of taxation. And poor enforcement of the law, especially poor enforcement of contracts, makes investment activities costly, uncertain, and risky for domestic and (perhaps especially) foreign investors.

Discussion of the effect of democracy on growth (if any) would require an entire paper. In a nutshell the evidence indicates that the direct effect of democracy (essentially voting rights and the existence of multiparty political competition) on growth is hard to measure and probably insignificant (Helliwell 1994; Barro 1996a; Alesina and others 1996; Perotti 1996). Tavares and Wacziarg (1996) point out, however, that democracy may have a positive influence on growth through a variety of indirect channels, such as the accumulation of human capital. When civil liberties are defined more generally (to include political rights) the evidence is stronger: civil rights, which are probably closely related to economic freedom, are positively associated with growth (see Barro 1996b). The regressions presented here are consistent with this picture. Barro (1996a) convincingly argues that the level of income is overwhelmingly the strongest predictor of democratization. It seems to become increasingly difficult for countries below a certain level of income to maintain democratic institutions.

Finally, there are the variables measuring initial income inequality and ethnolinguistic fractionalization. A large body of literature (Alesina and Rodrik 1994; Persson and Tabellini 1994; Perotti 1996; Deininger and Squire 1996) has shown that initial income or wealth inequality is associated with lower growth through a variety of political-economic channels. One channel is taxation and redistribution (Alesina and Rodrik 1994; Persson and Tabellini 1994). In a more unequal society a large impoverished majority will demand (by voting or other forms of political action) redistributive policies. Such policies, requiring distortionary taxes, will reduce growth.

A second channel emphasizes the effect of income inequality on political instability (Alesina and Perotti 1994). More inequality creates sociopolitical unrest, which hurts investor confidence and growth. A third channel emphasizes education (Perotti 1993; Galor and Zeira 1993). In more unequal societies (with imperfect capital markets) only a small portion of the population has the resources to invest in education. If education has positive externalities, societies with greater income inequality will grow less rapidly, because only a small portion of the population will acquire education. A fourth channel emphasizes higher fertility in more unequal societies, perhaps because of the lower level of education of women (Perotti 1996). Perotti (1996) presents a careful empirical analysis that tries to disentangle these different channels. In the regression shown in appendix table A.6 the coefficient on income inequality has the expected sign (negative) and is sometimes significant.[5]

The coefficient for ethnolinguistic fractionalization is negative and significant, as Easterly and Levine (1996) also found. They argue that the effect of ethnolinguistic fractionalization is crucial in explaining the poor performance of African economies. Much of the ethnic fractionalization in Sub-Saharan Africa is the result of the ethnically insensitive national borders drawn by European colonizers. Ethnic fractionalization may make it difficult to achieve consensus on policies, may reduce trust and social capital, and may be associated with a poor policy environment, in which the "public good" is seen not as a common good but as something to be allocated to conflicting groups. Ethnic fractionalization is strongly and negatively associated with various measures of institutional quality and positively associated with the occurrence of revolutions and coups.

A few other variables have recently been brought into the picture of cross-country growth regressions. Keefer and Knack (1996) consider measures of social capital and trust using data from surveys of individual attitudes. They find that measures of trust, which are probably correlated with enforcement and credibility of contracts, are positively and significantly associated with growth. Borner, Brunetti, and Weder (1995) use survey data to assess directly the credibility of the policy environment and of contract enforcement and conclude that these variables measuring institutional quality are very important.

Government Size, Growth, and Poverty

The two previous sections have shown that government consumption has a negative effect on growth and that the quality of institutions is an important determinant of growth. Viewed together, these results suggest that a large government in countries with weak institutions is particularly harmful for growth. This is precisely the point made recently in a study by Commander, Davoodi, and Lee (1997). Using the same data set used here, they reach the staggering conclusion that it would take 22 years for a country with a small government and good institutions to double its per capita income, whereas it would take 239 years for a country with a large government and weak institutions to do the same. They find similarly striking results when they consider the effect of policy distortions (measured by the black market premium) in countries with weak and those with good institutions. To show that these numbers are not unrealistic they note that it took the United States 31 years to double its per capita GDP after 1870. Between 1960 and 1990 many East Asian economies more than doubled their GDP. In contrast, Sub-Saharan African countries increased per capita GDP by only about 50 percent over that period.

These results are consistent with recent research on the role of foreign aid. Boone (1994a, b) presents the results of several cross-country regressions showing that foreign aid has generally increased government consumption while having no positive effect on growth and only weak, at best, effects on social indicators. Boone argues that foreign aid will not change the incentives of governments that have poor records in reducing poverty and achieving social goals. Aid tends to go to countries with the worst records in terms of improving social indicators, but in many of these countries the elites have the fewest incentives to improve the quality of life of their populations.

A recent study by Burnside and Dollar (1997) provides interesting results along the same lines. They show that aid has a positive effect on growth only in countries that have adopted good policies—that is, trade openness and a stable macroeconomic outlook. But foreign aid has no effect on policy choices: countries that choose good policies do so with or without aid. In general, the allocation of aid has not rewarded good policies but has been determined by donors' political agenda. In summary, government consumption, often supported by foreign aid, has no positive effect on growth and can be harmful in countries where a large government coexists with weak institutions.

These negative consequences for growth might be worth bearing if they were incurred to achieve social objectives, such as reducing poverty or inequality. That has not been the case, however. Rather, mistargeting, corruption, inefficiencies, and policy distortions have meant that the poor do not benefit much from government spending even on social programs, which instead favors special interests, vocal groups, and sections of the middle class.

Both a macro and a micro approach can be used to evaluate the effects of government programs on social indicators. The macro approach draws from the type of cross-country regressions examined above. The micro approach relies on single-country studies on the incidence and distributive effects of government spending. Commander, Davoodi, and Lee (1997) studied the effect of government spending on two measures of well-being: infant mortality and life expectancy. Following a macro approach, they found that government consumption has a small positive effect but that per capita income has a much stronger effect. To the extent that, as documented above, government consumption reduces growth (and thus future per capita income), the net long-run effect of government consumption on measures of well-being is not clear.

My own analysis on this point (available on request) is consistent with their conclusions: government consumption reduces growth and has a moderately positive effect on life expectancy and infant mortality. On the one hand, since income levels are positively associated with reductions in infant mortality and increases in life expectancy, government consumption has a negative long-run effect on these two health variables through this growth effect. On the other hand, government consumption may moderately lower infant mortality and increase life expectancy. The net effect of these two channels linking government consumption and health statistics is hard to compute, but it is unlikely to be large because the two effects pull in different directions.

To see whether there are strong effects of government consumption on income inequality, I used data from Deininger and Squire (1996) and regressed the change in income inequality on the level of government consumption (the average of the sample period), controlling for other economic variables. The coefficient on government size has the wrong sign and is not quite statistically significant (appendix table A.7). Because causality problems and endogeneity issues abound (in addition to measurement problems for changes in income inequality), this regression should not be taken at face value; however, it suggests that a large government has not been effective in reducing income inequality.

Much more reliable conclusions can be drawn using micro country studies. After studying several Latin American countries, Tanzi (1972, p. 75) concluded that "first, it appears that even the supposedly pro-poor social type expenditure has little effect on income distribution. Second, the group that seems to be getting the greater advantage from public spending is the urban middle class." In a paper written a few years ago (and soon to be published), I examined a large body of micro-empirical evidence on the effects of government programs in developing countries and concluded that Tanzi was correct and that little has changed (Alesina forthcoming). I examined evidence from a variety of sources (including World Bank studies) on the effect of public education, public health, public employment, and social security systems in many developing countries, especially in Latin America and Africa, and found that government spending is often nonprogressive, does not reach the poor (particularly in rural areas), is often mistargeted, and implies large policy distortions and waste.

Those conclusions were reconfirmed in a recent set of studies on the effect of government spending on the poor (van de Walle and Nead 1995). A brief review of the conclusions of that volume is instructive. In a chapter on Indonesia, Pitt, Rosenzweig, and Gibbons find that public education programs "cannot account for a large part of the actual growth of human capital outcomes in Indonesia in the 1980s" (p. 145). In a chapter on public education in Peru, Seldon and Wasylenko conclude that public spending on education is "only mildly pro-poor" (p. 180) (a fairly optimistic conclusion, given the evidence presented in the chapter). A chapter on public education in Pakistan by Adelman and others reaches more encouraging conclusions, but they are somewhat harder to interpret because they focus on the elimination of regional inequalities. In a chapter on public spending on health in Indonesia, van de Walle and Deolalikar note that "the availability of health services continues to vary significantly across . . . regions and to be inequitable" (p. 230), and that health subsidies were "not particularly well targeted" and only "mildly progressive" (p. 249). These findings imply that the poor in Indonesia do not benefit from government health expenditures. Indeed, the evidence indicates that increased government expenditure is actually associated with lower use of health services by the children of the poor (p. 283).

In a chapter on the effects of transfers in the Philippines, Cox and Jimenez find that household behavior can greatly offset the effect of public transfers (p. 322) and that as a result these schemes are much less effective than one would expect unless they are extremely well designed—perhaps to an unfeasible degree. Ravallion and Datt examine the effects of public employment schemes in two villages in India and conclude that such schemes were no more effective at reducing poverty than "a uniform (untargeted) allocation of the same gross budget across all households" (p. 435). Not much to write home about.

In summary, both macro regressions and micro evidence strongly suggest that large governments coupled with weak institutions are harmful for growth and are at best neutral in reducing inequality.

Policy Implications

The lessons from the results reviewed here should be clear: the international community in general and the World Bank in particular should not support government consumption in countries that do not satisfy some minimum standard of institutional quality. This requirement could be called *institutional conditionality*. The difference between this type of conditionality and the traditional one is that traditional conditionality implies imposing conditions based on policy performance regardless of the institutional setting. But below a minimum level of institutional quality the chances that policy conditionality will work are very low, suggesting that assistance should be denied to countries with poor records of institutional development and policy success, regardless of their promises.

Foreign aid, below-market loans, and general financial and even technical assistance should not be provided to countries that have very corrupt bureaucracies, do not enforce protection of property rights, and have poor records of directing government spending toward the poor. If a government continues to receive assistance regardless of its institutional development, it has no incentive to change. Many current recipients of aid would be penalized if aid depended on institutional quality, which could help them in the medium term by generating incentives for institution building.

Despite the convincing evidence that large government programs combined with weak institutions simply do not work, bureaucracies have an incentive to maintain these programs and to maximize the budgets they control in order to increase their influence and justify their existence. Even those that are motivated by the best intentions—to reach the poor and improve the appalling degree of inequality in many developing countries—must come to terms with the fact that without a moderate level of institutional development, foreign aid and government programs are largely ineffective.

The World Bank recognizes this point. World Bank (1996) concludes that "local institutional capacity is often too weak to implement policy interventions" (pp. 49–50). The solution advocated there is to help governments by supporting initiatives from nongovernmental organizations and local communities and by involving the private sector. The problem of poor institutional development and the need to cut assistance to create incentives for reform are not explicitly recognized. The World Bank should be much more explicit in punishing governments that are below a certain threshold of institutional transparency and quality.

The problem is how to measure institutional quality objectively. The evidence above suggests that progress has been made in addressing measurement problems and that more can be done. With the personnel and brainpower available to the World Bank, these measures of institutional quality could easily be improved and made usable for policy purposes.

Another mistake to be avoided is giving the impression that every problem has a quick solution and can be addressed with yet another World Bank mission, another assistance program, another loan. To the extent that institution building depends on history, degree of ethnic fractionalization and conflict, and level of trust and social capital, it will take time. Spending more on mistargeted government programs is counterproductive and will simply increase opposition to any type of help, even to deserving countries.

The World Bank should provide technical assistance for institution building and withdraw financial assistance for countries that have weak institutions and bad policies. Incentives and technical help may be the best combination of carrot and stick.

Appendix

The main variables used in the basic regression on cross-country growth rates (which was heavily influenced by the work of Barro 1991, 1996a, b) are described in table A.1. Results for samples for 1960–89 and 1970–89 are shown in table A.2. The first sample is the longest available sample for the economic variables used in the regression. The shorter sample is used when political-institutional variables are introduced and the longer sample cannot be used because too few of the political variables are available.

Table A.2 presents ordinary least squares estimates of the sample mean of each variable and shows seemingly unrelated regressions in which different equations are used for each five-year sample (six equations for the longer sample and four equations for the shorter). The parameters are constrained to be the same across equations. Results are also shown for a three-stage least squares procedure, which is identical to the seemingly unrelated regressions procedure except that the regressors are instrumented to control for endogeneity biases.

Table A.1. Description of Main Variables Used in Basic Regression

Variable	Number of observations	Description	Source	Period
Growth	125	Growth rate of real GDP per capita	Summers and Heston (1991)	1960–92
Log initial income	125	Log of real GDP per capita in 1985 international prices	Summers and Heston (1991)	1960–92
Trade openness	125	Imports and exports as a share of GDP	Summers and Heston (1991)	1960–85
Male human capital	106	Average number of years of secondary and higher schooling in male population over 25	Barro and Lee (1993)	1960–85
Female human capital	106	Average number of years of secondary and higher schooling in female population over 25	Barro and Lee (1993)	1960–85
Government consumption	125	Real government spending on goods and services as a percentage of GDP	Summers and Heston (1991)	1960–92
Investment	125	Real investment as a percentage of GDP	Summers and Heston (1991)	1960–92
Ethnolinguistic fractionalization	112	Index of ethnic and linguistic fractionalization	Mauro (1995)	1960
Gini coefficient	85	Measure of income inequality	Deininger and Squire (1996)	1960–92
Risk of contract repudiation	100	Index (1–10), where higher value represents lower risk of contract repudiation	Knack and Keefer (1995)	1982–95
Rule of law index	100	Index (1–6), where higher value represents better enforcement of the rule of law	Knack and Keefer (1995)	1982–95
Bureaucratic quality	100	Index (1–6), where higher value represents better quality of bureaucracy	Knack and Keefer (1995)	1982–95
Risk of expropriation	100	Index (1–10), where higher value represents lower risk of expropriation	Knack and Keefer (1995)	1982–95
Corruption index	100	Index (1–6), where higher value represents less corruption	Knack and Keefer (1995)	1982–95
Democracy index	138	Index (0–1), where higher value represents more political rights	Freedom House	1960–92
Civil liberties	138	Index (1–7), where higher value represents fewer civil liberties	Freedom House	1970–92
Political assassinations	123	Number of political assassinations a year	Banks (various years)	1960–92
Purges	123	Number of political purges a year	Banks	1960–92
Government crises	123	Number of government crises a year	Banks	1960–92
Guerrilla movements	123	Number of active guerrilla movements a year	Banks	1960–92
Revolutions and coups	123	Number of revolutions and coups a year	Banks	1960–92
Demonstrations	123	Number of antigovernment demonstrations a year	Banks	1960–92

Table A.1. Description of Main Variables Used in Regression (cont.)

Variable	Number of observations	Description	Source	Period
Riots	123	Number of riots a year	Banks	1960–92
Strikes	123	Number of general strikes a year	Banks	1960–92
Government changes	119	Dummy = 1 if at least one government change during a year	Alesina and others (1996)	1960–82
Major government changes	119	Dummy = 1 if at least one major government change (coup or political switch) during a year	Alesina and others (1996)	1960–82
Black market premium	110	Black market premium on the official exchange rate (percentage of official rate)	World Bank (1995)	1960–92

Table A.2. Base Economic Growth Regression Results

	1960–89			1970–89		
Variable	Seemingly unrelated regressions	Three-stage least squares[a,b]	Ordinary least squares on means[a]	Seemingly unrelated regressions	Three-stage least squares[a,b]	Ordinary least squares on means[a]
Constant	10.299 (6.28)	19.325 (7.35)	4.346 (2.63)	11.483 (5.24)	26.525 (7.13)	5.685 (2.35)
Log initial income	–1.373 (–5.90)	–2.882 (–7.17)	–0.568 (–2.46)	–1.425 (–4.73)	–3.666 (–6.46)	–0.800 (–2.47)
Male human capital	0.695 (1.82)	–0.011 (–0.02)	2.057 (4.19)	0.665 (1.42)	1.045 (0.93)	1.691 (3.10)
Female human capital	–0.568 (–1.34)	0.597 (0.82)	–1.845 (–3.69)	–0.549 (–1.09)	–0.211 (–0.18)	–1.475 (–2.72)
Government share	–0.084 (–4.45)	–0.106 (–2.86)	–0.048 (–2.15)	–0.126 (–5.61)	–0.219 (–3.72)	–0.064 (–1.93)
Investment rate	0.211 (9.74)	0.379 (10.92)	0.100 (3.86)	0.174 (6.66)	0.357 (8.56)	0.112 (3.67)
Openness	0.005 (1.49)	0.005 (0.90)	0.011 (3.66)	0.014 (3.35)	0.018 (1.90)	0.014 (4.02)
Number of observations	82	82	98	94	94	103
Adjusted r^2	.07 .30 .32 .09 .22 .31	.05 .28 .27 .08 .21 .29	.53	.35 .09 .23 .22	.30 .08 .25 .20	.42

Note: Numbers in parentheses are t statistics.
a. Heteroskedastic-consistent t statistics.
b. Variables used are terms of trade shocks, log of area, share of population over 65, ethnolinguistic fractionalization, Latin America dummy, Sub-Saharan Africa dummy, East Asia dummy, log of initial income, and log of population.

Table A.3. Summary Statistics for the Main Political-Institutional Variables

Variable	Mean	Standard deviation	Minimum	Maximum
Ethnolinguistic fractionalization	41.821	29.683	0.000	93.000
Gini coefficient	42.227	10.155	22.365	63.700
Risk of contract repudiation	5.852	2.010	2.419	9.875
Rule of law index	3.111	1.690	0.750	6.000
Bureaucratic quality	3.182	1.673	0.750	6.000
Risk of expropriation	6.246	2.012	2.000	9.875
Corruption index	3.273	1.591	0.000	6.000
Democracy index	0.484	0.333	0.000	1.000
Civil liberties	3.981	1.798	1.000	6.900
Political assassinations	0.239	0.551	0.000	3.350
Purges	0.114	0.193	0.000	1.000
Government crises	0.181	0.232	0.000	1.400
Guerrilla movements	0.241	0.341	0.000	1.450
Revolutions and coups	0.168	0.236	0.000	1.100
Demonstrations	0.629	1.101	0.000	5.800
Riots	0.499	1.095	0.000	8.850
Strikes	0.166	0.299	0.000	1.350
Government changes	0.256	0.181	0.000	0.867
Major government changes	0.105	0.108	0.000	0.489
Black market premium	72.703	302.998	−0.848	3,219.856

Note: Period covered is 1970–89 or as available.

Table A.4. Correlation Matrix for Selected Political Variables, Growth, and Human Capital

Variable	Growth	Ethnolinguistic fractionalization	Rule of law	Bureaucratic quality	Corruption
Growth	1.00				
Ethnolinguistic fractionalization	−0.23	1.00			
Rule of law	0.45	−0.33	1.00		
Bureaucratic quality	0.44	−0.32	0.88	1.00	
Corruption	0.36	−0.36	0.84	0.91	1.00
Democracy	0.22	−0.45	0.71	0.75	0.71
Political assassinations	−0.19	0.01	−0.22	−0.15	−0.11
Government crises	0.03	−0.12	0.08	0.11	0.10
Revolutions and coups	−0.27	0.23	−0.50	−0.48	−0.46
Government changes	0.11	−0.28	0.40	0.43	0.45
Strikes	−0.10	−0.05	−0.06	0.05	0.06
Black market premium	−0.32	−0.01	−0.20	−0.22	−0.05
Human capital	0.22	−0.32	0.68	0.70	0.68
Gini coefficient[a]	−0.35	0.20	−0.56	−0.54	−0.51

Note: Period covered is 1970–89 or as available. Results are based on seventy-eight observations.

Table A.5. Political Variables for the Ten Slowest- and Ten Fastest-Growing Economies

Economy/group	Growth	Ethnolinguistic fractionalization	Rule of law	Bureaucratic quality	Corruption
Slowest growing	−1.34	54	1.73	1.77	2.13
Nicaragua	−2.34	18	1.50	1.50	4.00
Iraq	−1.91	36	1.21	1.59	2.42
Zaire	−1.80	90	1.00	1.50	0.25
Guyana	−1.48	58	0.75	0.75	1.00
Liberia	−1.47	83	1.71	1.00	0.83
Zambia	−1.46	82	2.21	1.59	1.59
Venezuela	−1.16	11	3.59	2.75	2.59
Iran	−0.89	76	1.34	1.75	2.50
Peru	−0.47	59	1.25	2.25	2.59
Argentina	−0.44	31	2.75	3.00	3.59
Fastest growing	5.35	37	4.00	3.86	3.68
Korea, Republic of	7.51	0	2.54	3.67	2.50
Singapore	7.34	42	5.09	5.25	5.58
Taiwan (China)	6.98	42	5.25	4.17	4.25
Botswana	5.60	51	5.00	4.00	3.63
Indonesia	5.10	76	1.59	1.00	0.63
Malaysia	5.02	72	4.17	4.00	4.88
Thailand	4.37	66	3.25	3.84	3.25
Portugal	4.10	1	5.25	3.85	3.88
Tunisia	3.83	16	2.50	3.00	2.92
Japan	3.69	1	5.34	5.88	5.25

— Not available.
Note: Table includes only economies for which political data were available.

	Democracy	Political assassinations	Government crises	Revolutions and coups	Government changes	Strikes	Black market premium	Human capital
	1.00							
	0.05	1.00						
	0.22	0.44	1.00					
	−0.36	0.40	0.20	1.00				
	0.57	0.33	0.66	0.01	1.00			
	0.17	0.53	0.62	0.22	0.42	1.00		
	−0.19	0.00	−0.07	0.21	−0.09	−0.03	1.00	
	0.67	−0.09	0.12	−0.29	0.34	0.06	−0.16	1.00
	−0.55	−0.02	−0.16	0.13	−0.33	−0.07	0.23	−0.54

a. Based on sixty four observations only.

	Democracy	Political assassinations	Government crises	Revolutions and coups	Government changes	Strikes	Black market premium	Gini coefficient
	0.36	0.57	0.24	0.25	0.22	0.28	439.54	48.82
	0.32	0.25	0.15	0.45	0.18	0.20	3,219.86	—
	0.02	0.15	0.20	0.40	0.07	0.00	123.61	62.88
	0.07	0.05	0.05	0.25	0.11	0.00	94.52	—
	0.47	0.25	0.05	0.00	0.11	0.05	192.16	56.16
	0.21	0.05	0.40	0.30	0.18	0.00	0.00	43.00
	0.32	0.00	0.00	0.05	0.11	0.00	128.78	51.00
	0.95	0.05	0.05	0.00	0.13	0.00	49.34	44.82
	0.27	1.25	0.25	0.25	0.42	0.20	405.93	45.18
	0.49	0.85	0.45	0.15	0.24	0.95	63.22	47.46
	0.53	2.75	0.80	0.65	0.62	1.35	118.01	40.08
	0.53	0.04	0.20	0.12	0.26	0.06	6.53	40.60
	0.42	0.10	0.15	0.30	0.07	0.00	16.80	36.39
	0.41	0.00	0.00	0.00	0.18	0.00	0.80	39.92
	0.29	0.10	0.00	0.05	0.13	0.00	4.99	29.45
	0.83	0.00	0.00	0.00	0.11	0.00	18.35	53.90
	0.33	0.00	0.10	0.05	0.00	0.00	4.09	33.23
	0.66	0.05	0.15	0.05	0.44	0.00	0.81	49.84
	0.48	0.05	0.55	0.40	0.44	0.10	−0.47	44.06
	0.75	0.00	0.75	0.25	0.56	0.25	7.30	38.69
	0.23	0.00	0.15	0.05	0.18	0.05	12.24	45.75
	0.92	0.10	0.15	0.00	0.49	0.15	0.43	34.80

Table A.6. Regression Estimates of Coefficients on the Political Variables

Variable	Seemingly unrelated regressions Co-efficient	No. of observations	Adjusted r²	Three-stage least squares[a] Co-efficient	No. of observations	Adjusted r²	Ordinary least squares on means[a] Co-efficient	No. of observations	Adjusted r²
Bureaucratic quality and rule of law									
Black market premium	−0.0007 (−2.90)	92	.34 .09 .23 .27	−0.0007 (−1.22)	92	.30 .08 .25 .24	−0.0012 (−2.63)	99	0.43
Bureaucratic quality	0.374 (2.66)	81	.34 .10 .36 .30	0.245 (1.03)	81	.33 .10 .34 .27	0.341 (2.25)	87	0.49
Corruption	0.454 (3.23)	81	.35 .09 .38 .30	0.552 (1.84)	81	.34 .09 .37 .28	0.268 (1.62)	87	0.47
Risk of expropriation	0.502 (4.51)	81	.29 .08 .38 .45	0.383 (1.76)	81	.31 .09 .36 .35	0.380 (3.20)	87	0.52
Repudiation of contracts	0.580 (4.93)	81	.26 .07 .38 .48	0.408 (2.38)	81	.30 .09 .35 .37	0.355 (3.06)	87	0.51
Rule of law	0.345 (2.51)	81	.34 .11 .34 .31	0.250 (1.07)	81	.33 .11 .33 .27	0.343 (2.26)	87	0.49
Political rights and civil liberties									
Civil liberties	−0.149 (−1.16)	94	.33 .09 .23 .26	−1.138 (−2.93)	94	.22 .07 .21 .30	−0.214 (−1.55)	103	0.43
Democracy	0.696 (1.04)	94	.34 .09 .23 .25	1.624 (1.05)	94	.29 .08 .25 .23	1.387 (1.95)	103	0.44
Political instability									
Antigovernment demonstrations	−0.155 (−1.36)	93	.34 .10 .22 .20	−0.746 (−2.77)	93	.30 .10 .21 .12	0.060 (0.39)	99	0.36
Guerrilla movements	0.209 (0.79)	93	.35 .09 .23 .22	−0.176 (−0.40)	93	.30 .08 .24 .20	0.353 (0.71)	99	0.37
Political assassinations	−0.448 (−2.45)	93	.35 .10 .25 .21	−1.963 (−2.61)	93	.29 .09 .22 .18	−0.235 (−0.81)	99	0.37
Purges	0.739 (1.71)	93	.35 .09 .22 .22	1.739 (1.75)	93	.29 .08 .24 .21	0.224 (0.24)	99	0.36
Revolutions and coups	−1.194 (−2.23)	93	.34 .10 .24 .23	−1.804 (−1.47)	93	.30 .08 .25 .21	−1.143 (−1.39)	99	0.38
Riots	−0.050 (−0.45)	93	.35 .09 .22 .21	−0.402 (−1.25)	93	.31 .09 .19 .16	0.087 (0.61)	99	0.37
Strikes	−0.471 (−1.29)	93	.35 .10 .23 .22	−1.378 (−1.51)	93	.30 .09 .23 .19	−0.208 (−0.39)	99	0.36
Government crises	−0.102 (−0.25)	93	.35 .09 .23 .22	1.289 (1.32)	93	.28 .06 .23 .20	−0.161 (−0.23)	99	0.36
Major government changes	−0.963 (−0.97)	93	.38 .09 .24 .26	−1.096 (−0.42)	93	.32 .08 .25 .24	0.382 (0.25)	100	0.45
Government changes	−1.140 (−1.65)	93	.39 .09 .24 .26	−0.796 (−0.42)	93	.32 .08 .25 .24	−0.207 (−0.20)	100	0.45
Inequality and ethnolinguistic fractionalization									
Ethnolinguistic fractionalization	−0.014 (−2.11)	94	.37 .12 .23 .23	−0.019 (−1.77)	94	.30 .10 .26 .20	−0.015 (−2.18)	95	0.43
Gini coefficient	−0.025 (−1.36)	69	.34 .15 .42 .37	−0.049 (−2.00)	69	.31 .13 .43 .36	−0.021 (−1.10)	76	0.52

Note: Numbers in parentheses are t statistics.
a. Heteroskedastic-consistent t statistics.

Table A.7. Changes in Income Inequality and Size of Government, 1960–89 and 1970–89

Variable	1960–89 (n = 76)	1970–89 (n = 53)
Government size (period average)	0.0321	0.107
	(2.45)	(1.11)
Log initial income	−1.370	−0.533
	(−2.96)	(−1.55)
Per capita GDP growth (period average)	−0.071	0.134
	(−0.13)	(0.37)
Human capital (period average)	1.803	0.769
	(1.73)	(0.98)
Adjusted r^2	0.08	0.02

Note: A positive sign in the coefficient on the size of government variables indicates that larger government implies an increase in income inequality. Numbers in parentheses are t statistics.

Notes

1. The effect of education levels on growth has received much attention in the literature, particularly in terms of measurement. Alternative measures of education attainment include enrollment rates, changes in average years of schooling, and attainment rates by education levels, in addition to the Barro-Lee variable used in appendix table A.2. The results on the effects of education on growth are somewhat sensitive to the measure used.

2. Commander, Davoodi, and Lee (1997) find that an increase of 1 standard deviation in the share of government consumption implies a 0.65 percent decline in annual growth—close to the 0.7 found by Barro (1996b) and the 0.5 obtained here. Note that using the three-stage least squares estimate instead of the ordinary least squares estimates results in much larger values for the negative effect of government size on growth (on the order of 1.5 rather than 0.5). The lower 0.5, which is closer to the value found by others, seems much more sensible.

3. See, for example, the r^2 for 1970–89 in appendix table A.2.

4. This result is consistent with research by Mauro (1995), Keefer and Knack (1996), Knack (1994), Barro (1996b), and Commander, Davoodi, and Lee (1997), among others.

5. As discussed in Perotti (1996) and Deininger and Squire (1996), issues of data quality are particularly problematic. Here I use the most recent available data set assembled by Deininger and Squire.

References

Alesina, Alberto. Forthcoming. "The Political Economy of Macroeconomic Stabilization and Income Inequality: Myths and Reality." In Vito Tanzi, ed., *High-Quality Growth*. Cambridge, Mass.: MIT Press.

Alesina, Alberto, Sule Ozler, Nouriel Roubini, and Philip Swagel. 1996. "Political Instability and Economic Growth." *Journal of Economic Growth* 1 (June): 188–212.

Alesina, Alberto, and Roberto Perotti. 1994. "The Political Economy of Growth: A Critical Survey of the Recent Literature." *The World Bank Economic Review* 8 (3): 351–71.

———. 1996. "Income Distribution, Political Instability and Investment." *European Economic Review* 40: 1203–28.

Alesina, Alberto, and Dani Rodrik. 1994. "Distributive Politics and Economic Growth." *Quarterly Journal of Economics* 109 (May): 465–90.

Banks, Arthur. Various years. *Political Handbook of the World*. Binghamton, N.Y.: Center for Social Analysis of the State University of New York.

Barro, Robert. 1991. "Economic Growth in a Cross-Section of Countries." *Quarterly Journal of Economics* 106 (2): 407–33.

———. 1996a. "Democracy and Growth." *Journal of Economic Growth* 1: 1–27.

———. 1997. *The Determinants of Economic Growth*. Cambridge, Mass.: MIT Press.

Barro, Robert, and Jong-Wha Lee. 1993. "International Comparisons of Educational Attainment." *Journal of Monetary Economics* 32 (December): 363–94.

Barro, Robert, and Xavier Sala-i-Martin. 1995. *Economic Growth*. New York: McGraw-Hill.

Boone, Peter. 1994a. "The Impact of Foreign Aid on Savings and Growth." London School of Economics, Department of Economics.

———. 1994b. "Politics and the Effectiveness of Foreign Aid." London School of Economics, Department of Economics.

Borner, Silvio, Aymo Brunetti, and Beatrice Weder. 1995. *Political Credibility and Economic Development*. New York: St. Martin Press.

Brunetti, Aymo. 1995. "Political Variables in Cross-Country Growth Regression." University of Basel, Department of Economics.

Burnside, Craig, and David Dollar. 1997. "Aid, Policies, and Growth." Policy Research Working Paper 1777. World Bank, Washington, D.C.

Commander, Simon, Hamid Davoodi, and Une Lee. 1997. "The Causes of Government and the Consequences for Growth and Well-Being." Policy Research Working Paper 1785. World Bank, Washington, D.C.

Deininger, Klaus, and Lyn Squire. 1996. "A New Data Set Measuring Income Inequality." *The World Bank Economic Review* 10 (3): 565–91.

Easterly, William, and Ross Levine. 1996. "Africa's Growth Tragedy: Policies and Ethnic Divisions." World Bank, Policy Research Department, Washington, D.C.

Easterly, William, and Sergio Rebelo. 1993. "Fiscal Policy and Economic Growth: An Empirical Investigation." *Journal of Monetary Economics* 32 (December): 417–58.

Freedom House. Various years. *Freedom in the World Report.* New York.

Galor, Oded, and Joseph Zeira. 1993. "Income Distribution and Macroeconomics." *Review of Economic Studies* 60: 35–52.

Helliwell, John. 1994. "Empirical Linkage between Democracy and Growth." *British Journal of Political Science* 24: 225–48.

Keefer, Philip, and Steve Knack. 1996. "Does Social Capital Have an Economic Payoff? A Cross-Country Investigation." University of Maryland, College Park, Department of Economics.

Knack, Steve. 1994. "Institutions and the Convergence Hypothesis: The Cross-National Evidence." IRIS Working Paper. University of Maryland, College Park, Department of Economics.

Knack, Steve, and Philip Keefer. 1995. "Institutions and Economic Performance: Cross-Country Tests Using Alternative Institutional Measures." *Economics and Politics* 7: 207–27.

Levine, Ross, and David Renelt. 1992. "A Sensitivity Analysis of Cross-Country Growth Regressions." *American Economic Review* 82 (September): 942–63.

Mauro, Paolo. 1995. "Corruption and Growth." *Quarterly Journal of Economics* 110 (August): 681–712.

Perotti, Roberto. 1993. "Political Equilibrium, Income Distribution, and Growth." *Review of Economic Status* 60 (3): 755–76

———. 1996. "Growth, Income Distribution, and Democracy." *Journal of Economic Growth* 1 (2): 149–88.

Persson, Torsten, and Guido Tabellini. 1994. "Is Inequality Harmful for Growth?" *American Economic Review* 84 (June): 600–21.

Rodrik, Dani. 1995. "Getting Interventions Right: How South Korea and Taiwan Grew Rich." *Economic Policy* 20 (April): 55–107.

———. 1996. "Coordination Failures and Government Policy: A Model with Applications to East Asia and Eastern Europe." *Journal of International Economics* 40: 1–22.

———. 1997a. "The Paradoxes of the Successful States." *European Economic Review* 41 (3): 235–57.

———. 1997b. "TFPG Controversies, Institutions, and Economic Performance in East Asia." NBER Working Paper 5914. National Bureau of Economic Research, Cambridge, Mass.

Summers, Robert, and Alan Heston. 1991. "The Penn World Table (Mark 5): An Expanded Set of International Comparisons, 1950–1988." *Quarterly Journal of Economics* 106 (8): 327–68.

Tanzi, Vito. 1972. "Redistributing Income through the Budget in Latin America." *Banca Nazionale del Lavoro Quarterly Review* 42: 65–87.

Tavares, José, and Romain Wacziarg. 1996. "How Democracy Fosters Growth." Harvard University, Department of Economics, Cambridge, Mass.

van de Walle, Dominique, and Kimberly Nead, eds. 1995. *Public Spending and the Poor.* Baltimore, Md.: The Johns Hopkins University Press.

World Bank. 1993. *The East Asian Miracle: Economic Growth and Public Policy.* A Policy Research Report. New York: Oxford University Press.

———. 1996. *Poverty Reduction and the World Bank.* Washington, D.C.

Comment on "The Political Economy of High and Low Growth," by Alberto Alesina

T. Ademola Oyejide

Alberto Alesina's article makes an important contribution to the literature on growth—especially to the search for the variables that together may explain why economic growth rates differ so markedly across countries. While I agree with many of Alesina's points, my interpretations of and conclusions on some of these issues differ, and I believe several areas require further elaboration. My comments relate specifically to Sub-Saharan Africa, the region for which Alesina's analysis and policy recommendations are perhaps of greatest significance.

Alesina's Argument

Alesina begins with a widely acknowledged finding: the explanations offered by purely economic variables in the indigenous growth literature do not fully account for differences in country growth rates. Thus he offers four types of political-institutional variables to better explain these differences: sociopolitical instability, quality of government and institutions, institutional variables, and socioeconomic characteristics. He finds that weak institutions (as indicated by fragile government, political instability, and social conflict) have strong and significantly negative effects on growth.

In addition, Alesina finds that government consumption has negative consequences for growth and that big governments are particularly harmful for growth when institutions are weak. Noting other evidence showing that government consumption, often supported by foreign aid, has no positive effect on growth, Alesina concludes that the international community (especially the World Bank) should provide financial support only to countries that satisfy minimum standards of institutional quality. Countries unable to meet these standards should be denied financial assistance, even if they might have benefited from technical assistance targeted at institution building.

T. Ademola Oyejide is professor of economics at the University of Ibadan.

Differences in Interpretation

In a recent review Collier and Gunning (1997) offer a general critique of the emerging growth literature that is relevant to Alesina's argument. While conceding that the growth literature offers a more powerful tool for analyzing cross-country economic performance than the case-study approach used previously, Collier and Gunning claim that this literature misses an important point: Africa's performance has been strongly episodic.

This tendency has two significant implications for growth models and their results. First, episodes of severe decline may not receive sufficient analysis if their characteristics are averaged over decades. If, instead, such episodes are identified separately, nonlinearities and hysteresis may be found. Second, the fact that African countries are often concentrated in the extreme range of the explanatory variables during episodes of collapse may account for the significant unexplained residual (the "Africa dummy variable") that many researchers have found.

The literature relating economic performance to the underlying social structure generally supports Alesina's thesis regarding the influence of political-institutional factors (see Putnam, Leonardi, and Nanetti 1993). Civil society may be important partly because it affects politics (and hence public policy and service delivery) and partly because it influences social cohesion and trust (and hence the cost of transactions). This literature confirms that Africa has, on average, higher levels of corruption than other developing countries, longer bureaucratic delays, and weaker contract enforcement (Collier and Gunning 1997).

It is not clear, however, that these deficiencies are related to the most striking feature of the region's social structure—that is, ethnic fractionalization. Mauro (1995) shows that measures of corruption and judicial ineffectiveness are correlated with ethnic fractionalization, and Easterly and Levine (1995) find that fractionalization accounted for 35 percent of Africa's growth shortfall. But Collier and Hoeffler (1996) conclude that ethnic diversity is actually an asset in reducing the risk of war and that Africa's high incidence of war emanates from its severe poverty rather than its diverse social structure. Moreover, Alesina finds that good institutions are strongly correlated with per capita income and that income is overwhelmingly the strongest predictor of an important institutional variable—that is, democratization.

Alesina's finding on government consumption also merits a closer look. Public spending accounts for a larger share of GDP in Africa than in other developing regions (21 percent compared with 16–17 percent). Despite high public spending, however, Africa has poor infrastructure. Railways, telephones, electricity, and water are in short supply. Internal transport costs are higher than in other regions (Kanbur 1995). African trade faces high international transport costs (Amjadi and Yeats 1995). And the rate of return on public projects is significantly lower than that in other regions (Isham, Kaufmann, and Pritchett 1995).

Several factors have been suggested to explain why the level of Africa's public services is so low. These range from basic aspects of economic policies that reduce the returns on public projects (Isham and Kaufmann 1995) to elements of the social structure (Gelb, Knight, and Sabot 1989; Gersovitz and Paxson 1996). In the end it is not entirely clear that the size and productivity of government spending are unilaterally and significantly influenced by a country's social structure independent of the policy regime.

Issues Requiring Further Elaboration

An assessment of the explanatory power of growth regressions must answer two questions: are the selected explanatory variables the right ones, and are the proxies used in the aggregate model consistent with those indicated by the more detailed evidence from micro studies? Alesina's article suggests variables that are consistent with those of other research. In general, the literature on African growth highlights four key constraints: lack of openness in product markets, lack of social capital, high risk, and poor public services. Because these variables still leave a significant unexplained residual, I agree with Collier and Gunning (1997)—we need more case studies that exploit the indigenous growth literature and use country-level knowledge to shed light on the unexplained variances. Premature judgments and conclusions based entirely on growth regressions should be resisted.

In any case, it can be argued that three of the main constraints suggested as hindering African growth (lack of social capital, high risk, and poor public services) are endogenous to the first (lack of openness in product markets; Collier and Gunning 1997). Thus a significant increase in openness could be expected to bring about desirable changes in the others, although creating and strengthening social capital takes time.

Thus a more legitimate policy conclusion than Alesina's would recognize that good institutions are a function of a country's income and that institution building takes time and deserves support. Setting arbitrary minimum standards of institutional performance without reference to these two considerations and using such standards to punish developing countries is a fundamentally flawed proposal, especially given the shaky research foundation on which such advice is based.

References

Amjadi, Azita, and Alexander J. Yeats. 1995. "Have Transport Costs Contributed to the Relative Decline of Sub-Saharan African Exports? Some Preliminary Empirical Evidence." Policy Research Working Paper 1559. World Bank, International Economics Department, Washington, D.C.

Collier, Paul, and J.W. Gunning. 1997. "Explaining African Economic Performance." CSAE Working Paper 97-2. Oxford University, Centre for the Study of African Economies.

Collier, Paul, and Hoeffler. 1996. "On the Economic Causes of Civil War." CSAE Discussion Paper 183. Oxford University, Centre for the Study of African Economies.

Easterly, William, and Ross Levine. 1995. "Africa's Growth Tragedy: A Retrospective, 1960-89." Policy Research Working Paper 1503. World Bank, Washington, D.C.

Gelb, A.H., J.B. Knight, and R.H. Sabot. 1989. "Public Sector Employment, Rent Seeking and Economic Growth: Some New Evidence." *Oxford Bulletin of Economics and Statistics* 58: 9-28.

Gersovitz, M., and C.H. Paxson. 1996. "The Revenues and Expenditures of African Governments: Modalities and Consequences." *Journal of African Economies* 5: 199-227.

Isham, Jonathan, and Daniel Kaufmann. 1995. "The Forgotten Rationale for Policy Reform: The Productivity of Investment Projects." Policy Research Working Paper 1549. World Bank, Europe and Central Asia Country Department IV, Washington, D.C.

Isham, Jonathan, Daniel Kaufmann, and Lant Pritchett. 1995. "Government and Returns on Investment." Policy Research Working Paper 1550. World Bank, Policy Research Department, Washington, D.C.

Kanbur, Ravi. 1995. "A Continent in Transition." World Bank, Africa Technical Department, Washington, D.C.

Mauro, Paolo. 1995. "Corruption and Growth." *Quarterly Journal of Economics* 110 (August): 681–712.

Putnam, Robert D., Robert Leonardi, and Raffaella Y. Nanetti. 1993. *Making Democracy Work: Civic Traditions in Modern Italy.* Princeton, N.J.: Princeton University Press.

Comment on "The Political Economy of High and Low Growth," by Alberto Alesina

Ravi Kanbur

In exploring differences in growth, Alberto Alesina puts forward five propositions:
- Institutional quality, suitably defined, is good for growth and poverty reduction.
- High government consumption is bad for growth and poverty reduction.
- High government consumption is particularly bad for growth and poverty reduction when institutions are weak.
- Foreign aid increases government consumption, and this is especially so, and especially bad, when institutions are weak.
- Aid agencies should provide technical assistance for institution building and withdraw financial assistance from countries that do not satisfy minimum standards of institutional quality.

In discussing these propositions, I would like to consider the complementarity between the cross-country statistical regularities perspective of Alesina's article and the more country-specific and operational perspective that emerges from development practice.

An Operational Perspective

The cross-country regression literature that Alesina surveys has performed a useful service by putting on the development agenda the effect of institutions on growth and poverty reduction. The "normal science" of this enterprise—thousands of regressions with every conceivable specification, though often based on the same data set—has borne fruit in establishing that the nature of institutions and the channels through which they affect economic outcomes merit careful study.[1] Alesina makes the point that we must take institutions seriously. If support were needed for that proposition, the cross-country regression literature provides it.

Ravi Kanbur is T.H. Lee Professor of World Affairs and professor of economics at Cornell University. At the time of the conference he was principal adviser in the Office of the Senior Vice President, Development Economics, at the World Bank.

Annual World Bank Conference on Development Economics 1997
©1998 The International Bank for Reconstruction and Development / THE WORLD BANK

The second proposition—that high government consumption is bad for growth—is also based on Alesina's review of the cross-country regression literature. Despite the standard caveats on conceptual and empirical problems in measuring government consumption, I am happy to accept Alesina's conclusion as a fair summary of the literature. The issue here has to do with the range over which this finding is plausible. Plainly, zero government consumption is not good for growth and poverty reduction. Ghana's 5 percent share of government revenue in GDP in 1983 (and expenditure to match) did not indicate a thriving, dynamic economy but one that was in serious trouble (Kanbur 1995b). The rise in this share to 15 percent in 1991 (and the concomitant rise in expenditure) reflected recovery in the economy, as basic infrastructure services began to function.

In contrast, the huge 1992 pay increase to civil servants, which amounted to several percentage points of GDP, could by no stretch of the imagination be seen as good for growth or poverty reduction. (The pay award was given under the pressure of transition to constitutional rule—a transition that would, on the face of it, improve many of the institutional quality variables referred to in the literature.) The point here is that the specification of the relationship between government consumption and growth (and poverty reduction) needs to be looked at more carefully. Is there an optimal size of government? Are there threshold effects? What are the guidelines for size and composition of government consumption? Within its own terms the cross-country regression literature can easily begin to answer these questions—but first they have to be posed.

The third proposition—that poor institutional quality magnifies the adverse effects of large government—is clear from a country-specific and, particularly, an operational perspective. But very little cross-country regression evidence is cited in Alesina's article, presumably because very little work has been done on this issue. This is surprising, since the data sets compiled to investigate the two variables separately could in principle easily be used to investigate the effect of interactions between them. Some more "normal science" is clearly needed here!

A similar point can be made about the fourth proposition—that foreign aid increases government consumption and that this is particularly so, and has a particularly bad effect, when institutions are weak. While this proposition has much to recommend it from the operational perspective, the evidence marshaled in its favor in the article is limited. Few studies are referenced on the cross-country regression front because few address this question; those referenced do not necessarily speak to the proposition. The work of Burnside and Dollar (1997), for example, addresses the policy, not the institutional, environment.

Implications for Aid Policy

I have three observations about the fifth proposition—that aid agencies should withdraw financial assistance from countries that do not satisfy minimum standards of institutional quality. First, an injunction to withdraw aid if minimum standards of institutional quality are not met is not particularly useful. What exactly are these standards? And what happens when we go above them—how is the graduation of aid to improvements (or deterioration) in institutional quality to be modulated? It can be argued that the World Bank's operations staff are making judgments about institutional quality and aid flows all the time. The politics of aid cutoffs aside, it would be useful for them to have some guidelines and rules of thumb. In my view the normal science of the cross-country regression literature is well placed to make a start in answering this question, but the question first has to be posed.

Second, there is a tendency to jump from the kinds of results surveyed in Alesina's article to the conclusion that financial assistance is bad and technical assistance is good. There is little evidence in the article that speaks to this part of the proposition beyond the general point that institutions are important. In recent years practitioners have begun to document and discuss the vast failures of technical assistance, particularly in Africa (see, for example, Kanbur 1995a).

Finally, Alesina's article does not pose the truly radical question: is there something inherent in aid, particularly in large volumes of aid, that destroys local institutional quality? This question is not new to those who study the literature on absorptive capacity constraints or aid dependence, and it is often posed by those on the right and on the left of the political spectrum. Given the data sets marshaled already, it seems to me that the normal science of the cross-country regression literature could usefully contribute to this debate. But again, the question first has to be posed. There is much to be gained by combining the data and technology of the cross-country regression literature with the questions that arise from a deeper knowledge of country-specific and operational realities.

Note

1. Of course, each of us can find something to complain about in this literature. My own favorites are regression equations that have growth on the left side and inequality on the right side. This approach reverses the causality focus of the earlier literature (such as Anand and Kanbur 1993) but uses the same flawed data sets. These days I find it difficult to take seriously any cross-country regression that contains an inequality variable.

References

Anand, Sudhir, and Ravi Kanbur. 1993. "Inequality and Development: A Critique." *Journal of Development Economics* 41 (June): 19–43.

Burnside, Craig, and David Dollar. 1997. "Aid, Policies, and Growth." Policy Research Working Paper 1777. World Bank, Washington, D.C.

Kanbur, Ravi. 1995a. "A Helping Hand? The Problem of Technical Assistance in Africa: A Review Article." *Journal of African Economies* 5 (2): 289–306.

———. 1995b. "Welfare Economics, Political Economy and Policy Reform in Ghana." *African Development Review* 7 (June): 35–49.

Floor Discussion of "The Political Economy of High and Low Growth," by Alberto Alesina

A participant from the Bangladesh Institute of Development Studies asked Alberto Alesina (presenter) whether it was appropriate to make aid conditional on the strength of a country's institutions. What if, for example, a country inherited many of its institutions from its colonial past?

Alesina said he recognized that a country may not be to blame for its weak institutions. And, as he said in his article, he believed that a country should receive aid if it is making honest efforts to strengthen its institutions.

A participant from Argentina followed up with a similar point about conditionality, asking whether it was realistic to expect aid recipients to comply with formal indicators of institutional quality. Alesina acknowledged that it would be difficult to measure a country's compliance with such indicators. But given the World Bank's resources and the caliber of its staff, he believed that it could gauge countries' compliance.

Ravi Kanbur (discussant) added that many of the issues raised by institutional conditionality were related to monitoring and incentives. The problem, he said, is not that conditions are too stringent but rather that aid is given regardless of whether conditions have been met. In many cases aid is released because of political pressures from within donor countries. True, there are incentive problems within weak institutions, but many of the problems with conditionality arise because it is susceptible to international pressures.

Moreover, Kanbur continued, conditionality can send confusing signals to the private sector, which has no way of knowing whether a government is committed to reform or is merely paying it lip service in order to secure aid. A potential remedy would be to make aid conditional on a country's past performance—say, over the previous three years—and to release it in a single tranche. Under this approach only deserving countries would receive aid, but they would not have to commit themselves to future reforms. If performance slipped, however, future aid would be jeopardized.

The participant from Bangladesh noted that Alesina's presentation seemed to imply that the World Bank should rethink its approach to education lending, partic-

---

This session was chaired by Mieko Nishimizu, vice president, South Asia Region, at the World Bank.
Annual World Bank Conference on Development Economics 1997
©1998 The International Bank for Reconstruction and Development / THE WORLD BANK

ularly for higher education. Although an emphasis on primary and secondary education is appropriate, he said, countries seeking to create institutions for better governance must have high-quality managers. University education and research are required to produce such managers.

Extending that point, a participant from the African Economic Research Forum noted that the upper tail of the skills distribution in developing countries often overlaps with the lower end of the skills distribution in industrial countries. As a result a brain drain occurs—for example, the best doctors from developing countries often end up working in industrial countries. To enhance skills formation and retain needed skills, he asked, should donors subsidize the retention of highly qualified professionals in developing countries while macroeconomic reform is under way?

The issue, Kanbur replied, is the extent to which government policies and a lack of professionalism in the civil service have driven professionals away, and the likelihood that subsidies would help convince them to stay. The World Bank already provides institutional support and various subsidies that address the brain drain, he said. The problem with linking such assistance to higher education systems—for example, by boosting a country's budget for universities in order to produce better-trained professionals—is that these systems are so institutionally weak that the money would be wasted. In the medium term, he said, efforts should be made to strengthen these systems and then channel resources to them. But in the short term resources should be targeted to simply retaining qualified professionals.

A participant, noting that Alesina's regressions measured institutional variables starting in 1982 and growth variables starting in 1960, asked him about the apparent link between growth and institutional development. Is it safe to say that growth leads to good institutions? Alesina replied that it is, but that institutional development is a lengthy process. Moreover, data on institutions (like those used in his article) have a short history. So, while he agreed with her point, the limited data make it somewhat difficult to prove empirically.

A participant from the World Bank asked whether the discussion should be focusing on political instability, or whether policy instability was in fact the more relevant concern for discussions of growth. Alesina responded that in many cases political instability can cause policy instability. As an example he cited the link between coups d'etat and low growth.

Bruce Weinberg (presenter in another session) asked whether government spending was more efficient at some levels than at others. If local governments compete for clients, he asked, do they provide better services? Alesina said that the question is important but impossible to answer. As things stand the paucity of data on local governments makes it extremely difficult to compare countries. Even within countries little data are available to compare local and national governments. Thus, he said, an enormous investment is needed in collecting such data.

Alesina, responding to Kanbur's points, agreed that small government was not always the secret to rapid growth and that some governments need to grow in order to be more effective. But, Alesina said, he had been talking about the negative effects of excessive government consumption, not investment. Many of Kanbur's points about the important role larger government can play in promoting growth centered around its potential investment in infrastructure, enabling institutions, and the like. A bloated bureaucracy, on the other hand, does not promote growth. More research is needed on the optimal size and type of government, said Alesina, and better data are needed to distinguish government consumption from investment. He encouraged the World Bank to step up its efforts in both areas.

A participant from Russia countered that there is no reason to believe that government investment is any more efficient than government consumption. And while there is room for debate on the optimal size of government, in the late nineteenth century and early twentieth century today's advanced economies had per capita incomes similar to those in developing countries today (in current dollars)—yet government spending did not exceed 10 percent of GDP. Although this is not necessarily the optimal level everywhere, these countries managed to achieve fairly rapid growth and to deliver basic public services.

Alesina replied that he had not meant to imply that all government investment is beneficial. Rather, he meant that there is an optimal size of government and that government should provide infrastructure and make certain investments—in public education, for example.

Speaking as one involved in the World Bank's lending operations, Mieko Nishimizu (chair) thanked Alesina and Kanbur for their emphasis on good governance and institution building. Because the quality of institutions is determined by the quality of their staff, Nishimizu said, the discussion had reaffirmed her conviction that improving the quality of education—particularly for girls and women—remains an important challenge for developing countries.

Poverty and Environment

Environment, Poverty, and Economic Growth

Karl-Göran Mäler

There are two kinds of demand for environmental resources. One is as an amenity—that is, as something that directly affects people's well-being. The other is as an input in production. Environmental resources that are used in production are of great importance for poor people, and the income elasticity for such resources is less than one. The role of environmental resources is less clear when they are viewed as amenities. A few studies, however, have found that even then the income elasticity may be less than one—suggesting that for poor people such resources are necessities, not luxuries.

But demand is only one side of the coin. To fully understand the relationship between environmental management and poverty, supply issues must also be taken into account. The supply of environmental resources is determined by how the resource base is managed and exploited. By strengthening the institutional structures responsible for such decisions—for example, by improving property rights, implementing land tenure schemes, and establishing new markets—developing countries may reap substantial gains for the rural poor. Moreover, changes in the resource base may have consequences for fertility rates, and so may affect the future of the resource base.

Webster's *New World Dictionary* defines *environment* as the conditions, circumstances, and influences surrounding, and affecting the development of, an organism or group of organisms. For the purpose of this article that organism is primarily human beings, and the group of organisms is generally a group of human beings. The environment of other groups of organisms is also of major concern, however—particularly groups called ecological systems, or ecosystems. Both when they are humanmade (agriculture) and when they occur naturally, such

Karl-Göran Mäler is director of the Beijer International Institute of Ecological Economics of the Swedish Royal Academy of Sciences and professor at the Stockholm School of Economics. This article is based on a number of studies carried out at the Beijer International Institute of Ecological Economics, including Dasgupta and Mäler (1991, 1995); Dasgupta, Folke, and Mäler (1994); Mäler, Aniyar, Casler, and Weir (1996); Mäler (1991); Mäler, Gren, and Folke(1994); Arrow and others (1995); and Lindahl-Kiessling and Landberg (1994).

systems can profoundly affect human well-being. Thus this article takes a close look at ecosystem services and functions and environmental resources.

Environmental quality is often seen as a luxury good—something only the wealthy can afford. This is a misconception. In particular, it is important to distinguish between environment as an input in production and environment as an amenity. For people in developing countries, who are much more dependent on natural resources than people in industrial countries, environment is largely a necessity. I will show this theoretically and illustrate it with examples. Although there is theoretically no reason for amenities to be seen as either luxuries or necessities, the few studies on the demand for amenities suggest that some amenities may be necessities.

The demand for environmental resources is only one side of the coin, however. The other side is, of course, the supply of such resources. A number of mechanisms—including property rights, population growth, and discount rates—must be considered to understand the relation between poverty and environmental management.

A weak structure of property rights may completely negate the value of environmental resources, with potentially devastating effects in small local communities. There may also be consequences for population growth (Dasgupta and Mäler 1997). Finally, it is generally believed that poor people have high discount rates, which implies that they would discount future consequences from current degradation of the resource base.

Ecosystem Functions and Services

The ecological services produced by ecosystems are generated by interactions among organisms, populations of organisms, communities of populations, and the physical and chemical environment in which they reside. Many ecosystem functions and services are indispensable because they underpin all human activities. Ecosystems provide water, animal and plant food, and other renewable resources. They also recycle nutrients, control floods, filter pollutants, assimilate waste, pollinate crops, maintain a genetic library, preserve and regenerate soil, operate the hydrological cycle, and maintain the gaseous composition of the atmosphere. The world's ecosystems represent a large part of our natural capital base.[1] (In what follows I also refer to it as our environmental resource base.)

Since these services are essential for our survival, it would clearly be prudent to monitor the environmental resource base in much the same way that we monitor our manufactured capital stocks, such as roads, buildings, and machinery. This has not been standard practice, however, and even today such monitoring is not conducted in any systematic way. Instead, researchers often rely on trends in an economy's gross output (crops, fisheries, forest products) and on the prices of these outputs to assess whether the resource base is being depleted. This is a mistake. Agricultural output, for example, can rise even if soils are being mined. The environmental resource base is dynamic and complex, consisting of biological communities that interact with the physical and chemical environment in time and space.

Moreover, these interactions are often nonlinear. Thus the resource base can display threshold effects—meaning that the flow of services can be interrupted.

Degradation of the environmental resource base (excessive resource extraction, intensive land use, and so on) not only affects the quantity and quality of the services produced by ecosystems, it also challenges their resilience. An ecosystem's resilience is its capacity to absorb disturbances without undergoing fundamental changes. If a system loses its resilience, even a small perturbation can change it into a wholly new state. Thus the economist's panacea—that there are limitless substitution possibilities among resources and that society will be able to move smoothly from one resource base to another as each is degraded beyond its usefulness—is at odds with ecological truths. Ecosystems have limited resilience, and reductions in resilience are not easily observed. This is what makes ecological economics so difficult.

An ecosystem's carrying capacity is the maximum stress that it can absorb without changing to a vastly different state. Ecosystems are endemically subject to natural shocks and surprises—fires, floods, storms, and so on. Thus it is wrong to regard ecosystems as fixed stocks of capital that can be relied on to provide humans with a steady flow of resources. Our natural capital base has evolved over millions of years and has adapted to modifications and fluctuations in the background environment. The self-organizing ability of ecosystems determines their capacity to respond to the perturbations to which they are continually subjected (Wilson 1992).

Biological diversity, or biodiversity, plays two central roles in the evolution of ecosystems. First, it provides the units through which energy and materials flow, giving the system its functional properties. Second, it provides the system with resilience (Wilson 1992).

An ecosystem's carrying capacity is not fixed but is subject to change, usually in ways that are impossible to predict. This is because ecosystems are continually evolving. Economic policies that use static rules to achieve constant yields (for example, fixed sizes of cattle herds or fixed yields of fish) can lower an ecosystem's resilience. A system that loses too much resilience could break down in the face of disturbances that earlier would have been absorbed (Holling and others 1994).

Grazing patterns in the semiarid grasslands of East and southern Africa illustrate these points. Under natural conditions these grasslands are periodically subject to intensive grazing by large herbivores. The episodes are much like pulsations, and they result in a dynamic balance between two functionally different groups of grasses. One group can tolerate grazing and drought and has the capacity to hold soil and water. The second group is more productive in terms of plant biomass and enjoys a competitive advantage over the first group during periods when grazing is not intensive.

The diversity of grass species that is thus maintained serves two ecological functions: productivity and drought protection. Grazing by large herbivores that periodically shifts from intensive pulses to periods that allow recovery is part of the ecosystem's overall dynamic. But when fixed management rules are applied to the ecosystem (for example, the stocking of ranch cattle at a sustained and moderate level), that can cause grazing to shift from periodically intensive pulses to more moderate but persistent levels. This persistent mode, occasioned by deliberate economic policy, supports the competitive advantage of the productive but drought-sensitive grasses over the drought-resistant grasses, reducing functional diversity. As a result the grasslands can be transformed, becoming dominated by woody shrubs that are of little value for grazing.

Many environmental management policies—in agriculture, fisheries, and forestry—share this shortcoming (Holling and others 1994). The significance and value of the environment's "infrastructure" and its dynamics have received scant attention from economists. This is surprising because, as noted, the production capacity of the resource base forms the foundation for human life and development.

One challenge is to estimate the benefits that are lost when an ecosystem's resilience contracts. The main difficulty in such an exercise lies in the limitations of the models commonly used in applied environmental economics. Most do not consider nonlinearities in the ecological processes that are modeled, insulate the economic system from its environment, and ignore the evolutionary tendencies of the resource base, thereby missing some of the most important features of self-organizing systems (that is, environmental feedbacks, thresholds, and discontinuities). An ecosystem's evolutionary nature and the existence of threshold effects make it hard to predict these feedbacks, except within ranges in which the system exhibits local stability. In other words, economists tend to ignore or not to perceive certain dynamic effects when they attempt to aggregate values derived from partial observations of spending patterns in the wake of some change in the level of ecological resources or services. In the remainder of this article I identify the implications of these observations for economic and environmental policies in developing countries.

Rural Production and Demand for Resources

Most people in developing countries are agrarian and pastoral. In 1988 some 65 percent of the population in what the World Bank classifies as low-income countries lived in rural areas. The share of the labor force engaged in agriculture in these countries was a bit higher, and agriculture accounted for about 30 percent of GDP. In industrial countries, by contrast, agriculture accounted for 6 percent of the labor force and 2 percent of GDP (Dasgupta and Mäler 1995).[2]

For the most part developing countries have biomass-based subsistence economies, in that rural inhabitants eke out a living from products obtained directly from plants and animals. For example, a survey of villagers in a microwatershed of the Alaknanda River in the central Himalayas in India found that 30 percent of working hours were devoted to cultivation, 20 percent to fodder collection, and about 25 percent (evenly distributed) to fuel collection, animal care, and grazing (CSE 1990). Some 20 percent of time was spent on household chores (cooking took up much of that time), and the remaining 5 percent was spent on other activities, such as marketing. Studies in Central and West Africa have shown how vital forest products are to the lives of rural inhabitants (Falconer and Arnold 1989; Falconer 1990). Come what may, developing countries will remain largely rural economies for some time.

Thus it seems obvious that any analysis of rural productive activity in developing countries should take into account the enormous importance of these countries' environmental resource base. Yet forty years of research on poverty in developing countries has failed to do so. Until recently environmental resources made only perfunctory appearances in government planning models, and they were blithely ignored by most development economists.[3]

The situation has changed. Today no account of economic development would be considered complete without mention of the environmental resource base. What implications does this new focus have for emerging development issues?

Environmental Resources and Their Degradation

Environmental problems are almost always associated with resources that are regenerative (that is, renewable) but in danger of exhaustion from excessive use.[4] The earth's atmosphere is an example of such a resource. In the normal course of events the atmosphere regenerates itself. But the speed of regeneration depends on, among other things, the current state of the atmosphere and the rate at which pollutants are deposited. It also depends on the nature of the pollutants. (Smoke emissions, for example, differ in effect from the release of chemicals or radioactive material.)

To establish environmental guidelines, we need to be able to measure such resources. In the preceding example we must establish an atmospheric quality index. The net rate of regeneration of the atmospheric stock is the rate at which this index changes over time. Regeneration rates of atmospheric quality are complex and often poorly understood. This is because a great deal of synergism is associated with the interaction between different pollutants in the atmospheric sink, which makes the underlying relationships almost certainly nonlinear and, for certain compositions, perhaps greatly so. In the ecological literature these are referred to as nonlinear dose-response relationships.[5] These are merely qualifications, however, and the analytical point I am making—that pollution involves the degradation of renewable natural resources—is both true and useful (Ehrlich, Ehrlich, and Holdren 1977).

Animal, bird, plant, and fish populations are other examples of renewable natural resources, and a number of studies have addressed the reproductive behavior of different species under a variety of "environmental" conditions, including the presence of parasitic and symbiotic neighbors. Land is another such resource, since arable and grazing land can be maintained only through careful use. Population pressures can result in an extended period of overuse—meaning not only an unsustainable shortening of fallow periods but also deforestation and the cultivation and grazing of marginal lands. Such practices cause land to deteriorate until it eventually becomes wasteland.

The symbiotic relationship between soil quality and vegetative cover is central to the agricultural and environmental challenges facing Sub-Saharan Africa, especially in the Sahel (Anderson 1987). Drylands management must be sensitive to such relationships. For example, it is useful to distinguish between a reduction in soil nutrients and humus on the one hand and the loss of soil due to wind and water erosion on the other. The depletion of soil nutrients can be countered by fertilizers (which can have adverse effects elsewhere in the ecological system), but in drylands a loss in topsoil cannot be recovered. Under normal vegetative cover it can take from 100 to 500 years to form 1 centimeter of topsoil. Admittedly, what I am calling erosion is a redistribution of soil. But even when the relocation is from one agricultural field to another, there are adjustment costs. Moreover, the relocation is often into oceans and nonagricultural land—which amounts to erosion.[6]

Soil degradation can also occur if the wrong crops are cultivated. Contrary to general belief, in subtropical climates export crops are less damaging to soils than are cereals and root crops. (Groundnuts and cotton are exceptions.) Many export crops, including coffee, cocoa, palm oil, and tea, grow on trees and bushes that have a continuous root structure and provide continuous canopy cover. With grasses planted underneath, the soil erosion associated with such crops is substantially less than that associated with basic food crops (Repetto 1988, table 2). But problems are compounded in developing countries. In many cultures men control cash income while women control food. Studies in India, Kenya, Nepal, and Nigeria suggest that to the extent that women's incomes decline as cash cropping increases, the family's nutritional status (especially that of children) deteriorates (Gross and Underwood 1971; von Braun and Kennedy 1986; Kennedy and Oniang'o 1990). Public policy has a bewildering array of indirect effects in developing countries, where ecological and technological factors intermingle with behavioral norms that respond very slowly to changing circumstances (Dasgupta 1993).

The ecological literature also has devoted considerable attention to the link between irrigation and the process by which land becomes increasingly saline (see Ehrlich, Ehrlich, and Holdren 1977). In the absence of adequate drainage, continued irrigation slowly but surely destroys agricultural land because of the salts left behind by evaporating water. Worldwide, the surface area of agricultural land removed from cultivation through salinization is thought by some to equal the amount added by irrigation (see United Nations 1990). And desalinization of agricultural land remains enormously expensive.

The environment is also affected by the fact that the rural poor have limited access to credit, insurance, and capital markets. Because of such constraints, domestic animals are an extremely important asset (Binswanger and Rosenzweig 1986; Rosenzweig and Wolpin 1989; Hoff and Stiglitz 1990; Dasgupta 1993). But because such animals are vulnerable during periods of scarce rainfall, farmers and nomads in Sub-Saharan Africa carry extra cattle as insurance against droughts. Herds are larger than they would be if capital and insurance markets were open to the rural poor, imposing an additional strain on grazing lands, especially during droughts. That this link between capital and credit markets (or rather, their absence) and environmental degradation is quantitatively significant should come as no surprise (World Bank 1992). The environment is an enormous capital asset. The portfolio of assets that a household manages depends on what is available to it. In fact, one can argue that even the fertility rate is related to the extent of the local environmental resource base, such as fuelwood and water sources. Later in this article I show why we should expect this to be so and what the implications are for public policy (see also Dasgupta 1993).

Underground water basins can also be considered a renewable natural resource if they are recharged over the annual cycle. The required analysis is a bit more problematic, though, because we are interested in both quality and quantity. Under normal circumstances an aquifer undergoes a self-cleansing process as pollutants are deposited into it. But the effectiveness of the process depends on the nature of the pollutants and the rate at which they are discharged. Moreover, the recharge rate depends on annual precipitation, the extent of underground flows, and the rate of evaporation. Evaporation, in turn, is a function of soil cover. In drylands reduced soil cover lowers both soil moisture and the rate of recharge of underground basins, reducing soil cover still more, which reduces the rate of recharge, and so on (Falkenmark 1986 and 1989; Olsen 1987; Nelson 1988; Reij, Mulder, and Begemann 1988; and Falkenmark and Chapman 1989). With a lowered underground water table, the cost of water extraction rises.

Aquifers display another unique characteristic. On occasion the destructive factor is not the pollutants deposited into them. When groundwater is allowed to drop to too low a level because of excessive extraction, saltwater can intrude into coastal aquifers, destroying the basin.

Environmental resources such as forests, the atmosphere, and the seas have multiple competing uses. This accentuates management problems. Forests are a source of timber, bark, saps, and pharmaceuticals. Tropical forests also provide a habitat for a rich genetic pool. In addition, forests influence local and regional climates, preserve soil cover on site, and in the case of watersheds, protect soil downstream from floods. The increased runoff of rainwater that results from deforestation strips away soil, depriving agriculture of nutrients and clogging water reservoirs and irrigation systems. The social value of a forest usually exceeds the value of its direct products, sometimes by a considerable amount (Ehrlich, Ehrlich, and Holdren 1977; Dasgupta 1982; Hamilton and King 1983; and Anderson 1987).

The resources I am referring to here are sometimes used directly in consumption (as with fisheries), sometimes in production (as with plankton, which serves as food for fish), and sometimes in both (as with drinking and irrigation water). Their stocks are measured in different ways, depending on the resource: in mass units (for example, biomass units for forests, cow dung, and crop residues), quality indexes (water and air quality), volume units (acre-feet for aquifers), and so on. Concern about environmental resources often reflects a decline in their stock. But on its own a decline in stock is not a cause for concern. In the case of exhaustible resources such as fossil fuels, the only way to avoid reducing stocks is to not use them, and this is unlikely to be the right approach. Much has been written about optimal patterns of use (see, for example, Dasgupta and Mäler 1997). But even a casual look at the foregoing examples suggests that a number of issues in environmental economics are "capital-theoretic."

Environment as an Input

Most of the environmental economics literature treats environment mainly as an amenity—that is, as a factor that increases human enjoyment directly and not as a factor used in producing something beneficial. When Rachel Carson's *Silent Spring* appeared in 1962, the disappearance of birds brought about by pollution was regarded as a loss of important amenities. The beauty of nature was being degraded and, if the degradation continued, people would no longer have the pleasure of watching and listening to birds each spring. When Buzz Holling (1994) analyzed the disappearance of migrating birds in North America, he looked at the effects on insect populations and the possible destruction of boreal forests from the increasing numbers of these pests. Using simple ecological modeling, Holling predicted that a reduction of about two-thirds in the migratory bird population would cause a qualitative and quantitative change in insect populations, with drastic consequences for Canadian forests. Carson's amenity losses obviously differ from Holling's timber production losses, but they have the same cause—a reduction in bird populations. And while both the loss in amenity and the loss in timber production reduce well-being, the implications for equity may be quite different. Thus an informed discussion of environment and poverty must define values of amenities as well as values of environmental resources as inputs in production.

It is not obvious, however, how to analytically distinguish amenity values from input values. There is no problem as long as we focus on production units. Almost by definition these units have no amenity value, and the only value that can be attributed to an environmental resource as a production unit is its value as an input in production. I will refer to this as the production value of the environment. The value of a marginal change in an environmental resource is then simply the value of the marginal productivity of that resource.

The analytical difficulty in distinguishing between amenity and production values arises in households. Usually we start with an arbitrary preference structure, defined over a commodity set (where environmental resources are regarded as commodities), and with a utility function representing the preferences. Sometimes this utility function can be decomposed as a function of outputs from household production functions (see appendix).[7]

A typical household will make the best use of its resources within its feasibility set, which can be represented as a utility maximization process. The feasibility set is defined by the household's production functions, the supply of environmental resources (which I assume are exogenous to the household), prices, and outside income (remittances from children and so on). We can now use this simple framework to discuss the demand for environmental resources and how that demand depends on income and wage rate.

We consider the simplified case in which there are only two marketed goods, consumption good z and input good y, and one environmental resource, S. The household maximization problem can then be written as:

(1) $$\text{Max } u[z, f(y, S)]$$

subject to

(2) $$p_z z + p_y y = I$$

where p is price and I is income. We are interested in how income changes will affect the demand for the environmental resource. We will measure this demand as the marginal willingness to pay for the resource, where the willingness to pay is simply the value of the marginal productivity of the environmental resource. The consumption good is the numeraire.

What are the relations between changes in income and the marginal willingness to pay? To simplify further, we assume that household output and the consumption good are approximately perfect substitutes. Thus if the demand for the input good has a positive income elasticity (which seems likely) and if the purchased input is a complement to the environmental resource, the value of the resource will increase with income. In most cases, however, we should expect substitutability between the resource and the purchased input. Thus we should expect that as income rises, the value of the resource as an input also rises. In this sense environmental resources are more important for the poor than for the wealthy.

This is a rather strong result. Discussions of income elasticity of environmental resources have generally focused on whether that elasticity is greater than one. Here we have seen that it can even be negative under the stated assumption.

The intuition behind this is obvious. If by purchasing more of a good a household can compensate for a deteriorated resource, increased income will enable the household to compensate for that deterioration more easily. Note that this result is the effect of the assumption that the environmental resource is not yielding well-being directly but is being used as an input.

Soil and fertilizers are the most obvious examples of such resources. Farmers who can afford to compensate for soil erosion will be less affected by it. Fishers and their equipment are another example. If the stock of fish is depleted, fishers with higher incomes can more easily compensate for the depletion by using more expensive equipment. Many other examples could be presented.

But all this depends on what we mean when we say that the environment is important for the poor. Here importance has been defined as the marginal value of the resource. Another interpretation could be the total value of the resource— that is, the willingness to pay to avoid complete destruction of the resource. Since a household's well-being depends partly on what it can buy on markets and partly on what it produces, increased income will improve a household's ability to compensate for the total collapse of the resource. Let us consider an example of this connection between an environmental resource and income: mangroves and fisheries.

Mangroves are an example of an ecosystem under severe threat. Mangrove forests occur in coastal areas in the tropics where waters are shallow and river deltas receive suspended sediment (mud). Mangrove prop-roots trap sediment from ebb and flood tidal currents, gradually extending land seaward. Mangrove forests commonly consist of several shoreward belts of red, black, and white mangroves.

Mangroves are highly productive marine and estuarine ecosystems. Yet although society benefits, directly or indirectly, from their ecological functions, many policymakers and developers consider mangroves as wastelands except when they are reclaimed for other uses "of greater value." Such practices fail to recognize the natural value of these ecosystems.

Primary productivity in estuaries may be twenty times higher than in the deep sea and ten times higher than in near-shore waters or deep lakes. Mangroves produce a large amount of waste (leaves, stems, and the like) that is rapidly degraded into small particles called detritus, the primary energy source for tropical coastal marine ecosystems. Colonies of microscopic life feed on these particles and are in turn eaten by estuarine species such as shrimp, some fish, and small crustaceans, which serve as forage for birds, predatory fish, and eventually people.

Mangroves also act as natural storage systems for energy supplies in one or more of their component units (leaves, flowers, stems). Throughout the year mangroves generate a continuous stock of nutrient matter for other organisms. Mangroves also affect productivity in adjacent coastal waters by exporting litter, thereby enhancing near-shore primary and secondary production. The capability of mangroves to support major inshore or offshore fishery industries, as well as the *in situ* harvesting of oysters, mussels, clams, and other mollusks is widely recognized. Fish also act as storage units within the mangrove ecosystem, exchanging energy with neighboring ecosystems through exportation and importation. And because mangrove ecosystems discourage oceanic predators (which avoid shallow waters), they are important nursery areas for larval stages of commercial shrimp and fish species. The roots of mangrove trees provide shelter from wave action, enabling shellfish larvae to attach themselves to the roots. The shelter also permits the retention of suspended life and nutrients. Tidal energy provides an important driving force. Tidal flow transports nutrients and suspended life and dilutes and flushes wastes.

Mangrove forests provide many "free" services, including storm protection, erosion control, wastewater cleanup, and areas for educational and leisure activities, as well as many direct products (fuel, construction timber) and indirect products (food from fish, shrimp, and birds). Moreover, mangroves are self-maintaining and renewable at no cost. Any damage they sustain in a storm is self-repairing. Sustainable yields of fish and timber can be derived on a continual basis if the ecological processes governing the system are properly maintained (Hamilton and Snedaker 1984).

The relation between mangroves and fisheries is especially interesting. A change in a mangrove area affects the productivity of nearby fisheries and thus the well-being of fishers and their families. A number of studies have shown that the widespread destruction of mangrove forests has a significant economic impact on local communities (see Mäler and others 1996 for a survey). In many areas the conversion of mangrove forests into shrimp farms can be seen as a redistribution of wealth from poor communities to wealthy investors and to consumers of prawns in industrial countries. Fishers are quite aware that the destruction of mangrove forests means the destruction of their fisheries, which will force them to pursue other economic activities or to become almost permanently unemployed (personal communication with Sara Aniyar, who interviewed fishers in Los Olivitos, Venezuela).

We can conclude from this analysis that rural populations in developing countries depend extensively on environmental resources as production inputs. Maintaining this resource base is thus crucial to the economic development of developing countries.

Environment as an Amenity

In Europe and North America the environment is usually considered an amenity, something that directly affects human well-being. It has generally been assumed that amenities are luxury goods—that is, that their income elasticity is greater than one. For example, McFadden and Leonard (1992, p. 22) state that "environmental protection should be a 'luxury' good that in poor families is displayed by basic needs for food and shelter, and in wealthy families is more affordable."

There is, however, no theoretical reason for the environment's income elasticity to be greater than one. Contrary to some statements in the literature, it is purely an empirical matter. Although there have been few studies on the sensitivity of demand (interpreted as the marginal willingness to pay) for environmental quality to changes in income, some indicate that the elasticity may be less than one. Kriström and Riera (1996), for example, examined a set of valuation studies to find whether the elasticity is greater or less than one. The studies were all from Europe and were all contingent valuation studies. The result is striking: in almost all cases the elasticity was found to be less than one. Kanninen and Kriström (1993) analyzed data sets from Africa and the United States and found essentially the same outcome. These results suggest that environmental quality is not a luxury good and thus that environmental protection is progressive because low-income groups benefit relatively more than high-income groups.

Of course, these studies raise many questions and potential objections. One concerns the validity of contingent valuation methods. But even those who object strongly to contingent valuation methods can hardly argue that the estimates they provide are less valid than statements built on prejudice. A more relevant objection is that almost all the studies were undertaken in industrial countries. Thus it may not be valid to extend Kriström and Riera's conclusion to developing countries. The main message, however, is that the income elasticity of demand for environmental improvements is an empirical issue.

Supply of Environmental Resources

The supply of environmental resources is determined by how people manage and exploit the resource base. Of the many factors that affect environmental management, I focus on three: property rights, population growth, and discounting and access to markets.

Property Rights

The absence of well-defined property rights to a resource almost inevitably results in its degradation.[8] In southern and East Africa, for example, the lack of well-defined property rights is the main force driving overgrazing, soil degradation, and overfishing. No single individual or organization can be held responsible for the effect that the collective activities of these individuals or organizations have on the land, soil, or fish stock.

In most developing countries people have been using communal lands for centuries and over time have developed social norms that support efficient management of these lands. Yet however efficient these norms are (and however well adapted to variations in precipitation and other climatic variables), they are not robust to external disturbances (Dasgupta and Mäler 1991, 1997; Dasgupta 1993). Norms break down with population growth, technological change, and changing market conditions, so that what was once a valid way of managing land or water no longer works. In other words, these resources switch over into open-access regimes.

Many observers have recommended technical fixes to restore the resource base. Such fixes may work for a while, but in the long run countries need to redefine their property rights in order to create incentives for the people who use resources to do so in a sustainable way. Large-scale land redistribution may be required to give each household a sufficiently large entitlement to the resource to ensure a viable future. The poorest households are in particular need of institutional and land reform. In Zimbabwe cattle ranchers are exposed to the variability of natural conditions, but they are much better able to cope with these risks than are poor peasants living on communal land. Even after good rains, parts of the communal lands are barren and cannot be used for further grazing, while commercial ranches are green and provide space for expansion of cattle herds. Thus institutional reforms to protect the resource base are needed to improve the situation for the poor.

Population Growth

Rapid population growth directly contributes to environmental degradation. And as noted, population growth may break down social norms and resource management systems, further contributing to environmental degradation.

Yet environmental degradation can also increase population growth. Dasgupta and Mäler (1991) hypothesize that children are "produced" not only for consumption purposes (the pleasure of having children) and for retirement and insurance purposes, but also to increase the workforce. This hypothesis is further developed and summarized in Dasgupta (1993). Moreover, there is empirical evidence that the hypothesis is true, at least in some countries and some circumstances.

In an econometric analysis of the factors determining fertility in rural Lesotho (based on a survey of 300 rural households), Bakane-Tuoane (1997) showed that the economic value of children to households is a major determinant of fertility. Her hypotheses were that households demand children to provide old-age support and general social security, to serve as full-time productive agents, and to generate income to supplement household earnings. Thus the demand for children that determines the fertility rate will to some extent mirror the demand for labor in rural households.[9]

If fertility is positively related to the need for workers, there are clear implications for the relation between poverty and the environment. If environmental degradation increases the demand for workers, as seems reasonable to expect, then fertility will increase. For example, if land becomes overgrazed, cattle may have to be moved long distances, which will require more workers; if local water sources are polluted or depleted, more people will be needed to fetch water; and if deforestation reduces the local supply of firewood, more workers will be required to collect the same amount of wood as before.

Here there is apparently a vicious circle that affects mainly the poor: environmental degradation increases population, which increases degradation, and so on. But it is possible to make this circle virtuous. An improved environment would reduce fertility, further improving the environment. Thus the effects of the institutional reforms discussed in the previous section would probably be magnified through the effects on fertility. Thus any reduction in fertility resulting from better land tenure systems and a general increase in efficiency could also lower rural-urban migration if, as Bakane-Tuoane hypothesized (1997), rural households demand children to supplement income, often sending them to urban areas to earn incomes. Lower migration improves the urban environment as well as the well-being of urban citizens.

Discounting

The rate at which rational individuals, acting under certainty, discount future costs and benefits is determined by their pure rate of time preference and expected growth of well-being. Thus individuals expecting a constant or falling rate of well-being discount the future with a small or even negative rate. Even with positive growth the consumption discount is rather low (see Markandya and Pearce 1988). This result seems to contradict the generally held view that poor people generally have a high discount rate. The contradiction is only superficial if the discount rate is assumed to account for risk and if the individual is assumed to be uncertain about survival to the next period. In this case discounts of future costs and benefits would be higher than otherwise. However, it is in general better to deal with uncertainty and risk in other ways than to adjust the discount rate. What about people who expect no growth in well-being? Their consumption discount rate will be high only if their pure rate of time preference is high enough. Thus it is of interest to determine household time preferences.

Kundhande (1995) studied the time preferences of rural households in Zimbabwe by questioning their hypothetical choices between bundles of commodities—maize and fuelwood—today and tomorrow. Future use of fuelwood was consistently discounted at a lower rate than future use of maize. This finding could be explained by anticipated changes in relative prices: fuelwood was expected to be available without serious limitations in the future. Moreover, implicit discount rates, although they varied considerably among households (reflecting lack of markets for these goods), were extremely high. If these results are valid, the consumption discount rate in rural households may be a strong force driving environmental degradation. When people do not care much about the future, they will not take steps to protect the future environment.

If this rather popular theory—that high discount rates in poor societies contribute to environmental degradation—is accurate, policymakers should look for ways to change the behavior of households. One way to do this would be to establish organized credit markets for rural households. Giving people access to credit markets will induce them to change their behavior in ways that are compatible with rates on the markets. Credit markets will allow them to smooth their consumption over time, resulting in less pressure on resources during times of low production. And establishing even simple insurance schemes and giving households ways to diversify risks will result in even less pressure on resources.

Thus institutional reform of property rights should be accompanied by institutional reforms aimed at establishing markets for credit and insurance.

Growth and the Environment

Ever since publication of the World Bank's *World Development Report 1992: Development and the Environment,* it has been increasingly popular to study so-called inverse Kuznets curves. These curves relate a particular kind of environmental damage to per capita income. They are based on cross-country data—that is, environmental damage and per capita incomes in different countries are plotted and a curve is fitted to the scatter diagram. The curves show that countries with very low incomes have limited environmental damage. As incomes rise, the environment gets worse—but only up to a point. Beyond that point, further increases in per capita income are associated with an improved environment.

The intuitive explanation is as follows. When income is low, the economy does not affect the environment much. As income rises, environmental damage increases, but because income remains relatively low, demand for a cleaner environment does not increase much. But at a certain stage income is sufficiently high for the demand for environmental improvements to catch up, so further income growth will be accompanied by improvements in the environment. This argument is based on the assumption that the income elasticity for environmental demand is greater than one. Above I argued that, at least for environmental resources that are used as inputs in household production, the elasticity is less than one. This is, however, consistent with the estimated inverse Kuznets curves because almost all studies examine pollution problems in industrial countries, not the resource base in developing countries.

Arrow and others (1995) subjected the studies of environmental Kuznets curves to critical review. One of their main conclusions was that:

> Economic growth is not a panacea for environmental quality; indeed, it is not even the main issue. What matters is the content of growth—the composition of inputs (including environmental resources) and outputs (including waste products). This content is determined by, among other things, the economic institutions within which human activities are conducted.

Thus instead of discussing growth or no growth, we should focus on how to improve the efficiency of economic systems in such a way that each country can make the best use of its resources, including environmental resources, regardless of its degree of development.

If, despite this conclusion, we want to discuss growth and the environment, the appropriate framework is based on net national product (NNP) rather than gross domestic product. With an appropriate NNP measure there would be no conflict between growth and the environment. Maximizing NNP would ensure that well-being is maximized within the space of available resources, not only now but in the future (theoretical studies of these properties of NNP include Weitzman 1974; Mäler 1974, 1991; Dasgupta and Mäler 1991, 1997; Hartwick 1990, 1994; and Asheim 1994).

Conclusion

In developing countries environmental resources are used mainly as inputs in household production or in small-scale production units. As inputs they are of considerable value to the people using them, particularly if they are essential for survival. Economic analysis of these inputs and their outcomes must be based on a sound understanding of the ecological functions and life-supporting services provided by ecosystems. Thus economists must recognize the irrefutable features of these systems and can no longer take liberties in modeling the natural world.

Because economic and ecological systems are complex and nonlinear, interactions between the two systems may be hard to understand. Thus more study of these interdependencies is needed. Still, even the limited information that is available suggests that, to alleviate poverty while protecting the environment, developing countries should:

- Introduce well-defined property rights.
- Establish markets—particularly capital and insurance markets—wherever they will support better management of environmental resources.
- Measure growth with better indexes than conventional GDP measures, including NNP.

In the long run these general reforms are much more important than technical fixes that solve specific problems but fail to change overall incentive structures.

Appendix. Simple Framework of Demand for Environmental Resources

The utility function representing households' preference structure can be decomposed as a function of outputs from household production functions:

(A.1) $$U = u(z, q_1, ..., q_m, L)$$

where the household production functions are

(A.2) $$v_j = f_j(y^j, L^j, S).$$

Here z is a vector of consumption goods consumed directly; q_j is the consumption of household outputs; L^j is the input of labor in producing v_j, the output of household commodity j; y^j is a vector of inputs bought on markets; and S is a vector of environmental resources. Then

(A.3) $$x = z + \Sigma_j y^j, \text{ and}$$
$$L = \Sigma_j L^j.$$

But this decomposition may not be unique, and that gives rise to some conceptual problems. Since these problems will not arise in applied studies because household production is defined as an observed variable, I will not go into this further. (For more details see Mäler 1985 and Mäler and others 1994.)

A typical household will make the best use of its resources within its feasibility set, which can be represented as a utility maximization process. The budget constraint can be written as:

(A.4) $$\Sigma_i p_i x_i \leq wL + I$$

where I is income and p_i is price. We can now use this simple framework to discuss the demand for environmental resources and how that demand depends on income and the wage rate. The household maximization problem can be written as:

(A.5) $$\text{Max } u[z, f(y, S)]$$

subject to

(A.6) $$p_z z + p_y y = I$$

for the simplified case of two marketed goods, a consumption good z and an input good y, and one environmental resource S (whose supply is assumed to be exogenous to the household). To see how income changes affect the demand for the environmental resource, we measure this demand as the marginal willingness to pay for the resource:

(A.7) $$\delta = p_z (u_q / u_z) f_S.$$

If we further assume that household output and the consumption good are approximately perfect substitutes, the effect on the marginal willingness to pay is:

(A.8) $$\partial \delta / \partial I = (u_q / u_z) f_{sy}'' (\partial y / \partial I).$$

Notes

1. The natural capital base also includes underground minerals and ores.
2. Cross-country data such as these are not entirely comparable, but they do suggest orders of magnitude. That is the only purpose for which I use them.
3. There were, of course, exceptions—for example, CSE (1982 and 1985) and Dasgupta (1982). Moreover, agriculture and fisheries economists have routinely studied environmental matters. In the text I am referring to a neglect of environmental matters in "official" development economics.
4. Minerals and fossil fuels are not renewable, but they raise a different set of issues. For an account of what resource allocation theory looks like when exhaustible resources are included in the production process, see Dasgupta and Heal (1979); Hartwick and Olewiler (1986); and Tietenberg (1988). For a nontechnical account of the theory and the historical role that has been played by the substitution of new energy resources for old, see Dasgupta (1989).
5. The economic issues arising from such nonlinearities are analyzed in Dasgupta (1982) and Dasgupta and Mäler (1997).
6. UNEP (1984) provides a notable—and controversial—estimate of global declines in livestock and agricultural productivity in drylands due to soil losses: $26 billion a year. For a discussion of the UNEP estimate see Gigengack and others in Dixon, James, and Sherman (1990). The estimate by Mabbutt (1984), that about 40 percent of the world's productive drylands are threatened by desertification, suggests the magnitude of the problem. For accounts of the economics and ecology of drylands see Falloux and Mukendi (1987) and Dixon, James, and Sherman (1989, 1990).
7. Becker (1981) introduced household production functions into economics, and they have become an indispensable tool in analyzing relations between environment and households. For an application to environmental economics see Mäler (1985) and Mäler and others (1994).
8. For detailed discussions of different property rights regimes see Hanna and Munasinghe (1995a, b) and Hanna, Folke, and Mäler (1996).
9. This was illustrated recently during a visit to Zimbabwe, where a farmer living on communal land explained recent reductions in fertility by saying that, in the past, households needed a huge labor force and could only get that labor by producing it themselves. Now children are considered almost a burden that households try to avoid. The farmer did not, however, explain why families no longer require a huge labor force.

References

Anderson, Dennis. 1987. *The Economics of Afforestation: A Case Study in Africa*. Baltimore, Md.: The Johns Hopkins University Press.

Arrow, K.J., B. Bolin, R. Costanza, P. Dasgupta, C. Folke, C.S. Holling, B.O. Jansson, S. Levin, K.G. Mäler, C. Perrings, and D. Pimentel. 1995. "Economic Growth, Carrying Capacity, and the Environment." *Sciences* 268: 520–22.

Asheim, Geir. 1994. "Net National Product as an Indicator of Sustainability." *Scandinavian Journal of Economics* 96 (2): 257–65.

Bakane-Tuoane, Manane. 1997. "The Economic and Fertility Interactions in Agricultural Production in Lesotho." Beijer Institute Discussion Paper Series 98. Stockholm.

Becker, Gary. 1981. *A Treatise on the Family*. Cambridge, Mass.: Harvard University Press.

Binswanger, Hans. 1989. "Brazilian Policies That Encourage Deforestation in the Amazon." Environment Department Working Paper 16. World Bank, Washington, D.C.

Binswanger, Hans, and Mark Rosenzweig. 1986. "Credit Markets, Wealth, and Endowments in Rural South India." Report 59. World Bank, Agriculture and Rural Development Department, Washington, D.C.

Carson, Rachel. *Silent Spring*. Boston: Houghton Mifflin.

CSE (Centre for Science and Environment). 1982. *The State of India's Environment: A Citizens' Report*. New Delhi: Centre for Science and Environment.

———. 1985. *The State of India's Environment: A Citizens' Report*. New Delhi: Centre for Science and Environment.

———. 1990. *Human-Nature Interactions in a Central Himalayan Village: A Case Study of Village Bemru*. New Delhi.

Dasgupta, Partha. 1982. *The Control of Resources*. Oxford: Basil Blackwell.

———. 1989. "Exhaustible Resources." In L. Friday and R. Laskey, eds. *The Fragile Environment*. Cambridge: Cambridge University Press.

———. 1993. *An Inquiry into Well-being and Destitution.* Oxford: Clarendon Press.

Dasgupta, Partha, and G.M. Heal. 1979. *Economic Theory and Exhaustible Resources.* Cambridge: Cambridge University Press.

Dasgupta, Partha, and Karl-Göran Mäler. 1991. "The Environment and Emerging Development Issues." In Stanley Fischer, Dennis de Tray, and Shekhar Shah, eds., *Proceedings of the World Bank Annual Conference on Development Economics 1990.* Washington, D.C.: World Bank.

———. 1995. "Poverty, Institutions, and the Environmental Resource-Base." In J. Behrman and T.N. Srinivasan, eds., *Handbook of Development Economics.* Amsterdam: Elsevier.

———, eds. 1997. *The Environment and Emerging Development Issues.* New York: Oxford University Press.

Dasgupta, Partha, Carl Folke, and Karl-Göran Mäler. 1994. "The Environmental Resource-Base and Human Welfare." In Kerstin Lindahl-Kiessling and Hans Landberg, eds., *Population, Economic Development, and the Environment.* Oxford: Oxford University Press.

Dixon, J.A., D.E. James, and P.B. Sherman, eds. 1990. *Dryland Management: Economic Case Studies.* London: Earthscan Publications.

Ehrlich, Paul, Anne Ehrlich, and John Holdren. 1977. *Ecoscience: Population, Resources, Environment.* San Francisco: W.H. Freeman.

Falconer, Julia. 1990. *The Major Significance of "Minor" Forest Products: The Local Use and Value of Forests in the West African Humid Forest Zone.* Rome: United Nations Food and Agriculture Organization.

Falconer, Julia, and J.E. Mike Arnold. 1989. *Household Food Security and Forestry: An Analysis of Socio-Economic Issues.* Rome: United Nations Food and Agriculture Organization.

Falkenmark, Malin. 1986. "Fresh Water: Time for a Modified Approach." *Ambio* 15.

———. 1989. "The Massive Water Scarcity Now Facing Africa: Why Isn't It Being Addressed?" *Ambio* 18.

Falkenmark, Malin, and Tom Chapman, eds. 1989. *Comparative Hydrology: An Ecological Approach to Land and Water Resources.* Paris: United Nations Educational, Scientific, and Cultural Organization.

Falloux, François, and Aleki Mukendi, eds. 1987. *Desertification Control and Renewable Resource Management in the Sahelian and Sudanian Zones of West Africa.* World Bank Technical Paper 70. Washington, D.C.

Gross, D.R., and B.A. Underwood. 1971. "Technological Change and Caloric Cost: Sisal Agriculture in North-Eastern Brazil." *American Anthropologist* 73.

Hamilton, L.S., and P.N. King. 1983. *Tropical Forested Watersheds: Hydrologic and Soils Response to Major Uses or Conversions.* Boulder, Colo.: Westview Press.

Hamilton, L.S., and S.C. Snedaker, eds. 1984. *Handbook for Mangrove Area Management,* United Nations Environment Programme and East-West Center, Environment and Policy Institute, Honolulu.

Hanna, Susan, and Mohan Munasinghe, eds. 1995a. *Property Rights and the Environment: Social and Ecological Issues.* Washington, D.C.: Beijer International Institute of Ecological Economics and World Bank.

———. 1995b. *Property Rights in a Social and Ecological Context: Case Studies and Design Applications.* Washington, D.C.: Beijer International Institute of Ecological Economics and World Bank.

Hanna, Susan, Carl Folke, and Karl-Göran Mäler, eds. 1996. *Rights to Nature: Ecological, Economic, Cultural, and Political Principles of Institutions for the Environment.* Washington, D.C.: Island Press.

Hartwick, John. 1990. "Natural Resources, National Accounting, and Economic Depreciation." *Journal of Public Economics* 43 (December): 291–304.

———. 1994. "National Wealth and Net National Product." *Scandinavian Journal of Economics* 96.

Hartwick, John, and Nancy Olewiler. 1986. *The Economics of Natural Resource Use.* New York: Harper & Row.

Hoff, Karla, and Joseph E. Stiglitz. 1990. "Introduction: Imperfect Information and Rural Credit Markets: Puzzles and Policy Perspectives." *The World Bank Economic Review* 4 (3): 235–50.

Holling, C.S. 1994. "An Ecologist View of the Malthusian Conflict." In Kerstin Lindahl-Kiessling and Hans Landberg, eds., *Population, Economic Development, and the Environment.* Oxford: Oxford University Press.

Holling, C.S., D.W. Schindler, B.W. Walker, and J. Roughgarden. 1994. "Biodiversity in the Functioning of Ecosystems: An Ecological Primer and Synthesis." In C. Perrings and others, eds., *Biodiversity Conservatism: Problems and Policies.* Boston: Kluwer Academic.

Kanninen, B.J., and B. Kriström. 1993. "Welfare Benefit Estimation and Income Distribution." Revised version of Beijer Discussion Paper 20. Beijer International Institute of Ecological Economics, Stockholm.

Kennedy, E., and R. Oniang'o. 1990. "Health and Nutrition Effects of Sugarcane Production in South-Western Kenya." *Food and Nutrition Bulletin* 12.

Kriström, B., and P. Riera. 1996. "Is the Income Elasticity of Environmental Improvements Less Than One?" *Environmental and Resource Economics* 7.

Kundhande, Godfrey. 1995. "Empirical Measures of Rates of Time Preference of Rural Households in Zimbabwe." Paper presented at a Beijer International Institute of Ecological Economics Research Seminar, Gozo, Malta, 10–13 July.

Lindahl-Kiessling, Kerstin, and Hans Landberg, eds. 1994. *Population, Economic Development, and the Environment*. Oxford: Oxford University Press.

Lindert, P. 1980. "Child Cost and Economic Development." In Richard Easterlin, ed., *Population and Economic Change in Developing Countries*. Chicago: University of Chicago Press.

———. 1983. "The Changing Economic Costs and Benefits of Having Children." In R.A. Bulatao and R.D. Lee, eds., *Determinants of Fertility in Developing Countries*. New York: Academic Press.

Mabbutt, J.A. 1984. "A New Global Assessment of the Status and Trends of Desertification." *Environmental Conservation* 11.

Mäler, Karl-Göran. 1974. *Environmental Economics: A Theoretical Inquiry*. Baltimore, Md.: The Johns Hopkins University Press.

———. 1985. "Welfare Economics and the Environment." In A. Kneese and J. Sweeney, eds., *Handbook of Natural Resources and Energy Economics*. Amsterdam: Elsevier.

———. 1991. "National Accounting and Environmental Resources." *Journal of Environmental and Resource Economics* 1 (1): 1–15.

———. 1993. "Multiple Use of Environmental Resources: A Household Production Function Approach to Valuing Resources." Beijer Discussion Paper 4. Beijer International Institute of Ecological Economics, Stockholm.

Mäler, Karl-Göran, and I.M. Gren. 1994. "Multiple Use of Environmental Resources: A Household Production Function Approach to Valuing Natural Capital." In A.M. Jansson, M. Hammer, C. Folke, and R. Costanza, eds., *Investing in Natural Capital: The Ecological Economics Approach to Sustainability*. Washington, D.C.: Island Press.

Mäler, Karl-Göran, S. Aniyar, C. Casler, E. Weir, and J. Fuenmayor. 1996. "Economic Model of Los Olivitos Mangrove Ecosystem in Venezuela." *Boletín del Centro de Estudios Biológicos de la Universidad de Zulia* (Maracaibo Venezuela) 30(2).

Markandya, Anil, and David Pearce. 1988. "Environmental Considerations and the Choice of the Discount Rate in Developing Countries." Environment Department Working Paper 3. World Bank, Washington, D.C.

McFadden, D.L., and G.K. Leonard. 1992. "Issues in the Contingent Valuation of Environmental Goods: Methodologies for Data Collection and Analysis." In *Contingent Valuation: A Critical Assessment*. Cambridge: Cambridge Economics.

Nelson, Ridley. 1988. "Dryland Management: The Desertification Problem." Environment Department Working Paper 8. World Bank, Washington, D.C.

Olsen, W.K. 1987. "Manmade 'Drought' in Rayalaseema." *Economic and Political Weekly* 22.

Reij, Chris, Paul Mulder, and Louis Begemann. 1988. *Water Harvesting for Plant Production*. World Bank Technical Paper 91. Washington, D.C.

Repetto, Robert. 1988. "Economic Policy Reform for Natural Resource Conservation." Environment Department Working Paper 4. World Bank, Washington, D.C.

Rosenzweig, Mark, and Kenneth Wolpin. 1985. "Specific Experience, Household Structure and Intergenerational Transfers: Farm Family Land and Labour Arrangements in Developing Countries." *Quarterly Journal of Economics* 100 (supplement): 961–87.

Tietenberg, Thomas. 1988. *Environmental and Natural Resource Economics*. 2d ed. Glenview, Ill.: Scott, Foresman.

United Nations. 1984. *General Assessment of Progress in the Implementation of the Plan of Action to Combat Desertification, 1978–1984. Report to the Executive Director*. Nairobi: UNEP (United Nations Environment Programme).

von Braun, J., and E. Kennedy. 1986. "Commercialization of Subsistence Agriculture: Income and Nutritional Effects in Developing Countries." Working Paper on Commercialization of Agriculture and Nutrition 1. International Food Research Institute, Washington, D.C.

Weitzman, M. 1976. "On the Welfare Significance of the National Product in a Dynamic Economy." *Quarterly Journal of Economics* 90: 156–62.

Wilson, Edward. 1992. *The Diversity of Life*. Cambridge, Mass.: Harvard University Press.

World Bank. 1992. *World Development Report 1992: Development and the Environment*. New York: Oxford University Press.

Comment on "Environment, Poverty, and Economic Growth," by Karl-Göran Mäler

Edward B. Barbier

Karl-Göran Mäler's article touches on a number of issues crucial to the relationships between environment, poverty, and economic growth. Here I focus on three:

- Land degradation and deforestation as critical economic problems facing developing countries.
- Poverty as a constraint on the incentives of rural households to control land degradation and deforestation.
- The role of ecological functions in supporting and protecting economic activity.

Land Degradation and Deforestation as Critical Economic Problems

Mäler refers several times to processes of land degradation in developing countries. In the past land degradation was too often the sole province of natural scientists. But far from being a purely technical problem of soil science or plant breeding, at its core land degradation is clearly an economic problem. In developing countries poor rural households often live in marginal agricultural areas, where land productivity—and thus household income—is stagnant or declining. With limited access to capital or to alternative economic opportunities, it may be rational for these households to extract short-term rents through resource conversion and degradation, so long as additional land and resources are available to exploit relatively cheaply and the cost of access remains low. The outcome is increased land degradation and expanded agricultural activity on frontier forests and other marginal lands, resulting in further degradation.

Recent evidence confirms that deforestation and land degradation in developing countries are linked. A study of global trends in human-induced soil erosion over 1945–90 found that more than 20 percent of the vegetated land in developing countries is degraded, much of it suffering from moderate, severe, or extreme degradation (Oldeman, van Engelen, and Pulles 1990). Deforestation appears to be a major

---

Edward B. Barbier is a reader in the Environment Department at the University of York, United Kingdom.
Annual World Bank Conference on Development Economics 1997
©1998 The International Bank for Reconstruction and Development / THE WORLD BANK

source of the problem, accounting for about 40 percent of erosion in Asia and South America, 22 percent in Central America and Mexico, and 14 percent in Africa. Studies throughout the tropics have shown that deforestation leads directly to degradation of soil structure, changes the chemical and biological properties of soil, decreases the porosity of the surface layer, increases soil compaction, and decreases the infiltration rate (Lal 1995).

Recent studies have shown that tropical deforestation is a human-induced problem related to poverty and underdevelopment (Brown and Pearce 1994). For example, Barbier and Burgess (1997) analyze fifty-three tropical countries in an attempt to explain the economic determinants of tropical deforestation. They find that rising population density increases forest clearance, while rising per capita incomes and agricultural yields reduce the demand for forest conversion. This finding suggests that pressure for deforestation falls as countries develop economically and the productivity of agricultural lands improves.

Finally, Leonard (1989) reports that the poorest fifth of the rural population in developing countries is concentrated on low-potential lands (defined as resource-poor or marginal agricultural lands where inadequate or unreliable rainfall, adverse soil conditions, fertility, and topography limit agricultural productivity and increase the risk of chronic land degradation). Nearly 75 percent of the poorest fifth of the rural population in Latin America, 57 percent in Asia, and 51 percent in Africa live on low-potential lands. Because these lands are prone to chronic degradation, Mäler is correct in identifying resource management by poor rural households as a crucial economic issue in solving the development and poverty problems facing low-income countries.

Poverty as a Constraint on Incentives to Control Land Degradation and Deforestation

Mäler notes that if poverty is associated with high rates of time preference, poor rural households may discount the future heavily and thus degrade resources today. Poverty constrains developing country farmers' ability to manage—much less exploit—their productive resource base in many ways. Land and unskilled labor are generally their principal assets, and human and physical capital endowments are limited. These households also depend on agricultural production as their main source of income, although the importance of off-farm income increases as the size of holdings declines. As a result poor households with limited holdings often face labor, land, and cash constraints on their ability to invest in land improvements. For example, in a review of farmer adoption of agroforestry systems in Central America and the Caribbean, Current, Lutz, and Scherr (1995) conclude that poorer farmers may find agroforestry profitable, but their rate of adoption is often constrained by limited land, labor, and capital resources and their need to ensure food security and reduce risks.

A recent analysis by Deininger and Heinegg (1995) of sources of income for Mexico's rural poor illustrates the formidable incentive problems presented by poverty. Mexico's 1.3 million farm households with holdings of less than 2 hectares (34 percent of all producers) are extremely poor and highly dependent on off-farm income. Their agricultural systems are unproductive and lack diversity. Almost two-thirds of output value is derived from maize and beans, which occupy an average 84 percent of the land area available to these producers. Faced with such constraints, poor rural farmers have a limited ability and willingness to invest in improved land management or to adopt new farming systems.

A study in Malawi also highlights the unique incentives and constraints facing poor rural households in combating land degradation (Barbier and Burgess 1992). Female-headed households account for 42 percent of Malawi's "core-poor" households. They typically cultivate small plots of land (less than 0.5 hectare), and many are often marginalized onto less fertile soils and steeper slopes. Moreover, they often cannot finance agricultural inputs such as fertilizer, and have insufficient labor to rotate crops, plant "green manure" crops, or conserve soil and water. As a result most poor, female-headed farming households face declining soil fertility and crop yields, further exacerbating their poverty and increasing their dependence on land.

As Mäler notes, poor farming households may be able to overcome such constraints if they have access to credit. But throughout the developing world the ability of poor farmers to obtain credit for land improvements is limited by restrictions on the availability of rural credit for this purpose or by insecure property rights that make poor farmers ineligible for credit. In Honduras, for example, the introduction of legal land titles has helped alleviate liquidity constraints affecting the purchase of working inputs and has boosted the rate of return to holdings by an estimated 12 percent a year (López forthcoming). Among rural producers in Mexico who had received rural credit, only 9.6 percent had holdings of less than 2 hectares (Deininger and Heinegg 1995). In Malawi, although about 45 percent of rural smallholders have holdings of less than 1 hectare and more than 21 percent are core-poor households with less than 0.5 hectare, only 17 percent of medium-term credit is allocated to households with less than 2 hectares (Barbier and Burgess 1992). In El Salvador fewer than 20 percent of small farmers are able to obtain agricultural credit, and only 0.3 percent of this credit is used for reforestation, soil conservation, irrigation and drainage, or on-farm improvement works. Small farmers commonly rely on credit from the agricultural wholesalers to whom they sell their products as collateral at below-market prices (World Bank 1994).

As noted, many migrants to frontier forests and other marginal lands in developing countries are landless or near-landless rural households that are searching for new land and economic opportunities. As is common among poor migrants, these households have low levels of human capital and low opportunity costs of migrating to the frontier—particularly if agricultural employment opportunities are scarce. For these households the decision to migrate involves comparing the returns to rural employment and income in their home areas with the potential net returns on frontier or marginal lands (Barbier forthcoming).

Heath and Binswanger (1996) discuss how increasing numbers of poor rural households in Colombia are migrating to marginal upland areas and equally fragile forest land. The result is continued unsustainable farming of the Andean slopes and the Amazon Basin and abandonment of land as yields decline, followed by further extensions of frontier and upland farming. The problem is exacerbated somewhat by failures in rural labor markets or labor policies but more so by the failure of agricultural and land policies to absorb rural labor, promote efficient land use, and, most important, generate higher returns to smallholder agricultural land.

Land abandonment for further conversion and exploitation of frontier forests has been long recognized as a major problem in the Brazilian Amazon. As argued by Schneider (1994), in the Brazilian Amazon the returns to sustainable farming on existing agricultural land rarely compare favorably with the returns to unsustainable farming on converted frontier forests. The problem has been exacerbated by high and highly variable real interest rates, which force Amazonian farmers to seek immediate (and thus unsustainable) profits from frontier land. Unless investments in sustainable farming can yield initial profits that are 50–70 percent higher than those from existing nutrient-mining farming practices, farming households on the frontier will continue to engage in these practices, abandon their land when yields decline, and move to new frontier land. Given the additional incentives to sell existing land to higher-income settlers for modest gains, the pressure to migrate further into the frontier appears almost inevitable.

Environment as an Input: Mangrove-Fishery Links

Mäler emphasizes the role of environmental resources as essential inputs in the production processes and livelihoods of poor rural populations in developing countries. And as Mäler notes, for too long economists have failed to assess and value the contribution of ecological services in supporting and protecting economic activity in developing countries (Barbier 1994). Mäler describes an especially significant ecological "service" in developing countries—the role of mangroves as breeding grounds and nurseries for coastal and marine fisheries. The threat posed by excessive clearance of coastal mangroves cannot be overstated. Throughout the developing world this precious resource is being destroyed by agricultural development, urban expansion, logging and other extractive activities, residential coastal housing and tourist facilities, and, above all, conversion to shrimp and fish farming.

A number of studies support Mäler's claim that the continued loss of mangroves will have substantial effects on economic activities in developing countries, especially coastal and marine fisheries. For example, Parks and Bonifaz (1994) analyze the competition between mangroves and shrimp aquaculture in Ecuador. They note that throughout the developing world shrimp ponds appear to be attractive short-term investments, with initial average yields ranging from 40 to 133 metric tons per square kilometer. As a result shrimp ponds are being established throughout the tropics through the conversion of mangrove systems, which are fairly extensive shrimp production systems but have lower average yields. Parks and Bonifaz show that in Ecuador such mangrove deforestation causes the loss of postlarval shrimp input for the ponds, indicating a tradeoff between short-term profits from shrimp farming and long-term productivity and sustainability.

When other economic effects are taken into account, the net economic benefits of mangrove deforestation are often found to be negative. For example, Ruitenbeek (1994) examines the effects of different approaches to harvesting mangrove trees for the wood chip industry in Bintuni Bay, Irian Jaya, Indonesia. He concludes that there is little economic advantage to cutting significant amounts (say, more than 25 percent) of the mangrove area. Similarly, Sathivathai (1997) analyzes the economic benefits of mangrove systems in southern Thailand in supporting offshore fisheries, coastline protection, and carbon sequestration and compares these with the economic returns from converting the mangroves to shrimp ponds. Although shrimp aquaculture is financially attractive, the overall economic returns are negative when the loss of mangrove benefits is taken into account.

Finally, although the degradation of essential ecological services (such as the mangrove support function for offshore fisheries) can be economically significant, that should not be the exclusive focus. Other economic factors, such as open-access overexploitation of fisheries, may be the more crucial management problem. This is demonstrated in a recent analysis of mangrove-fishery links in the state of Campeche, Mexico (Barbier and Strand forthcoming). During 1980–90 mangrove deforestation had a potentially sizable effect on the offshore shrimp fishery in Campeche, with an average annual decline in mangrove area of about 2 square kilometers resulting in a loss of about 14.4 metric tons of shrimp harvest and nearly $140,000 in revenue from the Campeche fishery each year. But given the relatively low rate of annual mangrove deforestation in the region during this period, the resulting loss in shrimp harvest and revenue does not appear to be substantial—only about 0.2 percent a year.

A far more significant influence on the shrimp fishery was its overexploitation through open access. For example, the number of industrial and artisanal vessels increased from about 4,500 in 1980 to more than 7,200 in 1990. The management implications are clear: as long as levels of fishing effort continue to rise, harvests will fall as a result of overfishing, even if mangroves are fully protected. Moreover, any increase in harvest and revenue from an expansion into mangroves is likely to be short-lived, as it would simply draw in more fishers. Better management of the Campeche shrimp fishery to control overexploitation may be the only short-term policy capable of returning production to acceptable levels, as well as of realizing the long-term economic benefits of protecting mangroves. With the increase in artisanal vessels operated by poor fishing households the main threat to the fishery, we are once again confronting a poverty-environment trap—although perhaps a slightly different one than Mäler envisioned in his article.

Conclusion

Mäler emphasizes the need for development economists to consider seriously environment, poverty, and development links. As recent research has indicated, these links are often complex—but not insurmountably so, provided we are willing to accept that they exist and devote effort to analyzing them. I hope that

Mäler's article inspires the World Bank and others to continue this line of research, finally destroying the myth that environment is a luxury for developing countries.

References

Barbier, E.B. 1994. "Valuing Environmental Functions: Tropical Wetlands." *Land Economics* 70: 155–73.

———. Forthcoming. "Rural Poverty and Natural Resource Degradation." In Ramón E. López and Alberto Valdés, eds., *Rural Poverty in Latin America*. Washington, D.C.: World Bank.

Barbier, E.B., and J.C. Burgess. 1992. "Malawi: Land Degradation in Agriculture." Environment Department Working Paper 37. World Bank, Washington, D.C.

———. 1997. "The Economic Analysis of Tropical Forest Land Use Options." *Land Economics* 73: 174–95.

Barbier, E.B., and Ivan Strand. Forthcoming. "Valuing Mangrove-Fishery Linkages: A Case Study of Campeche, Mexico." *Environmental and Resource Economics*.

Brown, Katrina, and David W. Pearce, eds. 1994. *The Causes of Tropical Deforestation: The Economic and Statistical Analysis of Factors Giving Rise to the Loss of the Tropical Forests*. London: University College London Press.

Current, Dean, Ernst Lutz, and Sara Scherr, eds. 1995. "Costs, Benefits, and Farmer Adaption of Agroforestry: Project Experience in Central America and the Caribbean." Environment Department Working Paper 14. World Bank, Washington, D.C.

Deininger, Klaus, and Ayo Heinegg. 1995. "Rural Poverty in Mexico." World Bank, Latin America and the Caribbean Region, Country Department II, Washington, D.C.

Heath, John, and Hans Binswanger. 1996. "Natural Resource Degradation Effects of Poverty and Population Growth Are Largely Policy-Induced: The Case of Colombia." *Environment and Development Economics* 1: 65–83.

Lal, Rattan. 1995. *Sustainable Management of Soil Resources in the Humid Tropics*. New York: United Nations University Press.

Leonard, H.J. 1989. *Environment and the Poor: Development Strategies for a Common Agenda*. New Brunswick, N.J.: Transaction Books.

López, Ramón E. Forthcoming. "Determinants of Rural Poverty: Land Titles and Income in Honduras." In Ramón E. López and Alberto Valdés, eds., *Rural Poverty in Latin America*. Washington, D.C.: World Bank.

Oldeman, L.R., V.W.P. van Engelen, and J.H.M. Pulles. 1990. "The Extent of Human-Induced Soil Degradation." In L.R. Oldeman, R.T.A. Hakkeling, and W.G. Sombroek, eds., *World Map of the Status of Human-Induced Soil Erosion: An Explanatory Note*. 2d ed. Wageningen, The Netherlands: International Soil Reference and Information Centre.

Parks, Peter, and Manuel Bonifaz. 1994. "Nonsustainable Use of Renewable Resources: Mangrove Deforestation and Mariculture in Ecuador." *Marine Resource Economics* 9: 1–18.

Ruitenbeek, H.J. 1994. "Modelling Economy-Ecology Linkages in Mangroves: Economic Evidence for Promoting Conservation in Bintuni Bay, Indonesia." *Ecological Economics* 10: 233–47.

Sathivathai, Suthawan. 1997. "Economic Valuation of Mangroves and the Roles of Local Communities in the Conservation of the Resources: Case Study of Surat Thani, South of Thailand." Report submitted to the Economy and Environment Program for Southeast Asia, Singapore.

Schneider, R.R. 1994. "Government and the Economy on the Amazon Frontier." Latin America and the Caribbean Technical Department Report 34. World Bank, Washington, D.C.

World Bank. 1994. "El Salvador: Natural Resources Management Study." World Bank, Latin America and the Caribbean Region, Agriculture and Natural Resources Operations Division, Washington, D.C.

Comment on "Environment, Poverty, and Economic Growth," by Karl-Göran Mäler

John A. Dixon

Karl-Göran Mäler's article links three important issues: environment, poverty, and economic growth. Two questions are central to this analysis: What links these three variables? And is it possible to predict the direction of causality between environment and poverty—that is, does a degraded environment make people poor, or do poor people degrade their environment?

These questions are not merely academic; policymakers must know the answers to design and implement effective policies. Mäler's article addresses the issues as a set, weaving them together in a discussion of natural resources, their uses, and the links between resources, people, and economic growth. Here I focus on three of his most important concerns.

From Necessity to Amenity

Mäler starts by considering whether the environment and environmental quality are normal goods or luxury goods. Environmental resources are obviously a bit of both, serving as an input into many production processes as well as an amenity or a consumption good. As an input, environmental resources are essential to development, and in developing countries there is considerable dependence on the environment and environmental quality to produce food and meet other basic needs.

As incomes rise, however, environmental resources increasingly take on amenity values. Richer people can demand (and afford) a cleaner environment (less air and water pollution, better solid waste disposal) as well as increasing quantities of environmental services (ocean recreation, protected forests, biodiversity). Make no mistake—both rich and poor people value these resources, but rich people can afford them more easily. Still, even poor farmers in upland Java plant teak trees that will not be harvested for seventy years. They do so because they believe that teak trees are an important part of the ecosystem (even if they produce no immediate economic benefits) that they want to leave for their children and grandchildren.

John A. Dixon is chief of the Indicators and Environmental Valuation Unit in the Environment Department at the World Bank.

Annual World Bank Conference on Development Economics 1997
©1998 The International Bank for Reconstruction and Development / THE WORLD BANK

This dual role of environmental resources as a source of primary production and as a source of amenity values is evident in a recent World Bank study of national wealth and natural capital in more than 100 countries (World Bank 1997). An analysis of the stock of wealth of individual nations—a measure that included produced assets, human and social capital, and natural capital—found that in 1994 natural capital accounted for 2–21 percent of wealth (with the Middle East an outlier with 39 percent; table 1). Not surprisingly, human resources were the most important source of wealth, followed by produced assets. There was less variation among nations in natural capital per capita (on average, a 3 to 1 difference between the richest and poorest regions) than in human resources (19 to 1) or produced assets (22 to 1). Thus it appears that economic development is less a function of initial resource endowment than of how that endowment is managed (sustainably or not) and how the proceeds are invested (say, in education and health or in luxury automobiles).

The distribution of natural capital varies with the level of national income (table 2). In poorer countries agricultural lands (croplands and pastures) accounted for between 50 and 90 percent of the value of natural capital (again with the exception of the oil-rich Middle East), while minerals and fossil fuels accounted for between 5 and 25 percent (World Bank 1997). Forests and protected areas made up the balance. In richer countries agricultural lands are less important and forests, protected areas, and minerals and fossil fuels are more important. As incomes increase, countries shift from production-based benefits from the environment to amenity-based, nonconsumptive benefits.

Thus economic development can be considered to be a process of managing a portfolio of assets—assets that include produced capital, natural capital, and human capital as well as institutional arrangements that are part of social capital. The development challenge is to use the natural resource base, physical environment, and a

Table 1. Stock of Wealth by Region, 1994

Region	Total	Human resources	Produced assets	Natural capital	Human resources	Produced assets	Natural capital
	Amount (U.S. dollars per capita)				*Share of total wealth (percent)*		
North America	326,000	249,000	62,000	16,000	76	19	5
Pacific OECD	302,000	205,000	90,000	8,000	68	30	2
Western Europe	237,000	177,000	55,000	6,000	74	23	2
Middle East	150,000	65,000	27,000	58,000	43	18	39
South America	95,000	70,000	16,000	9,000	74	17	9
North Africa	55,000	38,000	14,000	3,000	69	26	5
Central America	52,000	41,000	8,000	3,000	79	15	6
Caribbean	48,000	33,000	10,000	5,000	69	21	11
East Asia	47,000	36,000	7,000	4,000	77	15	8
East and southern Africa	30,000	20,000	7,000	3,000	66	25	10
West Africa	22,000	13,000	4,000	5,000	60	18	21
South Asia	22,000	14,000	4,000	4,000	65	19	16

Source: World Bank 1997.

Table 2. Components of the Value of Natural Capital by Income Group, 1994
(percentage shares)

Income group	Croplands	Pastures	Timber benefits	Nontimber forest benefits	Protected areas	Metals, minerals, oil, coal, gas
High	41	15	10	4	11	19
Upper middle	28	10	6	5	2	48
Lower middle	56	5	5	3	4	27
Low	80	4	3	2	2	8

Source: World Bank 1997.

country's population in a way that adds value to natural resources and fosters growth. How the environment is managed and how the proceeds from that management are invested explain a lot about each country's development path.

Does Poor Have to Mean Polluted?

A puzzling question remains, however. If the environment is important both as an input into production (and source of investment funds) and for its amenity values, why is it so often degraded? Are developing countries likely to follow the path of industrial countries that also started out with natural resource–dependent economies? The second part of Mäler's article addresses this issue and offers a possible explanation as it explores poverty and its links to the environment.

A paradox: poor people value the environment, and their well-being is directly linked to the productivity and health of the environment. Yet poor people often live in degraded environments. Perhaps this is partly explained by the fact that being poor usually means having few options. Mäler identifies three important variables to explain observed resource management patterns: population growth, property rights, and discounting. These variables offer insights into much that can be observed about the link between poverty and resource management, and why something as important to the poor as the natural resource base can also be so degraded.

As shown in the Bank's work on the components of natural capital, poorer societies are more directly dependent on natural resources and their management and are disproportionately affected by environmental pollution (World Bank 1997). The opposite is true in richer societies: there is less direct dependence on natural resources, and environmental quality is higher. How easy is it to grow out of a degraded environment? Or is this the environmental equivalent of a "low-level equilibrium trap," whereby rapidly growing poor countries are destined to remain polluted?

An important factor is the size of populations—rapid population growth, especially in cities, can overwhelm the capacity of natural or human-made systems to clean the air and water. Moreover, the world's booming megacities (populations above 10 million people) are largely in developing, not industrial, countries. In fact, by 2015 nine of the world's ten largest cities will be in developing countries. Such high population densities mean that the traditional response to pollution—to spread it around—is no longer feasible. Major investments in capital infrastructure are required.

But rapid population growth is also putting pressure on natural resources. In fact, in some cases increased resource degradation may even lead to increased fertility, in a doomed attempt to combat declining productivity by creating more hands to work a dwindling resource base. Such a situation can lead, in the extreme case, to a vicious circle with a Malthusian exit.

Environmental Kuznets Curves and Causality

The third major theme of Mäler's article is the role of economic growth (and the importance of policies) in reducing poverty. If it is possible to break out of the low-level equilibrium trap noted above—poverty, leading to increased resource degradation, leading to more pollution, leading back to more poverty—economic growth is an essential ingredient.

Mäler discusses what have been called inverse Kuznets curves (or environmental Kuznets curves), which chart the observed relationship between per capita GNP and environmental degradation. In most cases these curves show an initial increase in environmental pollution or resource degradation with initial economic growth, then a plateau at intermediate levels of development, and then finally a turn down, producing a concave curve (figure 1). Thus economic growth first contributes to environmental problems (more production, more pollution), then contributes to their solution. In figure 1 the middle curves, for particulate and sulfur dioxide concentrations, exhibit the classic shape. The two curves at the top are reassuring because access to safe water and sanitation increases with income. The two bottom curves, for solid waste and carbon dioxide emissions, are more troubling because they do not level off.

The real question about these curves, however, is whether there is causality in the relationship. They are, after all, based on cross-sectional, not time-series, data. Some analysts believe that it is possible, through wise investments and policies, to leapfrog or dramatically flatten these curves—and so avoid some of the most serious environmental damage associated with economic growth. With modern communications and technology it is increasingly possible to avoid the worst "peaks" associated with environmental Kuznets curves.

As Mäler (citing Arrow and others 1995) notes, it is not economic growth, but the form that growth takes, that determines environmental quality. But even if economic growth is not the answer, it does make possible much of what people and societies desire and holds the potential for environmentally sustainable development. Initial resource endowments are important, and wise policy decisions and investments (especially in people) can help avoid many problems. Environmental Kuznets curves are merely a heuristic device, and we must remember that they represent neither optimal paths nor preordained fate in the process of economic development.

Figure 1 Environmental Indicators at Different Country Income Levels

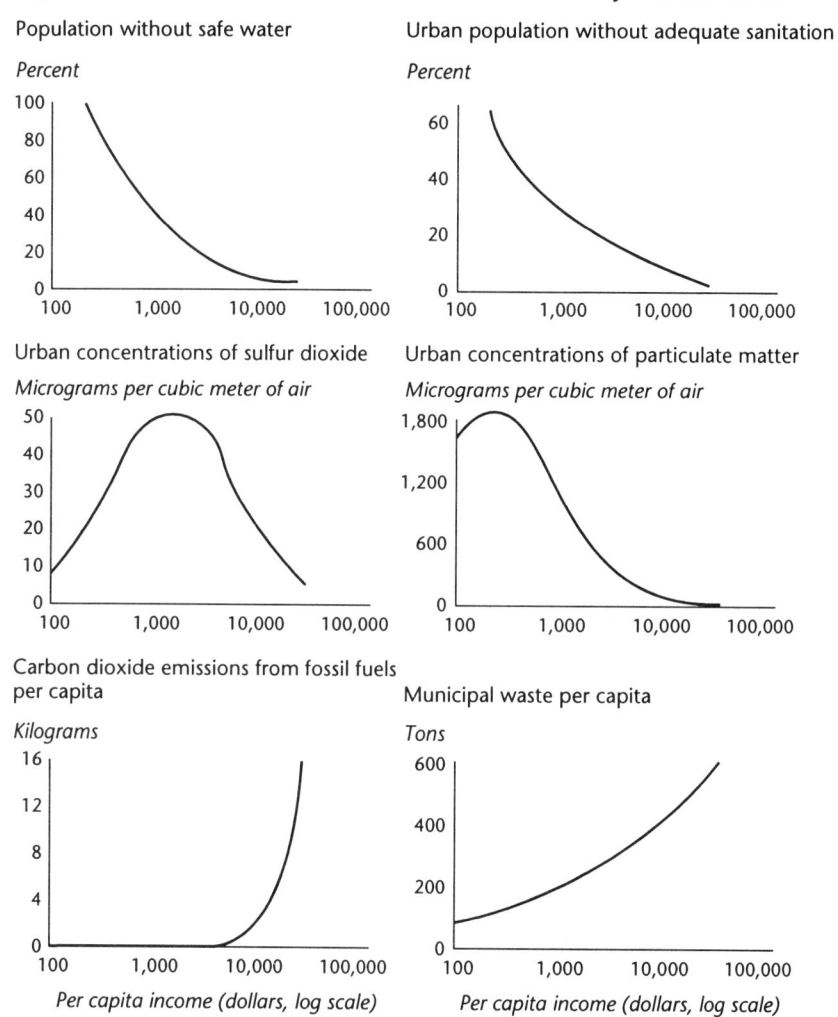

Population without safe water

Urban population without adequate sanitation

Urban concentrations of sulfur dioxide

Urban concentrations of particulate matter

Carbon dioxide emissions from fossil fuels per capita

Municipal waste per capita

Note: Estimates based on cross-country regression of data from the 1980s.
Source: World Bank 1992, based on Shafik and Bandyopadhyay 1992.

References

Arrow, K.J., B. Bolin, R. Costanza, P. Dasgupta, C. Folke, C.S. Holling, B.O. Jansson, L. Levin, K.G. Mäler, C. Perrings, and D. Pimentel. 1995. "Economic Growth, Carrying Capacity, and the Environment." *Science* 268 (5210): 520–22.

World Bank. 1992. *World Development Report 1992: Development and the Environment.* New York: Oxford University Press.

———. 1997. *Expanding the Measure of Wealth: Indicators of Environmentally Sustainable Development.* Environmentally Sustainable Development Studies and Monograph Series 17. Washington, D.C.

Floor Discussion of "Environment, Poverty, and Economic Growth," by Karl-Göran Mäler

Deborah Bräutigam (discussant in another session) asked whether the links between poverty, environment, and growth were less an economic problem and more a political one. For example, Bräutigam said, she had flown over Chiapas, Mexico, a few years earlier and had been struck by the contrast between land inhabited by the rich and that inhabited by the poor. The poor were concentrated in hilly, marginal lands, while the rich lived in fertile valleys. When the poor are confined to substandard land, she said—often as a result of resource allocation decisions that are made by politicians—they have neither the incentive nor the opportunity to cultivate that land in a sustainable way.

Karl-Göran Mäler (presenter) agreed that regard for environment is an inherently political issue, just as any discussion of property rights and land tenure raises political issues. The goal, he said, is to devise strategies that make resource management more efficient—and without changes in resource allocation policies, such strategies serve no purpose. If politicians are unwilling to create incentives that increase efficiency, economic analysis is of no use.

A participant from the University of Cambridge asked the speakers for their views on bottom-up planning mechanisms. Local people understand the importance of the environment, he said, but rarely have the power to protect it. Thus, he said, efforts to reduce poverty while protecting the environment should leave decisions about property rights and resource allocation to the people most affected by them, rather than to the state or to international organizations.

Mäler responded that, in fact, he had been describing a bottom-up approach. He had never advocated central planning for environmental issues. Rather, he had talked about the need to develop systems and institutions that give individuals and local communities the right to determine their own futures. People at all levels, he said, should be able to make their own decisions—and be held accountable for them. John Dixon (discussant) concurred, noting that government rarely leads the call for a change in the status quo. Rather, people seeking change—in

---

This session was chaired by Robert T. Watson, senior scientific adviser in the Environment Department at the World Bank.

environmental policies or elsewhere—must get involved and put pressure on their elected officials.

Edward B. Barbier (discussant) added that decentralized environmental planning may be useful, but it should not be considered a panacea for environmental problems. Local decisionmaking is not immune to corruption or to the abuse of power. Moreover, he added, households and communities can harbor weak incentive structures.

A participant asserted that many people in developing countries stay poor because of unfair terms of trade with industrial countries. Thus, for example, developing country exporters of primary products do not receive the full value of their exports. Even within the North American Free Trade Area, he said, high protection favors U.S. sugar producers over Mexican exporters. The European Union is similarly discriminatory, producing unnecessary primary products and dumping them in the world market. How, he asked, can poor exporters in developing countries be guaranteed a fair value for their products?

Mäler agreed that industrial country policies often deprive developing countries of markets for their primary exports. Moreover, he said, the issue goes beyond terms of trade and trade agreements. Members of the European Union, for example, pay taxes that subsidize European farmers. Meanwhile, developing country competitors who could provide the same commodities at a lower price cannot compete with subsidized production. As with environmental policies, people need to take a stand against these kinds of policies—convincing, for example, the French government to stand up to French farmers (who demand subsidies) so that Europe's agricultural policies can change.

Barbier countered that he took issue with the blanket claim that terms of trade determine who stays poor in developing countries. What about Malaysia and Indonesia, the world's leading producers of plywood? Certainly, he said, their products are not being discriminated against. Moreover, the recent Uruguay Round of the General Agreement on Tariffs and Trade had removed much of the discrimination faced by developing countries.

Dilip Mookherjee (presenter in another session) asked the speakers about the effect rising incomes have on the use of common property resources. What if poverty falls among fishers, for example, so that more fishing boats come into use and overexploitation increases? In Mookherjee's view, designers of credit programs and other types of assistance must take into account the programs' potential for increasing environmental degradation.

Mäler replied that, in terms of environment, the issue is whether access to common property resources is open or managed. Resources that are well managed are less susceptible to degradation. For example, he said, local fishing communities in Chile oversee local fishers and monitor intruders. As a result higher incomes do not necessarily result in overexploitation.

Barbier agreed that local resource management is essential to ensuring sustainable yields, but he noted that additional research is needed to learn how communities move away from open-access arrangements. To learn more about resource management decisions in developing countries, he said, researchers must have a better understanding of the incentives facing poor rural producers—in terms of both poverty and environmental degradation.

A participant from the World Bank said that he believed that Mäler had correctly identified two determinants of small farmers' decisionmaking (risk and discount rate) but had overlooked two others: variability of soil erosion and of demand for income. In many parts of the world, he said, 75 percent of the soil erosion that occurs over a twenty-five year period takes place in a five-year window. And specific events—such as a child entering a university—increase the need for immediate income. Either pressure can create enormous incentives for poor farmers to take unsustainable risks in exploiting their land and resources.

That is an important point, Dixon agreed. In some societies such pressures can upset a system's equilibrium. Moreover, economists often fail to account for these pressures because economic models tend to average events over time. To understand and overcome such problems, he said, ecologists and economists must work together.

Robert Watson (chair) closed by noting that many of the links between poverty, environment, and growth will continue to be shaped by political concerns. Still, he said, fostering a better dialogue between scientists and economists would help inform decisionmaking at both the local and global levels. Working together, he concluded, the two groups can find solutions that protect the environment while meeting people's needs.

Where Development Can or Cannot Go: The Role of Poverty-Environment Linkages

Ramón E. López

While rising population density has often been associated with higher incomes and better environments in industrial countries, it has caused massive poverty and ecological disaster in many developing countries. Evidence suggests that different interactions between environmental, institutional, and population dynamics explain the different outcomes. Where population growth is rapid, the environment is fragile, and institutions do not evolve quickly, ecological disaster and large-scale poverty are likely. To avoid these outcomes, governments should implement measures that restrain population growth, slow environmental dynamics, and accelerate institutional dynamics. Moreover, they should guard against external upheavals that undermine the evolution of communities. Finally, they should minimize the environmental and efficiency losses associated with rural-urban migration and the transition to private property rights.

In developing countries poverty is more prevalent and usually deeper in rural regions than in urban areas. The rural poor depend on natural resources for their subsistence, and their behavior affects a significant portion of those resources. Agriculture and other extractive resource–based activities are important sources of income for the rural poor, and in both low- and middle-income countries the poor's welfare is closely linked to the availability of drinking water, soil fertility, biomass as a source of fuelwood, and other subsistence goods. In low-income countries, however, a much larger share of the population is poor and lives in rural areas than is the case in middle-income countries, and overall economic performance is more affected by the economics of the poor.[1]

The Boserup Sequence

Poverty and resource degradation are widespread in developing countries, and population growth is widely regarded as an exacerbating factor. Boserup (1965, 1981),

Ramón E. López is professor of agricultural and resource economics at the University of Maryland at College Park. The author is grateful to two anonymous referees as well as to Claudia Binder, Dan Gilligan, Marc Nerlove, Claudia Romano, and Carmen Scoseria for helpful comments.

however, in one of the most influential approaches to the study of rural communities, suggests that population growth, far from being inimical to poverty and the environment, triggers agricultural intensification, improved natural resource management, and increased per capita income of the rural poor.[2] According to Boserup's theory, the evolution of rural communities starts with resource-abundant, hunting-gathering stages and culminates in modern communities characterized by an intensive pattern of resource utilization, investment, and innovation. Given the wide acceptance of Boserup's ideas and the consistency of her model with certain evidence, it is useful to consider her model as a benchmark for analyzing poverty and environmental degradation.

According to Boserup, as population grows, land and other natural resources become scarcer relative to labor, and access to markets improves. As a result agricultural intensification occurs. Relative prices change, and food prices increase as demand for food rises. At first (implicit) wages decline to reflect the increased supply of labor. This process generates the need for new institutions, such as private property rights, which somehow emerge. The new institutions facilitate the adoption of more intensive techniques and greater investments, which increase yields. Rather than deteriorating, the natural resource base improves as it becomes more valuable. Moreover, economies of specialization and of scale associated with the provision of infrastructure and public services (education, health care, and the like) emerge, leading to a greater supply of these services. These improvements promote increases in labor productivity that eventually reverse the initial wage decline induced by population growth.

Boserup's model seems to accurately describe the evolution of today's industrial countries in temperate parts of the world. Although the experience in some parts of the developing world has been consistent with Boserup's model, many developing countries have seen very different outcomes. Indeed, if the Boserup sequence were the norm in developing countries, we would not be concerned with sustainability and poverty.

One of the most striking pieces of evidence in support of Boserup's model in developing countries is a longitudinal study of the Machakos district in Kenya (Tiffen, Mortimore, and Gichuki 1994). That study shows that despite a fivefold increase in population, per capita income was higher, soil erosion was less severe, and more trees existed in Machakos in the 1990s than in the 1930s.[3] These improvements were the result of large investments in soil conservation and afforestation.

Other evidence is inconsistent with Boserup's model. In a review of case studies from Africa, Asia, and Latin America, Kates and Haarmann (1992) found that the evolution of rural communities led to increasing poverty and environmental destruction, possibly because of the failure of institutional evolution. In most cases the evolutionary sequence of rural communities stopped far short of achieving the investment and technical innovation predicted by Boserup. This gives rise to an important question: What goes wrong with the Boserup sequence in many developing countries?

The evolution of rural communities in most developing countries differs from the historical experience in industrial countries in three important ways. First, the integration of rural communities with the rest of the economy and even with the global economy is much more important in developing countries than it was in industrial countries. Moreover, this integration is increasing much more rapidly in developing countries than it did in industrial countries after agricultural intensification occurred there. The fact that an industrial world exists and that transportation, communications, and trade mechanisms are much more effective implies that the current evolutionary process is subject to much greater external influences.

Second, in today's industrial countries population density increased gradually over long periods. In contrast, population growth in the developing world over the past four or five decades has been explosive—even in rural areas that have been subject to significant emigration.

Third, most developing countries are located in tropical, semitropical, or semiarid parts of the world, where the natural resource base is much more fragile and unstable than that in the mostly temperate areas where industrial countries are located (Sanchez 1976; Webster and Wilson 1980). This fragility may impose serious restrictions on the pace of agricultural intensification and may require major investments to improve the stability and resilience of tropical soils and other natural resources.

Using evidence from cross-country studies, Sachs (1997) confirmed that tropical location has a strong negative effect on economic growth. According to Sachs, after controlling for the usual variables used in cross-country analyses (labor, human and physical capital) as well as for economic policies, long-run incomes in tropical countries would reach only 53 percent of incomes in temperate zone economies. Like Michael Todaro and other development economists writing in the 1960s and 1970s,[4] Sachs attributes this tropical shortfall to the high incidence of infectious disease and to the poor quality of tropical soils, which have prevented sustained agricultural development.

This article analyzes the possible factors underlying the divergent evolutionary paths of agrarian communities in developing countries. A key question is why some agrarian societies have evolved in line with Boserup's expectations and why many others have not. In particular, to what extent are the three contrasts between industrial and developing countries identified above associated with the success or failure of agrarian evolution? Using evidence from micro case studies rather than cross-country aggregate data, I provide micro foundations for the observed growth disadvantages of tropical areas found by Sachs and others, showing that these disadvantages stem from interactions between institutional, environmental, and population dynamics. The analysis goes beyond mechanistic formulas commonly derived from macro or cross-country evidence by showing that the historical experience of agrarian development in tropical zones does not necessarily imply that future growth will follow a similar pattern.

An Organizing Framework

Developing countries vary widely in the speed of population growth, the degree of integration of rural communities with the rest of the economy, and the fragility of the natural resource base. Based on these characteristics a taxonomy can be developed that is useful as an organizing framework for analysis:

- *Type 1: Low but rapidly growing rural population density, limited integration of rural areas with the rest of the economy, and a fragile natural resource base.* Production is dominated by small private holdings that depend on communal and even open-access resources (communal grazing lands, fallow lands, water resources, wood and forest lands) for their subsistence. Most of Sub-Saharan Africa, less populated parts of Asia, and indigenous communities in the tropical forests of South America are examples of type 1 areas.
- *Type 2: High rural population density, few opportunities for rural areas to integrate with the overall economy, and a fragile natural resource base.* Small private holdings with moderate dependence on communal resources are the dominant form of economic organization. Parts of East and South Asia, including parts of Bangladesh, China, India, and Pakistan, are examples of type 2 areas.
- *Type 3: Moderate to high rural population density, a high degree of integration with the national and international economy, and a fragile natural resource base.* A combination of a large number of small private holdings *(minifundia)* and large-scale commercial farms is most prevalent. Type 3 areas are found in Central America, parts of Mexico, parts of tropical South America, and some Asian countries (such as the Philippines).
- *Type 4: Moderate to high rural population density, a high degree of integration with the national economy, and a robust and stable natural resource base.* Large-scale and family-size private commercial farms dominate the agrarian structure. Examples of type 4 areas include Argentina, Uruguay, most of Chile, parts of Brazil (the southern regions), and most industrial countries. Type 4 regions are found largely in nontropical areas, where natural resources are generally stable and soils are rich in organic matter and able to retain nutrients well. Most successful intensification has occurred in areas where the resource endowment has been able to accommodate increasing numbers of people with remarkable resilience.

This article focuses on type 1, 2, and 3 areas. Most of these areas are found in tropical, subtropical, and semiarid parts of the world where institutional structures are still evolving. Individual private ownership of land and other natural resources coexists with common property resources and even with resources (such as forests) that nominally belong to the state but in practice are open access. The importance of common property resources and open-access resources is generally greater in type 1 than in type 2 areas. But as Dasgupta (1995) emphasizes, the poor depend heavily on common property resources in most parts of the world, including China, India, and several other highly populated Asian countries.

Determinants of Agrarian Institutional Change

What conditions are needed to trigger the institutional change that determines the evolution of rural communities? The Boserup sequence implies two types of change: the emergence and subsequent improvement of communal institutions for the efficient management of common property resources and the development of exclusionary individual property rights to resources that were originally common property. This section reviews the factors that are conducive to collective action in the management of common property resources. Privatization of common lands and open-access areas is considered in the next section.

Community Dynamics and Understanding

Although economics has a lot to say about the motivations for discarding old institutions and replacing them with new, usually more efficient ones, it has little to say about the dynamics of institutional reform (Bardhan 1991). The fact that an institution is inefficient does not necessarily mean that rational individuals will discard it. Similarly, rational individuals may not adopt institutions that are socially desirable. The theoretical and empirical literature points to a number of factors that may delay or even indefinitely postpone the adoption of socially desirable institutions.

Drawing on case studies, Baland and Platteau (1996) conclude that many traditional communities, particularly in type 1 areas, fail to perceive the relationship between stocks of natural resources and flows of extracted resources. They also fail to comprehend the causal links between their actions and the level of stocks. Recognition of this link is essential if institutional arrangements are to be established to control the degradation of natural resources.

It is not clear why some communities seem to appreciate the need for institutional reform while others do not, although education, external influences, and pure random events (such as the emergence of a visionary leader) may be factors. Even more important may be the stability of the relationships that affect communities: communities that have faced similar environmental, social, and technological conditions for a long period may have had time to understand such relationships. In contrast, communities affected by variable patterns may have difficulty connecting their actions with subsequent outcomes. Characteristics of the resource (such as its visibility) and the rate of population growth may also be relevant (Baland and Platteau 1996).

History and Cultural Norms

It may be difficult to change institutions that have become part of a group's cultural heritage, even if they are no longer efficient as the population increases. If social sanctions for individuals who deviate from group norms are sufficiently strong, breakaway coalitions may not gain adherents because of fear of social reprisals, thus leading to the preservation of the institutional status quo (Bauer and Yamey 1957; Akerlof 1984). The strong tradition of communal ownership of land and other resources that developed in type 1 regions because of their land abundance may impede the development of private property rights.

In addition, although the social disparities in poor agrarian societies may be large, many of these societies place a high value on equality. Thus even if the income gap between the rich and the poor is enormous, there is a degree of homogeneity among the rural poor that is appreciated as a social value. Increasing efficiency may require limiting rights over the use and appropriation of resources. Since the need for exclusive private property rights normally arises because of the relative scarcity of resources, institutional changes demanding these rights have serious effects on the distribution of wealth. The social norms of the poor may not allow for this change, preventing this type of institutional reform. (As is well known, it is very difficult to compensate the losers from such reform.)

Incomplete Information and Absence of Markets

Incomplete information and an absence of markets may lead to the development of "functional but imperfect institutions" such as sharecropping (Stiglitz 1991). These institutions may not necessarily cause greater environmental degradation, but some do reinforce such degradation. A lack of financial institutions, for example, induces peasants to use livestock as savings and a store of value, leading to oversized herds that increase pressures on the natural resources associated with production activities.

The development of insurance and other markets may require significant economies of scale in transactions—scale economies that a poor agrarian economy may not have. Thus market failure may be associated with initial poverty and low population density, which do not allow for the development of markets that require a large scale of operations. In the absence of rapid income growth, population growth may not be sufficient to permit the development of these markets. Hence imperfect institutions, which reduce the income potential of these communities, tend to persist until per capita income reaches a certain level.

Collective Action

Even if agrarian communities fully understand the relationship between their actions and natural resources and are able to overcome their attachment to traditional norms, collective action for the management of the commons may still fail. The vast theoretical and case study literature suggests that successful collective action depends on several conditions that are not always present in poor rural communities. Collective action is generally more likely to succeed with small, homogeneous groups than with large, heterogeneous ones. Failures of collective action have been observed not only in type 1 areas but in type 2 areas as well.

Parametrically testing the hypothesis that agricultural communities use biomass resources efficiently in Côte d'Ivoire and Ghana (both type 1 countries), López (1993 and 1997) found that although the communities restrict the use of common resources by both local and external populations, these controls are not always sufficient to induce biomass efficiency. Individual cultivators consider only a fraction (generally less than 30 percent) of the total social cost of expanding the area cultivated (and hence reducing the fallow periods). This evidence is inconsistent with the conclusion of other researchers that traditional communities, which have elaborate rules and enforcement mechanisms for regulating the use of common resources, use those resources efficiently. The evidence for Côte d'Ivoire and Ghana shows that the existence of rules is not sufficient to induce a socially efficient use of common resources.

A recent study econometrically tested various hypotheses regarding the determinants of collective action using data from seventy-five villages in Côte d'Ivoire (Ahuja 1996). Only ethnic heterogeneity and population size were consistently (negatively) correlated with efficiency in the use of common property resources. Interestingly, the correlation between resource scarcity and efficiency was weak and highly dependent on the specification used.

Studies in type 2 regions have shown that collective action for the management of the vast resources still held as common property does not always arise autonomously. Using data from several villages in Rajasthan's Udaipur district in India, Chopra and Gulati (1996) found that participation by village households in maintaining or improving common water and land resources was negligible in the absence of external intervention by nongovernmental organizations (NGOs) and other agencies. A significant contribution of labor to communal resource maintenance was observed only in villages with prolonged exposure to the work of NGOs and other external agencies that promote institutional development. Similar findings were reported by Intal (1991) for villages in the northwestern state of Haryana, India, where common lands suffered serious degradation until effective external intervention by a government agency occurred in the early 1980s. This intervention created the ground rules for a new institutional setup that dramatically altered how resources are used and increased the contribution of village members to the improvement and maintenance of common resources.

Implications

These findings imply that:

- A scarcity of resources does not seem to induce better resource management.
- Population growth by itself may not induce institutions to improve natural resource management.
- Collective action has at least partly failed in many developing regions.
- Collective action may become more difficult as geographical integration, social mobility, and market integration increase (Baland and Platteau 1996).

If these results are representative of rural communities in developing countries, the prospects for a Boserup sequence diminish significantly.

Although external market forces tend to make collective management of the commons more difficult, NGOs or government agencies that explicitly target institutional development can dramatically improve common property resource management. This is certainly one of the most positive findings of the case study literature. Still missing, though, is an evaluation of the costs and benefits of external intervention oriented toward improving community institutions.

Environmental and Institutional Dynamics

The resources available to the rural poor are either environmentally fragile and highly susceptible to degradation or extremely limited in quantity. That is, the rural poor in developing countries generally fall into one of three categories: rural communities with large volumes of natural resources that are degraded or very fragile; *minifundistas,* or people with very little land; or landless people, who depend wholly on their labor for survival. Many minifundistas and the landless are descendants of people disenfranchised from common lands. This disenfranchisement may have been caused by the privatization accompanying the evolution of rural communities or by external forces associated with commercial interests, governments, or both.

Environmental Dynamics

Communities that only have access to fragile and degradable resources often fail to evolve. To be sustainable, the intensification of production in fragile areas requires large volumes of fixed investments (in building terraces, bunds, diversion ditches, dams, and the like) and labor-intensive practices (contour cultivation, alley cropping, perennial intercropping).[5] Similarly, intensification of grazing lands requires significant investment to avoid excessive deterioration of natural pastures. Most of these investments take a long time to pay off (Lutz, Pagiola, and Reiche 1993; Current, Lutz, and Scherr 1995). Continuous cultivation in fragile areas without such investments causes the natural resource base to deteriorate rapidly, with a consequent loss in the productive capacity of soils.

The investment required for intensification is usually smaller in areas where natural resources are less fragile and more stable. These conditions are found mainly in valleys and in temperate areas, where soils are deeper, more stable, and better able to retain nutrients than in sloped tropical soils. Thus the more fragile are an area's natural resources, the larger are the investments required to achieve a sustainable transition to more intensive modes of cultivation.

Communal cooperation in fragile areas therefore requires dramatic changes. Traditional cooperation consists mainly of the community exerting control over the allocation of common property resources across households. In contrast, sustainable intensification requires greater cooperation, since community members must contribute their labor to build the required fixed investments in community lands. Sustainable intensification also requires more labor-demanding cultivation norms, which will affect both the current and the future productivity of the soil. The incentives of individual cultivators who lack private and permanent usufruct rights over the common resources are not necessarily consistent with these norms.[6] Even if these conditions are met, poverty, combined with the absence of credit markets, can impede the implementation of these investments. Poor households may not devote much effort to investments that pay off only in the long run if by doing so they risk not meeting basic subsistence needs in the short run.

Hence there is a need to monitor not only households' access to common resources but also their cultivation practices. This change implies a much more demanding and complex form of cooperation—one for which traditional village institutions may be poorly suited. While the traditional institutions for cooperation may continue to be effective in the context of a solid environmental base, on which sustainable intensification can be achieved with little fixed investment, they may not be useful under environmentally fragile conditions that require large investments. Thus the Boserup sequence is likely to proceed smoothly where natural resources are stable but not where they are fragile.

Given these findings, it might be argued that intensification will cause privatization of the common resources, solving the institutional problem. As noted earlier, however, the fact that there is a need for a new institution does not ensure its development. Even if a new institution emerges, the process may take a long time, depending on the sociocultural conditions discussed earlier. The dynamics of institutional change relative to the natural resource base are crucial in determining the evolutionary path of rural communities.

Boserup argues that population-induced intensification causes lower per capita consumption as natural resources become relatively scarcer but that the use of new inputs, innovation, and economies of scale offsets this scarcity. This process, in turn, increases per capita income. The effectiveness of modern inputs in environmentally fragile areas, however, depends on investments that enable soils to resist intensification without too much degradation. Increased applications of modern inputs without these investments might not raise or even maintain the productivity of these soils.[7]

Irreversibility is also important. Soil may become permanently damaged if it is used intensively beyond a certain threshold without proper investment. The more fragile and unstable is the soil, the greater is the risk of irreversible damage after a short period of intensive use. Thus institutional reform may have a tight time deadline in the context of fragile resources prone to irreversible damage.

Institutional Dynamics

The profound institutional reforms that sustainable intensification requires—privatization or considerable tightening of the institutions dealing with common property resources—may be slow to emerge. Meanwhile, increased population leads to unsustainable intensification, and the deterioration in environmental quality makes it even harder to develop new institutions, for several reasons. First, the degradation of natural resources makes them less valuable, lowering the demand for institutions that sanction their privatization. Second, the drop in per capita income caused by resource degradation and the failure of modern inputs may increase the discount rate among community members, making it even harder to reach consensus on labor contributions for the fixed investments. Third, the required scale economies for the development of credit, insurance, and other markets are less likely to be attained, because population growth is not accompanied by an increase in per capita income. Thus imperfect subsidiary institutions remain in lieu of the missing markets.

The nature of customary institutions is another determinant of the evolutionary path of agrarian communities when population growth accelerates. Initial institutional conditions affect the speed at which rural institutions adapt to increasing population and intensification. Institutions are more likely to evolve rapidly in communities where customary relationships have been close and cooperation has been intense than they are in communities where cooperation has been less intense and more sporadic. Similarly, indigenous communities that developed customary land rights akin to private property rights before the acceleration of population growth (perhaps as a result of external influences, such as proximity to European settlers), such as the Machakos district in Kenya, may make a swift transition to private property, allowing the investments needed for sustainability. History and culture are important determinants of the evolution of rural poverty and resource degradation.

Another important dynamic element that affects the final outcome is the velocity of population growth. The higher is the rate of population growth, the more rapidly will demands for intensification grow and the more likely it will be that environmental dynamics will dominate institutional dynamics.

Interactive Dynamics between Institutions and the Environment

The evolutionary path of rural communities depends on the race between environmental and institutional dynamics. When the natural resource base is fragile and the communal institutions in place before the acceleration of population growth are weak, environmental dynamics are swift and institutional dynamics are slow. The threshold of irreversible damage to the resource base is likely to be reached before institutions adapt to population growth. In this case the community ceases to be a viable economic entity, and massive migration and abandonment occur. The result is a vicious cycle of environmental degradation and increasing poverty.

Conversely, if initial institutions are strong (favorable to cooperation or with customary land rights akin to private property rights), the evolution can follow the Boserup sequence even if the environmental base is fragile, as illustrated in the Machakos district. When the environmental base is solid, institutional dynamics dominate environmental dynamics, leading to the successful intensification of production and to increasing per capita income—even if population is growing fast. This pattern, in turn, facilitates the emergence of important markets that come to replace the subsidiary institutions that emerged in response to the missing markets.

Privatization

An increase in per capita income does not necessarily mean that poverty disappears from evolving communities. In fact, the increased value of natural resources resulting from sustainable intensification leads to increased demands for private and exclusive rights to those resources. Privatization normally takes place when population density is high, causing a large portion of the population to end up with little or no land. The part of the population that loses access to the disappearing common resources becomes even poorer; indeed, the elimination of the common resources implies the loss of an important insurance against extreme poverty (Bassett 1993). Several studies in developing countries have documented the high correlation between poverty and lack of access to land (López and Valdés forthcoming).

Other qualitative dynamic considerations are relevant to the privatization of common resources in addition to the speed of adjustment of institutions and of environmental deterioration. As common lands become scarcer, individuals are likely to invest in acquiring exclusive private access to the land. Where property rights are up for grabs, competition among individuals for actual or potential land rents can cause a dissipation of these rents in the process of privatization. The means used to ensure exclusive land rights might cause significant efficiency losses that could even offset the long-run efficiency gains of private property.

Anderson and Hill (1990) examined what was probably the largest land privatization in history, the privatization of more than 1 billion acres in the United States between 1790 and 1920. They show that privatization by sale to the highest bidder without any conditions attached resulted in much slower, less intensive land development than privatization through preemption (squatting) or homesteading. The reason is clear: unlike people who bought land through auctions, squatters and homesteaders had to establish definitive rights by exploiting the land before it was profitable to do so or by exploiting it more intensively than was optimal. Thus competition for property rights among squatters and homesteaders resulted in a socially inefficient pattern of resource exploitation and in rent dissipation.

The U.S. experience is particularly relevant for type 1 and 3 regions, since privatization of common lands and of public (effectively open-access) lands in such regions is taking place largely through processes analogous to squatting and homesteading (see, for example, evidence presented by Shepherd 1991 for parts of Africa). The acquisition of private rights to (usually forested) public lands also involves premature and excessively intensive development that results in deforestation beyond the socially optimal level. In contrast, privatization of common (fallow) lands usually involves more continuous cultivation, minimizing the risk that the land will revert to the community. The continuous cultivation of common lands may, however, occur before alternative techniques for sustainable continuous land exploitation are available. While the net effect of the "race for property rights" in a relatively resilient environment (such as the United States) is mainly a temporary efficiency loss, in a more fragile environment (such as many tropical and semiarid areas) it could be dramatic, irreversible degradation of the natural resource base—frustrating or significantly delaying successful intensification.[8]

The long-run outcome may depend crucially on the nature of the adjustment to privatization. De facto processes that require premature and excessively intensive exploitation of resources may result in highly degraded resources and extreme poverty over the long term. Even if the environmental damage is reversible, poverty may prevent the investment needed to recuperate the productive capacity of the resources. André and Platteau (forthcoming) illustrate how the impressive evolution toward privatization associated with rapid population growth has not prevented Rwanda from falling into a poverty and resource degradation trap. The process of privatization of common lands is likely to have at least partly conditioned this outcome.

External Influences

The evolution of rural communities is affected not only by internal forces but also by external factors, mainly commercial interests and the state. Heath and Binswanger (1996), Tiffen, Mortimore, and Gichuki (1994), and others identify government policies as the main factor preventing the Boserup sequence from occurring in developing countries. But government policies are just one of many external and internal forces that may disrupt the intensification sequence.

Commercial Interests

In type 3 regions the dynamics of rural poverty appear to have been affected more by external influences than by population growth. López (1992) reviews case studies in Latin America and Asia that illustrate the role of external forces in resource degradation and in the increased impoverishment of large segments of the rural population. In almost all the studies the intrusion of commercial interests (often with the tacit or explicit support of the government) resulted in established rural communities' displacement and loss of entitlement to their lands and in the destruction of their institutions.

This process, which can be called perverse land reform, appears to have had a greater effect on the rural poor than conventional land reforms. Some of the displaced rural poor have been absorbed by the new commercial activities established on their original lands; others have migrated to cities or to marginal agricultural areas. Marginal agricultural areas are usually quite fragile, and the new cultivators lack the institutions and understanding needed for the new environment. The result? Much greater resource degradation and deeper poverty among the cultivators.

The extent of migration, whether into urban or marginal rural areas, partly depends on the labor intensity of the new commercial activities on the old community lands. Commercial activities are often much less labor intensive than communities' production activities. Stonich (1989), for example, describes how a temporary boom in export commodity prices—mainly in low-quality beef—led to a massive expansion of large-scale, export-oriented agriculture in southern Honduras in the late 1960s and early 1970s. Major public infrastructure and credit subsidies facilitated this process but apparently were not the main cause. The result was a significant reallocation of land from forest, fallow, and food crops to pastures for livestock. At the same time many small producers lost their lands, through both legal and illegal means, to the land-intensive commercial livestock operations. (Peasants' lack of legal land titles greatly facilitated expropriation of their land.)

Because the new livestock activities were much less labor intensive than traditional activities, only a small portion of the population could be employed in the new activities, and emigration was massive. Emigration increased again when the commodity boom went bust and livestock production contracted. Moreover, the new commercial producers' overexploitation of natural resources resulted in the environmental destruction of the peasants' lands; the development of agriculture in steeper, more fragile areas, with consequent deforestation; the loss of important institutional capital; and a dramatic increase in the extent and intensity of poverty. All this damage in exchange for a temporary increase in exports and the enrichment of a small number of entrepreneurs.

Perverse land reform is not unique to Honduras. The environmental destruction and increased poverty induced by such perverse reforms are most common in tropical Latin America and the resource-rich countries of Asia (see Browder 1988; Anderson 1987; Binswanger 1991; and Heath and Binswanger 1996).

Government Policies

In many developing countries, particularly in type 3 regions, land ownership is extremely concentrated, and a large portion of the rural population has little or no access to land. Lack of access to good land by the poor is partly associated with imperfections in land and credit markets and with other distortions, often induced by the government. The value of land reflects a number of benefits not related to its productive potential. Among the most important are credit subsidies and tax write-offs that are capitalized into land prices. Many of these benefits apply much less to poor farm households than to large farm operators. The result is a segmented land market and an inability of poor farm households to expand their land area (Heath and Binswanger 1996).

In addition to exacerbating poverty, tax concessions and credit subsidies have contributed to extensive deforestation in tropical countries, particularly in Latin America. Binswanger (1991) estimates that much of the deforestation in the Brazilian Amazon has been caused by these policies. Barbier (forthcoming) also concludes that rural poverty and resource degradation in Latin America are largely a reflection of policy failures. Along with trade policies, tax and credit policies bias the structure of incentives in favor of land-intensive, labor-extensive outputs such as cattle production. These incentives contribute to a decrease in rural employment and an increase in deforestation.

Several African governments have taxed agricultural exports. Yet most agricultural export crops in Africa are tree crops that are not land intensive and that protect land against degradation, while most import substitutes are annual, land-intensive crops, such as cereals. Thus trade protection may exacerbate deforestation and land degradation by inducing a structure of production that demands more land and is less protective of the soil. These policy distortions could be replaced by policy reforms that both increase economic efficiency (including environmental efficiency) and reduce poverty.[9] Several governments in Asia and Latin America have managed to significantly reduce such distortions.

The net effect of policy distortions on natural resources and poverty is not always clear-cut, however. Eliminating trade distortions is likely to reduce poverty and improve the environment when an economy's comparative advantages are in unskilled labor-intensive industries (type 2 countries), since trade distortions tend to tax labor-intensive activities relative to capital-intensive activities. Removing these distortions is good for labor and, to the extent that capital-intensive activities are natural resource intensive, may be good for the environment. But for countries that have comparative advantages in natural resource–intensive activities, such as most type 3 countries, eliminating trade distortions may not reduce poverty or improve the environment. If access to good-quality land and other natural resources is highly concentrated and property rights to marginal or frontier lands are weak, as in most type 3 countries, eliminating trade distortions will widen income disparities and harm the environment, since the wealthy have access to the best resources and inadequate property rights will induce more rapid exploitation of marginal lands beyond sustainable levels.

The lack of access to land not only increases rural poverty. It also forces the poor to concentrate their productive efforts on hillsides and other extremely fragile lands, leading to environmental degradation. Furthermore, in countries where frontier lands are still available, the rural poor tend to migrate to these areas, causing deforestation. Governments in many countries, including Brazil and Indonesia, colonize forested frontier areas with the rural poor to relieve political pressures for land redistribution.

Governments often restrict the land tenure security of the poor, sometimes with disastrous consequences for the poor and the environment. African governments have repeatedly denied land ownership to rural communities. In many African countries land has been nationalized, and producers have received implicit but uncertain rights over the land they cultivate. (Until recently Ethiopia and Mozambique employed this practice.) Elsewhere the problem of tenure security stems from a failure to legally formalize de facto tenure arrangements. A large portion of poor farmers in Latin America and Asia do not have legal title to their lands. For example, more than half of small farmers lacked legal land titles in five Latin American countries analyzed by López and Valdés (forthcoming). Lack of tenure security restricts the incomes of the poor by reducing their access to collateralized credit and lowers their incentives to make land-related investments, including soil conservation investments (Feder 1987).

It is not clear how important government failures are in disrupting the Boserup sequence. Not all policy distortions are inimical to the poor and the environment, and the net effect of policy distortions in developing countries may not be to exacerbate poverty and environmental degradation. Distortions that increase poverty and hurt the environment should be identified so that reforms that yield the largest social returns can be adopted. But the inherent sample selection bias of this exercise should not be forgotten when the net effects of economic liberalization are evaluated.[10] Moreover, the fact that successful intensification paths frequently coexist with failures within the same countries and during the same periods suggests that the effects of government or policy are not necessarily the definitive determinant of the evolution of rural poverty and of natural resources. Thus the removal of government distortions should not be expected to be sufficient to significantly reduce environmental degradation and rural poverty.

Economic Growth and Rural Poverty

Not all external factors exacerbate rural poverty. In fact, an accelerated growth rate can be an important source of poverty reduction. Although growth is usually associated with an increasing share of nonrural activities in national income, that is not always the case. There are several examples of long growth episodes in which the rural economy has expanded as fast as or even faster than the urban economy. (A good example is Chile over the past two decades; another is Belize, which has experienced a continuously increasing share of rural employment and production over the past ten years.) Still, growth is usually concentrated in urban areas, and the returns to labor and other factors of production tend to expand faster in urban than in rural areas. A key distinction between balanced and unbalanced growth is that unbalanced growth implies the increasing mobility of people and other factors of production from rural to urban areas.

The opportunity cost of labor and other mobile factors of production owned by the rural poor increases rapidly in a growing economy. Where growth is biased toward urban areas, an increasing number of the rural poor decide to shift these factors of production from rural to nonrural sectors. In the long run this shift may reduce pressures on the natural resources that provide sustenance to the rural poor. In some cases, however, the short-run dynamics may work in the opposite direction. The increase in the opportunity cost of labor and capital induced by growth creates incentives to withdraw them from rural areas. Rural inhabitants who perceive these opportunities will want to liquidate their resources, including both their individually owned resources and part of those under communal control, so that they can be transferred to other, more profitable activities. If land markets work, people who have individual legal titles to their land can sell their assets to people who have a lower opportunity cost outside the rural areas. If land markets do not work, the only way to transform natural resource stocks into liquid assets is by extracting greater flows from them—that is, by exploiting them beyond sustainable levels.

The need to transform natural resource stocks into liquid assets is likely to be enhanced by the fact that migration is costly. Transportation costs and the costs of supporting oneself in the new place of residence while searching for a job may be large. Even where capital markets exist, lending to poor peasants to finance their migration is unlikely. Hence migrants will need to finance their migration costs from their own savings (perhaps complemented by contributions from relatives). Liquid savings are usually not significant among the rural poor, whose main source of wealth is their natural assets. Thus where land markets are lacking or imperfect and legal or some other recognized form of land title is absent, peasants may opt for accelerated extraction of their natural stocks to facilitate the mobility of their factors of production into other activities.

So far the analysis has focused on the effect of increasing nonrural opportunities for poor, independent cultivators. The increased outside opportunities for a subset of the rural population (typically the young and better educated) also have important implications for rural communities that own common property resources. Increased migration may lead to greater degradation of common property resources even though it alleviates population pressures. This result follows for two reasons. First, greater outside opportunities increase the desire of potential emigrants for liquid assets. Without established contractual arrangements between people who want to migrate and the remaining members of the community for trading "shares" of common property resources, migrating individuals may be tempted to overexploit common resources and will be less inclined to participate in village conservation activities. These individuals may feel that they can bypass community rules because after they migrate they will be less affected by the sanctions established in the communities for people who transgress communal norms.

Second, increased outside opportunities for some members of the community may further weaken communal institutions. Several case studies have concluded that communal institutions tend to become less effective as the community becomes more integrated with the market economy (Baland and Platteau 1996). The weakening of traditional institutions, in turn, tends to render controls on the use of common resources less effective and, hence, to cause greater degradation. That is, greater migration opportunities are likely to induce more intensive extraction of common resources and less conservation investment not only by the potential migrants but also by the remaining members of the community.

To the extent that growth is manifested in higher rural wages, however, it may also have positive environmental effects. In many countries poor small farmers depend on off-farm labor income as a source of subsistence. In most Latin American countries, for example, off-farm income accounts for a larger share of poor farmers' than rich farmers' total income (López and Valdés forthcoming). This relationship is particularly pronounced in fast-growing economies. Thus poor farmers in Latin America are likely to benefit considerably from increasing rural growth. Increased rural off-farm income opportunities are likely to complement better resource management, particularly for farmers who have been unable to implement conservation investments because of liquidity constraints.[11]

In summary, while growth that is biased against rural areas may reduce rural poverty, it may also induce greater environmental degradation by the poor. In contrast, more balanced growth that promotes rapid expansion of the rural economy both reduces rural poverty and provides greater incentives for the poor to protect their environmental resources. In the most common case, in which growth is biased toward the urban economy, the environmental effects will depend crucially on the effectiveness of the land market and the specification of property rights. If the rural poor are able to trade their stocks of natural resources, urban-based growth may also induce less environmental degradation by the poor.

Conclusion and Policy Implications

Several mechanisms may cause agrarian communities to fall into a vicious cycle of increased poverty, environmental degradation, and eventual abandonment of land. Understanding the interactive dynamics of certain key variables is essential to understanding the evolution of agrarian communities.

Conventional comparative statics cannot be used to analyze agrarian evolution because it is a dynamic process characterized by multiple potential long-run equilibria, path dependency, and the existence of environmental thresholds that, if exceeded, can push the agrarian system into disastrous—and in many cases irreversible—outcomes. Whether agrarian evolution ends in a desirable or undesirable long-run equilibrium depends on the dynamics and interactions of three key factors: the resilience of the natural resource base, initial institutional conditions (based on history and culture), and the rate of population growth. External forces (including government policies) affect the evolution of rural communities largely by affecting the dynamic interactions among these three factors.

Most tropical and subtropical areas have the inherent disadvantage of natural resource fragility, but this disadvantage can be overcome through adequate and timely protective investments, as shown by some successful intensification episodes in these areas. Peasants require incentives to invest in soil protection, and these investments must be made early enough to prevent irreversible environmental degradation. The rapid emergence of new institutions is a necessary condition for appropriate investment incentives, and gradual (rather than explosive) population growth is essential to allow enough time for protective investments to have an effect. The important point to recognize is that no mechanistic determinism prevents agrarian development—even in highly fragile tropical zones.

The policy implications of this conceptual framework are straightforward. Government should devise measures that slow the environmental dynamics, accelerate the institutional dynamics, and help make population growth more gradual. External influences that undermine the internal evolution of communities should be prevented, and measures that minimize the environmental and efficiency losses associated with rural-urban migration and the transition to private property rights should be promoted. The following recommendations for public policy are consistent with the approach presented here:

- Support the institutions of agrarian communities. Provide legal title to land and other resources to communities or individuals. Do not impose institutions that communities do not understand or want.

- Promote privatization and other mechanisms that reduce rent seeking and the likelihood of a "race for property rights." Identify public lands to be privatized and impose no conditions other than price for sanctioning privatization.
- Encourage and facilitate the definition of legal communal rights over common property resources. The establishment of legal communal ownership that can be enforced through the justice system will allow communities that want to privatize part of their common resources to do so through price or market mechanisms rather than through traditional mechanisms that promote overutilization of common lands.
- Devise measures to slow environmental dynamics. Identify areas that are environmentally vulnerable and concentrate extension services, supportive infrastructure, and (nonsubsidized) credit in those areas—which are usually where the poorest people are concentrated. Focus on supporting community investments in natural resource conservation and measures that could help stabilize the environment.
- Promote measures that reduce the rate of population growth. Provide information on family planning methods, and support women's groups that promote the status of women in communities and households. Given the rapid dynamics of environmental degradation, these long-term measures will need to be supplemented by short-term measures, such as identifying areas where population is expanding most rapidly and making these areas a priority in rural nonfarm job creation, so that population pressure on natural resources is relieved.
- Target land reform. Since land reform is very expensive when large landowners receive full compensation, efforts should focus on areas where the poor's access to land is especially limited and where there are large private landholdings in the surrounding areas.
- Target subsidies for land diversion and tree planting in areas affected by serious degradation. In some areas agricultural production is no longer viable because of excessive degradation. A frequent policy response in these areas has been to promote large rehabilitation investments and technical assistance from governments and NGOs to bolster agricultural production. These investments are bound to yield low returns when agroecological conditions have deteriorated substantially. A better response is to provide subsidies for farmers to plant trees and not to cultivate the land.

Much more empirical research is needed on how agrarian institutions evolve and on the consequences for the environment and the poor of the evolutionary paths followed. Studying factors that determine the demand for institutional innovation is not enough, since the same institutions can have dramatically different effects on income, poverty, and the environment depending on the adjustment path followed. Future research should focus on explaining the dynamics of adjustment rather than on showing that institutional laissez-faire is sufficient to ensure that the successful evolutionary experiences of industrial countries can be replicated in developing countries.

The dynamic paths to privatization and rural migration are only beginning to be understood. Much more analysis, both empirical and conceptual, is required. Important policy implications may arise from a better understanding of these processes.

Systematic analysis of the best interventions for promoting institutional development in agrarian communities is also needed. Much can be learned from both successful and unsuccessful interventions by NGOs and government agencies.

Notes

1. According to the World Bank (1996), in 1994 about 70 percent of the population of low-income countries lived in rural areas; excluding India and China the share of agriculture in GDP was 38 percent. For middle-income economies these figures were 49 percent and 10 percent.

2. Boserup assumes that population changes exogenously. I retain that assumption in this article, for several reasons. First, over the past three or four decades decreases in mortality have contributed more to increases in population than have increases in fertility. To a large extent the decline in mortality in developing countries can be considered exogenously induced. Second, endogenizing population growth would greatly increase the complexity of the analysis, with little effect on the qualitative results of interest here. Finally, consideration of endogenous population changes is probably important for analyses over the very long run, but such changes are much less important for the shorter periods (three or four decades) considered here.

3. Some characteristics of the study site are unique, however, and atypical for Africa. As the authors recognize, in contrast to most of Africa, customary land rights in the Machakos district were akin to private ownership as early as 1930. Customary rights in the Machakos district held that the first person to clear a piece of land was allowed to retain the land, sell it, or leave it to his sons without restrictions. More important, these rights were retained even if the land was left fallow.

4. According to Todaro (1977, p. 129), "it is a historical fact that almost every successful example of modern economic growth has occurred in a temperate zone country. . . . One obvious climatic factor is that extremes of heat and humidity contribute to deteriorating soil qualities . . . and weaken workers' health."

5. See, for example, the papers in Moldenhauer and Hudson (1988) that describe the investments and cultural practices required for intensive cultivation in Jamaica, Kenya, Malawi, Peru, and Taiwan (China). Evidence of the magnitude of the investments for resource conservation in agricultural intensification is also available in case studies of highland communities (see, for example, the evidence from Oaxaca, Mexico, in Garcia-Barrios and Garcia-Barrios 1990 and the evidence from Puno, Peru, in Collins 1987). These studies show that resource conservation in the highlands requires large labor-intensive investments. See also Chopra and Gulati (1996) and Intal (1991) for evidence from India.

6. Individual exclusive land rights or efficient common property institutions are necessary conditions for the implementation of these vital investments. Studies in Asia (Feder 1987) and Latin America (López 1996; Carter and Olinto 1996) illustrate the importance of land rights security for investment and productivity on privately owned lands. The evidence for Sub-Saharan Africa is less clear. A study by Migot-Adholla and others (1991) using data for Ghana, Kenya, and Rwanda found that investment and productivity on private plots with different degrees of indigenous land rights are not much different. Using the same Ghana data, Besley (1995) found that land rights facilitate investment in one of the regions considered (Wassa) but not in the other (Anloga). This may be due to the lack of credit markets in Sub-Saharan Africa. Most of the advantages of tenure security in private lands found elsewhere are associated with the collateral value of land in the credit market. Also, these studies compared land rights only on private lands, where differences in tenure security are relatively minor; they did not compare investment levels on private lands with those on common lands. As several studies have shown, common property resources are still an important source of subsistence for the poor in most developing countries, including those in Sub-Saharan Africa. Despite the gradual evolution in Sub-Saharan Africa toward individualization of land rights, a large portion of the natural resources available to the poor is still held as common property.

7. Highly productive processes are typically more demanding of soil quality. The failure of the green revolution in parts of Africa, for example, may be associated with the inability to preserve the natural characteristics of soils as more intensive techniques are applied. Even in temperate areas, such as the Palouse region in the northwestern United States, intensification without measures to protect the topsoil in sloped areas causes a significant reduction in the capacity to benefit from improvements in agricultural technology (Taylor and Young 1985).

8. The race for property rights may also induce more continuous cultivation with tree crops or other fixed investments rather than with annual crops. In this case the effects could be positive for the environment. But given the uncertainties about the final outcome of the property rights race, it is doubtful that individual cultivators will use these rather expensive means when the cheaper alternative of more continuous cultivation with annual crops is available.

9. This outcome is not guaranteed, however. Trade liberalization, for example, not only changes the relative prices of agricultural exports and agricultural import substitutes; it also reduces protection of the industrial sector, which is usually based on import substitution. This implies that agriculture as a whole would benefit from trade liberalization (including land-intensive, import-substitute crops). The net effect on export agriculture is unambiguous, but the effect on agricultural import substitutes is not. López shows that the net effect for the environmental base is positive in Côte d'Ivoire (1998) but negative in Ghana (1997). Most of the supply response of farmers to trade liberalization comes from expanding the area cultivated with both annuals and perennials (and reducing fallow) rather than from using more modern inputs on established lands.

10. There is no reason to believe that world prices are always better for the environment and for poverty reduction than distorted domestic prices. Distorted prices may ameliorate poverty and improve the environment.

11. Lutz, Pagiola, and Reiche (1993) provide evidence of highly profitable conservation investments that are not implemented because the payback period is too long. This is normally due to lack of access to credit.

References

Ahuja, Vinod. 1996. "Efficiency of Resource Use in Common Property: A Case of Land in Sub-Saharan Africa." Ph.D. dissertation. University of Maryland at College Park, Department of Agricultural and Resource Economics.

Akerlof, George. 1984. *An Economic Theorist's Book of Tales.* Cambridge: Cambridge University Press.

Anderson, James. 1987. "Lands at Risk, People at Risk: Perspectives on Tropical Forest Transformation in the Philippines." In Peter Little and Michael Horowitz, eds., *Lands at Risk in the Third World.* Boulder, Colo.: Westview Press.

Anderson, Terry, and Peter Hill. 1990. "Race for Property Rights." *Journal of Law and Economics* 33 (April): 177–97.

André, Catherine, and Jean-Philippe Platteau. Forthcoming. "Land Relations under Unbearable Stress: Rwanda Caught in the Malthusian Trap." *Journal of Economic Behavior and Organization.*

Baland, Jean-Marie, and Jean-Philippe Platteau. 1996. *Halting Degradation of Natural Resources: Is There a Role for Rural Communities?* New York: Oxford University Press.

Barbier, Edward. Forthcoming. "Rural Poverty and Natural Resource Degradation." In Ramón E. López and Alberto Valdés, eds., *Rural Poverty in Latin America.* Washington, D.C.: World Bank.

Bardhan, Pranab. 1991. "Alternative Approaches to the Theory of Institutions in Economic Development." In Pranab Bardhan, ed., *The Theory of Agrarian Institutions.* Oxford: Clarendon Press.

Bassett, Thomas. 1993. "Introduction: The Land Question and Agricultural Transformation in Sub-Saharan Africa." In Thomas Bassett and Donald Crummay, eds., *Land in African Agrarian Systems.* Madison: University of Wisconsin Press.

Bauer, Peter, and Basil Yamey. 1957. *The Economics of Under-Developed Countries.* Chicago: University of Chicago Press.

Besley, Timothy. 1995. "Property Rights and Investment Incentives: Theory and Evidence from Ghana." *Journal of Political Economy* 103 (October): 903–37.

Binswanger, Hans. 1991. "Brazilian Policies That Encourage Deforestation in the Amazon." *World Development* 19 (July): 821–29.

Boserup, Ester. 1965. *The Conditions of Agricultural Growth: The Economics of Agrarian Change under Population Pressure.* New York: Aldine.

———. 1981. *Population and Technological Change: A Study of Long-Term Change.* Chicago: University of Chicago Press.

Browder, John. 1988. "Public Policy and Deforestation in the Brazilian Amazon." In Robert Repetto and Malcolm Gillis, eds., *Public Policies and the Misuse of Forest Resources.* Cambridge: Cambridge University Press.

Carter, Michael, and Pedro Olinto. 1996. "The Impact of Land Titling on Agricultural Productivity in Paraguay." World Bank, Latin America and the Caribbean Technical Department, Washington, D.C.

Chopra, Kanchan, and S.C. Gulati. 1996. "Environmental Degradation, Property Rights and Population Movements: Hypotheses and Evidence from Rajasthan." Institute of Economic Growth, New Delhi.

Collins, J.E. 1987. "Labor Scarcity and Ecological Change." In Peter Little and Michael Horowitz, eds., *Lands at Risk in the Third World*. Boulder, Colo.: Westview Press.

Current, Dean, Ernst Lutz, and Sara Scherr, eds. 1995. *Costs, Benefits, and Farmer Adoption of Agroforestry: Project Experience in Central America and the Caribbean*. Environment Paper 14. Washington, D.C.: World Bank.

Dasgupta, Partha. 1995. *An Inquiry into Well-Being and Destitution*. Oxford: Clarendon Press.

Feder, Gershon. 1987. "Land Ownership and Farm Productivity: Evidence from Thailand." *Journal of Development Studies* 24 (1): 16–30.

Garcia-Barrios, Raul, and Luis Garcia-Barrios. 1990. "Environmental and Technological Degradation in Peasant Agriculture: A Consequence of Development in Mexico." *World Development* 18 (November): 1569–85.

Heath, John, and Hans Binswanger. 1996. "Natural Resource Degradation Effects of Poverty Are Largely Policy-Induced: The Case of Colombia." *Environment and Development Economics* 1: 65–84.

Intal, Ponciano. 1991. "Commentary on 'Environmental Consequences of Agricultural Growth.'" In Stephen A. Vosti, Thomas Reardon, and Winfried von Urff, eds., *Agricultural Sustainability, Growth and Poverty Alleviation: Issues and Policies*. Washington, D.C.: International Food Policy Research Institute.

Kates, Robert, and Viola Haarmann. 1992. "Where the Poor Live: Are the Assumptions Correct?" *Environment* 34 (May): 4–28.

López, Ramón E. 1992. "Environmental Degradation and Economic Openness in LDCs: The Poverty Linkage." *American Journal of Agricultural Economics* 74 (December): 1138–45.

———. 1993. "Resource Degradation, Community Controls and Agricultural Productivity in Tropical Areas." University of Maryland at College Park, Department of Economics.

———. 1996. "Land Titles and Farm Productivity in Honduras." University of Maryland at College Park, Department of Economics.

———. 1997. "Environmental Externalities in Traditional Agriculture and the Impact of Trade Liberalization: The Case of Ghana." *Journal of Development Economics* 53 (June): 17–39.

———. 1998. "The Tragedy of the Commons in Côte d'Ivoire Agriculture: Empirical Evidence and Implications for Evaluating Trade Policies." *The World Bank Economic Review* 12 (1).

López, Ramón E., and Alberto Váldes, eds. Forthcoming. *Rural Poverty in Latin America*. Washington, D.C.: World Bank.

Lutz, Ernst, Stefano Pagiola, and Carlos Reiche, eds. 1993. *Economic and Institutional Analysis of Soil Conservation Projects in Central America and the Caribbean*. Environment Paper 8. Washington, D.C.: World Bank.

Migot-Adholla, Shem, Peter Hazell, Benoit Blarel, and Frank Place. 1991. "Indigenous Land Rights Systems in Sub-Saharan Africa: A Constraint on Productivity?" *The World Bank Economic Review* 5 (1): 155–75.

Moldenhauer, W.C., and N.W. Hudson, eds. 1988. *Conservation Farming in Steep Lands*. Ankeny, Iowa: World Association of Soil and Water Conservation.

Sachs, Jeffrey. 1997. "The Limits of Convergence: Nature, Nurture and Growth." *The Economist* 343 (8021): 19–22.

Sanchez, Pedro. 1976. *Properties and Management of Soils in the Tropics*. New York: J. Wiley.

Shepherd, Gill. 1991. "Communal Management of Forests in the Semi-Arid and Sub-Humid Regions of Africa: Past Practice and Prospects for the Future." *Development Policy Review* 9 (June): 151–76.

Stiglitz, Joseph. 1991. "Rational Peasants, Efficient Institutions, and the Theory of Rural Organizations: Methodological Remarks for Development Economics." In Pranab Bardhan, ed., *The Theory of Agrarian Institutions*. Oxford: Clarendon Press.

Stonich, Susan. 1989. "The Dynamics of Social Processes and Environmental Destruction: A Central American Case Study." *Population and Development Review* 15 (2): 269–96.

Taylor, Daniel, and Douglas Young. 1985. "The Influence of Technological Progress on the Long-Run Farm Level Economics of Soil Conservation." *Western Journal of Agricultural Economics* 10: 63–76.

Tiffen, Mary, Michael Mortimore, and Francis Gichuki. 1994. *More People, Less Erosion: Environmental Recovery in Kenya.* New York: J. Wiley.

Todaro, Michael. 1977. *Economic Development in the Third World.* New York: Longman.

Webster, Cyril Charles, and Peter Northcote Wilson. 1980. *Agriculture in the Tropics.* London: Longman.

World Bank. 1992. *World Development Report 1992: Development and the Environment.* New York: Oxford University Press.

———. 1996. *World Development Report 1996: From Plan to Market.* New York: Oxford University Press.

Comment on "Where Development Can or Cannot Go: The Role of Poverty-Environment Linkages," by Ramón E. López

Cielito F. Habito

Poverty, environmental degradation, and rapid population growth are three mutually reinforcing forces in developing countries, in many cases seeming to perpetuate one another. Ester Boserup (1965, 1981) observed that today's industrial countries avoided this trap through seemingly natural forces that fostered institutional change, which in turn increased investments in land productivity (through agricultural intensification), eventually leading to higher rural incomes. Alas, that pattern no longer seems to hold. In fact, it seems more the exception than the rule in developing countries today. Ramón E. López explores why in his comprehensive article.

The Colonial Influence

At the outset López identifies three important differences between rural communities in developing countries and those in industrial countries at similar points in their evolution: rural communities in today's developing countries are more closely integrated with the domestic and international economy, experience much more rapid population growth, and have more fragile and unstable natural resource bases (because of their location in tropical, semitropical, and semiarid regions). I see one more crucial difference that is relevant to much of the developing world: a colonial history that brought about highly feudalistic rural structures in societies already characterized by private ownership (albeit by a privileged few).

Thus while López tends to trace the story of rural economies from an initial situation marked either by open access to land and other primary resources or by common ownership over those resources, this precondition does not apply to many postcolonial rural economies in developing countries. Moreover, while Boserup's and López's theses seem to be premised on farmers being independent actors (acting either individually or collectively), this was not necessarily the case in postcolonial societies, where the relationship between a few landlords and

Cielito F. Habito is secretary of socioeconomic planning, Republic of the Philippines.

large numbers of tenant farmers tended to be paternalistic. As I argue below, this backdrop reinforces the obstacles López identifies to fulfilling the Boserup sequence.

As López asserts, we must examine the dynamics, not just the comparative statics, of rural change to understand the many deviations from the Boserup sequence. In these deviations institutions do not change or investments in productivity are not made, or both. There are many reasons why, and many circumstances in which, these failures occur; understanding them helps identify appropriate interventions for overcoming rural poverty and environmental degradation.

Observations on Policy Implications

I summarize my comments in six observations related directly to the points raised by López.

1. *Exclusive land rights (privatization) may generate stronger incentives for soil conservation and environmental sustainability, but they will not automatically lead to economic efficiency.* Achieving economic efficiency requires appropriate policies as well. Highly protectionist policies, for instance, tend to perpetuate inefficiencies even under a private enterprise system. In the Philippines high levels of protection in the sugar industry—through quantitative trade restrictions and, more recently, high import tariffs—have led to persistent inefficiencies that are forcing painful adjustments. Despite active research and development in farm productivity and improved sugarcane varieties conducted in public institutions since the 1950s, few farms have adopted new technologies. High effective protection has retarded innovation and perpetuated inefficient institutional arrangements in the industry.

2. *Governments and their policies are often important obstacles to institutional change and investments in efficiency.* The role of government in Boserup's sequence, both as obstacle and as facilitator, is much more crucial than López acknowledges. He identifies history and cultural norms, incomplete information and absence of markets, and failure of collective action as obstacles to institutional change. But policies that distort economic behavior—such as excessive trade protection or inappropriate pricing of natural resources—also can inhibit adjustments in institutions or investments in productivity. Thus "functional but imperfect institutions" (Stiglitz 1991) may be perpetuated, inhibiting improvements in productivity and efficiency that could otherwise lead to the increases in rural income posited by Boserup. Share tenancy, which originated in the colonial feudalistic structure of rural communities, is one such institution.

In some cases inefficient institutional arrangements are even fixed by legal mandate. In the Philippine sugar industry, for example, a decades-old law mandates a cane-sharing system between sugar planters and millers in which planters pay the mills a fixed percentage of the sugar recovered from the sugarcane (typically 30 percent) regardless of the quality of the cane and the efficiency of the mill. This system has led to underinvestment in cane improvements by planters and underinvestment in milling improvements by millers. The situation has persisted because of the high degree of trade protection enjoyed by the industry. As a result the industry finds itself uncompetitive internationally, and incomes have been falling.

Similarly, much of the forest degradation in the Philippines was the result of extremely low forest extraction charges. If pricing of natural resources such as forests and minerals is inappropriate, providing exclusionary rights to their extraction will lead to unsustainable production and rapid degradation of the resources. Only in the 1980s did the Philippine government raise forest charges to levels consistent with more sustainable forest utilization.

3. *Governments often must play an active role in effecting institutional change.* Because government policies often stand in the way of the fulfillment of the Boserup sequence, government must play an active role in facilitating that process. More often than not, institutional change must be induced, since conditions often prevent such change. In the Philippine sugar industry a desirable institutional change (shifting to a toll milling system based on a cane valuation scheme that accounts for quality) should be effected through legislation, since the inefficient cane-sharing system was itself mandated by legislation.

Interlinked credit is another example of a persistent imperfect institution in many rural economies that originated in a feudalistic agrarian structure. Traditionally, the landlord was the main source of credit for tenant farmers, reinforcing the farmers' dependence on the landlord. After agrarian reform redistributed land to small farmers, the creditor role shifted to agricultural traders (many of them landlords). When traders are also farmers' primary source of credit, farmers are caught in a monopsony (single-buyer) situation—they are left with no choice but to sell their crop to their creditors, who invariably pay them less than they would receive in a more competitive market. Like the cane-sharing system, this institution has long been recognized as inhibiting the growth of farm incomes. Nonetheless, it has persisted in the Philippines and many other countries. Changing some inefficient agrarian institutions can be extremely difficult and requires determined and sustained efforts from outside, most likely from government.

4. *Investments in productivity (intensification) and environmental sustainability often must be undertaken directly by government, particularly when those investments take on the nature of public goods. At the very least, communities must be induced to invest in such facilities—something that usually requires government intervention.* Communal irrigation is a case in point. Small farmers normally would not invest in irrigation on their own, except where individual tubewell irrigation makes technical and economic sense. Thus government must intervene to ensure the provision of irrigation facilities, either by undertaking the public investments directly or by facilitating the formation of farmers associations (if they do not exist) and their access to investment resources.

In the Philippines responsibility for communal irrigation has been devolved to local governments, but a lack of capability and resources has necessitated intervention by the national government. In some cases the National Irrigation Administration builds irrigation systems; in others it provides farmers associations or irrigators associations with access to concessional foreign loans to build communal systems. In these situations investments in intensification will not happen automatically with increasing population density.

5. *Governments must develop policies that facilitate private investment in intensification and productivity, encourage more judicious use of natural resources, and foster institutional change.* Governments must reduce trade protection to increase the impetus for productivity improvements. Appropriate pricing of natural resources—forest charges, mineral concession fees, irrigation charges—is also necessary. Market-based instruments for controlling other forms of environmental degradation, such as pollution (with tradable pollution permits and pollution charges, for example), must be part of the standard policy framework. And support should be provided for nongovernmental organizations (NGOs), which often help to induce desirable institutional change.

One important rationale for land reform that has not received enough emphasis is its role in promoting environmental protection. By providing wider access to land, governments can inhibit the tendency for the landless rural population to migrate to uplands—an important cause of forest degradation in the Philippines and elsewhere. Indeed, encroachment into upland forests is believed to have caused more forest degradation than commercial logging.

6. *Communal management may be preferable to exclusive individual rights when population growth and density are so high that they lead to uneconomic units—but the institutional requirements for success are much more challenging.* The government has a crucial role in steering institutional change. Cooperative farming, widely owned corporate farms, and nucleus estate schemes will not develop without government intervention.

Conclusion

I have focused on the crucial role governments must play in bringing about the Boserup happy ending. (I suppose this is not surprising coming from an academic economist turned government policymaker like myself.) This role consists of eliminating policy distortions and government-induced obstacles to desirable institutional change, making public investments in productivity, resource intensification, and environmental protection, and facilitating institutional change, including providing support for NGOs.

Though the rosy Boserup scenario may have unfolded in years past without much help from government in today's industrial countries—and in some exceptional cases in developing countries, such as the much-cited Machakos district in Kenya—it is not likely to be achieved in the current environment without government action. López provides a useful framework in which to assess the proper role of government in alleviating rural poverty and environmental degradation.

References

Boserup, Ester. 1965. *The Conditions of Agricultural Growth: The Economics of Agrarian Change under Population Pressure*. New York: Aldine.

———. 1981. *Population and Technological Change: A Study of Long-Term Change*. Chicago: University of Chicago Press.

Stiglitz, Joseph. 1991. "Rational Peasants, Efficient Institutions, and the Theory of Rural Organizations: Methodological Remarks for Development Economics." In Pranab Bardhan, ed., *The Theory of Agrarian Institutions*. Oxford: Clarendon Press.

Comment on "Where Development Can or Cannot Go: The Role of Poverty-Environment Linkages," by Ramón E. López

Jeffrey R. Vincent

Ramón E. López asks an important question: If Ester Boserup (1965, 1981) was right—if population growth stimulates agricultural intensification and institutional evolution, which in turn raise rural incomes—why is there still so much poverty and environmental degradation in rural areas of the developing world?

López's inquiry focuses on regions with a fragile resource base. He classifies such regions into three types based on population density and integration with the rest of the economy. This typology comes early in the article and, at least superficially, appears to support Boserup's hypothesis. Population density and economic integration increase as one moves from type 1 to type 3 areas, while the relative importance of private property rises and the relative importance of communal and open-access property declines—just what Boserup predicted in terms of institutional responses to rising population density and economic integration. Thus the typology makes one wonder if in fact there is any puzzle to solve.

López's Two Questions

A close reading of the article suggests, however, that López is less interested in a global test of the Boserup hypothesis than in two more interesting, and more researchable, questions. First, even if the hypothesis holds in many cases, why do the cases in which it does not hold account for such a large share of the total? And second, why does the hypothesis often seem to hold partially—that is, why does institutional evolution occur but not result in reduced poverty and improved resource management?

López develops a dynamic model for exploring these issues. He argues that, given initial conditions determined by the degree of fragility of the environment and the degree of development of property rights institutions, the path of rural development is driven by the rate of population growth. In effect, environmental fragility determines the direction of the path, and institutions determine whether the path is

---

Jeffrey R. Vincent is a fellow at the Harvard Institute for International Development.

Annual World Bank Conference on Development Economics 1997
©1998 The International Bank for Reconstruction and Development / THE WORLD BANK

smooth or bumpy and how rapidly it is being extended. Population growth determines how fast rural areas speed along the path. If population growth is too rapid, rural areas may either skirt environmental thresholds too closely and skid off into irreversible environmental degradation or drive off the end of the path and get stuck in a swamp of poverty.

The rate of population growth is the driving force in this model. López adds three shocks that also influence dynamic behavior: the effects of government policies, commercialization of resources by external interests (often through forcible seizure), and growth in the rest of the economy.

The model is simple, which gives it a certain elegance. Simplicity is certainly desirable when there is a mountain of case study evidence to sort through (directly or indirectly, López reportedly reviewed some 200 studies). I am concerned, however, that the model omits four key factors that are needed to understand the institutional links between population, poverty, and environment in developing countries.

Four Omitted Factors

The first point relates to the assumption that the population growth rate is exogenous is dubious. Public health programs have already caused mortality rates to fall in most of the developing world. Future population trends are likely to reflect primarily fertility rates. Women in the developing world have varying degrees of control over their fertility rates, and they face varying incentives to exercise that control.

I would be more comfortable with López's model as a device for understanding the population-poverty-environment nexus if it reflected the endogeneity of fertility decisions and the existence of potential feedback mechanisms from institutions and the environment to those decisions. Dasgupta (1995) describes in considerable detail how institutional factors within households and communities can cause fertility decisions to be socially inefficient. Panayotou (1994) argues that the closing of the commons can induce a drop in the fertility rate, as the relative benefits of having more children to capture the freely available resources decline.

The second point has to do with the environmental component of López's model. Cross-country variations in evidence for and against Boserup's hypothesis might be less informative than variations within countries—in fact, within communities. Highly evolved property rights for agricultural land often exist side-by-side with open access for forests, pastures, fisheries, and water. This variation appears to be related to resource characteristics other than fragility or resilience. The common-sense economic explanation is that property rights evolve more rapidly when the benefit-cost ratio for changing them is higher. This ratio is likely to be higher for easily demarcated, highly productive agricultural land in the immediate vicinity of a village than for distant, marginally productive forests that are difficult to monitor. López's model sheds no light on these issues, as it lumps all resources together and ignores characteristics other than fragility.

The third point has to do with external shocks. López ignores a critically important one, technology. In Boserup's model households gradually adopt new technologies (implicitly, from an existing technology set) in response to resource scarcity and improved institutions. In practice, however, technologies are often introduced suddenly from the outside before appropriate institutions have evolved. This can derail Boserupian evolution, with a dynamic effect much more rapid than that of population growth. For example, the introduction of modern fishing equipment has dissipated rents in traditional open-access fisheries around the world, thus generating only ephemeral increases in income. The ending can be more Boserupian when appropriate institutions already exist. The introduction of tree crops in Malaysia, which has had well-defined property rights for agricultural land since early in this century, enabled both commercial estates and smallholders to enjoy substantial increases in farm income. Although much lowland rainforest gave way to plantations of the exotic crops, their introduction ultimately saved the remaining forests by providing a sustainable alternative to the small-scale subsistence shifting cultivation and large-scale commercial shifting cultivation that plagued Malaysia in the late 1800s (Vincent and Hadi 1993).

The final point has to do with an external shock that López considers but, I think, does not emphasize adequately—namely, growth in the rest of the economy. In Asia, the region I know best, growth in the rest of the economy is arguably the most important external factor affecting rural areas. And I believe, furthermore, that its effects are by and large positive for both rural poverty and the rural environment. Let me clarify that I am referring to growth that derives from countries pursuing their comparative advantage in labor-intensive industries, not from an urban bias. Forest areas have stabilized in some fast-growing countries in Southeast Asia, such as Malaysia, for reasons having little to do with institutional evolution. What has happened instead is that rapid urban growth has induced rural-urban migration. This change has driven up the opportunity cost of rural labor and driven down the returns to land clearing. This process has occurred quickly, in a single generation. It is remarkably similar to the stabilization of the agricultural frontier that occurred in the United States earlier this century.

López rightly expresses concern that migrants might damage the environment by liquidating natural resources to obtain financial resources for migration. Although this is certainly a possibility, I am not aware of substantial evidence that it has occurred in Asia. Instead, families have either chosen the other option that López describes, selling off their land (which should reduce poverty, since it facilitates land consolidation and thus economies of scale), or, more commonly, an option he does not consider, in which some members of the family (typically the parents and one or two elder siblings) stay on the farm while others migrate to urban areas. This is a second important aspect of household decisionmaking (the first being fertility) that López's highly aggregated model cannot capture.

I am not arguing that economic growth is a cure-all, least of all for environmental problems, but I would certainly choose it over the alternative. A rising tide may toss some boats to the shore, but it is more likely to lift the remaining ones than is a stagnant economy, much less an economy going down the drain. If few benefits of economic growth for poverty alleviation and environmental improvement have been observed in rural parts of Latin America and Africa, it may simply be because those regions have experienced so little growth.

References

Boserup, Ester. 1965. *The Conditions of Agricultural Growth: The Economics of Agrarian Change under Population Pressure.* New York: Aldine.

———. 1981. *Population and Technological Change: A Study of Long-Term Change.* Chicago: University of Chicago Press.

Dasgupta, Partha. 1995. "The Population Problem: Theory and Evidence." *Journal of Economic Literature* 33 (4): 1879–1902.

Panayotou, Theodore. 1994. "The Population, Environment, and Development Nexus." In Robert Cassen, ed., *Population and Development: Old Debates, New Conclusions.* New Brunswick, N.J.: Transaction Publishers.

Vincent, Jeffrey R., and Yusuf Hadi. 1993. "Malaysia." In National Research Council (Committee on Sustainable Agriculture and the Environment in the Humid Tropics), *Sustainable Agriculture and the Environment in the Humid Tropics.* Washington, D.C.: National Academy Press.

Floor Discussion of "Where Development Can or Cannot Go: The Role of Poverty-Environment Linkages," by Ramón E. López

A participant from the Bangladesh Institute of Development Studies asked Ramón E. López (presenter) about his assertion that rural emigration has adverse effects on the rural environment. Although there is not much data on the topic, the participant believed that, if such costs do exist, rural nonagricultural development was one way to lower them.

López agreed on the absence of data on the link between migration and rural environmental degradation. But two studies—one in Mexico and one in Peru—had shown that conservation falters when rural land is abandoned by migrants, for two reasons. First, conservation is labor intensive. Second, migration provides the opportunity and the incentive to sell natural resources, particularly if urban growth is pushing up the opportunity cost of those resources. The long-term environmental objective may be to have fewer people putting fewer pressures on natural resources, he said. But trying to achieve that objective may actually increase environmental degradation.

Community controls over common property (water, fuelwood, grazing lands) are some of the most effective ways to contain environmental damage, López continued. But it is precisely when such controls are most needed—when people are migrating to urban areas or when population density has increased considerably—that they collapse most often. There is increasing evidence, he said, that a growing population and increasing external influence, particularly for migration, weaken the community organizations that are crucial to promoting the efficient use of natural resources.

A participant from Cornell University noted that a growing number of researchers, particularly archaeologists, are finding evidence of groups—from small villages to entire cultures—that have disappeared without any obvious signs of strife, invasion, or environmental disaster. Rather, gradual environmental degradation appears to have been the cause. In many cases these groups could even have been prospering from the environmental harm they were causing, unaware of its long-term effects. Eventually they reached a point of environmental degradation from which they never recovered, and their society simply vanished. Thus, the presenter concluded, in con-

---

This session was chaired by Caio Koch-Weser, managing director, Operations, Policies, and Programs at the World Bank.

Annual World Bank Conference on Development Economics 1997
©1998 The International Bank for Reconstruction and Development / THE WORLD BANK

trast to the inverted Kuznets curve that some researchers use to plot environmental and growth paths, some societies go up the curve but do not come back down. They disappear somewhere along the top because of environmental damage.

Dilip Mookherjee (presenter in another session) took note of the tradeoffs between rural environmental damage and urban environmental damage. Urban migration and growth may alleviate rural environmental damage, but the increased concentration of urban populations may offset those gains. If, for example, a river flows through a series of towns and rural areas, and pollutant discharges into the river remain constant even as populations shift, the water will always be polluted by the time it reaches the sea.

Jeffrey Vincent (discussant) agreed that environmental damage in urban areas often mirrors what happens in rural areas. If people move from rural areas where they are degrading the environment to urban areas with open-access resources—as in the form of a river to take away waste—environmental degradation will continue. Thus the overall environment does not improve.

López added that such a tradeoff is important, but that the problem may be even more complex. It might be that degradation continues in rural areas as it worsens in urban areas. As he had noted, urban migration can have a deleterious effect on the rural environment.

A participant noted that everyone agrees that economic growth is admirable and desirable. Economists, however, often fail to make a distinction between growth that is genuine and growth that comes from the sale of environmental capital. When environmental capital is sold, growth rates rise and people prosper. But over the long term such growth is neither desirable nor sustainable. Thus, the participant said, economists should better distinguish between these two types of growth.

Caio Koch-Weser (chair) closed the discussion by noting three links between the research being presented and the World Bank's work for its country clients. First, he said, the interactions among population dynamics, environmental change, and institutional evolution are one of the Bank's most complex and possibly least understood areas of research. Accordingly, in recent years Bank projects have evolved from a sustainable development paradigm that included the environment toward one that also embraces social development. This move has involved greater support for institutional development and its social underpinnings and changes in Bank services, modes of operation, and support for participatory development. And much of the work on the social underpinnings of development has been applied first in the environmental and human resources areas.

Second, the World Bank's country assistance strategies need to pay more attention to political economy—to overall policies, their supporting institutional framework, and their sustainability. To that end, part of the Bank's new approach to rural development involves focusing more on institutional reforms in rural communities.

Finally, Koch-Weser concluded, the Bank needs more systematically accumulated knowledge about countries in which virtuous circles of institutional evolution and social capital development have occurred. Acquiring such knowledge will require research, but such research will pay rich dividends in the Bank's operational work.

Distributors of World Bank Publications

Prices and credit terms vary from country to country. Consult your local distributor before placing an order.

ARGENTINA
Oficina del Libro Internacional
Av. Cordoba 1877
1120 Buenos Aires
Tel: (54 1) 815-8354

AUSTRALIA, FIJI, PAPUA NEW GUINEA, SOLOMON ISLANDS, VANUATU, AND WESTERN SAMOA
D.A. Information Services
648 Whitehorse Road
Mitcham 3132
Victoria
Tel: (61) 3 9210 7777

AUSTRIA
Gerold and Co.
Weihburggasse 26
A-1011 Wien
Tel: (43 1) 512-47-31-0

BANGLADESH
Micro Industries Development Assistance Society (MIDAS)
House 5, Road 16
Dhanmondi R/Area
Dhaka 1209
Tel: (880 2) 326427

BELGIUM
Jean De Lannoy
Av. du Roi 202
1060 Brussels
Tel: (32 2) 538-5169

BRAZIL
Publicações Tecnicas Internacionais Ltda.
Rua Peixoto Gomide, 209
01409 Sao Paulo, SP.
Tel: (55 11) 259-6644

CANADA
Renouf Publishing Co. Ltd.
5369 Canotek Road
Ottawa, Ontario K1J 9J3
Tel: (613) 745-2665

CHINA
China Financial & Economic Publishing House
8, Da Fo Si Dong Jie
Beijing
Tel: (86 10) 6333-8257

China Book Import Centre
P.O. Box 2825
Beijing

COLOMBIA
Infoenlace Ltda.
Carrera 6 No. 51-21
Apartado Aereo 34270
Santafé de Bogotá, D.C.
Tel: (57 1) 285-2798

COTE D'IVOIRE
Center d'Edition et de Diffusion Africaines (CEDA)
04 B.P. 541
Abidjan 04
Tel: (225) 24 6510; 24 6511

CYPRUS
Center for Applied Research
Cyprus College
6, Diogenes Street, Engomi
P.O. Box 2006
Nicosia
Tel: (357 2) 44-1730

CZECH REPUBLIC
USIS, NIS Prodejna
Havelkova 22
130 00 Prague 3
Tel: (420 2) 2423 1486

DENMARK
SamfundsLitteratur
Rosenoerns Allé 11
DK-1970 Frederiksberg C
Tel: (45 31) 351942

ECUADOR
Libri Mundi
Libreria Internacional
P.O. Box 17-01-3029
Juan Leon Mera 851
Quito
Tel: (593 2) 521-606; (593 2) 544-185

CODEU
Ruiz de Castilla 763, Edif. Expocolor
Primer piso, Of. #2
Quito
Tel: (593 2) 507-383; 253-091

EGYPT, ARAB REPUBLIC OF
Al Ahram Distribution Agency
Al Galaa Street
Cairo
Tel: (20 2) 578-6083

The Middle East Observer
41, Sherif Street
Cairo
Tel: (20 2) 393-9732
Fax: (20 2) 393-9732

FINLAND
Akateeminen Kirjakauppa
P.O. Box 128
FIN-00101 Helsinki
Tel: (358 0) 121 4418

FRANCE
World Bank Publications
66, avenue d'Iéna
75116 Paris
Tel: (33 1) 40-69-30-56/57

GERMANY
UNO-Verlag
Poppelsdorfer Allee 55
53115 Bonn
Tel: (49 228) 949020

GHANA
Epp Books Services
P.O. Box 44
TUC
Accra

GREECE
Papasotiriou S.A.
35, Stournara Str.
106 82 Athens
Tel: (30 1) 364-1826

HAITI
Culture Diffusion
5, Rue Capois
C.P. 257
Port-au-Prince
Tel: (509) 23 9260

HONG KONG, MACAO
Asia 2000 Ltd.
Sales & Circulation Department
Seabird House, unit 1101-02
22-28 Wyndham Street, Central
Hong Kong
Tel: (852) 2530-1409

HUNGARY
Euro Info Service
Margitszgeti Europa Haz
H-1138 Budapest
Tel: (36 1) 350 80 24, 350 80 25

INDIA
Allied Publishers Ltd.
751 Mount Road
Madras - 600 002
Tel: (91 44) 852-3938

INDONESIA
Pt. Indira Limited
Jalan Borobudur 20
P.O. Box 181
Jakarta 10320
Tel: (62 21) 390-4290

IRAN
Ketab Sara Co. Publishers
Khaled Eslamboli Ave., 6th Street
Delafrooz Alley No. 8
P.O. Box 15745-733
Tehran 15117
Tel: (98 21) 8717819; 8716104

Kowkab Publishers
P.O. Box 19575-511
Tehran
Tel: (98 21) 258-3723

IRELAND
Government Supplies Agency
Oifig an tSoláthair
4-5 Harcourt Road
Dublin 2
Tel: (353 1) 661-3111

ISRAEL
Yozmot Literature Ltd.
P.O. Box 56055
3 Yohanan Hasandlar Street
Tel Aviv 61560
Tel: (972 3) 5285-397

R.O.Y. International
PO Box 13056
Tel Aviv 61130
Tel: (972 3) 5461423

Palestinian Authority/Middle East
Index Information Services
P.O.B. 19502 Jerusalem
Tel: (972 2) 6271219

ITALY
Licosa Commissionaria Sansoni SPA
Via Duca Di Calabria, 1/1
Casella Postale 552
50125 Firenze
Tel: (55) 645-415

JAMAICA
Ian Randle Publishers Ltd.
206 Old Hope Road, Kingston 6
Tel: 876-927-2085

JAPAN
Eastern Book Service
3-13 Hongo 3-chome, Bunkyo-ku
Tokyo 113
Tel: (81 3) 3818-0861

KENYA
Africa Book Service (E.A.) Ltd.
Quaran House, Mfangano Street
P.O. Box 45245
Nairobi
Tel: (254 2) 223 641

KOREA, REPUBLIC OF
Daejon Trading Co. Ltd.
PO. Box 34, Youida, 706 Seoun Bldg
44-6 Youido-Dong, Yeongchengpo-Ku
Seoul
Tel: (82 2) 785-1631/4

LEBANON
Librairie du Liban
P.O. Box 11-9232
Beirut
Tel: (961 9) 217 944

MALAYSIA
University of Malaya Cooperative Bookshop, Limited
P.O. Box 1127
Jalan Pantai Baru
59700 Kuala Lumpur
Tel: (60 3) 756-5000

MEXICO
INFOTEC
Av. San Fernando No. 37
Col. Toriello Guerra
14050 Mexico, D.F.
Tel: (52 5) 624-2800

Mundi-Prensa Mexico S.A. de C.V.
c/Rio Panuco, 141-Colonia Cuauhtemoc
06500 Mexico, D.F.
Tel: (52 5) 533-5658

NEPAL
Everest Media International Services (P) Ltd.
GPO Box 5443
Kathmandu
Tel: (977 1) 472 152

NETHERLANDS
De Lindeboom/InOr-Publikaties
P.O. Box 202, 7480 AE Haaksbergen
Tel: (53) 574-0004

NEW ZEALAND
EBSCO NZ Ltd.
Private Mail Bag 99914
New Market
Auckland
Tel: (64 9) 524-8119

NIGERIA
University Press Limited
Three Crowns Building Jericho
Private Mail Bag 5095
Ibadan
Tel: (234 22) 41-1356

NORWAY
NIC Info A/S
Book Department, Postboks 6512
Etterstad
N-0606 Oslo
Tel: (47 22) 97-4500

PAKISTAN
Mirza Book Agency
65, Shahrah-e-Quaid-e-Azam
Lahore 54000
Tel: (92 42) 735 3601

Oxford University Press
5 Bangalore Town
Sharae Faisal
PO Box 13033
Karachi-75350
Tel: (92 21) 446307

Pak Book Corporation
Aziz Chambers 21, Queen's Road
Lahore
Tel: (92 42) 636 3222; 636 0885

PERU
Editorial Desarrollo SA
Apartado 3824, Lima 1
Tel: (51 14) 285380

PHILIPPINES
International Booksource Center Inc.
1127-A Antipolo St, Barangay,
Venezuela
Makati City
Tel: (63 2) 896 6501; 6505; 6507

POLAND
International Publishing Service
Ul. Piekna 31/37
00-677 Warzawa
Tel: (48 2) 628-6089

PORTUGAL
Livraria Portugal
Apartado 2681, Rua Do Carmo 70-74
1200 Lisbon
Tel: (1) 347-4982

ROMANIA
Compani De Librarii Bucuresti S.A.
Str. Lipscani no. 26, sector 3
Bucharest
Tel: (40 1) 613 9645

RUSSIAN FEDERATION
Isdatelstvo <Ves Mir>
9a, Kolpachniy Pereulok
Moscow 101831
Tel: (7 095) 917 87 49

SINGAPORE, TAIWAN, MYANMAR, BRUNEI
Ashgate Publishing Asia Pacific Pte. Ltd.
41 Kallang Pudding Road #04-03
Golden Wheel Building
Singapore 349316
Tel: (65) 741-5166

SLOVENIA
Gospodarski Vestnik Publishing Group
Dunajska cesta 5
1000 Ljubljana
Tel: (386 61) 133 83 47; 132 12 30

SOUTH AFRICA, BOTSWANA
For single titles:
Oxford University Press Southern Africa
Vasco Boulevard, Goodwood
P.O. Box 12119, N1 City 7463
Cape Town
Tel: (27 21) 595 4400

For subscription orders:
International Subscription Service
P.O. Box 41095
Craighall
Johannesburg 2024
Tel: (27 11) 880-1448

SPAIN
Mundi-Prensa Libros, S.A.
Castello 37
28001 Madrid
Tel: (34 1) 431-3399

Mundi-Prensa Barcelona
Consell de Cent, 391
08009 Barcelona
Tel: (34 3) 488-3492

SRI LANKA, THE MALDIVES
Lake House Bookshop
100, Sir Chittampalam Gardiner Mawatha
Colombo 2
Tel: (94 1) 32105

SWEDEN
Wennergren-Williams AB
P.O. Box 1305
S-171 25 Solna
Tel: (46 8) 705-97-50

SWITZERLAND
Librairie Payot Service Institutionnel
Côtes-de-Montbenon 30
1002 Lausanne
Tel: (41 21) 341-3229

ADECO Van Diermen
EditionsTechniques
Ch. de Lacuez 41
CH1807 Blonay
Tel: (41 21) 943 2673

THAILAND
Central Books Distribution
306 Silom Road
Bangkok 10500
Tel: (66 2) 235-5400

TRINIDAD & TOBAGO AND THE CARRIBBEAN
Systematics Studies Ltd.
St. Augustine Shopping Center
Eastern Main Road, St. Augustine
Trinidad & Tobago, West Indies
Tel: (868) 645-8466

UGANDA
Gustro Ltd.
PO Box 9997, Madhvani Building
Plot 16/4 Jinja Rd.
Kampala
Tel: (256 41) 251 467

UNITED KINGDOM
Microinfo Ltd.
P.O. Box 3, Alton, Hampshire GU34 2PG
England
Tel: (44 1420) 86848

The Stationery Office
51 Nine Elms Lane
London SW8 5DR
Tel: (44 171) 873-8400

VENEZUELA
Tecni-Ciencia Libros, S.A.
Centro Cuidad Comercial Tamanco
Nivel C2, Caracas
Tel: (58 2) 959 5547; 5035; 0016

ZAMBIA
University Bookshop, University of Zambia
Great East Road Campus
P.O. Box 32379
Lusaka
Tel: (260 1) 252 576

ZIMBABWE
Academic and Baobab Books (Pvt.) Ltd.
4 Conald Road, Graniteside
P.O. Box 567
Harare
Tel: 263 4 755035